Perspectives on Mormon Theology

Perspectives on Mormon Theology

Perspectives on Mormon Theology is designed to facilitate and advance the academic study of Latter-day Saint thought. As Mormon Studies continues to develop as an academic field, there is increasing demand for scholarship that engages theological studies and the philosophy of religion. This series is a response to this need and is designed to provide interested readers additional resources in understanding this rich and intriguing religious tradition. Each volume engages a specific theological topic and exhibits a variety of perspectives in the topic area. The series is not intended to defend any particular position, but rather to provide a forum within which a range of approaches and methodologies are given voice.

Other titles in the series:

Scriptural Theology, edited by James E. Faulconer and Joseph M. Spencer
Grace, edited by Sheila Taylor and Robert L. Millet
Atonement, edited by Deidre Green and Eric D. Huntsman
Revelation, edited by Brian D. Birch and Richard Livingston

Perspectives on Mormon Theology

Apologetics

Edited by
Blair G. Van Dyke
and Loyd Isao Ericson

Volume 2 of the Perspectives on Mormon Theology series
Series edited by
Brian D. Birch
and Loyd Isao Ericson

GREG KOFFORD BOOKS
SALT LAKE CITY, 2017

Copyright © 2017 Greg Kofford Books
Cover design copyright © 2017 Greg Kofford Books, Inc.
Cover design by Loyd Isao Ericson

Published in the USA.

All rights reserved. No part of this volume may be reproduced in any form without written permission from the publisher, Greg Kofford Books. The views expressed herein are the responsibility of the authors and do not necessarily represent the position of Greg Kofford Books.

Paperback ISBN: 978-1-58958-580-5
Harccover ISBN: 978-1-58958-581-2
Also available in ebook.

Greg Kofford Books
P.O. Box 1362
Draper, UT 84020
www.gregkofford.com
facebook.com/gkbooks

Library of Congress Control Number: 2017948568

Contents

Preface. A Brief Introduction and Orientation	vii
1. Critical Foundations of Mormon Apologetics *Blair G. Van Dyke*	1
2. A Brief Defense of Apologetics *Daniel C. Peterson*	27
3. Boundary Maintenance that Pushes the Boundaries: Scriptural and Theological Insights from Apologetics *Neal Rappleye*	43
4. I Think, Therefore I Defend *Michael R. Ash*	63
5. A Wall Between Church and Academy *Benjamin E. Park*	83
6. Mormon Apologetics and Mormon Studies: Truth, History, and Love *Ralph C. Hancock*	91
7. The Intellectual Cultures of Mormonism: Faith, Reason, and the Apologetic Enterprise *Brian D. Birch*	119
8. The Role of Women in Apologetics *Juliann Reynolds*	139
9. Avoiding Collateral Damage: Creating a Woman-Friendly Mormon Apologetics *Julie M. Smith*	155
10. "The Perfect Union of Man and Woman": Reclamation and Collaboration in Joseph Smith's Theology Making *Fiona Givens*	171
11. Lamanites, Apologetics, and Tensions in Mormon Anthropology *David Knowlton*	193

12. Conceptual Confusion and
    the Building of Stumbling Blocks of Faith   209
    Loyd Isao Ericson

13. Shifting Intellectual and Religious Paradigms:
    One Apologist's Journey into Critical Study   223
    David Bokovoy

14. Toward a New Vision of Apologetics   235
    Joseph M. Spencer

15. Apologetics as Theological Praxis   247
    Seth Payne

Contributors   267
Index   271

PREFACE

A Brief Introduction and Orientation

This volume is an exploration of theology and, to a lesser degree, the practical engagement of Mormon apologetics—or defense of the faith—in the twenty-first century. Given the mix of spiritualism, personal revelation, communalism, strong ecclesiastical hierarchy, an ongoing identity fettered to religious persecution, and a commission to defend, apologetics in Mormonism is part of the fabric of the tradition. The contributing authors in this volume constitute diverse voices in the field of apologetics, and their writings comprise an informative spectrum of thought. A brief overview of the organization of the chapters may be serviceable.

On the heels of Blair Van Dyke's introduction that provides a theological and historical backdrop for subsequent chapters, one finds groupings of authors that address apologetics at large. Daniel Peterson, Neal Rappleye, and Michael Ash consider the contributions of apologetics, including their usefulness and scope—an apologetic for apologetics if you will.

Juliann Reynolds, Julie Smith, and Fiona Givens consider women's voices—or the lack thereof—in Mormon apologetics. Their writings discuss the import of apologetics as an act of devotion, challenge the predominantly-male defenses of gendered roles and beliefs within the LDS tradition, and offer unique insights and apologetics of priesthood authority and feminine identity.

Ralph Hancock, Benjamin Park, and Brian Birch deliberate the role of apologetics in the academy. The boundaries of inclusion for defense of faith in scholarly circles is one of the most dynamic discussions surrounding apologetics in Mormonism—particularly as schools of higher education have become increasingly secular and ideologically left over the past decades. These debates in higher education frequently carry significant implications for the way apologists are received as scholars and often reflect viewpoints prevalent at the respective institutions. However, the dialogues and deliberations on the place of apologetics in the academy are frequently conducted amongst insiders unbeknownst to Mormons at large. These authors present issues for any reader—academic or otherwise—to consider.

Loyd Ericson, David Knowlton, and David Bokovoy offer varying criticisms of Mormon apologetics. They indict aspects of the endeavor for attempting to police and define the boundaries of faithfulness, failing to sufficiently depict the religious nature of Joseph Smith's restoration, and unnecessarily threatening the faith that apologists are supposed to defend.

Finally, Joseph Spencer and Seth Payne, while offering their own criticisms of apologetics for occasionally rendering defenses that are not critical in thought or abandoning the very principles of Christian civility espoused by Mormonism, focus instead on presenting their own visions of apologetics going forward.

As illustrated by the groupings above, there is no attempt to forge a common view of apologetics in this volume. This is as it should be since a sterilized rendering of the actual status of apologetics serves no one well. As editors, we aimed to portray the breadth and width, the borders and boundaries of Mormon Apologetics, and thus intentionally employed limited editorial touch to allow readers the opportunity to encounter authors as they present themselves in their own style. This includes the possible use of rhetoric that some may find unnecessarily antagonistic—even inimical—which itself is an issue that is frequently discussed and debated (as it is in this volume). As such, the author's work is their own and readers are encouraged to engage each chapter critically.

Finally, we made every effort to bring diverging perspectives together in this way so that astute readers may observe the textures and contours of apologetics in Mormonism where deep theological and ideological fissures are sometimes manifest and vigorous disagreements are consistently on display. It is essential to note, however, that in spite of pressing differences, what each author has in common is a passion for Mormonism and how it is presented and defended. This volume captures that reality and allows readers to encounter the terrain of Mormon apologetics at close range.

Blair G. Van Dyke
Loyd Isao Ericson

ONE

Critical Foundations of Mormon Apologetics

Blair G. Van Dyke

> Because of our sacred regard for each human intellect, we consider the obtaining of an education to be a religious responsibility.
> —Russell M. Nelson[1]

> As LDS scholars you must speak with authority and excellence to your professional colleagues in the language of scholarship, and you must also be literate in the language of spiritual things.
> —Spencer W. Kimball[2]

The word "apologetic" comes from the Greek *apologia*, and in the Christian tradition it has been used to describe the "defense by argument of Christian belief and of the Christian way of life against criticism."[3] Apologetics is understood by practitioners to function in the realm of intractable and non-negotiable truth claims. In broad terms it involves defending claims such as the reality of God, legitimacy of scripture, the creation of the earth, the Fall, the preeminence of grace, and the eschatology of end times. Luther referred to these central truths as the *loci communes* or "common places."[4] In addition to these intractable truths, Mormon

---

1. Russell M. Nelson, "Where Is Wisdom?" *Ensign*, November 1992, available at https://www.lds.org/ensign/1992/11/where-is-wisdom.

2. Spencer W. Kimball, "Second Century Address," *BYU Studies* 16 (Summer 1976): 446.

3. *Oxford Concise Dictionary of the Christian Church* (Oxford: Oxford University Press, 2006), s.v. "apologetics."

4. The concept of *loci communes* is grounded in classical Aristotelian rhetoric. Aristotle held that certain universal truths, or common places, provide basic launching points for logical argumentation on any given subject. Similarly, Luther established common places of first order theological premises from which dialogists

apologists frequently defend important issues such as Joseph Smith's First Vision, an embodied God, continuing revelation, extra-biblical scripture, priestly temple rituals, and social positions of the LDS Church. Certainly, to back away from these common places is, in their view, a denial of faith and undercuts the Church's divine charge to strengthen her own and bring others to belief. Mormon apologists do not see defense as optional. They take Peter at his word when he declared: "Be ready always to give an answer to every man that asketh you a reason of the hope that is in you with meekness and fear" (1 Pet. 3:15). Simply, Mormon apologetics attempt to present arguments for the legitimacy of the tradition's faith claims and show that they are not duplicitous or deceptive but are reasonable and laden with truth and God's approbation. Because the development of Mormon apologetics is commonly influenced by time and place, we cannot escape a light overview of key periods in the history of the enterprise.

Apologetic Method: Negative and Positive

On the face, there are two basic approaches to apologetics. First, responses to criticism already levied against Mormonism (such as the implausibility of Lehi's transoceanic voyage in the sixth century BCE) is called *negative apologetics*. This approach intends to neutralize attacks. Second, crafting arguments that justify the faith and fortify her position ahead of disagreements and criticisms (such as chronicling Joseph Smith's prophesies that have been fulfilled to carefully establish his status as a seer) is known as *positive apologetics*.[5] Generally, Mormon apologists practice defensive (negative) apologetics with greater frequency than positive apologetics.[6] Indeed, there is a sense among many Mormon apologists that "rational arguments are valuable only in so far as they dismantle criticisms of Church doctrine, history, or practice."[7]

---

may ground arguments to establish the legitimacy of Christianity. See Christof Rapp, "Aristotle's Rhetoric," *Stanford Encyclopedia of Philosophy*, February 1, 2010, https://plato.stanford.edu/entries/aristotle-rhetoric/.

5. William Lane Craig, *Reasonable Faith: Christian Truth and Apologetics* (Wheaton, Ill.: Crossway Books, 1994), xv.

6. See Daniel C. Peterson, "The Role of Apologetics in Mormon Studies," *Interpreter: A Journal of Mormon Scripture* 2 (2012): http://www.mormoninterpreter.com/the-role-of-apologetics-in-mormon-studies/.

7. Brian D. Birch, "Philosophical Musings on Mormon Apologetics" (paper delivered at the at the Tenth Annual Mormon Apologetics Conference Organized

Faith vs. Reason

The heat, smoke, sparks, and fire of apologetics most frequently emerge at friction points between faith and reason and how each should be considered and employed in the defense of Christianity. Determining the jurisdictions of the two is a matter of continual debate. Degrees of accommodation for reason abound, but with the exception of some natural theologians and Christian rationalists, when decisions of ultimate import reach their climax, faith presides as the primary tenet of Christianity. However, the epistemological implications of faith's supremacy are many and varied. For instance, second-century apologist Justin Martyr maintained that all knowledge (Christian or otherwise) emanates from Christ, hence there is no cause to fear reason, as it may strengthen Christians and bring pagans to believe.[8] Augustine held that humanity possesses rational capacities but that those capacities must be enlightened by God to His uses.[9] Arguably, the most celebrated expression of the relationship between faith and reason was articulated by Anselm, the eleventh-century Benedictine monk who intoned, *"fides quaerens intellectum"* or "faith seeking understanding." Again, faith precedes humanity's intellectual yearnings—one understands because one first believes. Five centuries later, however, Martin Luther colorfully decried reason as the "Devil's greatest whore" unless checked by faith in Jesus Christ. For Luther, faith presides in *magisterial power* over reason which serves a *ministerial* role.[10] John Calvin held that God places in the human soul *sensus divinitatis* (sense of divinity) and, therefore, the things of God are prima facie reasonable.[11] To be sure, Christian apologists enjoy different levels of agreement on the relationship between faith and reason.

---

by the Foundation for Apologetic Information and Research (FAIR), in Sandy, Utah, on July 8, 2008).

8. Alvin Platinga, *Christianity and Plurality: Classic and Contemporary Readings*, (Oxford: Blackwell Publishers, 1999), 29–30.

9. Of his extensive learning of Greek philosophy Augustine wrote: "I prated as one well skilled; but had not I sought Thy way in Christ our Saviour, I had proved to be not skilled, but killed. . . . Most eagerly then did I seize that venerable writing of Thy Spirit: and chiefly the Apostle Paul. . . . So I began; and whatsoever truth I had read in those other books, I found here amid the praise of Thy Grace . . ." Augustine, *The Confessions of St. Augustine*, trans. E. B. Pusey (New York: Dutton, 1951), bk. 7, 141.

10. Steven A. Hein, "Reason and the Two Kingdoms: An Essay in Luther's Thought," *The Springfielder* 36, no. 2 (1972), 138–48.

11. John Calvin, *Institutes of a Christian Religion* (1536), trans. Henry Beveridge, (1845; rpt. Grand Rapids, Mich.; Christian Classics Etherial Library,

Whence Cometh Mormonism?

When Joseph Smith was born in 1805, the reverberations of the European Enlightenment continued to shake centuries-old epistemological and theological premises. An overarching theme of the Enlightenment was the insistence on evidential validation of truth claims. Further, Thomas Jefferson was president of the United States and his attending Deism also shaped America. In 1804, he published his revised version of the Bible. Commonly referred to as the *Jefferson Bible*, he literally took a razor to the text and cut out teachings and miracles that were inconsistent with natural laws. After more than fifteen hundred years, the Western world no longer found its orbit exclusively around God. Established religious authority was giving way to the authority of reason. *Evidentialism* demanded that religious claims be grounded in evidentiary proofs.

Apologetic Method: Evidentialism

Evidentialism serves a purpose in Mormon apologetics that may be analogous to forensics in criminal investigations. It aims to temper superfluous attention on supernatural phenomenon in order to observe *what is* and draw suitable conclusions. According to Peter Kreeft and Ronald Tacelli, evidence is a broadcast, of sorts, of God's divinity.[12] The veracity of Christianity may be observed by common investigators of phenomena that exist in the natural world around them. This epistemological stance is called natural theology.

A Mormon apologetic for the Book of Mormon might use this methodology because it may be unreasonable to expect others to take the book seriously *until* credible evidence indicates that it deserves consideration in the first place. Arguments made to show the alignment of Middle Eastern geography with the Lehite escape narrative is one example.[13] Or, consider the 1987 discovery of a steel sword just north of the ruins of ancient Jericho that dated to the seventh century BCE. This find debunked common criticism that the Book of Mormon's description of Laban's sword of fine steel

---

n.d.), 454–55; available at http://www.ccel.org/ccel/calvin/institutes.pdf.

12. Peter Kreeft and Ronald Tacelli, *Handbook of Christian Apologetics* (Downers Grove, Ill.: Intervarsity Press, 1994), 204–6.

13. See S. Kent Brown, *Voices from the Dust: Book of Mormon Insights* (American Fork, Utah: Covenant, 2004), 27–63. See also, *Journey of Faith*, (Provo, Utah: Foundation for Ancient Research and Mormon Studies, 2005), film.

could not be true since the processes of crafting steel had not yet reached ancient Palestine by that time. Mormon apologists were quick to point out the significance of the evidence. An article in the June 1987 *Ensign* drew the following conclusion: "The find demonstrates that the Jews had the ability to make or means to obtain sophisticated weaponry. It thus helps to authenticate historical records that refer to steel weapons."[14] It is interesting that this evidence indicates that the Book of Mormon narrative is accurate relative to steel *and* indirectly suggests that the Book of Mormon is a historical document. Combining evidence and rational justifications in this way to show legitimacy of faith claims is often called Classical Apologetics, as it is a method frequently employed by the earliest Christian apologists.[15]

Evidentialist-Fideist Split

Yet running parallel to the Enlightenment's brand of evidentialism was a persistent incredulity for propositions that God's primary revelations to humanity were bound in rational thought and evidence. On the contrary, these thinkers held that faith (Latin: *fide*) was the most suitable epistemology by which to know God—inasmuch as that is possible. As such, fideism is a "belief in the incapacity of the intellect to attain to knowledge of divine matters and correspondingly put an excessive emphasis on faith."[16] Fideism occupies the opposite end of the epistemological spectrum from evidentialism.

Certainly not the first to express fideistic thought, but arguably the most pointed voice, was Søren Kierkegaard (1813–1855), a Danish philosopher and contemporary of Joseph Smith. He proposed that mankind's relationship to God is deeply personal, a matter of individual conscience and feeling. Therefore, only transcendent experience of conviction can facilitate a sense for the reality of God and His supernal status. Furthermore, Kierkegaard's religious heritage is grounded in Martin Luther's conception of total depravity—that humanity is terminally fallen. Hence, any attempt to analyze and formulate arguments based in evidence and rational proofs could only produce misrepresentations of the nature of God. Therefore,

---

14. "Iron Sword from the Time of Jeremiah Discovered near Jericho," *Ensign*, June 1987, available at https://www.lds.org/ensign/1987/06/research-and-perspectives/iron-sword-from-the-time-of-jeremiah-discovered-near-jericho.

15. William Lane Craig, "Classical Apologetics," in *Five Views on Apologetics*, (Grand Rapids: Zondervan, 2000), 26–55.

16. *Oxford Concise Dictionary of the Christian Church*, s.v. "fideism."

the attempt is futile.[17] Truth, fideists hold, is paradoxical; as Kierkegaard explains: "the supreme paradox of all thought is the attempt to discover something that cannot think."[18] In other words, fideism demands a "leap of faith."[19]

The Problem of Fideism as an Apologetic Method

Mormons consistently manifest strains of fideism, and in many cases this manifestation washes over into apologetics. As such, a primary tactic involves establishing distance between truth claims and systematic theological tests. The religious experience of Mormons, as outlined by an essay published on the Church's Newsroom, is "based on a spiritual witness from God that inspires both heart and mind, creating an interpersonal relationship directly with the divine."[20] That relationship is not ultimately centered on scholarly investigation or intellect but through an internal quest to find the will of God. As former Church president Ezra Taft Benson affirmed: "The Lord works from the inside out. The world works from the outside in. . . . Christ changes men, who then change their environment. The world would shape human behavior, but Christ can change human nature."[21] Further, Mormon apostle Dallin H. Oaks advanced that "there are grounds for believing in the existence of God simply because the spiritual life confirms it." While there are some "evidences" for truth, "scientific methods will not yield spiritual knowledge. . . . We gain or strengthen testimony by

---

17. Richard Amesbury, "Fideism," *The Stanford Encyclopedia of Philosophy*, September 21, 2016, https://plato.stanford.edu/archives/win2016/entries/fideism/.

18. Søren Kierkegaard, *Philosophical Fragments or A Fragment of Philosophy*, trans. David F. Swenson (Princeton: Princeton University Press, 1962), 46.

19. Perhaps the most prominent contemporary scholar that maintains strong fideist leanings is Alvin Platinga of the University of Notre Dame. He argues that it is "properly basic" and entirely rational to believe in God independent of objective verification. See Alvin Platinga, *Reason and Belief in God* (London: University of Notre Dame Press, 1983). Reformed Epistemology is related to fideism but due to its complexities, exceeds the scope of this piece. In short, it suggests that evidentialism is insufficient to fully articulate humanity's experience with God because it stands in a secondary and subordinate relationship to personally held sensibilities of divinity that are innate and stirred by God to draw souls to him.

20. "The Religious Experience of Mormonism," Mormon Newsroom, June 1, 2008, http://www.mormonnewsroom.org/article/the-religious-experience-of-mormonism.

21. Ezra Taft Benson, "Born of God," *Ensign*, November 1985, available at https://www.lds.org/ensign/1985/11/born-of-god.

bearing it. Someone even suggested that some testimonies are better gained on the feet bearing them than on the knees praying for them."[22]

Of course, the glaring snag of fideism is that it is removed from rational proofs that make it possible to present Christianity as a viable option to anyone who contests its claims. And as such, many maintain that it cannot be employed as a suitable apologetic from the start. For Mormon apologetics specifically, Brian Birch observes that "Latter-day Saints cannot, on the one hand, claim to share with some broader community the same conception of reason, and then, on the other hand, under pressure of criticism, appeal to an idiosyncratic conception of rationality to preserve doctrinal orthodoxy."[23] To be sure, serious inquiries that rightly merit rational responses are not served well by a fideist approach and its attached mantra to "just believe." And it is largely impotent as a means of defense in the face of criticism.[24]

Negotiating World View

The rise of Mormonism transpired within this evidentialist-fideist split. On the one hand, many truth claims espoused by Joseph Smith defy

---

22. Dallin H. Oaks, "Testimony," *Ensign*, May 2008, available at https://www.lds.org/ensign/2008/05/testimony. See also, Dallin H. Oaks, "On Learning and Becoming," in *Learning in the Light of Faith: The Compatibility of Scholarship and Discipleship* (Salt Lake City: Bookcraft, 1999), 79, and Joseph B. Wirthlin, "Pure Testimony," *Ensign*, November 2000, available at https://www.lds.org/ensign/2000/11/pure-testimony. For decades this epistemology has been part of Church-correlated instruction for young men and young women. For example, see "Lesson 45: Strengthening Testimonies by Bearing Them," in *Aaronic Priesthood Manual 3* (Salt Lake City: The Church of Jesus Christ of Latter-day Saints, 1995), 182–84, and "Testimony," in *Young Women Manual 1* (Salt Lake City: The Church of Jesus Christ of Latter-day Saints, 2002), 113–16.

23. Brian D. Birch, "'Faith Seeking Understanding': Mormon Atheology and the Challenge of Fideism," in *Mormonism at the Crossroads of Philosophy and Theology*, ed. Jacob T. Baker (Salt Lake City: Greg Kofford Books, 2014), 68.

24. It is not unreasonable to connect Mormon fideism to what is commonly called a "crisis of faith." Church history, doctrine, or social positions can run contrary to contemporary narratives and create dissonance. When fideist responses to concerns are used to resolve dissonance many are dissatisfied and leave the faith. The work of Terryl and Fiona Givens comes to mind as a response to this crisis. They attempt to ease the jarring effects of dissonance through rational approaches that are also intended to foster faith. See Terryl Givens and Fiona Givens, *Crucible of Doubt: Reflections on the Quest for Faith* (Salt Lake City: Deseret Book, 2014).

rational explanations and call for something beyond strict evidentialism. This approach constituted a significant milieu of the day and accommodation of broader definitions of proof made for a loosening of the grip of what Peter Forrest calls the "hegemony of evidentialism."[25] Understandably then, Joseph Smith and early Mormons accepted visions and miracles as evidentiary proofs. This was especially the case with the Book of Mormon. When opponents attacked the Church, early Mormon apologists were quick to appeal to the book as tangible proof to legitimize their claims. The question then was whether or not this constituted suitable evidence. On the other hand, declarations of the transcendence of the Book of Mormon come through spiritual confirmation, frequently on the heels of deep mediation and prayer. It is a conversion of the heart and soul that for many Mormons—perhaps most—supersedes evidential proof because it is existential and beyond rationalism's webs.

And so, Mormonism straddled the evidentialist-fideist split and, according to Davis Bitton, enjoyed decades of "comfortable alignment" with "the values of rationalism, science, education and social reform" while simultaneously maintaining its fantastic and otherworldly visionary beginnings.[26] As Jan Shipps notes, Mormonism is not an ordinary story but an "extraordinary" and "supernatural" one.[27] Mormon apologetics began within, and continue to be shaped by, this multifaceted nineteenth-century landscape that Avery Dulles described as "one of the most fruitful in the entire history of Christian apologetics. . . . In this period apologetics overcomes the sterile rationalism that had affected it in the previous century."[28]

---

25. Peter Forrest, "The Epistemology of Religion," *The Stanford Encyclopedia of Philosophy*, April 24, 2013, https://plato.stanford.edu/entries/religion-epistemology/. For example, see D. Michael Quinn's explorations of what he calls "the magic world view." D. Michael Quinn, *Early Mormonism and the Magic World View*, 2nd ed. (Salt Lake City: Signature Books, 1998).

26. Davis Bitton, "Anti-intellectualism in Mormon History," *Dialogue: A Journal of Mormon Thought* 1, no. 3 (Fall 1966): 119. Bitton notes further: "It would be absurd to claim that Mormonism in the nineteenth century was a thoroughly intellectual religion, compatible in every respect with the intellectual fashions of that tumultuous age. But we have seen enough, I think, to recognize that, for the Mormons, there was a greater compatibility than we had been led to believe . . . for their religion was shot through with the values of rationalism, science, education and social reform."

27. Jan Shipps, *Mormonism: The Story of a New Religious Tradition* (Chicago: University of Illinois Press, 1987), 1.

28. Avery Cardinal Dulles, *A History of Apologetics* (San Francisco: Ignatius, 2005), 267.

Mormonism, Faith, and Reason

One can argue that Mormons are divinely commissioned to employ reason in their undertakings. In December 1832 Joseph Smith received a revelation that directed him to organize what came to be known as the School of the Prophets. The revelation states that Mormons are to teach one another with diligence and aim to more perfectly understand all things

> both in heaven and in earth, and under the earth, things which have been, things which are, things which must shortly come to pass; things which are at home, things which are abroad; the wars and the perplexities of the nations, and the judgments which are on the land and a knowledge also of countries and kingdoms. . . . That ye may be prepared in all things. (D&C 88:78–80)

Later in that same revelation Mormons are commissioned to ". . . seek ye diligently and teach one another words of wisdom; yea, seek ye out of the best books words of wisdom; seek learning even by study and also by faith" (v. 118).

These instructions commend a broad range of disciplines including astronomy, geology, history, political science, law, and international relations. It appears that God expects intellectual exertion to be coupled with spiritual direction in order to become conversant in these disciplines. This is confirmed in a "Gospel Topics" essay published on the LDS Church's website, which states that "while gospel study does not require formal academic training, it does involve reason and mental exertion. . . . In our search for truth, we read, ponder, and analyze information and weigh its reliability. We examine the assumptions behind various theories, as well as our own thoughts, and seek to place facts in their proper context."[29]

And yet there is more. When quoting the revelation above, a clause in the revelation is frequently omitted. This is the recognition that "*as all have not faith*, seek ye diligently . . ." From this, it seems apparent that if an individual practices *fuller and more earnest faith* the need to teach one another out of the best books would diminish because, as Smith claimed in public discourse, the highest and most comprehensive way to gain knowledge is not to read books but to "gaze in heaven" to be taught directly by God.[30]

---

29. "Gospel Learning," The Church of Jesus Christ of Latter-day Saints, November 2013, https://www.lds.org/topics/gospel-study.

30. Quoted in Andrew F. Ehat and Lyndon W. Cook, eds., *The Words of Joseph Smith* (Orem, Utah: Grandin Book Company, 1994), 254.

Intellect yes, but faith indeed! The implications are that the evidentialist-fideist split persists.

The research and publications of Lester Bush on race and priesthood stand as an illustration of these competing interests. Five years before the priesthood and temple ban for black Mormons was lifted in 1978, Bush strongly demonstrated that it did not originate with Joseph Smith or revelatory channels but instead emerged from the culture in which the Church was immersed in the latter half of the twentieth century—and he was criticized by Church leaders for doing so.[31] Today the Church has largely accepted his findings, and in 2013 it renounced its former racialist doctrines—a full forty years after Bush published his scholarly work.[32] Why did it take four decades to close the gap between Bush's scholarship and the doctrine of the Church?

This example, one of many that could be provided, indicates that one may use reason selectively when it unfavorably contradicts Church practices or beliefs. In other words, the acceptance of scholarship may be deferred. When Mormon apologists employ this strategy it brings into question the very use of arguments anchored in credible scholarly findings. If they can be dismissed without rational justification, then why employ the methodology in the first place? William Lane Craig suggests that a common default position is that apologists "will not lose faith but will persevere in the hope and expectation that further evidence will once again tip the balance."[33] However, in the case of blacks and the priesthood ban, that did not happen. Such are the common complexities of the relationship between faith and reason.

Modernism

Modernism, as used here, is an intellectual bent unbeholden to any particular organization or ecclesiastical license. It is a broad canopy of epistemological conceptions that affords primacy to the strengths of reason and intellect, and celebrates the merits of the scientific method. Within modernism, religion is largely privatized; as such, the view that religion was the sole means for determining truth was brought into question.

---

31. Lester E. Bush Jr., "Mormonism's Negro Doctrine: An Historical Overview," *Dialogue: A Journal of Mormon Thought* 8, no. 1 (Spring 1973): 11–68.

32. See "Race and the Priesthood," The Church of Jesus Christ of Latter-day Saints, December 2013, https://www.lds.org/topics/race-and-the-priesthood.

33. Craig, "Classical Apologetics," 37.

Modernism's varied tenets were integrated into theological views, ecclesiastical structures, and authoritative interpretations. As it began to hold sway in the first decades of the twentieth century, American Christianity became intellectualized. This strained the threads of religious cloth in America. The so-called liberal-fundamentalist split emerged amidst these developments, and it had a significant influence on Mormonism.

Liberal-Fundamentalist Split

The split fractured American Protestants into two general camps beginning in about 1880, which became a fixed part of American religious life by 1920.[34] Epistemologically, liberal theology holds that the Bible, general spiritual phenomena, and ecclesiastical systems are most profitably anchored in humanism, scientific thought, and social progressivism.[35] Essentially, faith, scriptural interpretation, and religious practice evolves with human discovery and is not necessarily bound by constraints found in the ancient world of the Bible or bygone eras of the church. In other words, liberal theology maintains modernism and energetically carried it into the twentieth century. Rationalism and scientific discovery are thus not a threat to faith but provide the backdrop for coming religious quests for further enlightenment.

Fundamentalists, on the other hand, held that liberal theology eviscerated Christian faith at a baseline level. They intended to break away from the rigid rationalism of modernism (as they understood it) and return instead to what they viewed as the fundamentals of Christianity, including biblical literalism, the Atonement of Christ and his physical resurrection, unflinching characterizations of sin and grace, the virgin birth of Christ, the Second Coming, and so forth. Epistemologically, fundamentalists view scripture as the premier source of truth—the ultimate authority—that scientists and intellectuals must submit to. According to Dulles, they became "conscious of the weakness of apologetics when it pretends to be

---

34. Mark A. Noll, *A History of Christianity in the United States and Canada* (Grand Rapids: Eerdmans, 1992), 381–86. See also George M. Marsden, *The Soul of the American University* (Oxford: Oxford University Press, 1994).

35. Harry Emerson Fosdick, "Shall the Fundamentalists Win?" *Christian Work* 102 (June 10, 1922): 716–22. See also Robert Moats Miller, *Harry Emerson Fosdick: Preacher, Pastor, Prophet* (Oxford: Oxford University Press, 1985); chapters 21–26 are particularly salient.

able to prove the *fact* of revelation on historical grounds. We can only be sure of divine revelation with the experience of faith."[36]

As one would expect, the split had a significant effect on Mormon apologetics. Fundamentalism was very influential and provided epistemological and theological lenses through which Mormonism was interpreted through the twentieth and into the twenty-first centuries. Bitton noted that at this time "the comfortable alignment which nineteenth-century Mormonism had enjoyed with science began to fall apart," and the vacuum was filled with an "upsurge of anti-intellectualism."[37] Efforts to yoke faith and reason, such as those presented by Elders James E. Talmage, B. H. Roberts, and John A. Widtsoe dissipated. Arguably, the strongest responses to liberal theology were offered by Joseph F. Smith and his son Joseph Fielding Smith who identified "false educational ideas" as a threat to the Church from within and branded some tenets of liberal theology as "pernicious and soul-destroying doctrines."[38] The latter's eventual response was a five-hundred page apology for biblical literalism and the place of faith in the face of the secular philosophies of men.[39]

The split affected studies in Mormon theology, history, economics, science, and social science. Perhaps the greatest impact was felt in the Church's

---

36. Dulles, *History of Apologetics*, 326–27.

37. Bitton, "Anti-intellectualism," 119.

38. Joseph F. Smith, *Gospel Doctrine* (Salt Lake City: Deseret Book, 1986), 312–13; Joseph Fielding Smith, *Man . . . His Origin and Destiny* (Salt Lake City: Deseret, 1954), 36. Others, including J. Reuben Clark, Ezra Taft Benson, Mark E. Peterson, Bruce R. McConkie, and Boyd K. Packer adopted similar perspectives. Many scholars have explored this development in detail. For further reading see D. Michael Quinn, *J. Reuben Clark: The Church Years* (Provo, Utah: Brigham Young University Press, 1983), 173–95; Armand Mauss, *Shifting Borders and a Tattered Passport: Intellectual Journeys of a Mormon Academic* (Salt Lake City: University of Utah Press, 2011), chs. 7–9; Terryl L. Givens, *People of Paradox: A History of Mormon Culture* (Oxford: Oxford University Press, 2007), chs. 5 and 11; Leonard J. Arrington, *Adventures of a Church Historian* (Chicago: University of Illinois Press, 1998); and Gregory A. Prince, *Leonard Arrington and the Writing of Mormon History* (Salt Lake City: University of Utah Press, 2016).

39. See Smith, *Man*. It is important to note Richard Bushman's observations of the work of Smith and others: "Mormon objections to science are all particular, not general. The scientific enterprise as a whole is never discredited, only its errors in particular realms where it contradicts Mormon belief." Richard L. Bushman, "On Being Ill at Ease in the World," *SquareTwo* 2, no. 2 (Summer 2009): http://squaretwo.org/Sq2ArticleBushmanIllAtEase.html.

Seminaries and Institutes of Religion (the private educational system that serves Mormon high school and university students throughout the world). Early in its history, modernism was accommodated in the curriculum and general pedagogical approaches to gospel instruction—so much so that the Church sent some teachers to liberal graduate schools like Chicago Divinity to receive the most recent training in biblical studies and theology so that they could effectively teach and defend Mormonism in rationally grounded perspectives.[40] However, those sands shifted dramatically, and since the mid-twentieth century the system has become overwhelmingly devotional and manifests strains of anti-intellectualism that rival ultra-conservative American Evangelicals and Pentecostals in their approach.[41]

Speaking to these educators in 1938, J. Reuben Clark of the First Presidency declared that the youth of the Church must be inoculated against toxic contagions carried by intellectualism.[42] In 1980, Ezra Taft Benson named intellectuals as one of two groups that "have the greatest difficulty in following the prophet."[43] In 1983, Mark E. Peterson of the Quorum of the Twelve Apostles launched what at the time was dubbed the "witch hunt" involving individual scholars being singled out for their natural approaches to Mormon history or work that questioned official

---

40. The Church of Jesus Christ of Latter-day Saints, *By Study and also By Faith: One Hundred Years of Seminaries and Institutes of Religion* (Salt Lake City: Intellectual Reserve Inc.: 2015), 56–71. It is noteworthy that during this time period John A. Widtsoe served as Commissioner of Church Education for two different terms. See also, Casey Paul Griffiths, "The Chicago Experiment Finding the Voice and Charting the Course of Religious Education in the Church," *BYU Studies* 49, no. 4 (Winter 2010), 91–130.

41. Armand Mauss, *The Angel and the Beehive: The Mormon Struggle with Assimilation* (Chicago: University of Illinois Press, 1994), chs. 6, 10–11; Prince, *Leonard Arrington*, 408–16.

42. J. Reuben Clark, "The Charted Course of the Church in Education," August 8, 1938, available at https://www.lds.org/manual/the-charted-course-of-the-church-in-education/the-charted-course-of-the-church-in-education. It is reasonable to view this speech as the turning point of the LDS Church's Seminaries and Institutes of Religion (formerly Church Educational System) away from general interests to employ intellectual approaches in the classroom. Instead, Seminaries and Institutes of Religion continues to be entirely devotional and employ a pedagogy of indoctrination.

43. Ezra Taft Benson, "Fourteen Fundamentals in Following the Prophet" (presented at Brigham Young University on February 26, 1980), available at https://speeches.byu.edu/speakers/ezra-taft-benson/.

Church positions on issues such as race, gender, and polygamy; local ecclesiastical leaders were even ordered to interview and investigate certain scholars.[44] In 1991, Boyd K. Packer suggested that scholarly work of academics and intellectuals (particularly in the field of history) were a threat to one's own faith, frequently destroyed the faith of others, and oft times furthered Satan's work to destroy the plan of God.[45] Further, in May 1993 Packer echoed Joseph F. Smith and identified "the ever-present challenge from the so-called scholars or intellectuals" as one of three threats to the Church.[46] According to Packer, a faithful scholar of history would not use her training to unveil weaknesses of prophets like Joseph Smith or Brigham Young; because "there is no such thing as an accurate or objective history of the Church which ignores the Spirit," the historical narrative should yield to the interests of the Spirit to shore up faith.[47] Hence, according to Packer, the real danger of a scholarly approach is that we may "first leave out of professional study the things of the Spirit. The next step soon follows: we leave the spiritual things out of our lives." He went on to explain that if we are not vigilant in such matters "we may lose our way in the world of intellectual and scholarly research."[48]

According to Armand Mauss, who was one of the scholars that Mark Petersen ordered to be questioned by his local leader, the absolutism employed through these years was particularly injurious on many levels but nowhere more so than among scholars that, understandably, "made the choice simply to put their academic interests in Mormon studies 'on hold' while burnishing their credentials as faithful members and leaders until it seemed

---

44. Prince, *Leonard Arrington,* 416–18. See also, Gregory A. Prince, Lester E. Bush Jr., and Brent N. Rushforth, "Gerontocracy and the Future of Mormonism," *Dialogue: A Journal of Mormon Thought* 49, no. 3 (Fall 2016): 89–108.

45. Boyd K. Packer, "The Mantle is Far, Far Greater than the Intellect" (presented at the Fifth Annual Church Educational System Religious Educators Symposium on August 22, 1981, at Brigham Young University), available at https://si.lds.org/bc/seminary/content/library/talks/ces-symposium-addresses/the-mantle-is-far-far-greater-than-the-intellect_eng.pdf.

46. Boyd K. Packer, "Talk to the All-Church Coordinating Council," May 19, 1993, transcript available at http://www.zionsbest.com/face.html. The two other threats were the gay-lesbian movement and the feminist movement.

47. Packer, "The Mantle."

48. Ibid. For a helpful treatment of "faithful scholarship," see John-Charles Duffy, "Can Deconstruction Save the Day? 'Faithful Scholarship' and the Uses of Postmodernism," *Dialogue: A Journal of Mormon Thought* 41, no. 1 (Spring 2008): 11–43.

safe to return to such studies without jeopardizing their standing with the leadership."[49] Mauss holds that these sequestered scholars constituted something of a "lost generation" of critical Mormon thought.[50] Their work, that a generation earlier would have been employed by Mormon apologists with Modernist leanings, was, for all intents and purposes, extinguished.

With such high-ranking Mormon leaders communicating animus toward intellectual approaches for so many years it is not surprising that from the mid-twentieth century on, hagiographic and devotional approaches waxed while natural historical and modernist attitudes waned. As such, the comfortable alignment which nineteenth-century Mormonism had enjoyed with science had almost entirely fallen apart; at the same time a corresponding apologetic developed.[51]

Presuppositionalism

Much of epistemology begins with presuppositions—a presumed truth. Presuppositionalism informed the liberal-fundamentalist split. It posits that human thought is flawed and lacks ability to accurately identify or analyze objectively. Hence, the most significant presupposition is that Jesus Christ is the source of all truth. Presuppositionalists then maintain that with this veracity in place, any other investigative pursuit

---

49. Mauss, *Shifting Borders*, 180–81. Mauss indicates that not all scholars involved in this melee were inculpable. Some, mostly well-meaning but injudicious, caused unnecessary damage as well.

50. Ibid.

51. It must be noted that many Mormons did not embrace fundamentalist perspectives. Possibly the most prominent Mormon philosopher that opposed the notion that rational study of religion is toxic to faith was Sterling M. McMurrin. He observed that "there seems to be obvious grounds for the view that it is the study of human beings, their ideas, and their behavior that really brings us face-to-face with the crucial problems of religion, and therefore the humane disciplines and arts rather than the natural sciences are religion's chief intellectual challenge. But more than that, and this is the crux of the matter, it is the study of religion itself that occasions the most difficult discomposing questions. It is when religion is studied and discussed seriously by rational, informed persons with open minds and honest intentions that it encounters its most severe questions." Sterling M. McMurrin, *Religion, Reason, and Truth: Historical Essays in the Philosophy of Religion* (Salt Lake City: University of Utah Press, 1982), 134. What McMurrin seems to communicate here is that religion may be openly scrutinized but the pressing threat is most likely dogmatism and not rationalism.

of truth eventually leads the inquirer to Christianity. A key thinker in this school of thought was Cornelius Van Til. He aimed to minimize effects of liberal theology and establish a biblical worldview that was heavily influenced by Calvinism. For Van Til, truth emanates from God's word as found in the Bible and is infused into every aspect of existence. Hence, its accuracy and veracity stand preeminent and, therefore, presupposed without reservation.[52]

Similarly, Gary Scott Smith recommends that God has absolute control over humanity in every facet of existence including politics, education, science, economics, business, and morality. Religious epistemology must be holistic or it runs the risk of failing to acknowledge God's supremacy in all human experience. Therefore, experience should be viewed and assessed through this lens.[53] Van Til argued that if one does not presuppose the absolute divinity of Christ and his holy word then they embrace a mere projection of reality through the general consciousness of man; such a starting point can only end in error.[54]

For example, presuppositionalists do not deny the importance of scientific exploration, but they also do not hold all scientific claims and associated methodologies as equal. As William Jennings Bryan (noted defender of fundamentalist Christianity during the Scopes "Monkey" Trial) indicated, "it is not scientific truth to which Christians object, for true science is classified knowledge and nothing can be scientific unless it is true." In this sense, "true science" is eternal and unchanging. It is safeguarded and dispensed by God.[55] As Van Til writes,

---

52. Cornelius Van Til, *The Case for Calvinism* (Phillipsburg, N.J.: Presbyterian and Reformed Publishing Company, 1963), 32.

53. Gary Scott Smith, *The Seeds of Secularization: Calvinism, Culture, and Pluralism in America 1870–1915* (Grand Rapids: Eerdmans, 1985), 48–49. For a related approach from a Mormon scholar, see James E. Faulconer, "The World and the Prophets: A Religious Response to Secularism," *Square Two* 2, no. 1 (Spring 2009): http://squaretwo.org/Sq2ArticleFaulconerSecularism.html.

54. Cornelius Van Til, *Christianity and Barthianism* (Phillipsburg, N.J.: Presbyterian and Reformed Publishing, 1962), 3. The writings of Benjamin B. Warfield are very important as he defends a God-centric worldview and legitimacy of the biblical text during rising tides of liberal theology and associated developments such as higher criticism of the Bible. See Benjamin B. Warfield, *The Inspiration and Authority of the Bible*, ed. Samuel G. Craig and Cornelius Van Til (Phillipsburg, N.J.: The Presbyterian and Reformed Publishing Company, 1948).

55. As quoted in George M. Marsden, *Fundamentalism and American Culture: The Shaping of Twentieth-Century Evangelicalism 1870–1925* (Oxford: Oxford

The natural man must not be encouraged to think that he can, in terms of his own adopted principles, find truth in any field. He must rather be told that, when he finds truth, even in the realm of the "phenomenal," he finds it in terms of principles that he has "borrowed," wittingly or unwittingly, from Christianity. The fact of science and its progress is inexplicable except upon the presupposition that the world is made and controlled by God through Christ and that man is made and renewed in the image of God through Christ.[56]

Indeed, presuppositionalism views God as the primary focus and force in all epistemological inquiry.

The challenge of presuppositionalism is that it frequently treats evidence preferentially. In other words, if evidence supports presuppositions then it is readily accepted and employed to shore up one's position. However, when evidence does not align with presuppositions then it may be skirted altogether. As such, one is left to wonder why presuppositionalists would employ arguments grounded in evidentiary claims at all. It certainly poses challenges for those that want to engage in scholarly discussions where traditional academic uses of evidence lie at the core of deliberations. Inconsistencies in how evidence is used can create formidable dialogical deterrents.

Apologetic Method: Presuppositionalism

Given the previously described influence of Fundamentalist Christianity on Mormonism, it is not surprising that presuppositionalism is often at play in Mormon apologetics. It is apparent in discussions about gender that spring out of the Church's 1995 missive, "The Family: A Proclamation to the World." In this document, which is commonly afforded scriptural status, the Church declares that "gender is an essential characteristic of individual premortal, mortal, and eternal identity and purpose."[57] This presupposition frequently undergirds arguments put forth by the Church to explain roles of men and women, best parenting practices, as well as policy and doctrinal positions relative to same-sex marriage and the general Lesbian-Gay-Bisexual-Transgender-Queer (LGBTQ) spectrum.

University Press, 1980), 213.

56. Van Til, *The Case for Calvinism*, 106.

57. "The Family: A Proclamation to the World," The Church of Jesus Christ of Latter-day Saints, https://www.lds.org/topics/family-proclamation.

In 2010, Boyd K. Packer, then president of the Quorum of the Twelve Apostles, taught that homosexuality is a deviation from natural law. He explained: "Some suppose that they were pre-set and cannot overcome what they feel are inborn tendencies toward the impure and unnatural. Not so! Why would our Heavenly Father do that to anyone? Remember he is our father."[58] This statement is informed by presuppositions articulated in the Proclamation and is a representative sample of how the Church employed public and private arguments based in natural law theory with accompanying evidence bound in that epistemological view.[59]

However, decades prior to the Church's release of the Proclamation, research and clinical studies concluded that human gender and sexual identity are fluid and exist on a multi-varied spectrum. As such, the American Psychological Association noted that findings lead "all mainstream medical and mental health organizations in this country to conclude that these orientations represent normal forms of human experience. Lesbian, gay and bisexual relationships are normal forms of human bonding."[60]

---

58. Boyd K. Packer, "Cleansing the Inner Vessel," *Ensign*, November 2010, https://www.lds.org/ensign/2010/11/cleansing-the-inner-vessel. Shortly after Packer gave this talk he amended his words to remove the rhetorical question of why God "would do that to anyone" and changed "tendencies" to "temptations." Furthermore, his defining the Proclamation as a *"revelation"* that members of the Church should read and follow was redefined as being simply a "guide." Both examples illustrate how presuppositions may allow claims to shift when placed under close scrutiny. A primary question is whether or not "The Family: A Proclamation to the World" is actually afforded revelatory status equal to a revelation that has been canonized in Mormon scripture. The answer, apparently, is no. Rather, it is an important "guide." See Peggy Fletcher Stack, "Packer Talk Jibes with LDS Stance After Tweak," *Salt Lake Tribune*, October 25, 2010, http://archive.sltrib.com/story.php?ref=/sltrib/home/50440474-76/packer-church-question-speech.html.csp.

59. Natural law arguments are compelling. Packer employed them consistently throughout his ministry. Robert P. George, an Oxford-trained professor at Princeton University, is arguably the most prominent scholar in the United States to support traditional views of marriage and gender from natural law arguments. A representative sample of his work is Robert P. George, *The Clash of Orthodoxies: Law, Religion, and Morality in Crisis* (Wilmington, Del.: ISI Books, 2001). Other prominent authorities in natural law theory commonly cited by the Church and apologists include: Ryan T. Anderson, Sherif Girgis, David Blankenhorn, Maggie Gallagher, Joshua K. Baker, Mark Regnerus, Ryan Anderson, Sherif Gerges, and David Popenoe to name a few.

60. "Answers to Your Questions: For a Better Understanding of Sexual Orientation and Homosexuality," *American Psychological Association*, 2008, www.apa.org/topics/lgbt/orientation.pdf.

Furthermore, extensive research and findings in social science have shown that claims that question the competence and suitability of same-sex married couples to raise children are generally grounded in prejudice and stereotypes about gay people and are unfounded. More to the point, "research indicates that the children of lesbian and gay parents do not differ markedly from the children of heterosexual parents in their development, adjustment or overall well-being."[61]

Yet given the presuppositions at play, Church leaders and other Mormon apologists generally do not acknowledge these findings. This may be seen in the Church's formal response to the 2013 ruling of the United States Supreme Court in favor of same-sex marriage. It reads as follows: "Regardless of the court decision, the Church remains irrevocably committed to strengthening traditional marriage between a man and a woman, which for thousands of years has proven to be the best environment for nurturing children."[62] But evidentiary proof does not bear out this claim. And as such, the associated presuppositions and unpredictable use of evidences fly in the face of intentions and purposes for citing evidence in the first place.

Hence, the primary weakness of presuppositionalism is illustrated in this case. Should the Church accept the latest research on gender, homosexuality, and their relationship to marriage and parenting they would necessarily have to deny critical content of "The Family: A Proclamation to the World." It is unlikely that the Church, or her apologists, will do this. In the end, therefore, the Church's defense in this point may be more profitably couched in theological, ecclesiastical, or devotional contexts where the burden of evidential proof is not necessarily the foundation of the argument.

The Pendulum Swings

Two factors combined to initiate a sea change wherein the LDS Church renewed emphasis on Evidentialist epistemological approaches. First, the ubiquity of the internet in the twenty-first century and the associated free and open flow of information about Mormon theology, history, and ecclesiastical governance. It effectively toppled long-standing pillars of intellectual isolationism sustained by central correlation and control

---

61. Ibid.

62. "Church Responds to Supreme Court Rulings," Mormon Newsroom, June 23, 2013, http://www.mormonnewsroom.org/article/church-responds-supreme-court-marriage-rulings.

over key Mormon narratives. Second, high-ranking leaders of the Church determined that traditional methods of scholarship should be more overtly fostered to ensure that official histories produced by the Church would promote intellectual credibility in circles outside and inside Mormonism.[63] Predominantly hagiographic and devotional writings were important yet insufficient in the face of access to historical and theological information in an internet-driven world. Simply, the story of Mormonism would be increasingly defined by outsiders if adjustments were not made.[64]

Evidentialism was again more comfortably seated at the table. In 2007 the Church published an essay stating that Mormonism "came about because of intellectual curiosity" and that the Church "encourages a deeper and broader examination of its theology, history and culture on an intellectual level" that will, in turn, "expand open dialogue and conversation between the Latter-day Saints and various scholarly communities."[65] Speaking to religious educators at universities and seminaries and institutes of the Church Educational System, Apostle M. Russell Ballard explained:

> Given the realities of today's world, pure testimony may not always be enough. . . . Our curriculum [of the past], though well meaning, did not prepare students for today—a day when students have instant access to virtually everything about the Church from every possible point of view. . . . And if necessary, we should ask those with appropriate academic training,

---

63. A watershed example of this shift was the work of three professional historians that were granted open access to the Church's archival documents associated with the Mountain Meadows Massacre. They produced what is now the definitive work on the subject. See Ronald W. Walker, Richard E. Turley, and Glen M. Leonard, *Massacre at Mountain Meadows* (Oxford: Oxford University Press, 2008).

64. For some implications of this difficulty see Patrick Q. Mason, *Planted: Belief and Belonging in an Age of Doubt* (Provo, Utah, and Salt Lake City: Neal A. Maxwell Institute for Religious Scholarship & Deseret Book, 2015), 11–23.

65. "'Mormon Studies' and the Value of Education," Mormon Newsroom, November 2, 2007, http://www.mormonnewsroom.org/article/mormon-studies-and-the-value-of-education. See also, "Academic Interest in Mormonism Rises," Mormon Newsroom, February 22, 2008, http://www.mormonnewsroom.org/article/academic-interest-in-mormonism-rises. It is noteworthy that Mormon Studies programs have been established (with appointed coordinators or chairs) at major universities including Utah Valley University, Claremont Graduate University, the University of Utah, the University of Virginia, and Utah State University. It is apparent that other universities will follow suit.

experience, and expertise for help. This is exactly what I do when I need an answer to my own questions that I cannot answer myself.[66]

This is a monumental leap from aforementioned warnings that such approaches abandon faith and may destroy the soul. It appears that the very scholarship that troubled earlier Church leaders is now viewed as essential to more clearly understand Mormonism and maintain faith.

Arguably, the current apex of this response is the Church History Department, with its cadre of professional historians, and the Neal A. Maxwell Institute for Religious Scholarship at Brigham Young University (formerly the Foundation for Ancient Research and Mormon Studies [FARMS]), which for years has endorsed a variety of apologetic approaches. In some ways, the work of both have been adjusted to more suitably fit conventional boundaries of the academy.

The Church History Department has undertaken a herculean task to compile, edit, and publish the extensive body of Joseph Smith's papers in a scholarly work befitting the standards of top-tier scholarship grounded in modernism. As stated by the general editors of the *Joseph Smith Papers*, the documents have "religious meaning to us as Latter-day Saints, we present them in these volumes without comment on their ultimate source. . . . Our aim is simply to reproduce the documents and their historical setting so far as we can reconstruct it."[67] In other words, even though those most closely associated with the project are Mormons, they bracket their faith so that the evidence stands independent and speaks for itself.[68] Further, there have been

---

66. M. Russell Ballard, "The Opportunities and Responsibilities of CES Teachers in the 21st Century," (address to CES Religious Educators in the Salt Lake Tabernacle on February 26, 2016), available at https://www.lds.org/broadcasts/article/evening-with-a-general-authority/2016/02/the-opportunities-and-responsibilities-of-ces-teachers-in-the-21st-century.

67. Dean C. Jessee, Mark Ashurst-McGee, and Richard L. Jensen, *Journals, Volume 1: 1832–1839*, Vol. 1 of the Journals series of *The Joseph Smith Papers*, ed. Dean C. Jessee, Ronald K. Esplin, and Richard Lyman Bushman (Salt Lake City: The Church Historians Press, 2008). Additionally the Church History Department has undertaken a four volume comprehensive history of the Church. This is the first official comprehensive history produced since B. H. Roberts published his landmark history in 1930. See "Church Historian Announces New 4-Volume History of the Church," *Church News*, June 4, 2017, https://www.lds.org/church/news/church-historian-announces-new-4-volume-history-of-the-church.

68. George M. Marsden recommends that in such instances faith functions as a "background belief" that is admissible in the academy. See George M. Marsden, *The Outrageous Idea of Christian Scholarship* (Oxford: Oxford University Press, 1997), 49.

few observers that do not heartily endorse the work of the Joseph Smith Papers Project, the bracketing of faith, and its scholarly foundations.

The mission statement of the Maxwell Institute declares a principal objective "to strive for excellence in furthering religious scholarship within the academic world."[69] Their aim is to foster growth in the academic study of Mormonism, with a specific intention to create what the namesake of the institute, LDS Apostle Neal A. Maxwell, called "disciple-scholars." Maxwell wrote that "for a disciple of Jesus Christ, academic scholarship is a form of worship. It is actually another dimension of consecration. Hence, one who seeks to be a disciple-scholar will take both scholarship and discipleship seriously; and, likewise gospel covenants."[70] In this spirit, the Institute says it will seek to promote "solid academic work which more directly commends and defends the faith by analyzing criticisms, misunderstandings, and other aspects of LDS history and belief"—noting that this would include engagement in apologetics.[71] However, the Institute affirms that "smashmouth" approaches (which have, from time to time, been employed in the past) have no place in the work of the Institute.[72]

These changes at the Maxwell Institute have not been seamless. Tensions over the nature of apologetics and its fit in the academy vis-a-vis the rise of academic study of Mormonism have not only percolated but

---

69. See "About the Maxwell Institute," Neal A. Maxwell Institute for Religious Scholarship, http://mi.byu.edu/about/.

70. Neal A. Maxwell, "The Disciple-Scholar," in *Learning in the Light of Faith: The Compatibility of Scholarship and Discipleship*, ed. Henry B. Eyring (Salt Lake City: Bookcraft, 1999), 5. Some examples of this approach include: publications in the *Mormon Studies Review* which are intended to be stridently academic and appeal to scholars and laymen alike whatever their religious or areligious convictions may be. The Maxwell Institute's Living Faith book series generally targets Latter-day Saints but strives to achieve the highest academic standards possible. Two titles published by the Maxwell Institute are representative samples of this approach: Adam S. Miller, *Letters to a Young Mormon* (2014) and Patrick Q. Mason, *Planted: Belief and Belonging in an Age of Doubt* (2015).

71. Blair Dee Hodges, "Apologetics at the Neal A. Maxwell Institute? No *and* Yes," Neal A. Maxwell Institute for Religious Scholarship (blog), November 11, 2015, https://mi.byu.edu/miapologetics/. For a strong defense of the disciple-scholar see Louis C. Midgley, "Defending the King and His Kingdom," *Interpreter: A Journal of Mormon Scripture*, 2 (2012): http://www.mormoninterpreter.com/defending-the-king-and-his-kingdom/.

72. Hodges, "Apologetics at the Neal A. Maxwell Institute?"

have, on occasion, boiled over. It is not surprising that many strains center on the classic question: What roles do faith and intellect play in explorations of Mormonism?

This question has been treated in a number of different ways, falling along a spectrum that runs from accommodating the language of revealed truth in academic parlance to the complete denial of any role of apologetics in the academy. Loyd Ericson concisely expresses a justification for the first perspective: "While religious beliefs are being rejected a priori because of their explicit metaphysical and epistemological assumptions, non-religious argumentation is being allowed even though they implicitly make similar, though opposing assumptions."[73] Extending this thinking, Ralph Hancock recommends a bilingualism that "speaks the language of the academy and the language of revealed truth." According to Hancock, the danger of Mormon scholars not adopting this bilingualism is that

> the secular framework, having been purged of old, integrating questions concerning the moral and religious dimensions of the human condition, can no longer be translated into the community's authoritative religious idiom. When this happens, faith is left speechless, defenseless, resourceless.[74]

Simply, an apologetic stripped of faith's language is not an apologetic at all.

The other end of the spectrum demands that faith claims be bracketed and the language of faith not employed. The rationale generally suggests that without such bracketing the apologetic is unsuitable for the academy and potentially constitutes an insider-to-insider echo chamber. Some in this camp would argue that apologetics and academics constitute an incompatible relationship—especially in light of the devotional intentions at the bedrock of any apologetic. The solution from this vantage may be a *public epistemic parity*, which claims that a lack of evidence proving or disproving a religious belief puts both the believer and non-believer on equal epistemic grounds. This approach invites apologists to position arguments in a rationale that involves only evidence that is available to any observer independent of private religious conviction. Such a methodology could

---

73. Loyd Ericson, "Where is the 'Mormon' in Mormon Studies?" *The Claremont Journal of Mormon Studies* 1, no. 1 (Spring 2011): 11.

74. Ralph Hancock, "Keeping Faith in Provo: Warning of the Dangers of Secularism for Brigham Young University," *First Things*, March 2014, https://www.firstthings.com/article/2014/03/keeping-faith-in-provo.

foster healthy respect and necessary humility.[75] As Brian Birch explains, apologetics in academia

> must be subjected to scrutiny regarding its grounds, consistency, and coherence, especially in light of other parts of the tradition or other approaches to the question of revelation. . . . Otherwise, the conversation risks sliding into self-contained confession without the publicity necessary for revision or correction. This situation may be acceptable or even desirable in serving *religious* ends; but its *academic* limitations must be recognized by parties on all sides.[76]

That being said, it may be more productive to avoid arguments involving beliefs that are privately held and, therefore, risk a certain triumphal tone—since the debate over what counts as evidence inevitably remains. Ultimately, the Maxwell Institute has rejected the binary either/or categorizations between faithful Mormons and scholarship, or the religiously devoted and secular. The lines and borders of each are oft-times blurred and, therefore, must be navigated nimbly, thoughtfully, and with charity.[77]

Conclusion

Mormon apologetics is said to be grounded in intractable and non-negotiable truth claims. Were it otherwise, it would hardly be compelling to observe or engage. To be sure, it constitutes remnants of the legitimacy of Joseph Smith's charismatic spiritualism in the face of Evidentialism, the rationalistic theologies of Widtsoe and Roberts, presuppositionalism prevalent in the second half of the twentieth century, and the internet-spawned revival of the importance of scholarship in pursuit and acquisition of truth and faith. It is apparent that the nature of apologetics is messy and complex. Further, as the Church continues to expand and encounter authentic questions about its history, doctrines, and positions on socio-political issues—including same-sex marriage, gender, race, and the place of religion

---

75. Peter Forrest, "The Epistemology of Religion," *The Stanford Encyclopedia of Philosophy*, April 24, 2013, https://www.plato.stanford.edu/archives/spr2014/entries/religion-epistemology/.

76. Brian D. Birch, "In Defense of Methodological Pluralism," *Mormon Studies Review* 1 (2014), 61.

77. Hodges, "Apologetics at the Neal A. Maxwell Institute?" A classic approach to civil and charitable apologetics is Robert D. Hales, "Christian Courage: The Price of Discipleship," *Ensign,* November 2008, available at https://www.lds.org/ensign/2009/11/seeking-to-know-god-our-heavenly-father-and-his-son-jesus-christ.

in the public square (to name a few)—the role and profile of Mormon apologetics will almost certainly garner greater attention in and out of the Church. This recommends that Mormons engaged in apologetics do so with care, precision, and thoughtfulness. As John G. Stackhouse suggests, the most difficult aspect of the venture going forward may be to maintain an unpretentious openness to contemplate all possibilities—including the outside chance that maybe, just maybe, you *might be wrong!*[78] As such, an ideal Mormon apologetic should be interpersonally civil, necessarily humble, and for scholars engaged in defense, academically admissible. As Elder Neal A. Maxwell explained, critics of Mormonism "must be met by the meekness and articulateness of believers. . . . If our shortcomings as a people are occasionally highlighted, then let us strive to do better."[79]

---

78. John G. Stackhouse Jr., *Humble Apologetics: Defending the Faith Today* (Oxford: Oxford University Press, 2002), 232.

79. Neal A. Maxwell, "Becometh as a Child," *Ensign,* May 1996, available at https://www.lds.org/ensign/1996/05/becometh-as-a-child.

TWO

A Brief Defense of Apologetics

Daniel C. Peterson

"Apologetics" (from the Greek word απολογία, "speaking in defense") is the practice or discipline of defending a position (usually—but not always—a religious one) through the use of some combination or other of evidence and reason. In modern English, those who are known for defending their positions (often minority views) against criticism or attack are frequently termed "apologists." In this essay, I will, unless I say otherwise, be using "apologetics" to refer to attempts to prove or defend religious claims. But the fact is that every argument defending any position, even a criticism of Latter-day Saint apologetics, is an apology.

Some people turn their noses up at the thought of apologetics. Apologists, they declare, are not concerned with truth; what apologists do isn't real scholarship, and anyhow, some say, apologetics is a fundamentally unethical and immoral enterprise.

I disagree. Like any other intellectual undertaking, of course, apologetics can be done competently or incompetently, logically or illogically, honestly or not. But religious apologetics has a quite venerable tradition behind it, including such notable writers, scholars, and thinkers as Socrates, Plato, St. Justin Martyr, Origen of Alexandria, St. Augustine, al-Ghazālī, Ibn Rushd [Averroës], Moses Maimonides, St. Anselm, St. Thomas Aquinas, Hugo Grotius, John Locke, John Henry Newman, G. K. Chesterton, Ronald Knox, C. S. Lewis, Richard Swinburne, Alvin Plantinga, Peter Kreeft, Stephen Davis, N. T. Wright, and William Lane Craig. Summarily dismissing the apologetic writings of such men as fundamentally unethical and immoral, flatly irrational, and unworthy of academic respect strikes me as dubious, at best. Moreover, although the term *apologetics* has rarely been used within the Church of Jesus Christ of Latter-day Saints, Mormons have engaged in apologetics from the very beginning of the Restoration. (The brothers Parley and Orson Pratt, Oliver Cowdery,

Orson Spencer, John Taylor, B. H. Roberts, and Hugh Nibley represent some of the high points.)

Still, even some communicant members of the Church disdain apologetics. A few, for instance, seem to believe it inherently evil. They seem to use "apologetics" to mean "trying to defend the Church but doing so badly," whether through incompetence, dishonesty, or mean-spiritedness. But, again, "apologetics," as such, is a value-neutral term. Just like historical writing, carpentry, and cooking, apologetics can be done well or poorly. Apologists—like attorneys and scientists and field laborers—can be pleasant or unpleasant, humble or arrogant, honest or dishonest, fair or unfair, civil and polite, or nasty and insulting.

If it's argued that apologetics promotes faith, a critic might respond that bad apologetics and "faith-promoting fictions," even lies, can strengthen faith too. And this is undoubtedly correct. It is possible, in science and politics and every other field, to hold correct views for faulty reasons. Young Latter-day Saint missionaries have, for instance, sometimes used questionable stories and quirky arguments, often passed down from one missionary generation to another, to build and sustain faith in their investigators as well as in themselves. That's one of the reasons why, for many decades now, they've been encouraged to use standard, Church-approved lesson plans in their work. Members of the Church of Jesus Christ of Latter-day Saints are almost certainly not alone in circulating edifying myths and rumors; probably no group is immune to such things.

But this seems no adequate reason, in itself, to oppose the enterprise of supporting beliefs via evidence and argument. After all, in medicine, placebos sometimes help. Does that mean that there's no value in real medicines or that medicine itself is worthless? Do bad philosophical arguments invalidate or discredit philosophy as a whole?

But most (if not all) bad apologetic arguments were once regarded by somebody, somewhere, as convincing. How can one be sure that a supposedly good apologetic argument is actually a good one and not a bad one? One must evaluate it as one evaluates any other form of reasoning from evidence, just as one distinguishes logically sound arguments from those that are not, and solid historical writing from poor or dishonest historiography. Most now-discredited scientific theories were once regarded as true by many if not all scientists. Catastrophism, the four bodily humors, the universal ether, stress-induced ulcers, steady-state cosmology, Lamarckianism, the Ptolemaic view of the solar system—all of these and many other now-abandoned scientific theories were, in their day, widely accepted. Some, in fact, enjoyed overwhelming consensus support for many centuries.

But this doesn't invalidate science. And even though one cannot claim infallibility for anything produced by humans, we move forward with cautious faith—something that apologetics will never supplant. We take elevators high up into buildings constructed by fallible workers on the basis of plans developed by fallible architects, and we allow ourselves to be inoculated with medicines that can guarantee neither complete effectiveness nor even complete safety; we cannot pause life or stop the presses until we've attained absolute human certainty.

Room for Faith and Reason

A few members of the Church appear to reject apologetics in principle, regarding it as inevitably—no matter how charitably and competently it's done—more detrimental than beneficial. They seem to do so on the basis of something resembling fideism, the view that faith is independent of reason, and even that reason and faith are incompatible with each other.

Now, obviously, to treat God solely as a hypothesis, a conjecture, or a topic for discussion is very different from reverencing or submitting to God in a spirit of religious devotion. There are few if any for whom reason is sufficient without faith. Ideally, from the believer's perspective, God comes to be known in a personal I–Thou relationship, as an experienced challenge and as a comfort in times of sorrow, not merely as a chance to show off in a graduate seminar or, worse, to grandstand on an internet message board. And many of those who know God in that way—certainly this must be true of simple, unlettered believers across Christendom and throughout its history—may neither need nor desire any further evidence. Moreover, most would agree—I certainly would—that it's impossible, using empirical methods, to prove the divine. And it's surely true that faith is best nurtured and sustained, not by immersion in clever arguments, but by the method outlined in Alma 32. Emulation of the Savior, loving service, faithful home and visiting teaching, generous fast offerings, earnest missionary work, prayerful communication—these are the fundamentally significant elements of a Christian life. Not everybody needs academic arguments in order to come to faith. And likely nobody would find such arguments sufficient by themselves.

For the vast majority of people, today as in premodern times, faith isn't a matter of reason or argumentation, but of hearing the testimonies of others and of coming to conviction on the basis of personal experiences. Each fast Sunday, Latter-day Saints are privileged to hear often-beautiful testimonies that offer neither syllogisms nor objective data. Missionaries quickly discover that it's testimony that changes hearts, not chains of scriptural references, let alone a book of reasoned arguments.

But that's not to admit that evidence and logic are wholly irrelevant to religious questions. Apologetics is no mere luxury or game. Someone who's been confused and bewildered by the sophistry of antagonists—and often, though not always, that's exactly what it is—might well justly regard apologetic arguments as a vital lifeline permitting the exercise of faith, as a way of keeping a spark of faith going long enough to rekindle a fire of robust belief. Testimony can see a person through times when the evidence seems against belief, but studied conviction can help a believer through spiritual dry spells, when God seems distant and spiritual experiences are distant memories. Even faithful members who're untouched by crisis or serious doubt can be benefited by solid apologetic arguments, motivated to stand fast, to keep doing the more fundamental things that will build faith and deepen confidence and strengthen their all-important spiritual witness. Why should such members be deprived of this blessing?

Will apologetic arguments save everybody? No. The Savior himself aside, *nothing* will—and, in fact, at least a few determined souls will apparently forgo salvation despite even his gracious atonement. But the fact that some remain unmoved by them no more discredits apologetic arguments as a whole than the enterprise of medicine is rendered worthless by the fact that some patients don't recover. Some illnesses are fatal.

The children of God have different temperaments, expectations, capacities, personal histories, interests, and paths, and we dare not, it seems to me, close a door on someone's journey that, though perhaps unnecessary to us, might be invaluable for that person. The fact that I can swim doesn't justify my standing on the shore watching while someone else drowns because she can't. As C. S. Lewis put it, speaking of and to well-educated British Christians,

> To be ignorant and simple now—not to be able to meet the enemies on their own ground—would be to throw down our weapons, and to betray our uneducated brethren who have, under God, no defence but us against the intellectual attacks of the heathen. Good philosophy must exist, if for no other reason, because bad philosophy needs to be answered.[1]

---

1. C. S. Lewis, "Learning in War-Time," in *The Weight of Glory and Other Addresses* (New York: HarperCollins, 2001), 58.

With Lewis expressly in mind, the English theologian and philosopher Austin Farrer (d. 1968) wrote:

> Though argument does not create conviction, lack of it destroys belief. What seems to be proved may not be embraced; but what no one shows the ability to defend is quickly abandoned. Rational argument does not create belief, but it maintains a climate in which belief may flourish.[2]

If the ground is encumbered with a lush overgrowth of critical arguments, the seed of faith of which Alma speaks cannot take root. It's the duty of the apologist, in that sense, to clear the ground and make it possible for the seed to grow. Faith is still necessary. (I'm unaware of anybody who claims that religious belief derives purely from reason; for that matter, I'm confident that unbelief doesn't either.) Apologetics is simply a useful tool that helps to preserve an environment that permits such faith to take root and flourish.

The Obligation to "Apologize"

"Be ready," says the New Testament epistle of 1 Peter, "always to give an answer (απολογιαν) to every man that asketh you a reason of the hope that is in you with meekness and fear" (1 Pet. 3:15). That's the King James Version rendering of the passage. "Always be prepared," reads the New International Version, "to give an answer to everyone who asks you to give the reason for the hope that you have. But do this with gentleness and respect." The Greek word rendered "answer" in both translations is *apologia*, which is manifestly cognate with the English word "apologetics."

One might, of course, respond that the author of 1 Peter is telling Christians to be willing to testify of Christ and their hope for salvation, something quite distinct from a call to use reason to defend a particular religious claim. And, obviously, the biblical apostles would indeed want us to stand as witnesses for Christ. But does 1 Peter 3:15 exclude the use of rational argument in such testifying?

It seems highly unlikely. The word that's translated as "reason" by both the King James Version and the New International Version, cited above, is the Greek λογος, or *logos*. It's an extraordinarily rich term, and much has been written about its meaning. *Logos* can refer to speech, a word, a computation or reckoning, the settlement of an account, or the indepen-

---

2. Austin Farrer, "The Christian Apologist," in *Light on C. S. Lewis*, ed. Jocelyn Gibb (New York: Harcourt, Brace and World, 1965), 26.

dent personified "Word" of God (as in most translations of John 1:1). A central meaning, however, is "reason," and it's from *logos* that the English word "logic" derives—as do the names of any number of fields devoted to systematic, rational inquiry (e.g., anthropology, archaeology, biology, cosmology, criminology, Egyptology, geology, meteorology, ontology, paleontology, theology, and zoology). It's rendered in the Latin Vulgate Bible's version of 1 Peter 3:15 as "ratio," which is obviously related to our English word "rational." Furthermore, when Paul spoke before King Agrippa at Caesarea Maritima—arguing that, among other things, Christ's resurrection fulfilled the predictions of Moses and the other prophets—he was making his "defense," and he used a Greek verb closely and directly related to *apologia*: *apologeisthai*. The *Apology* by Plato, similarly, reports the speech that Socrates offered before his Athenian accusers.

It seems that 1 Peter's exhortation to "be ready always to give an answer to every man that asketh you a reason of the hope that is in you" charters and legitimizes the use of reasoned argument in support of the gospel of Jesus Christ. Frankly, the idea that active Latter-day Saints might (or even should) feel no obligation to use what they know in order to defend the Church against its critics, or to help struggling Saints, strikes me as exceedingly strange. Our responsibility as members of the Church of Jesus Christ of Latter-day Saints to love and serve the Lord with all our heart, might, *mind*, and strength implies such an obligation, and our temple covenants absolutely *entail* that we sustain and defend the kingdom of God. In a sense, the scholar, thinker, teacher, or writer who places his or her skills on the altar as an offering to God is no different from the bricklayer, knitter, carpenter, counselor, administrator, dentist, accountant, youth leader, farmer, physician, linguist, genealogist, or nurse who donates time and labor and specific abilities in the service of God and the Saints and humanity in general.

> Now the body is not made up of one part but of many. If the foot should say, "Because I am not a hand, I do not belong to the body," it would not for that reason cease to be part of the body. And if the ear should say, "Because I am not an eye, I do not belong to the body," it would not for that reason cease to be part of the body. If the whole body were an eye, where would the sense of hearing be? If the whole body were an ear, where would the sense of smell be? But in fact God has arranged the parts in the body, every one of them, just as he wanted them to be. If they were all one part, where would the body be? As it is, there are many parts, but one body. The eye cannot say to the hand, "I don't need you!" And the head cannot say to the feet, "I don't need you!" (1 Cor. 12:14–21, NIV)

Now, one might conceivably argue that while, as a Christian, one is under a divine mandate to bear witness, one is not obliged to use reason to defend specific truth claims; or that, whatever covenants they may have taken upon themselves, Latter-day Saints are not obligated to defend their specific church by the use of such rational arguments as they can muster.

The scriptures, however, seem to teach otherwise. Jesus himself, for example, appealed to miracles and to fulfilled prophecy as evidence that his claims were true. To his disciples, he said, "Believe me that I am in the Father, and the Father in me: or else believe me for the very works' sake" (John 14:11). To the two Christian disciples walking along the road to Emmaus immediately after his resurrection, he said:

> O fools, and slow of heart to believe all that the prophets have spoken: Ought not Christ to have suffered these things, and to enter into his glory? And beginning at Moses and all the prophets, he expounded unto them in all the scriptures the things concerning himself. (Luke 24:25–27)

Speaking to other Jews, the original Christian apostles likewise employed fulfilled prophecy and the miracles of Jesus—particularly his resurrection—to demonstrate that Jesus was the Messiah. Consider, for example, how, in his sermon on the day of Pentecost, Peter appeals to all three:

> Men of Israel, listen to this: Jesus of Nazareth was a man accredited by God to you by miracles, wonders and signs, which God did among you through him, as you yourselves know. This man was handed over to you by God's set purpose and foreknowledge; and you, with the help of wicked men, put him to death by nailing him to the cross. But God raised him from the dead, freeing him from the agony of death, because it was impossible for death to keep its hold on him. David said about him:
>
>> "I saw the Lord always before me.
>> Because he is at my right hand,
>> I will not be shaken.
>> Therefore my heart is glad and my tongue rejoices;
>> my body also will live in hope,
>> because you will not abandon me to the grave,
>> nor will you let your Holy One see decay.
>> You have made known to me the paths of life;
>> you will fill me with joy in your presence."
>
> Brothers, I can tell you confidently that the patriarch David died and was buried, and his tomb is here to this day. But he was a prophet and knew that God had promised him on oath that he would place one of his descendants on his throne. Seeing what was ahead, he spoke of the resurrection of the Christ, that he was not abandoned to the grave, nor did his body see

decay. God has raised this Jesus to life, and we are all witnesses of the fact. (Acts 2:22–32, NIV)

In dealing with non-Jews, the apostles attempted to demonstrate the existence of God by appealing to evidence of it in nature. Thus, for instance, in Acts 14 when the pagans at Lystra were so impressed by the miracles of Barnabas and Paul that they mistook them for, respectively, Zeus and Hermes, the two apostles were horrified.

> They rent their clothes, and ran in among the people, crying out, and saying, Sirs, why do ye these things? We also are men of like passions with you, and preach unto you that ye should turn from these vanities unto the living God, which made heaven, and earth, and the sea, and all things that are therein: who in times past suffered all nations to walk in their own ways. Nevertheless he left not himself without witness, in that he did good, and gave us rain from heaven, and fruitful seasons, filling our hearts with food and gladness. (Acts 14:14–17)

Addressing the saints at Rome, Paul declared that

> the wrath of God is being revealed from heaven against all the godlessness and wickedness of men who suppress the truth by their wickedness, since what may be known about God is plain to them, because God has made it plain to them. For since the creation of the world God's invisible qualities—his eternal power and divine nature—have been clearly seen, being understood from what has been made, so that men are without excuse. (Rom. 1:18–20, NIV)

Such appeals to the evidence of nature are also found in the Old Testament: "The heavens declare the glory of God," says the Psalmist; "the skies proclaim the work of his hands" (Ps. 19:1, NIV).

Historical evidence also plays a role. Addressing the Saints at Corinth, the apostle Paul ticks off a list of witnesses to the resurrection of Jesus as evidence for the truth of what they've been taught:

> For what I received I passed on to you as of first importance: that Christ died for our sins according to the Scriptures, that he was buried, that he was raised on the third day according to the Scriptures, and that he appeared to Peter, and then to the Twelve. After that, he appeared to more than five hundred of the brothers at the same time, most of whom are still living, though some have fallen asleep. Then he appeared to James, then to all the apostles, and last of all he appeared to me also. (1 Cor. 15:3–8, NIV)

During his stay in Athens, Paul "reasoned in the synagogue with the Jews and the God-fearing Greeks, as well as in the marketplace day by day with those who happened to be there" (Acts 17:17, NIV).

And, most notably, he presented a logical case to some of the city's Epicurean and Stoic philosophers on Mars Hill, near the Acropolis, even citing proof texts from pagan Greek poets in support of his doctrine (Acts 17:18–34).

It's clear that both Jesus and the apostles were perfectly willing to supply evidence and to make arguments for the truth of the message they preached. Did this mean that they didn't trust the Holy Ghost to bring about conversion? Hardly. Instead, they trusted that the Holy Ghost would work through their arguments and their evidence to convert those whose hearts were open to the Spirit.

Moreover, according to the Book of Mormon, a similar mixture of preaching, testifying, and appealing to reason was employed by the inspired leaders of the pre-Columbian New World. Consider the case of the antichrist called Korihor:

> And he did rise up in great swelling words before Alma, and did revile against the priests and teachers, accusing them of leading away the people after the silly traditions of their fathers, for the sake of glutting on the labors of the people. Now Alma said unto him: Thou knowest that we do not glut ourselves upon the labors of this people; for behold I have labored even from the commencement of the reign of the judges until now, with mine own hands for my support, notwithstanding my many travels round about the land to declare the word of God unto my people. And notwithstanding the many labors which I have performed in the church, I have never received so much as even one senine for my labor; neither has any of my brethren, save it were in the judgment-seat; and then we have received only according to law for our time. And now, if we do not receive anything for our labors in the church, what doth it profit us to labor in the church save it were to declare the truth, that we may have rejoicings in the joy of our brethren? Then why sayest thou that we preach unto this people to get gain, when thou, of thyself, knowest that we receive no gain? (Alma 30:31–35)

Alma even appeals to a simple kind of natural theology to make his point:

> And then Alma said unto him: Believest thou that there is a God? And he answered, Nay. Now Alma said unto him: Will ye deny again that there is a God, and also deny the Christ? For behold, I say unto you, I know there is a God, and also that Christ shall come. And now what evidence have ye that there is no God, or that Christ cometh not? I say unto you that ye have none, save it be your word only. But, behold, I have all things as a testimony that these things are true; and ye also have all things as a testimony unto you that they are true; and will ye deny them? Believest thou that these things are true? Behold, I know that thou believest, but thou art possessed with a lying spirit,

and ye have put off the Spirit of God that it may have no place in you; but the devil has power over you, and he doth carry you about, working devices that he may destroy the children of God. And now Korihor said unto Alma: If thou wilt show me a sign, that I may be convinced that there is a God, yea, show unto me that he hath power, and then will I be convinced of the truth of thy words. But Alma said unto him: Thou hast had signs enough; will ye tempt your God? Will ye say, Show unto me a sign, when ye have the testimony of all these thy brethren, and also all the holy prophets? The scriptures are laid before thee, yea, and all things denote there is a God; yea, even the earth, and all things that are upon the face of it, yea, and its motion, yea, and also all the planets which move in their regular form do witness that there is a Supreme Creator. And yet do ye go about, leading away the hearts of this people, testifying unto them there is no God? And yet will ye deny against all these witnesses? And he said: Yea, I will deny, except ye shall show me a sign. And now it came to pass that Alma said unto him: Behold, I am grieved because of the hardness of your heart, yea, that ye will still resist the spirit of the truth, that thy soul may be destroyed. (Alma 30:37–46)

And the same mixture of preaching, testimony, and reasoning has been enjoined upon members of the Church of Jesus Christ of Latter-day Saints in this modern dispensation as well. "Behold," the Lord told William E. McLellin in a revelation given through the Prophet Joseph Smith on October 25, 1831, at Orange, Ohio,

> verily I say unto you, that it is my will that you should proclaim my gospel from land to land, and from city to city, yea, in those regions round about where it has not been proclaimed. . . . Go unto the eastern lands, bear testimony in every place, unto every people and in their synagogues, reasoning with the people. (D&C 66:5, 7)

McLellin was to proclaim the gospel, yes, and to bear testimony, but he was also to reason with his audience—which sounds very much like a description of a type of apologetic argumentation. Indeed, it is difficult to conceive of a method of testifying that in no way includes the faculty of reason. Even to say something as simple as "I have felt divine love, so I'm confident that there is a God who loves me" represents an elementary form of logical argument. Likewise, according to a revelation given at Hiram, Ohio, in November 1831,

> My servant, Orson Hyde, was called by his ordination to proclaim the everlasting gospel, by the Spirit of the living God, from people to people, and from land to land, in the congregations of the wicked, in their synagogues, reasoning with and expounding all scriptures unto them. (D&C 68:1)

A Brief Defense of Apologetics

Leman Copley, too, called along with Sidney Rigdon and Parley P. Pratt on a mission to his former associates among the Shakers by a revelation given at Kirtland, Ohio, in March 1831, was told to

> reason with them, not according to that which he has received of them, but according to that which shall be taught him by you my servants; and by so doing I will bless him, otherwise he shall not prosper. (D&C 49:4)

On December 1, 1831, in the wake of a series of newspaper articles written by an apostate named Ezra Booth, the Lord told the members of his little church:

> Wherefore, confound your enemies; call upon them to meet you both in public and in private; and inasmuch as ye are faithful their shame shall be made manifest. Wherefore, let them bring forth their strong reasons against the Lord. Verily, thus saith the Lord unto you—there is no weapon that is formed against you shall prosper; and if any man lift his voice against you he shall be confounded in mine own due time. (D&C 71:7–10)

Not surprisingly, the Church's contemporary missionary program, too, encourages and trains its representatives to give reasons, as the missionaries have always been expected to do. *Preach My Gospel*, the contemporary guide to missionary service, lists scriptural passages by the scores at appropriate places in its lessons for investigators. Missionaries are plainly intended to use these to reason with those they are teaching, to explain the claims of the Restoration and to support and ground them in revealed scripture.

Who Needs to Do Apologetics?

I have been arguing that there is an obligation "to give an answer to everyone who asks you to give the reason for the hope that you have."

Does that mean that every believer is under an obligation to engage in scholarship designed for apologetic use? No. Not everybody has the capacity to do it, frankly, and most are not interested. But I think that every believer is obliged to use what he or she knows in order to defend the Church against its critics when the occasion arises, or to help struggling Saints—and that believers should be steadily improving their knowledge of Church doctrine, Mormon history, and the standard works so as to (among other things) meet obligations more effectively. (If we are to do something, it seems to me obvious that we should try to do it well.) Is every believer obligated to seek out opportunities to engage critics? Again, no. Some may feel so inclined. Most do not, will not, and should not.

To the critic of apologetics who contends that apologetics is neither necessary nor essential to the gospel of Jesus Christ, an obvious rejoinder is that an ability to speak Samoan isn't essential to the gospel either. But the fact that at least one member of the Church has been able to speak Samoan has certainly helped Samoan speakers find salvation. In much the same way, those who may need reasons and evidence to help them along their path to a spiritual witness of the gospel—who, as it were, speak that language—can be benefitted by those able to communicate with them in the most appropriate manner. In this, as in every other way, members of the Church do well to imitate their Lord, who speaks "unto [his] servants in their weakness, after the manner of their language, that they might come to understanding" (D&C 1:24).

There are very many Latter-day Saints who will never write a book or an article in a journal or make a conference presentation but who nevertheless, in their own sphere and style, stand as witnesses for God and defend the cause of God as they understand it. They would seldom if ever label such a thing "apologetics." They may well not know the term.

This is as it should be. And we should all be continually improving our ability to be such witnesses, in whatever manner suits our abilities, interests, and inclinations. (There's no one, single, right way.) In a revelation given through Joseph Smith at Kirtland, Ohio, on or about December 27, 1832, the Saints were given

> a commandment that you shall teach one another the doctrine of the kingdom. Teach ye diligently and my grace shall attend you, that you may be instructed more perfectly in theory, in principle, in doctrine, in the law of the gospel, in all things that pertain unto the kingdom of God, that are expedient for you to understand; of things both in heaven and in the earth, and under the earth; things which have been, things which are, things which must shortly come to pass; things which are at home, things which are abroad; the wars and the perplexities of the nations, and the judgments which are on the land; and a knowledge also of countries and of kingdoms—that ye may be prepared in all things when I shall send you again to magnify the calling whereunto I have called you, and the mission with which I have commissioned you. Behold, I sent you out to testify and warn the people, and it becometh every man who hath been warned to warn his neighbor. Therefore, they are left without excuse, and their sins are upon their own heads. He that seeketh me early shall find me, and shall not be forsaken. Therefore, tarry ye, and labor diligently, that you may be perfected in your ministry to go forth among the Gentiles for the last time. (D&C 88:77–84)

It seems axiomatic that if one is going to hold a position, one has the responsibility to defend it. And, unless we're catatonic or asocial, we all routinely do it. We all give reasons. We don't just say, "Because!" Even someone arguing that we ought not to do apologetics is, ironically, offering an apologetic for that position.

Now, a critic of apologetics might respond that she prefers carrots to broccoli but that she sees no reason to defend her position against somebody who likes broccoli better than carrots. The problem with this implicit analogy is that taste in food is entirely personal and subjective; famously, *De gustibus non disputandum est*—"There is no disputing about tastes." But religious truth is not merely a matter of taste—at least to most believers. There must be and really is something Out There, however difficult it may be to verify, that is objectively real.

Positive Apologetics

As I've said, I believe that some form of apologetics is incumbent upon all Christians, and because of the covenants that they've taken upon themselves, perhaps even more so upon Latter-day Saints. Those covenants culminate in the temple, but they begin at baptism. "Behold," said the prophet Alma,

> here are the waters of Mormon (for thus were they called) and now, as ye are desirous to come into the fold of God, and to be called his people, and are willing to bear one another's burdens, that they may be light; yea, and are willing to mourn with those that mourn; yea, and comfort those that stand in need of comfort, and to stand as witnesses of God at all times and in all things, and in all places that ye may be in, even until death, that ye may be redeemed of God, and be numbered with those of the first resurrection, that ye may have eternal life—Now I say unto you, if this be the desire of your hearts, what have you against being baptized in the name of the Lord, as a witness before him that ye have entered into a covenant with him, that ye will serve him and keep his commandments, that he may pour out his Spirit more abundantly upon you? (Mosiah 18:8–10)

But how, precisely, are we to "stand as witnesses of God at all times and in all things, and in all places"? I answer, "in various ways." Defense is good and necessary, with regard to advancing the gospel as in playing football, chess, soccer, basketball, checkers, rugby, and baseball. However good one's offense may be, if there is no defense one will lose. The story of Nehemiah's rebuilding of the temple and other structures in Jerusalem following the Babylonian captivity, accomplished against considerable local opposition, offers an instructive metaphor:

> And it came to pass from that time forth, that the half of my servants wrought in the work, and the other half of them held both the spears, the shields, and the bows, and the habergeons; and the rulers were behind all the house of Judah. They which builded on the wall, and they that bare burdens, with those that laded, every one with one of his hands wrought in the work, and with the other hand held a weapon. For the builders, every one had his sword girded by his side, and so builded. (Neh. 4:16–18)

Those builders would surely have preferred to devote their full attention to constructive labor, but, under the circumstances, they simply couldn't. I like to call the corresponding form of apologetics "*negative* apologetics," meaning not that it's mean-spirited but that its task is the negatively defined one of rebuttal and defense. I contrast such undertakings with what I term "*positive* apologetics," the constructive effort of affirmatively advocating the claims of the Restoration. It could be viewed as the act of planting the seed in the ground, while negative apologetics, rebutting the attacks of antagonists, is analogous to clearing the ground of weeds, and keeping it clear, so that the seed has a chance to take root and grow. Both kinds of apologetics are necessary, just as both sowing and weeding are required in the garden.

A good recent example of negative apologetics would be the responses of Latter-day Saint scientists to certain DNA-based arguments against Book of Mormon historicity. Contemporary genetic research was supposed to constitute a "Galileo moment" and to deliver a fatal blow to Mormonism. But upon examination, the critics' arguments were found to be deficient. They were based on misconceptions about what DNA can and cannot prove and upon long-held but unsustainable assumptions about Book of Mormon geography and populations. Thus, what looked like a bed of weeds that threatened to choke out the seed of faith was cleared away by good, solid apologetics. Plainly, occasional weeding is just as necessary to the flowering of faith and the harvest of testimony as are planting and cultivating.

But like those ancient postexilic workers in Jerusalem, most of us—I emphatically include myself in this, even though I've certainly devoted a great deal of time to countering critics—will naturally prefer affirmative apologetics, building a positive case for our beliefs. For most people worldwide, Mormonism is not what William James, in his classic essay "The Will to Believe," called a "live hypothesis." Belief in it simply isn't possible for them, given what they know, or believe they know, about the gospel and about the universe, and given where they are at in their lives.

It is the challenge of positive apologetics, or so it seems to me, to attempt to make the gospel a "live hypothesis" for as many more of the Father's children as we can.

How? There are innumerable ways. The positive task has (at least) two parts: (1) Obviously, those we hope to bring to Christ and to his church need to believe that the gospel is true. (2) But they also need to believe that it's desirable. (I suspect that the priority or order of these two aspects will vary from one person to the other and will even be mixed in various idiosyncratic ways. Conversion is always individual.) The second task opens up the realm of apologetics far beyond those who are specially skilled in scriptural argument or in building historical arguments. In fact, it may not require arguments at all. C. S. Lewis, for example, continues to show millions of people how a Christian worldview can satisfy, inspire, and fulfill—and, although he wrote many brilliant books of apologetic argument, he also does it, in very many cases, via his fictional Chronicles of Narnia series and his so-called Perelandra trilogy.

I argue that no expertise is required for demonstrating that the gospel is desirable. Or, rather, no *unique* expertise, no special training. All have the ability to do this.

Conclusion

The word may be offputting, but I contend that apologetics is an essential part of Christian discipleship. Moreover, I insist, we all engage in it. Even those who argue against apologetics are arguing for their own vision of what discipleship ought to be.

The question isn't whether we'll do apologetics, but how we'll do it. Will we be honest? Competent? Civil? Will we be effective, or not?

THREE

Boundary Maintenance that Pushes the Boundaries: Scriptural and Theological Insights from Apologetics

Neal Rappleye

Apologetics is, by definition, a defense of already held beliefs and points of view. As such, it is easy to see apologetics as an obstacle to new understandings of scriptural texts and theological concepts. This can and does happen, and some may even argue that defending a viewpoint inherently obscures or prevents new points of view from being considered. However, as counterintuitive as it may seem, the practice of apologetics by Latter-day Saint scholars has often done just the opposite: efforts to defend certain points of Latter-day Saint belief have often led to fresh perspectives on LDS scripture and theology.

My purpose here is not to defend or endorse any particular apologetic approach or argument, but rather to show how defending certain tenents of Latter-day Saint belief involves reinterpretations of scripture and doctrine—and that whatever the merits of any specific reinterpretation may be, this transformative effect is a net positive. Apologetics is at its best not when it is merely defending or providing supportive evidence, but when it can get Latter-day Saints to rethink their understanding of scriptural narratives and teachings, even as it defends certain fundamental premises.[1] My background makes me more familiar with LDS apologetic work on

---

1. Since "apologetic" and "apologist" have in certain venues become a pejorative, I simply want to clarify that my use of these terms here is not intended in a negative or derogatory sense. To the contrary, I myself identify as an apologist and have contributed apologetic works utilizing some of the approaches discussed in this paper.

the Book of Mormon, so I will largely draw my examples from there. Other apologetic work, however, has also provided its fair share of insights into LDS theology and scripture.

"As Far As It Is Translated Correctly": The Bible and the Book of Mormon

One place to start is by looking at how certain apologetic approaches to the Book of Mormon have changed how we read and understand the Bible. Despite rejecting biblical inerrancy and accepting the Bible only insofar "as it is translated correctly" (A of F 1:8), LDS approaches to the Old Testament have generally been rather conservative. Biblical narratives are typically taken at face value, and the Bible is theologically harmonized both internally—within the books of the Bible—and externally—with the rest of the LDS canon and contemporary teachings.

Some LDS scholars, however, have not only dealt with critical approaches to the Bible, but embraced them as part of their argument for the authenticity of the Book of Mormon. An example of this is found in the way Margaret Barker's work has become paradigmatic for some Latter-day Saint apologetic scholarship.[2] Throughout several books and articles, Barker has argued that pre-exilic Israelite religion was centered on the temple, where *El* or *Elohim* sat on his throne in the holy of holies as "Most High God" (*El Elyon*), amidst a divine council of gods. *Yahweh* (Jehovah) was one of the sons of El, appointed over Israel (i.e., the "God of Israel"), and he was manifest on earth through the Davidic king (i.e., the "Messiah"). Through temple ritual, the king (the Messiah), acting as Yahweh, would make atonement for the people. According to Barker, these original Israelite beliefs were lost or repressed for centuries, and Christianity marked a return to this older faith.[3]

Barker's reconstruction of ancient Israelite belief, and her notion of Christianity as a "restoration" of that belief, bears an uncanny resemblance to traditional Mormon theology. Her work has therefore possessed a natural attraction for LDS apologists, and they've used it in a variety of ways.

---

2. See Kevin Christensen, "'Paradigms Regained': A Survey of Margaret Barker's Scholarship and its Significance for Mormon Studies," *FARMS Occasional Papers* 2 (2001).

3. Barker's views on this are scattered throughout numerous publications, but can be found conveniently summarized on her website in Margaret Barker, "Temple Theology," online at http://www.margaretbarker.com/Temple/default.htm.

In particular, Barker's reconstruction of pre-exilic Israelite theology is used to defend the Book of Mormon from criticisms about its overtly Christian theology in 600 BC, and to argue that the Book of Mormon fits this pre-exilic context better than a nineteenth-century context.[4] Yet adopting Barker's work as a paradigm for understanding the Book of Mormon and LDS theology introduces some new wrinkles.

According to Barker, the loss or repression of this ancient Israelite religion began under the direction of King Josiah during his religious reformation, ca. 622 BC. The biblical narrative presents Josiah as a righteous king, who responds to the discovery of a lost "book of the law" (Deuteronomy) by restoring and implementing its lost religious teachings (2 Kgs. 22–23). Barker, however, would have it the other way around: older Israelite religious traditions were stamped out and purged by Josiah and his supporters, and biblical texts, most especially Deuteronomy through 2 Kings, were written or edited by Josiah's supporters and their ideological descendants to eliminate or suppress the older, messianic faith.[5] In LDS parlance, Josiah's reforms were not a restoration but an apostasy.

Placing Lehi, Nephi, and the Book of Mormon within this paradigm acknowledges competing theological views within the Old Testament and sets the Book of Mormon at odds with some of them. It also dramatically changes how we understand King Josiah. Within typical LDS pedagogy, the positive portrayal of Josiah found in the Old Testament is accepted at face value.[6] While LDS scholars who have embraced Barker's paradigm

---

4. See Kevin Christensen, "The Temple, the Monarchy, and Wisdom: Lehi's World and the Scholarship of Margaret Barker," in *Glimpses of Lehi's Jerusalem*, ed. John W. Welch, David Rolph Seely, and Jo Ann H. Seely (Provo, Utah: FARMS, 2004), 449–522; Kevin Christensen, "The Deuteronomist De-Christianizing of the Old Testament," *FARMS Review* 16, no. 2 (2004): 59–90; Brant A. Gardner, *Second Witness: Analytical and Contextual Commentary on the Book of Mormon*, 6 vols. (Salt Lake City: Greg Kofford Books, 2007), 1:214–22. Barker herself reviews the Book of Mormon and other LDS beliefs in light of her views on pre-exilic Israel in Margaret Barker, "Joseph Smith and Preexilic Israel," in *The Worlds of Joseph Smith: A Bicentennial Conference at the Library of Congress*, ed. John W. Welch (Provo, Utah: BYU Press, 2005), 69–82.

5. See Margaret Barker, "What Did King Josiah Reform?" in *Glimpses of Lehi's Jerusalem*, ed. John W. Welch, David Rolph Seely, and Jo Ann H. Seely (Provo, Utah: FARMS, 2004), 521–42.

6. See, for instance, the treatment of Josiah in *Old Testament: Gospel Doctrine Manual* (Salt Lake City: Intellectual Reserve, 2001), 144–50.

have not completely rejected Josiah and his reforms as mistaken, it has certainly required a more nuanced approach.[7]

Apologetic approaches like this give weight to a theological concept—that the Bible is not perfect and contains errors—that often feels hollow within typical Mormon approaches. They also serve to illustrate to Latter-day Saints that critically approaching the composition of scripture need not be something to fear. Seeing multiple, and even contending points of view within scripture is not necessarily a bad thing. In fact, it can bolster faith as it provides better context for the Book of Mormon and improves understanding of how the Book of Mormon relates to different traditions within the Old Testament.

Authorial Bias in the Book of Mormon: Laman and Lemuel as a Case Study

These kinds of approaches also invite us to look for competing traditions and viewpoints within the Book of Mormon itself—since it is, after all, believed to be written by several different persons who lived in different places over the course of 1,000 years. Taking the Book of Mormon seriously on those terms has led LDS scholars to consider the circumstances in which specific authors within the text are said to have written, and reflect on how those circumstances shape their writing. Noel Reynolds, for example, has noted that when Nephi wrote his additional account (First and Second Nephi) in the small plates, his father Lehi had already passed away and his brothers Laman and Lemuel had made competing claims of leadership within the Lehite community (2 Ne. 4:12; 5:3). Reynolds thus argues that this separate account was written as a "political tract" intended

---

7. This subject was discussed by a pair of apologists with different perspectives in 2013. See Benjamin L. McGuire, "Josiah's Reform: An Introduction," *Interpreter: A Journal of Mormon Scripture* 4 (2013): 160–63; William J. Hamblin, "Vindicating Josiah," *Interpreter: A Journal of Mormon Scripture* 4 (2013): 165–76; Kevin Christensen, "Prophets and Kings in Lehi's Jerusalem and Margaret Barker's Temple Theology," *Interpreter: A Journal of Mormon Scripture* 4 (2013): 177–93. For another approach, see the personal note in Daniel C. Peterson, "Nephi and His Asherah: A Note on 1 Nephi 11:8–23," in *Mormons, Scripture, and the Ancient World: Studies in Honor of John L. Sorenson*, ed. Davis Bitton (Provo, Utah: FARMS, 1998), 218–19. My own personal thoughts on this can be seen in Neal Rappleye, "The Deuteronomist Reforms and Lehi's Family Dynamics: A Social Context for the Rebellions of Laman and Lemuel," *Interpreter: A Journal of Mormon Scripture* 16 (2015): 89–90.

to establish the legitimacy of Nephi's rule over the competing claims of his brothers.[8] For the apologist, this demonstrates complexity in the narrative and motives for writing, and it ties those motives to specific circumstances in Nephi's life—thus arguing that First and Second Nephi were written by someone who really experienced those conditions (i.e., Nephi himself), rather than being a fictional account written by someone far removed from such a situation (i.e., Joseph Smith).

The suggestion that Nephi's account, which he says is for the "more sacred" things (1 Ne. 19:5) is actually a highly political document by itself is a remarkable insight into the Book of Mormon text, but it also opens further possibilities. If Nephi's text is a political tract meant to establish his own legitimacy, how might that impact how he portrays the political opposition—Laman and Lemuel? Grant Hardy notes that in Nephi's account, "Laman and Lemuel are stock characters, even caricatures."[9] Using Barker's reconstruction of pre-exilic Israelite religion, if Lehi and Nephi are seen as being at least partly opposed to Josiah's reforms, Laman and Lemuel it seems were all in.[10] But this means that Laman and Lemuel were not paragons of wickedness or decadence, as modern readers tend to assume, but "orthodox, observant Jews" from their time.[11] Even their attempts to kill Nephi and Lehi can be seen in the context of Deuteronomic laws regarding false prophets, rather than nefarious or murderous designs (Deut. 13:1–11; 18:20).[12] None of this means that Laman and Lemuel were right or that Latter-day Saints today should agree with them, but it does make them more understandable as real people who held beliefs and points of view that, in context, were entirely rational.

A Divine Mother in the Book of Mormon

Given Latter-day Saint belief in a Heavenly Mother,[13] it is no surprise that LDS apologetic scholars have also taken interest in the proposal, made

---

8. Noel B. Reynolds, "The Political Dimension in Nephi's Small Plates," *BYU Studies* 27, no. 4 (Fall 1987): 20–33.

9. Grant Hardy, *Understanding the Book of Mormon: A Reader's Guide* (New York: Oxford University Press, 2010), 33.

10. See Rappleye, "The Deuteronomist Reforms," 87–99.

11. Hardy, *Understanding*, 39.

12. See Rappleye, "The Deuteronomist Reforms," 93–94; Hardy, *Understanding*, 40.

13. See David L. Paulsen and Martin Pulido, "'A Mother There': A Survey of Historical Teachings about Mother in Heaven," *BYU Studies* 50, no. 1 (2011): 71–97.

by Barker and many others, that many ancient Israelites worshipped a Mother Goddess named *Asherah*, wife of El or Yahweh.[14] David L. Paulsen drew on this work to argue that theologians and scholars are now coming around to the doctrines within LDS theology—such as the belief in a divine mother—that have traditionally been seen as pushing the boundaries.[15] But more interesting—and somewhat surprising—than the use of Asherah to support LDS belief in Heavenly Mother is the way this ancient Israelite belief has been used to argue for the antiquity of the Book of Mormon.

A connection between Heavenly Mother and the Book of Mormon doesn't seem obvious; no blatant appearance of an ancient Israelite goddess shows up within its pages. Yet Daniel Peterson has argued that in Nephi's vision (1 Ne. 11), the spirit draws explicitly on the imagery of Asherah in order to instruct Nephi on the meaning of his father's dream.[16] When Nephi asked to know the meaning of the tree, he is shown "the mother of God . . . bearing a child in her arms" (1 Ne. 11:18, 20).[17] Throughout ancient Near Eastern cultures, goddesses are symbolized by a sacred tree,[18] and Asherah in Israel appears to be no exception to this.[19] In the broader Canaanite cultures, these tree-goddesses were heavily sexualized, but in

---

14. See William G. Dever, *Did God Have a Wife? Archaeology and Folk Religion in Ancient Israel* (Grand Rapids: Wm. B. Eerdmanns, 2005).

15. David L. Paulsen, "Are Christians Mormon? Reassessing Joseph Smith's Theology in His Bicentennial," *BYU Studies* 45, no. 1 (2006): 104–7.

16. For the most recent iteration of his argument, see Daniel C. Peterson, "A Divine Mother in the Book of Mormon?" in *Mormonism and the Temple: Examining an Ancient Religious Tradition*, ed. Gary N. Anderson (Logan, Utah: Academy for Temple Studies and USU Religious Studies, 2013), 109–24. See also Daniel C. Peterson, "Nephi and His Asherah," *Journal of Book of Mormon Studies* 9, no. 2 (2000): 16–25.

17. I am following the wording found in the original text, which did not include "son of" in 1 Nephi 11:18. For discussion of this variant, see Royal Skousen, *Analysis of Textual Variants of the Book of Mormon, Part 1: 1 Nephi–2 Nephi 11*, 2nd ed. (Provo, Utah: FARMS and BYU Studies, 2017), 235–38.

18. John S. Thompson, "The Lady at the Horizon: Egyptian Tree Goddess Iconography and Sacred Trees in Israelite Scripture and Temple Theology," in *Ancient Temple Worship: Proceedings of The Expound Symposium, 14 May 2011*, ed. Matthew B. Brown, et al. (Orem, Utah, and Salt Lake City: Interpreter Foundation and Eborn Books, 2014), 217–41.

19. See Margaret Barker, "The Fragrant Tree," in *The Tree of Life: From Eden to Eternity*, ed. John W. Welch and Donald W. Parry (Salt Lake City and Provo, Utah: Deseret Book and Neal A. Maxwell Institute, 2011), 55–79.

both Israel and Egypt, the tree-goddess took on a more motherly role—specifically, the mother of the gods in heaven and the king on earth—and tree-goddesses are often depicted nursing a child.[20]

Peterson acknowledges, of course, that Mary is not Asherah or Heavenly Mother. But with the association of Mary with the same symbolism and title as Asherah, Mary becomes a representation on earth of the divine Mother in Heaven.[21] Furthermore, Nephi's sudden understanding that the tree in his father's vision is the "love of God" (1 Ne. 11:22) potentially takes on additional meaning. As Allison Skabelund Von Feldt noted, "the 'love of God' could also mean not merely a possession of God's . . . but rather the object of God's love—the person whom he loves. . . . A beloved wife, perhaps."[22] In any case, an allusion to Heavenly Mother in the Book of Mormon is a significant insight, one that could, with further exploration, provide a means for bringing the divine feminine more to the forefront in contemporary Mormon thought.[23]

The Temple in Scripture and Antiquity

As of June 2017, there are 182 temples either in operation, currently under construction, or announced by the LDS Church.[24] As with so many other things, Joseph Smith believed that he was restoring something ancient but lost or corrupted with the building of temples and the introduction of rituals performed there. So, starting with Hugh Nibley,[25] ancient temple studies has been a major component to LDS apologetic scholar-

---

20. See Thompson, "The Lady at the Horizon," 225, 228–229; Peterson, "Nephi and His Asherah," *JBMS* 19; Peterson, "A Divine Mother," 110–11; Barker, "The Fragrant Tree," 72.

21. Barker, "Joseph Smith and Preexilic Israel," 76; Samuel Zinner, *Textual and Comparative Explorations in 1 & 2 Enoch* (Orem, Utah, and Salt Lake City: Interpreter Foundation and Eborn Books, 2014), 265.

22. Alyson Skabelund Von Feldt, "Does God Have a Wife?" *FARMS Review* 19, no. 1 (2007): 114.

23. Overall, this potential has scarcely been tapped. For one effort to further seek out Heavenly Mother in scripture, however, see Val Larsen, "Hidden in Plain View: Mother in Heaven in Scripture," *SquareTwo* 8, no. 2 (2015), http://squaretwo.org/Sq2ArticleLarsenHeavenlyMother.html.

24. See "Statistics," at *Temples of the Church of Jesus Christ of Latter-day Saints*, June 3, 2016, http://ldschurchtemples.org/statistics/.

25. For a collection of Nibley's temple-related studies, see Hugh Nibley, *Temple and Cosmos* (Salt Lake City and Provo, Utah: Deseret Book and FARMS, 1992).

ship.²⁶ Given the nature of temple ritual and commitments, arguments are often more implicit than explicit, but the (usually implied) argument is that ancient temple rituals parallel the ceremonies performed in the modern LDS temples, thus supporting Joseph Smith's claims of restoring ancient traditions and countering claims of more modern derivation from sources such as Masonry.²⁷ Recognizing ancient similarities to LDS temple practices, however, also has the potential to enrich and add meaning to the temple experience of Latter-day Saints.

Understanding the meaning and symbolism in similar ancient Near Eastern and early Christian rituals can yield insights for temple-attending Latter-day Saints. William Hamblin, for example, has pointed out that in ancient Israel, Yahweh's "secret" plan (Amos 3:7) was revealed to prophets in the divine council, which usually took place in a temple setting. Noting that the pattern followed in these visions was similar to the pattern followed in the LDS temple endowment ceremony, Hamblin suggested that participants in the Endowment should see themselves as ritually participating in the divine council, where the initiate enters into God's presence, has His plan revealed, and is commissioned to fulfill that plan.²⁸ Through this insight, a fairly typical Latter-day Saint can see themselves as receiving the same experience and commission as the ancient prophets.

Insights from ancient temple studies have also been extended to the unique LDS scriptural works. Mormon scholars have identified ancient temple themes and patterns in the Book of Mormon,²⁹ the Book of

---

26. See the papers in Donald W. Parry, ed., *Temples in the Ancient World* (Salt Lake City and Provo, Utah: FARMS, 1994); Donald W. Parry and Stephen D. Ricks, ed., *The Temple in Time and Eternity* (Provo, Utah: FARMS, 1999).

27. See Blake Ostler, "Clothed Upon: A Unique Aspect of Christian Antiquity," *BYU Studies* 22, no. 1 (1982): 31–45; Jeffrey M. Bradshaw, "Freemasonry and the Origins of Modern Temple Ordinances," *Interpreter: A Journal of Mormon Scripture* 15 (2015): 159–237.

28. See William J. Hamblin, "The *Sôd* of YHWH and the Endowment," *Interpreter: A Journal of Mormon Scripture* 4 (2013): 147–54.

29. John W. Welch, *Illuminating the Sermon at the Temple and the Sermon on the Mount: An Approach to 3 Nephi 11–18 and Matthew 5–7* (Provo, Utah: FARMS, 1999); LeGrand L. Baker and Stephen D. Ricks, *Who Shall Ascend in the Hill of the Lord? The Psalms in Israel's Temple Worship in the Old Testament and the Book of Mormon* (Salt Lake City: Eborn Books, 2010).

Moses,[30] and the Book of Abraham.[31] Apologetically, these observations are used both as evidence that these scriptural works are genuinely ancient, and that the modern LDS temple rituals were not later innovations of Joseph Smith but in fact baked into his earliest revelations.[32] Going beyond these apologetics, such connections can inform how we read these scriptural works, and they can help Latter-day Saints connect their temple worship experience to their daily worship and scripture study.

Recognizing temple themes in LDS scriptural texts also leads to specific insights into scriptural meanings. An illustration of this can be seen with the "tongue of angels" in Joseph Spencer's reading of First and Second Nephi as a temple text.[33] The phrase "speak with the tongue of angels" in 2 Nephi 31:13–14 and 32:2–3 is customarily understood to mean speaking under inspiration of the Holy Spirit.[34] Read as a temple text, however, the "tongue of angels" comes as a part of Nephi's reflections on passing through the veil and entering into the Lord's presence (2 Ne. 30–33). Coupling this context with the fact that Nephi uses similar phraseology when describing both speaking with the tongue of angels and his father's encounter with the divine council (1 Ne. 1:8; 2 Ne. 31:13), Spencer argued that speaking with the "tongue of angels" should be un-

---

30. See Jeffrey M. Bradshaw, *Temple Themes in the Book of Moses* (Salt Lake City: Eborn Books, 2014); David Bokovoy, *Authoring the Old Testament: Genesis–Deuteronomy* (Salt Lake City: Greg Kofford Books, 2014), 147–49.

31. See Hugh Nibley, *The Message of the Joseph Smith Papyri: An Egyptian Endowment*, 2nd ed. (Salt Lake City and Provo, Utah: Deseret Book and FARMS, 2005); Stephen O. Smoot and Quinten Barney, "The Book of the Dead as a Temple Text and the Implications for the Book of Abraham," in *The Temple: Ancient and Restored* (Orem, Utah, and Salt Lake City: Interpreter Foundation and Eborn Books, 2016), 183–209.

32. Gerald E. Smith, *Schooling the Prophet: How the Book of Mormon Influenced Joseph Smith and the Early Restoration* (Provo, Utah: Neal A. Maxwell Institute for Religious Scholarship, 2015), 129–64; Don Bradley, "Piercing the Veil: Temple Worship in the Lost 116 Pages," (paper presented at the Annual FairMormon Conference on August 3, 2012 in Sandy, Utah), available at https://www.fairmormon.org/conference/august-2012/piercing-the-veil-temple-worship-in-the-lost-116-pages.

33. See Joseph M. Spencer, *An Other Testament: On Typology*, 2d ed. (Provo, Utah: Neal A. Maxwell Institute for Religious Scholarship, 2016), 33–52.

34. Robert L. Millet, "Tongue of Angels," in *Book of Mormon Reference Companion*, ed. Dennis L. Largey (Salt Lake City: Deseret Book), 757–58.

derstood as becoming divine and joining the council.³⁵ This interpretation is supported further by analysis of the patterns and phrasing in the divine council settings described in 1 Nephi 11 and 2 Nephi 16 (Isaiah 6), and Nephi's final conclusion, where he asserts that he himself will be among the divine council when the reader enters into the Lord's presence to be judged (2 Ne. 33:11). This comes right on the heels of his statement that he "speaketh by the power of the Holy Ghost" and that his writings are "the words of Christ" (2 Ne. 33:1, 10)—both conceptual equivalents to speaking with the tongue of angels (2 Ne. 32:3).³⁶ This new interpretation—that speaking with the tongue of angels refers to becoming a divine member of God's council—also gives Latter-day Saints one way to see deification (exaltation) in the Book of Mormon, a modern LDS belief not customarily thought to be present in the Nephite text.

Geography and Gentiles

Transitioning from the esoteric to the more mundane and physical, studies in Book of Mormon geography often serve apologetic purposes, but also have valuable insights to offer. Most readers of the Book of Mormon pay little attention to geographic details, but if they do, they quickly find themselves lost in a dizzying array of details scattered across the 500-plus page narrative. Sorting out Book of Mormon geography can feel like putting together a 1000-piece puzzle without having the picture on the box for reference.³⁷ Not having paid much attention to the details, however, most readers assume that the book's geography is "obviously" hemispheric—with the "land northward" being North America, the "land southward" being South America, and Panama being the "narrow neck of land."

From very early on, however, some who carefully read and analyzed the geographic details in the text realized that Nephite geography must

---

35. Spencer, *An Other Testament*, 49–52.

36. See Neal Rappleye, "'With the Tongue of Angels': Angelic Speech as a Form of Deification," *Interpreter: A Journal of Mormon Scripture* 21 (2016): 303–23.

37. The leading Book of Mormon geographers have cited up to 1,068 passages while constructing geographical models. See Randall P. Spackman, "Verses in the Book of Mormon with Potential Geographical Relevance" (2003), available online at https://archive.bookofmormoncentral.org/content/verses-book-mormon-potential-geographical-relevance.

have been more limited in scope.[38] In 1909, even while upholding a hemispheric geography himself, B. H. Roberts realized that "the physical description relative to the contour of the lands occupied by the Jaredites and Nephites . . . can be found between Mexico and Yucatan with the isthmus of Tehuantepec between," and felt that shifting to that more limited region, "many of our difficulties as to the geography of the Book of Mormon—if not all of them in fact, will have passed away."[39] Using a more limited geography, a coherent picture emerges from that 1000-piece puzzle—a fact that is used in apologetics as evidence that the Book of Mormon was too complex to be written in rapid dictation by Joseph Smith.[40] The emergence of a coherent geography is also an impressive insight in its own right.

Even before attempting to correlate it to the real world, the "internal maps" that Book of Mormon geographers such as John Sorenson and John Clark have produced are useful study aids that can, at the very least, help readers make sense of the sometimes-dizzying geographical details.[41] The insight this can provide to the geographic-heavy war narratives or missionary journeys should be obvious. But there are also some more surprising ways understanding Book of Mormon geography can bring clarity to the text. In some instances, awareness of the geographic situation can help make sense of how Isaiah is being used in the Book of Mormon.

Consider the trial of Abinadi in Mosiah 12–17, where the priests of King Noah ask him to interpret Isaiah 52:7–10. Why would they ask him to interpret Isaiah in the middle of a legal trial? The typical assumption is

---

38. For the intellectual history of Book of Mormon geography, see Matthew Roper, "Limited Geography and the Book of Mormon: Historical Antecedents and Early Interpretations," *FARMS Review* 16, no. 2 (2004): 225–75; John L. Sorenson, *The Geography of Book of Mormon Events: A Source Book*, revised edition (Provo, Utah: FARMS, 1992), 7–35. For analysis of the travel distances in the Book of Mormon, see John L. Sorenson, *Mormon's Map* (Provo, Utah: FARMS, 2000), 55–78.

39. B. H. Roberts, *New Witnesses for God*, 3 vols. (Salt Lake City: Deseret News, 1909), 3:502–3.

40. John L. Sorenson, "How Could Joseph Smith Write So Accurately About Ancient American Civilization?" in *Echoes and Evidences of the Book of Mormon*, ed. Donald W. Parry, Daniel C. Peterson, and John W. Welch (Provo, Utah: 2002), 267–69. See also Hardy, *Understanding*, 6–7.

41. See Sorenson, *Mormon's Map*; John E. Clark, "Revisiting 'A Key for Evaluating Book of Mormon Geographies'," *Mormon Studies Review* 23, no. 1 (2011): 13–43. The utility in assisting readers make sense of the text is precisely why Grant Hardy, ed., *The Book of Mormon: A Reader's Edition* (Urbana, Ill., and Chicago: University of Illinois Press, 2003) included Sorenson's internal map (pp. 688–89).

that the wicked priests are witless pursuers of the scriptures who seek better understanding from the prophet Abinadi, even as they prepare to execute him.[42] To the contrary, however, understanding the topography of Nephite lands and geo-historical context reveals that the priests of Noah perhaps had a specific and sophisticated interpretation of Isaiah 52:7–10, and that they believed this interpretation proved Abinadi was a false prophet.[43]

This story takes place in the land of Nephi. This was the place Nephi and his first followers had settled and built a temple when they separated themselves from Nephi's brothers (2 Ne. 5:1–16). It was evidently amidst a mountainous region, high up in elevation.[44] After hundreds of years making this land their home, the Nephites left this land, coming down from the mountains and settling in the land of Zarahemla (Omni 1:12–13). Zeniff, Noah's father, led a group of Nephites back to what would have been, to them, their promised land, where they displaced the Lamanites and regained possession of the city and the temple (Mosiah 7:21; 9:1–9). As Noah began to rule, they were prospering in the land, as evidenced by Noah and his priests' opulence (Mosiah 11).

As John Welch and Joseph Spencer have argued, in this geographic, historical, and political context, Isaiah 52:7–10 was not just some random scripture that Noah's priests were curious about. It was a proof text. *They* were the messengers, whose feet were beautiful "upon the mountains," who preached the "good tidings of good." The Lord had, indeed, "brought again Zion" in the land of their fathers, their "Jerusalem" had been "redeemed."[45] And now, in the face of what they saw as clear pro-

---

42. See, for example, Monte S. Nyman, "Abinadi's Commentary on Isaiah," in *Mosiah, Salvation Only Through Christ*, ed. Monte S. Nyman and Charles D. Tate Jr. (Provo, Utah: BYU Religious Studies Center, 1991), 161.

43. See John W. Welch, *The Legal Cases of the Book of Mormon* (Provo, Utah: BYU Press and the Neal A. Maxwell Institute for Religious Scholarship, 2008), 139–209. Though I chose not to explore it in this paper, the legal analysis of Welch on not just Abinadi's trial, but also several other stories in the Book of Mormon, is another example of apologetic scholarship—Welch is arguing that the Book of Mormon reflects ancient Israelite legal perspectives—which has provided several rich insights into the Book of Mormon. Joseph M. Spencer, "Isaiah 52 in the Book of Mormon: Notes on Isaiah's Reception History," *Relegere: Studies in Religion and Reception* 6, no. 2 (2016): 203 n.40 praises Welch's analysis of Abinadi's trial as "some of the best available exegesis of the Abinadi story."

44. Sorenson, *Mormon's Map*, 32–34.

45. See Welch, *Legal Cases*, 176; Spencer, "Isaiah 52 in the Book of Mormon," 203–4.

phetic fulfillment, who was Abinadi to challenge them? The priests cited Isaiah 52:7–10 as evidence that the Lord was with them, and thus Abinadi must be a false prophet worthy of death. This insight further enlightens the rest of the Abinadi narrative.[46]

The realization that the geography is limited has other implications to how the text is read. The Book of Mormon's stage was in "a comparatively little theater," in the words of late-twentieth-century apostle Neal A. Maxwell,[47] and that little theater left a lot of room for other peoples to play out other stories. As with the limited geographical scope, there's been some awareness of this reality from very early on in Mormon history,[48] though most readers have generally assumed that Book of Mormon peoples inhabited an empty continent. To overcome that general impression, LDS apologetic scholars have scoured the text searching for hints of "others" in the text.[49] At the same time, the lack of more explicit reference to these "others" has been explained by defining the Book of Mormon as a "lineage history," a type of history found in ancient Mesoamerica (and many other places) that deals exclusively, or at least primarily, with the history of a specific lineage to the exclusion of all other peoples.[50]

Shrinking Book of Mormon geography and adding other populations into the picture has several apologetic advantages: no longer does the Book of Mormon or its defenders have to account for every artifact or every ruin, or explain all the linguistic diversity through the limited

---

46. For the full analysis, see John W. Welch, "Isaiah 53, Mosiah 14, and the Book of Mormon," in *Isaiah in the Book of Mormon*, ed. Donald W. Parry and John W. Welch (Provo, Utah: FARMS, 1998), 293–312; Welch, *Legal Cases*, 139–209.

47. Neal A. Maxwell, "The Book of Mormon: A Great Answer to 'The Great Question'," in *First Nephi, The Doctrinal Foundation*, ed. Monte S. Nyman and Charles D. Tate Jr. (Provo, Utah: BYU Religious Studies Center, 1988), 9; originally given at a symposium at BYU in 1986.

48. See Matthew Roper, "Nephi's Neighbors: Book of Mormon Peoples and Pre-Columbian Populations," *FARMS Review* 15, no. 2 (2003): 91–112

49. See John L. Sorenson, "When Lehi's Party Arrived in the Land, Did They Find Others There?" *Journal of Book of Mormon Studies* 1, no. 1 (1992): 1–34; Roper, "Nephi's Neighbors,"113–27.

50. John L. Sorenson, "The Book of Mormon as a Mesoamerican Record," in *Book of Mormon Authorship Revisited*, ed. Noel B. Reynolds (Provo, Utah: FARMS, 1997), 418–29. For examples of the cultural diversity that would often go unmentioned in hieroglyphic texts (which focused on the history of the ruling lineage), see Mark Alan Wright, "The Cultural Tapestry of Mesoamerica," *Journal of the Book of Mormon and Other Restoration Scripture* 22, no. 2 (2013): 11–12.

migrations mentioned in the text.[51] With the rise of modern genetics, the limited geography theory has become a semi-official apologetic to deal with the lack of Middle Eastern DNA in Native American populations.[52] Yet understanding the Book of Mormon as a lineage history—telling the story of one people among many—also brings several new perspectives to the table.

Consider Nephi trying to establish a people of God not in some kind of cultural vacuum, but rather in the midst of other nations, or "gentiles." In this light, John Gee and Matthew Roper review anew Nephi's selection of Isaiah chapters in 2 Nephi.[53] The Isaiah quotations begin with Jacob, who says he was assigned this text by Nephi, and encourages his people to liken it to themselves (2 Ne. 6:4–5). Despite stressing that they should liken Isaiah to themselves as the house of Israel, Jacob starts with Isaiah 49:22–23 (2 Ne. 6:6–7)—a text about gentiles who will be "nursing fathers" and "nursing mothers" to Israel. Jacob then taught, "blessed are the Gentiles . . . if it so be that they shall repent and fight not against Zion" (2 Ne. 6:12).

As Nephi begins his own extended quotation of Isaiah, he similarly stresses that Isaiah's words should be likened to his people (2 Ne. 11:2). He then begins with a quotation of Isaiah 2, which describes a time when "the mountain of the Lord's house shall be established in the top of the mountains" and "all nations shall flow unto it" (Isa. 2:2; 2 Ne. 12:2). Remembering that Nephi's people just settled in the land of Nephi, a mountainous region, and built a temple there (2 Ne. 5:1–16), this could be read as an invitation to all those among them who were not of Israelite descent to nonetheless "flow unto" the temple and make covenants with the Lord. Indeed, Nephi concludes his quotation with Isaiah 14, which begins by mentioning Israel being set "in their own land: and the strangers shall be joined with them" (Isa. 14:1; 2 Ne. 24:1). Then, while providing

---

51. See, for example, John W. Welch, "Finding Answers to B. H. Roberts's Questions and An Unparallel," FARMS Preliminary Reports, 1985, available at https://publications.mi.byu.edu/fullscreen/?pub=2839&index=71.

52. "Book of Mormon and DNA Studies," Church of Jesus Christ of Latter-day Saints, https://www.lds.org/topics/book-of-mormon-and-dna-studies.

53. See John Gee and Matthew Roper, "'I Did Liken All Scriptures Unto Us': Early Nephite Understandings of Isaiah and Implications for 'Others' in the Land," in *The Fulness of the Gospel: Foundational Teachings from the Book of Mormon*, ed. Camille Fronk, Brian M. Hauglid, Patty A. Smith, Thomas A. Wayment (Salt Lake City and Provo, Utah: Deseret Book and BYU Religious Studies Center, 2003), 51–65.

commentary on these Isaiah passages, Nephi taught that the Lord "inviteth them all to come unto him . . . and he remembereth the heathen; and all are alike unto God, both Jew and Gentile" (2 Ne. 26:33).

Understanding that Nephi and his family settled in an already populated and culturally diverse promised land, this use of Isaiah can be seen as part of Nephite efforts to incorporate "gentiles," "strangers," and other "nations" into their midst, extending the blessings of the Lord to those who joined with them.[54]

Finding Mesoamerica in the Book of Mormon

Beyond internal geographies, John Sorenson and others have tried to situate the Book of Mormon in the real world by identifying a location that fits or at least approximates the map constructed from all the geographic puzzle pieces in the text. Sorenson's work is the most comprehensive, fitting Book of Mormon geography to Mesoamerica using several hundred of the geographic clues in the Book of Mormon.[55] For apologists, the very fact that hundreds of scattered geographic references can not only form a coherent picture, but then that it can fit reasonably well with a real-world setting serves as evidence favoring the book's claims to legitimate history. If Joseph Smith made this up, they argue, it would not fit reasonably anywhere in the world.[56]

Sorenson also went beyond geography and sought to ground Nephite life and history within Mesoamerican archaeology and culture, arguing for several hundred "correspondences" between the Book of Mormon and Mesoamerica.[57] While such correspondences are typically exploited as evidence for apologetic purposes, this context has consequences. As evangelical biblical scholar Peter Enns recently observed:

> Nothing has changed our understanding of the Old Testament more dramatically than what we have learned over the past 150 years or so about what Israel's

---

54. Gee and Roper, "I Did Liken," 55–60.
55. See John L. Sorenson, *An Ancient American Setting for the Book of Mormon* (Salt Lake City and Provo, Utah: Deseret Book and FARMS, 1985).
56. See John E. Clark, "Archaeology, Relics, and Book of Mormon Belief," *Journal of Book of Mormon Studies* 14, no. 2 (2005): 47.
57. John L. Sorenson, *Images of Ancient America: Visualizing Book of Mormon Life* (Provo, Utah: Research Press, 1999); John L. Sorenson, *Mormon's Codex: An Ancient American Book* (Salt Lake City and Provo, Utah: Deseret Book and Neal A. Maxwell Institute for Religious Scholarship, 2013).

ancient neighbors thought and how they lived—and how much the Israelites not only resembled their neighbors but how indebted they were to modes of thinking that were well in place long before the Israelites ever existed. No corner of the Old Testament has remained unaffected: stories of origins, cosmology, theology, cult (worship), psalmody, wisdom, prophecy, and more.[58]

Likewise, if placed in a Mesoamerican context, every corner of the Book of Mormon must be reconsidered in light of Mesoamerican norms, beliefs, and practices. Sorenson laid the foundation, and began to work in this direction, but today LDS Mesoamericanists such as Brant Gardner, Mark Wright, and Kerry Hull are further exploring the impact that a Mesoamerican setting has on the Book of Mormon.[59] This work is adding new insights that can deepen a person's appreciation for and engagement with the text.

The story in Alma 20, for example, becomes particularly interesting in light of Mesoamerican political structures. In this chapter, King Lamoni's father, the "king over all the land," intercepts Lamoni traveling with Ammon toward Middoni to free Ammon's brethren from imprisonment there (Alma 20:2–8). Lamoni's father reacted by demanding that Lamoni kill Ammon, but when he refused, his father attempted to kill him—Lamoni being spared by the intercession of Ammon (Alma 20:14–18). Usually understood as a family quarrel, readers have been quick to condemn Lamoni's father as being so wicked he was willing to kill his own son simply for being with a Nephite![60] When read in the context of Classic Maya politics, however, a different view emerges.

Brant Gardner has pointed out that, among the Classic Maya, scholars have found a complex system of kings and "overkings," to whom lesser kings were subordinate.[61] The lesser king would be expected to make regu-

---

58. Peter Enns, "5 Modern Insights about the Old Testament that Aren't Going Anywhere," *Pete Enns: The Bible for Normal People*, June 6, 2017, https://www.peteenns.com/5-modern-insights-old-testament-arent-going-anywhere/.

59. See Brant A. Gardner, *Traditions of the Fathers: The Book of Mormon as History* (Salt Lake City: Greg Kofford Books, 2015); Mark Alan Wright, "Nephite Daykeepers: Ritual Specialists in Mesoamerica and the Book of Mormon," in *Ancient Temple Worship: Proceedings of The Expound Symposium, 14 May 2011*, ed. Matthew B. Brown, et al. (Orem, Utah, and Salt Lake City: Interpreter Foundation and Eborn Books, 2014), 243–57; Kerry Hull, "War Banners: A Mesoamerican Context for the Title of Liberty," *Journal of Book of Mormon Studies* 24 (2015): 84–118.

60. See, for example, D. Kelly Ogden and Andrew C. Skinner, *Verse by Verse: The Book of Mormon*, 2 vols. (Salt Lake City: Deseret Book, 2011), 1:427.

61. See, for example, Simon Martin and Nikolai Grube, *Chronicles of the Maya Kings and Queens*, 2nd ed. (New York: Thames and Hudson, 2008), 20–21.

lar "royal visits" and pay tribute to his overking. Failure to attend such an occasion would, at the least, be seen as a serious insult to the overking, and likely be taken be as a sign of rebellion.[62] In this setting, Lamoni's father was more than just a dad upset that his son wasn't home for dinner. Instead, he was an overking who felt insulted that one of his subordinate kings failed to attend an important diplomatic feast (Alma 20:9), where not only his presence but likely his payment was expected. Finding Lamoni currently traveling with the prince—Ammon was the son of King Mosiah—of an enemy state (Alma 20:10–13), about to use his political clout to help free others of Nephite nobility from captivity,[63] no doubt heightened his suspicions of rebellion. Lamoni's blatant insubordination upon being ordered to kill Ammon (Alma 20:14) all but confirmed Lamoni's treason. It is at this point that the overking attempts to kill Lamoni, not as a father upset at who his son is spending his time with, but as a ruler seeking to dispatch a treasonous vassal lord.[64] The actions of Lamoni's father suddenly become very understandable within a Mesoamerican political context.

A Mesoamerican context also explains a curiosity in the account of Abinadi's death. Abinadi's "death by fire" (Mosiah 17:20) is typically visualized as a burning at the stake. Yet before "flames began to scorch him" (v. 14), the text says that Abinadi's tormentors "scourged his skin with faggots" (v. 13). The oddity of this phrase compelled Royal Skousen to propose an emendation here to "*scorched* his skin with faggots."[65] Emendation, however, may not be necessary. Mark Wright and Kerry Hull have documented a practice among the various North American and Mesoamerican natives, including the ancient Maya, of torturing and executing people by physically beating them with firebrands. This form of torment could go on for days or even weeks, and Wright and Hull note that it was often prolonged deliberately to maximize the pain. This kind of death is aptly

---

62. See Gardner, *Traditions of the Fathers*, 300–302.

63. Royal captives were also significant in Mesoamerica, and would be kept and tormented for political reasons. See Gardner, *Traditions of the Fathers*, 302–3.

64. For further discussion of the political context, see Gardner, *Second Witness*, 4:311–19.

65. See Royal Skousen, "'Scourged' vs. 'Scorched' in Mosiah 17:13," *Insights: A Window on the Ancient World* 22, no. 3 (2002): 2–3; Royal Skousen, *Analysis of Textual Variants of the Book of Mormon, Part 3: Mosiah 14–Alma 17*, 2nd ed. (Provo, Utah: BYU Studies and FARMS, 2017), 1412–14.

described by the phrase "scourged his skin with faggots," and this dramatically changes one's perspective on Abinadi's death.[66]

The Mesoamerican setting can also provide insight into more spiritual principles. For example, LDS scripture declares that God "speaketh unto men according to their language, unto their understanding" (2 Ne. 31:3; cf. D&C 1:24). While it is one thing to say that the Lord adapts his messaging to the understanding of his people, it's hard to know what that looks like in practice. Since the Book of Mormon shares some material and an early cultural background with the Bible, ways in which things diverge from biblical patterns in the Book of Mormon might provide some clues. While several LDS scholars have argued that the early revelations of Lehi and Nephi follow the expected pattern of ancient Israelite theophanies,[67] Mark Wright noticed that a different pattern emerges by Alma's day—one that is more consistent with Mesoamerican modes of revelation.[68]

Wright also noticed a subtle difference in how Jesus Christ presented the wounds of his resurrected body in the account in 3 Nephi compared to those in the New Testament. In the biblical accounts, Christ either didn't mention (Luke 24:39–40), or mentioned secondarily (John 20:25–28), the wound in his side. In the Book of Mormon account, however, Christ mentioned the wound in his side *first*, and only secondarily mentioned the marks in his hands and feet (3 Ne. 11:14). Considering this difference in a Mesoamerican context, Wright noted that one common method of human sacrifice in Mesoamerica was to cut a large opening below the ribcage and remove the still-beating heart. Thus, to a Mesoamerican audience, it

---

66. See Mark Alan Wright and Kerry Hull, "Ethnohistorical Sources and the Death of Abinadi," in *Abinadi: "He Came Among Them in Disguise"*, ed. Shon D. Hopkin (Salt Lake City and Provo, Utah: Deseret Book and BYU Religious Studies Center, forthcoming 2018). I would like to personally thank the authors for allowing me to read a pre-publication draft of this paper. See also Brant Gardner, "Scourging with Faggots," *Insights: A Window on the Ancient World* 21, no. 7 (2001): 2–3.

67. See Blake T. Ostler, "The Throne-Theophany and Prophetic Commission in 1 Nephi: A Form-Critical Analysis," *BYU Studies* 26, no. 4 (1986): 67–95; Stephen O. Smoot, "The Divine Council in the Hebrew Bible and the Book of Mormon," *Studia Antiqua: A Student Journal for the Study of the Ancient World* 12, no. 2 (Fall 2013): 1–18.

68. Mark Alan Wright, "'According to Their Language, unto Their Understanding': The Cultural Context of Hierophanies and Theophanies in Latter-day Saint Canon," *Studies in the Bible and Antiquity* 3 (2011): 51–65.

was the wound on the side that would have primarily expressed the idea that Jesus had been killed as a sacrifice.[69]

For the believer who accepts the Book of Mormon as both historically authentic and divinely revealed, the way these divine communications within the text diverge from biblical patterns and conform to Mesoamerican ones provides concrete examples of what it really means for God to adapt His message to His audience's understanding.

Conclusion:
Boundary Maintenance or Pushing Boundaries?

As mentioned in the beginning of this paper, my purpose is not to defend or promote any of these particular approaches. It must be admitted, however, that the value of any one of these insights is at least somewhat contingent upon how much merit is granted to the paradigm that produced it. I do think, however, that even those who do not accept the historicity of the Book of Mormon or other Latter-day Saint claims can appreciate the ways LDS efforts to defend these points of view have yielded new insights and interpretations into LDS scripture and theology. Some may even be able to find the new perspectives interesting and meaningful, without necessarily accepting the apologetic arguments that often go with them.

My aim here, however, was simply to show that these new insights and perspectives exist, and are beneficial to the vitality of Latter-day Saint belief. New insights like the ones described above force believing Latter-day Saints to rethink aspects of their faith in light of new information and research, even while defending fundamental premises such as the historicity of the Book of Mormon or the antiquity of temple rituals. They help readers humanize scriptural characters, and thus better relate to the stories being told within the LDS canon. When readers have been engaging theses texts since childhood, the stories can begin to feel stale, but ancient paradigms can bring in fresh perspectives that help bring the stories to life.

In several cases, these new insights may challenge Latter-day Saints used to typical interpretations and approaches. Seeing scriptural texts and authors as being at odds with each other might seem uncomfortable. A tree-goddess might seem weird and pagan. The notion that Nephites thought Jesus was sacrificed by having his still beating heart ripped out of

---

69. Mark Alan Wright, "*Axes Mundi*: Ritual Complexes in Mesoamerica and the Book of Mormon," *Interpreter: A Journal of Mormon Scripture* 12 (2014): 89–91.

his chest might not only seem pagan, but also gruesome and distasteful, along with Abinadi's being "scourged" to death by burning sticks bound together. Thus, despite apologetics usually being a form of boundary maintenance, in many cases LDS apologetic approaches are actually pushing the boundaries of scriptural interpretation and theological understanding.

FOUR

I Think, Therefore I Defend[1]

Michael Ash

In Norse mythology, the god Loki came upon two dwarf brothers metal-smithing in a forge. He taunted the dwarves by betting them they couldn't produce three new creations that surpassed what other dwarves had created. If he were to lose, Loki offered his own head as the reward. The dwarves *did* create three amazingly magical items, one of which was Thor's hammer, Mjölnir. When the dwarves came to collect Loki's head, however, Loki claimed that they had a right to his head but not his neck. Loki kept his head because they couldn't agree on where the neck ended and the head began.

Loki's Wager,[2] as the tale has been dubbed, is analogous to the sometimes frustrating arguments that arise when competing parties disagree on the demarcations of a concept.[3] Some terms seem to defy concrete definitions. "Love," "big," "loud," "beautiful," "magic," and "anti-Mormon" are among those words which seem to resist universally accepted definitions. The term "apologetics" seems to suffer from a similar dilemma. LDS scholars and non-LDS scholars often disagree on the demarcation between apologetics and scholarship because there is no universal agreement about where one ends and the other begins.

---

1. Some of the material for this chapter was culled, in part, from a longer book-length project in which I am engaged tentatively entitled *God Is a Scientific Character*.

2. The term "Loki's Wager" can also refer to a logical fallacy wherein the claim is made that a topic is beyond discussion or criticism because the concept cannot be clearly defined.

3. See examples of the "demarcation problem" or problem determining the criteria for what qualifies as science vs. non-science or pseudo-science in Massimo Pigliucci and Marten Boudry, eds., *The Philosophy of Pseudo-Science: Reconsidering the Demarcation Problem* (Chicago and London: University of Chicago Press, 2013).

From a strictly etymological perspective, the English "apologetics" derives from the Greek *apologia*, which means to defend one's position and was originally used in early Greek law. Although in today's world the term is typically associated with religious arguments, it is still recognized as descriptive for the defense of non-religious arguments. We find, for example, that apologetics are used in the discussion of managerialism, biological diversity, the regulation of pornography, Japan's international relations, the deregulation of energy and telecommunications companies, and in many more discussions.[4] Some atheists even recognize that they defend their paradigms by engaging in apologetics.[5]

Granting to confine our definition to the realm of religious discourse, we are still faced with the problem that there is no unified methodology governing the practice of apologetics. Some prominent philosophers suggest that there are many different Christian apologetic methodologies. While the *Classic Method* believes that the hand of God can be observed in nature and through human reason,[6] the *Evidential Method* accumulates historical evidences for the truth of Christianity through "the careful application of historical principles, tempered by various sorts of critical analyses,"[7] and the *Reformed Epistemology Method* holds "that it is perfectly reasonable for a person to believe many things without evidence."

---

4. Edward S. Mason, "The Apologetics of 'Managerialism,'" *The Journal of Business* 31, no. 1 (January 1958): 1–11; Richard B. Norgard, "The Economics of Biological Diversity: Apologetics or Theory?" in *Sustainable Resource Development in the Third World*, ed. Douglas D. Southgate and John F. Disinger (Boulder and London: Westview Press, 1987), 95–109; Steven G. Grey, "The Apologetics of Suppression: The Regulation of Pornography as Act and Idea," *Michigan Law Review* 87, no. 6 (June 1988): 1564–634; Otto von Feigenblatt, *Japan and Human Security: 21st Century Official Development Policy Apologetics and Discursive Co-Optation* (Delray Beach: Academic Research International, 2007); Harry M. Trebing, "Apologetics of Deregulation in Energy and Telecommunications: An Institutional Assessment," *Journal of Economic Issues* 20, no. 3 (September 1986): 613–32.

5. See, for example, "Intellectual Ammo for Atheists" at AtheistApologist.com, and the Atheism.wikia.com which includes "apologetics for Naturalism," http://atheism.wikia.com/wiki/Apologetics.

6. Steven B. Cowan, *Five Views on Apologetics* (Grand Rapids, Mich.: Zondervan, 2000), 15.

7. Gary R. Habermas, "Evidential Apologetics," in *Five Views of Apologetics*, ed. Steven B. Cowan (Grand Rapids, Mich.: Zondervan, 2000), 95.

A "belief in God," the latter argues, "does not require the support of evidence or argument in order for it to be rational."[8]

Proponents of the *Cumulative Case Method* claim that "any belief must correspond with reality" and that the tests for determining truth are the same ones utilized by scientists, historians, and others who engage in rational discourse.[9] This methodology, notes one scholar, "pieces together several lines or types of data into a sort of hypothesis . . . that comprehensively explains that data . . . better than any alternative hypothesis."[10] Finally, the *Presuppositional Method* presupposes "the truth of Christianity as the proper starting point in apologetics," and it believes that the scriptures provide a "framework through which all experience is interpreted and all truth is known."[11]

To further muddy the waters, most apologists recognize the application of *negative* as well as *positive* apologetics.[12] Negative apologetics take the classical form of the word *apologia* and defends religious positions against criticisms. Personally I choose to refer to such methods as *defensive* apologetics because of the possible misunderstanding of the more ambiguous "negative." Positive apologetics, on the other hand, strengthens the validity of a religious position by demonstrating that a belief is bolstered by secular evidence. My personal taste would be to refer to this approach as *affirmative* apologetics.

An LDS example of defensive apologetics would include the DNA argument. To simplify, according to critics the Book of Mormon cannot be true because DNA studies demonstrate that Native Americans have Asiatic DNA instead of Israelite DNA. The apologetic defense is to point out that according to the best experts, DNA markers can and do disappear over time—especially in cases where the DNA of a small foreign group intermingles with a larger native population.[13]

An LDS example of affirmative apologetics would include the discovery of ancient altars in southern Arabia that are inscribed with the letters

---

8. Cowan, *Five Views*, 20.

9. Paul D. Feinberg, "Cumulative Case for Apologetics," *Five Views of Apologetics*, ed. Steven B. Cowan (Grand Rapids, Mich.: Zondervan, 2000), 154.

10. Cowan, *Five Views*, 18.

11. Ibid., 19.

12. Ibid., 375.

13. See *The Book of Mormon and DNA Research: Essays from the FARMS Review and the Journal of Book of Mormon Studies*, ed., Daniel C. Peterson (Provo, Utah: Neal A. Maxwell Institute for Religious Scholarship, 2008).

NHM. According to LDS scholars this supports the Book of Mormon's claim that the Lehites passed through a land known as Nahom where they buried Ishmael. The altars are in the right place, date to the right time, and designate an area that was commonly used as burial land by outsiders.[14] Like all other scholarly claims the arguments advanced in defensive or affirmative apologetics are open to discussion and debate.

Apologetic discourse is also open to anyone's input. While the Church has no official apologists, those who engage in LDS apologetics include scholars of renown and high caliber—many of whom are trained in fields that are pertinent to the areas in which they comment—as well as educated and uneducated amateurs. This open court of opinion is a double-edged sword. The past few decades have shown that a number of amateur scholars (including both believers and unbelievers) have made valuable contributions to the field of Mormon studies.[15] This eclectic mix, however, allows for the real possibility that some apologetic arguments, claims, or approaches could damage testimonies.

Social media and message boards, for example, can become breeding grounds for aggressive character assassinations, insults, and ad hominem attacks. Defensive apologetics played out in such an arena can quickly become *offensive* in the sense that it can turn people off to not only the apologist and apologetics, but also to the argument. The open-mic of affirmative apologetics allows for arguments that can be either illuminating or embarrassing. While a number of LDS apologists have advanced rigorous evidence-based arguments, others have made claims that are weak, specious, or egregiously out of sync with mainstream scholarship and science.

An LDS example of bad affirmative apologetics could include some of the early speaking tours by LDS authors who made outrageous claims regarding supposed "proof" of the Book of Mormon. Every ancient American pit was a baptismal font, every bone belonged to a Nephite, and every city (no matter when it was actually constructed or inhabited) was proof of the building expertise of Book of Mormon people.[16] Serious scholars who

---

14. See Warren P. Aston, "Newly Found Altars from Nahom," *Journal of Book of Mormon Studies* 10, no. 2 (2001): 56–61, 71.

15. See Michael R. Ash, "The Impact of Mormon Critics on LDS Scholarship," (presented at the 2002 FAIR Conference in Orem, Utah, on August 9, 2002), available at http://www.fairmormon.org/perspectives/fair-conferences/2002-fair-conference/2002-the-impact-of-mormon-critics-on-lds-scholarship.

16. See the comments of John L. Sorenson, "Instant Expertise on Book of Mormon Archaeology," *BYU Studies* 16, no. 3 (Spring 1976): 429.

engage in apologetics recognize, to quote Daniel Peterson, "that it is impossible, using empirical methods, to prove the divine."[17] When we lump all models and methodologies into one "Apologetics" label, it's no wonder that some people have difficulty deciding if the endeavor is good or bad.

Just as some serious scholars may engage in apologetics, other equally-serious scholars are critical of the endeavor for various reasons. These criticisms range from the belief that apologetics is simply out of the purview of generally accepted scholarly standards to the belief that apologetics can cause significant damage to LDS testimonies.[18] Perhaps due to the blurred definition of what qualifies as apologetics, some scholars appear to hold simultaneously conflicting views on the apologetic effort—at times expressing neutral observations or contributing their own writings to the LDS apologetic enterprise, while at other times asserting negative comments about the undertaking.[19] This occasional unevenness may arise from their reaction to the material they perceived to be apologetic at the time they make their comments.

FairMormon (originally known by the acronym FAIR—the Foundation for Apologetic Information and Research) was born in this message board environment and for the first few years of its existence continued to maintain a message board as part of its web presence. Not long after its inception, however, FairMormon distanced itself from the contentious message boards and focused on *educational* apologetics. FairMormon's mission is to create, collect, and provide a repository of *scholarly* arguments which answer criticisms as well as provide support for Mormon beliefs.

Matters of history and biblical studies are fields with varying degrees of scholarly consensus as well as debate. While a particular FairMormon article may take a position that agrees with one side of a debate, this does not mean that the approach to the topic is automatically antithetical to scholarship. Similarly, in more than one instance FairMormon has attempted to correct the kind of affirmative apologetics that take pseudo-

---

17. Daniel C. Peterson, "The Role of Apologetics in Mormon Studies," *Interpreter: A Journal of Mormon Scripture* 2 (2012), available at http://www.mormoninterpreter.com/the-role-of-apologetics-in-mormon-studies/.

18. For example, see contributions in this volume by Ben Park, David Bokovoy, and Loyd Isao Ericson.

19. As expressed in various internet discussions, the details of which were saved by this author.

scientific approaches to Mormon studies—positions which FairMormon agrees can actually damage testimonies.[20]

While apologists are often painted as anti-intellectual, that's typically not what we find among modern LDS apologists. The now-defunct *FARMS Review* was well-known as a scholarly publication that utilized apologetics to defend and affirm the faith. Ex-Mormon John-Charles Duffy, Visiting Assistant Professor of Comparative Religion at Miami University, pointed out in a 2004 *Sunstone* article[21] that six of the first eight volumes of the *Review* "contain critical responses to the anti-intellectual tradition" and disapprove of the way certain Mormon authors appear to attack biblical scholarship.[22] One *FARMS Review* contributor took such Mormons to task asking,

> If this is the attitude with which our university students are taught to approach the scriptures, can we really expect them to become the kind of people who can reconcile discovered and revealed truth without feeling they have to reject one or the other?[23]

Duffy notes that "[f]ar from seeing scholarship as a threat to faith," scholars of FARMS-apologetic-persuasion, "describe their faith as being 'enhanced,' 'enriched,' and 'deepened' by scholarship."[24] While apologists may, at times, disagree with other scholars (or each other) on various issues of debate, it is false to claim that they are anti-intellectual and eschew real scholarship.

I believe that in some ways, apprehension by critics of apologetics arise from shared concerns that have been voiced by FairMormon. Both are vexed about defensive apologetic approaches which take on war-like mentalities that are more interested in defeating "the enemy" than in com-

---

20. "Reviews of DNA Evidence for Book of Mormon Geography," FairMormon, http://www.fairmormon.org/reviews-of-dna-evidence-for-book-of-mormon-geography.

21. John-Charles Duffy, "Defending the Kingdom, Rethinking the Faith: How Apologetics is Reshaping Mormon Orthodoxy," *Sunstone* (May 2004). At the time Duffy wrote the article he was working on his doctorate, and while he had not at that time been excommunicated, he did not believe in the historicity of the Book of Mormon (p.43).

22. Ibid., 31.

23. J. Michael Allen, "Review of Joseph Fielding McConkie and Robert L. Millet, *Doctrinal Commentary on the Book of Mormon: Volume 3, Alma through Helaman*," *FARMS Review* 4 (1992): 151.

24. Duffy, "Defending the Kingdom," 33.

I Think, Therefore I Defend

ing to the truth. Likewise, both are concerned about affirmative apologetic approaches that are based on shoddy scholarship, bad science, or faulty logic. No scholar (believer or critic) is right all the time. Arguments must be engaged on an individual basis.

The *big* argument against apologetics—the one raised by most all of those who dislike apologetics—is the claim that unlike "real" scholarship—which simply follows the facts to wherever they lead—apologetics only embraces evidence that supports an already predetermined belief. Thus David Bokovoy writes in an online criticism of apologetics, "Mainstream scholarship adopts the historical critical method. This is an effort to read the material independent from a contemporary theological bias or agenda. An apologetic reading takes the exact opposite approach. When I engage in biblical scholarship, I avoid an apologetic reading that reflects my own religious assumptions."[25]

While it is certainly commendable and worthwhile to pursue assumption-free scholarship, unfortunately it's not something we humans are capable of doing very well. The more we know about the brain, for instance, the more we learn that apologetics is an unavoidable part of our human nature thanks to our evolutionary heritage.

Brains are designed to see patterns. Some animals instinctively see patterns in selecting which foods to eat and which to avoid. For example, the kiskadee, a bird that lives from Texas to south Argentina and eats snakes, has innate pattern recognition to help it avoid the venomous coral snake. Researchers raised several kiskadees in a laboratory and then tested their pattern recognition skills by painting various wooden dowels to resemble snakes. Some dowels were painted with solid colors and some with rings of colors. Even though these birds had never seen snakes and had never been taught by a parent bird which snakes to eat or avoid, the kiskadees attacked all of the dowels except those with patterns that matched the patterns of coral snakes.[26]

Human babies seem to have innate pattern recognition for faces, including the ability to recognize emotional expressions and direction of gaze. Research suggests that babies automatically respond to the basic pattern of a face—the three blobs of eyes and a mouth.[27]

---

25. David Bokovoy, post on Facebook March 29, 2015.
26. Susan M. Smith, "Coral-Snake Pattern Recognition and Stimulus Generalisation by Naive Great Kiskadees," *Nature* (February 10, 1977), 535–36.
27. Oliver Braddick, Janette Atkinson, and Georgio Innocenti, eds., "Gene Expression to Neurobiology and Behavior: Human Brain Development and

"Our brains," notes agnostic scholar Michael Shermer, "evolved to connect the dots of our world into meaningful patterns that explain why things happen. These meaningful patterns become beliefs, and these beliefs shape our understanding of reality."[28] Sometimes this can lead us down wrong paths, but without them we could not move at all. As anthropologist Stewart Guthrie explained, "it is better for a hiker to mistake a boulder for a bear than to mistake a bear for a boulder."[29] In other words, generating a false pattern, even when such a pattern doesn't actually exist, is better for the survival of the species than having no pattern-recognizing skills. Pattern-generating animals are more likely to live and to pass on their proclivities to their progeny.

Cognitive scientists have long known that our brains think at different, sometimes conflicting, levels—an instinctive level and a more analytical level. The psychologist Daniel Kahneman describes these two levels as a metaphorical System 1 and System 2. System 1 is the instinctive level that gives us our gut reactions, our knee-jerk responses, and sees initial patterns. It is ready to contribute at a moment's notice, is typically the first system called up in our brains, and creates a coherent interpretation of what's going on. System 2, on the other hand, is lazy (and thinking literally uses a lot of energy) so it usually kicks in when System 1 is overwhelmed, when more brain power is required, or when System 1 needs some confirming support. Because it's impossible to analyze everything all the time, we often must rely on instincts formed by past experiences and contexts; in other words, we have to rely on System 1's preconceptions, biases, pattern recognition, and predictions in order to think. "Because System 1 operates automatically and cannot be turned off at will," notes Kahneman, "errors of intuitive thought are often difficult to prevent."[30]

The instinctive process of pattern recognition often starts with the eyes and ears but is ultimately pieced together in the brain. *Pareidolia*, for instance, is the sensation of seeing or hearing patterns in meaningless ar-

---

Developmental Disorders," in *Progress in Brain Research*, Vol. 189 (Amsterdam: Elsevier, 2011), 175.

28. Michael Shermer, *The Believing Brain: From Ghosts and Gods to Politics and Conspiracies—How We Construct Beliefs and Reinforce Them as Truths* (New York: Times Books, 2011: Kindle Edition), 5.

29. Stewart Guthrie, *Faces in the Clouds: A New Theory of Religion* (New York: Oxford University Press, 1993), 6.

30. Daniel Kahneman, *Thinking, Fast and Slow* (New York: Farrar, Straus and Giroux, 2001: Kindle Edition), 28.

rangements. If you see the face of Jesus in your toast, that's an example of pareidolia. When you see a dinosaur shape in the clouds, or a human face on the surface of the moon, you are engaging in pareidolia. Rorschach (or inkblot) tests are examples of pareidolia. "We do not 'want' to see a man in the moon," explains psychologist Thomas Gilovich. "We do not profit from the illusion. We just see it."[31] Pareidolia typically relies on information and memories already in our brain and predicts what is coming next. As Stephen L. Macknik, Susana Martinez-Conde, and Sandra Blakeslee put it, "essentially, you are a prediction machine."[32]

"The measure of success for System 1," observes Kahneman, "is the coherence of the story it manages to create. The amount and quality of the data on which the story is based are largely irrelevant."[33] While we can't fully escape the instinctive pattern recognition our eyes and minds generate with pareidolia, most people engage System 2 to understand that what looks like a face on the moon is not really a face on the moon. Context helps us overcome System 1's pattern generation. When the context is less definitive, however, it's not so easy to brush off the pattern. If we walk through a dark alley and see what appears to be a person standing behind a dumpster, our System 1 response will dominate our thoughts until we get closer and discover that what we thought was a person is actually an old rolled up carpet that someone set against the wall.

What does this all have to do with apologetics? System 1's pattern-generation is not limited to our visual senses but also plays a big role in how we end up defending our own thoughts—even, and perhaps especially, to ourselves. An interesting example comes from research on split-brain patients. Our brains are bilateral symmetrical structures consisting of two hemispheres that mirror each other and communicate with each other through fiber tracts. The largest tract is the *corpus callosum* which is made up of about 200 million nerves and is the major neural pathway that allows communication between the left and right brain hemispheres.

In the 1960s some doctors discovered that severe cases of epilepsy could be remedied if the corpus callosum was severed. Thanks to better medications this procedure is almost never done today, but fifty years ago

---

31. Thomas Gilovich, *How We Know What Isn't So: The Fallibility of Human Reason in Everyday Life* (New York: Free Press, 1991), 10.
32. Stephen L. Macknik, Susana Martinez-Conde, and Sandra Blakeslee, *Sleights of Mind: What the Neuroscience of Magic Reveals about Our Everyday Deceptions* (New York: Henry Holt and Co., 2010: Kindle Edition), 9.
33. Kahneman, *Thinking, Fast and Slow*, 85.

it was a complicated surgical operation that helped many people who were unable to find relief elsewhere. About a dozen of those early patients became the subject of volumes on brain research. Thanks to that research, we know that the right side of your body is primarily controlled by the brain's left hemisphere (which typically controls verbal functions), while the left side of your body is primarily controlled by the brain's right hemisphere.[34]

Most of the higher forms of communication are lost in split brain patients because of the severed corpus callosum, but scientists believe that lower forms of communication still exist through some of the lesser fiber tracts. These smaller tracts, and the fact that both sides of the brain generally see the same thing when both eyes are open, allow split-brain patients to lead normal lives. When researchers isolated each hemisphere's input, however, they found a lack of communication between the two hemispheres.

For example, in one experiment a picture of a snowy meadow was shown to the patient's left eye which was then processed by their non-verbal right hemisphere. Simultaneously, a picture of a bird's claw was shown to the patient's right eye which was then processed in their verbal left hemisphere. Following the initial two photos another group of photos was shown to the volunteer. The subject was asked to point to a photo that related to the image they had seen previously in the first photo(s). Because the right hemisphere had seen a snowy meadow, the left hand pointed at a shovel. The left hemisphere, however, had seen a bird's claw so the right hand pointed to a picture of a chicken. What happened next is where it gets *really* interesting. The subject was asked why they had pointed to the shovel. The only half of the brain that could answer was the left hemisphere (the verbal half) which had only seen the bird's claw and the chicken, not the snowy meadow. So how did the brain respond? It fabricated a lie: "You need a shovel to clean out the chicken shed."[35]

It's important to understand that the subject wasn't lying to the researcher, but rather the brain was lying to the subject. It filled in the gaps in the story in order to make the story coherent. As Gilovich explains,

> Note that the real reason the subject pointed to the shovel was not given, because the snow scene that prompted the response is inaccessible to the left hemisphere that must fashion the verbal explanation. This does not stop the

---

34. Steven Rose, "The Human Brain," in *Consciousness: Brain, States of Awareness, and Mysticism*, ed. Daniel Goleman and Richard J. Davison (New York: Irvington Publishers Inc., 1979), 4.

35. Quoted in Jonah Lehrer, *How We Decide* (New York: Houghton Mifflin Harcourt Publishing Co., 2009), 211.

person from giving a "sensible" response: He or she examines the relevant output and invents a story to account for it. It is as if the left hemisphere contains an explanation module along with, or as part of, its language center—an explanation module that can quickly and easily make sense of even the most bizarre patterns of information. . . . It suggests that once a person has (mis)identified a random pattern as a "real" phenomenon, it will not exist as a puzzling, isolated fact about the world. Rather, it is quickly explained and readily integrated into the person's pre-existing theories and beliefs.[36]

While you and I are (likely) not split-brain subjects, the take-away message from these experiments is that our brains are story-generating machines that need to make sense of the world around them—even if that means filling in the gaps with information that could be accurate or inaccurate.

Another couple of interesting examples come from the 2005 research of a group of cognitive scientists at Lund University in Sweden. While sitting across a table from their volunteers, the scientists would show two playing-card-sized photos of two entirely different women's faces. The scientists would then ask the volunteers which person they believed was more attractive. Following the volunteer's selection, the scientist would slide the card face down to the volunteer who would pick up the card for closer inspection. Unbeknownst to the volunteer, however, the scientists—using sleight of hand—switched the cards so that the volunteer was actually looking at the face of the person they felt was *less* attractive.

In about 75% of the cases, the volunteers did not notice that the faces had been switched—even when the two faces on the cards were very different. This is referred to as *change blindness*. The scientists then asked the volunteers to explain why they found this face to be the more attractive. Not knowing that the cards had been switched, the volunteers would nevertheless create ad hoc explanations of what they liked better about the face card they held in their hands.[37]

To ensure that their experiment was not tainted by the specific act of judging attractive features, in 2010 they tried a similar experiment at a local supermarket with two flavors of jam: black currant and raspberry. One jar had a red label and the other a blue label. After the shopper tasted the jams and then told the researcher which jam they liked best, the re-

---

36. Gilovich, *How We Know What Isn't So*, 22–23.

37. Petter Johansson, Lars Hall, Betty Tärning, Sverker Sikström, and Nick Chater, "Choice Blindness and Preference Change: You Will Like This Paper Better If You (Believe You) Chose to Read It!" *Journal of Behavioral Decision Making* 27, no. 3 (2013): 281–89.

searcher would surreptitiously turn the jar upside down. The pots of jam were double-ended with a divider between the two halves and each pot contained both of the two different jams. The researcher would then give the shopper another spoonful of jam from the pot they had selected—this time from the bottom side of the pot containing the alternative jam—and ask the shopper to describe, while tasting the jam, why they liked this flavor better. As with the face-card experiment most of the shoppers would confidently describe what they liked better about the jam they tasted, not realizing that they were eating the jam they liked less.[38]

We would all like to think that we wouldn't fall for such a ruse, but the truth is that we probably would. Once we formulate opinions or ideas—often created by System 1—we tend to defend those positions—often with the more rigorous application of System 2. Generally, the more invested we are in an idea (because of religious, academic, or even community influences) the less likely we are to give up on the idea. That doesn't mean that people won't change their minds, but the truth is that pure intellectual reasoning does not drive all of our thoughts or decisions.

People defend their positions because their brains have constructed believable paradigms and because all people are susceptible to confirmation bias; we seek evidences to confirm and support what we already believe. "[T]he facts of the world," notes Shermer, "are filtered by our brains through the colored lenses of worldviews, paradigms, theories, hypotheses, conjectures, hunches, biases, and prejudices we have accumulated through living. We then sort through the facts and select those that confirm what we already believe and ignore or rationalize away those that contradict our beliefs."[39]

As Shermer notes for example, Christopher Columbus based his trip estimation on the miscalculation of others and, after 5,000 kilometers, "encountered land in the exact place where he had calculated the Indies would be, and thus he dubbed the people he engaged there 'Indians.'"[40] It didn't matter that the flora and fauna were nothing like what had been described by Marco Polo, Columbus was able to match the evidence to an already existing paradigm.

> Because of the power of the paradigm to shape perceptions, Columbus's cognitive map told him what he was seeing. When his men dug up some common garden rhubarb, *Rheum rhaponticum* (used in pies), for example, the ship's sur-

---

38. Tali Sharot, *The Optimism Bias: A Tour of the Irrationally Positive Brain* (New York: Pantheon Books, 2011), 18–20.
39. Shermer, *Believing Brain*, 36.
40. Ibid., 282.

geon determined that it was *Rheum officinale*, the medicinal Chinese rhubarb. The native American plant gumbo-limbo was mistaken for an Asiatic variety of the mastic evergreen tree that yields resin used to make lacquer, varnish, and adhesives. The South American *nogal de pais* nut was classified as the Asian coconut, or at least what Marco Polo had described as such. Columbus deemed a plant with the aroma of cinnamon to be that valuable Asian spice.[41]

"Ownership," observes psychologist Dan Ariel, "is not limited to material things. It can also apply to points of view. Once we take ownership of an idea—whether it's about politics or sports—what do we do? We love it perhaps more than we should. We prize it more than it is worth. And most frequently, we have trouble letting go of it because we can't stand the idea of its loss."[42]

To satisfy our confirmation bias we seek out like-minded reassurance for our beliefs. This can be found in the books and articles we read as well as in the social groups to which we gravitate. "We can often anticipate other people's general beliefs and overall orientations," notes Gilovich, "and thus can predict with some accuracy their views on a particular question. By judiciously choosing the right people to consult, we can increase our chances of hearing what we want to hear."[43]

> It is a fact of social life that we are selectively exposed to information that tends to support our beliefs. Conservatives read conservative periodicals and . . . religious fundamentalists tend to read "creationist" literature. . . . Indeed, similarity of beliefs, values, and habits is one of the primary determinants of those with whom we associate.[44]

Our biases not only affect our social circle, the books we read, and the authorities we respect, but they also affect how much effort we put into searching for answers. We get an "emotional boost" of confidence, notes Shermer, when we find evidence to confirm our beliefs. This in turn creates a loop that drives our search for confirmatory evidence.[45] "[W]hen the initial evidence is hostile," writes Gilovich, "we often dig deeper, hoping to find more comforting information, or to uncover reasons to believe that the original evidence was flawed."[46]

---

41. Ibid., 283.
42. Dan Ariely, *Predictably Irrational: The Hidden Forces That Shape Our Decisions* (New York: HarperCollins, Kindle Edition: 2009), 177–78.
43. Gilovich, *How We Know*, 81–82.
44. Ibid., 115.
45. Shermer, *Believing Brain*, 5.
46. Gilovich, *How We Know*, 82.

In 1979 three Stanford psychologists preformed an experiment to see how people would respond to disconfirmatory evidence on strongly held views—so they chose the topic of capital punishment. After screening possible volunteers they selected twenty-four people who favored capital punishment and twenty-four who opposed it. The volunteers were then asked to examine statements from two purported studies on the death penalty's effectiveness in deterring murder. One of the studies made claims that supported capital punishment as a deterrent, and the other made claims that capital punishment did not deter murder. Unbeknownst to the volunteers the data in both studies were fictional.

What the researchers found was that both groups "rated those results and procedures that confirmed their own beliefs to be the more convincing and probative ones."[47] In other words, the volunteers felt that the studies that supported their initial views were more convincing than those studies that opposed their initial view. Surprisingly, the Stanford psychologists found that both groups tended to *more strongly* hold to their original view. It seemed that the volunteers came to "regard the ambiguities and conceptual flaws in the data *opposing* their hypotheses as somehow suggestive of the fundamental *correctness* of those hypotheses."[48] Commenting on this experiment Gilovich points out that participants "correctly saw hostile findings as hostile findings" and didn't "simply ignore these negative results."

> Instead, they carefully scrutinized the studies that produced these unwanted and unexpected findings, and came up with criticisms that were largely appropriate. Rather than ignoring outright the evidence at variance with their expectations, the participants cognitively transformed it into evidence that was considered relatively uninformative and could be assigned little weight. Thus, the participants' expectations had their effect not through a simple process of ignoring inconsistent results, but through a more complicated process that involved a fair amount of cognitive effort.[49]

System 1 sees the pattern, System 2 looks for evidence to confirm the pattern.

Most religious topics of debate are in fields often referred to as the "soft sciences." We cannot prove, by secular means that Jesus rose from the dead, that Joseph Smith saw the Father and Son in a vision, or that a figure

---

47. Charles G. Lord, Lee Ross, and Mark R. Lepper, "Biased Assimilation and Attitude Polarization: The Effects of Prior Theories on Subsequently Considered Evidence," *Journal of Personality and Social Psychology* 37, no. 11 (1979): 2098.
48. Ibid., 2099.
49. Gilovich, *How We Know*, 54.

known to us as Abraham was asked to sacrifice his son. The most important points in our religion cannot be measured with secular tools. These tools, however, can shed light on when the Bible might have been written, what might have influenced the authors, how they might have perceived the world, and so forth. When we get into debates of history and literary analysis, however, not only are there different intelligent opinions, but paradigms invariably shape the interpretation and selection of the evidence and the *apologetic* methods used to promote and defend that evidence.

When a critic or believer argues for a position relating to Mormon Studies they act as apologists for that position. My agnostic friend Dan Vogel, for instance, correctly explains that for those like himself who do not believe in an historical Book of Mormon or the existence of Nephites, "then one is obliged to explain the plates and witnesses" with a theory "consistent with that conclusion."[50]

The conclusion—the paradigm—drives the interpretation of the evidence. When a scholar, believing or non-believing, argues that the Documentary Hypothesis is the best explanation for the creation of the Old Testament, then that scholar becomes an apologist for the Documentary Hypothesis. In an internet discussion, David Bokovoy claims that he can be both a believer *and critic* of the Documentary Hypothesis because although he currently believes that this theory presents the best case for the data, he is open to other theories if they make better sense of the data. "As such, apologetics may rely upon scholarship, but the second a person assumes a position that cannot be critiqued that person cannot engage in scholarship (at least the way I understand this term)."[51] Bokovoy, however, presents a false dichotomy. I don't know of any high-profile LDS apologists who believe that their position cannot be critiqued. While it's certainly true that an apologist (critic or believer) will seek evidence to defend their position, that does not mean that they aren't open to a superior position should one present itself.

Science is self-correcting. Attempts to falsify a theory help to either strengthen a good model or replace a bad model. According to Daniel Little, when scientists encounter anomalies to their theories, "they must

---

50. Quoted in Michael R. Ash, *Shaken Faith Syndrome: Strengthening One's Testimony in the Face of Criticism and Doubt*, 2nd ed. (Redding, Calif.: FairMormon, 2013), 70.

51. David Bokovoy, post on *Mormon Dialogue & Discussion Board*, February 28, 2013, http://www.mormondialogue.org/topic/60180-scholarship-versus-apologetics/?p=1209230715.

choose whether to abandon the theory altogether or modify it to make it consistent with the contrary observations. If the theory has a wide range of supporting evidence (aside from the contrary experience), there is a powerful incentive in favor of salvaging the theory" by modifying the original paradigm. These "progressive modifications" are integral to paradigm maintenance and anomaly management in typical science.[52]

This is what happens in Bokovoy's field as well. In my current opinion, as well as Bokovoy's, the evidence favors the Documentary Hypothesis as an accurate model. Anomalies are noted and engaged, and they are rejected or incorporated into modifications of the Documentary Hypothesis. That's good scholarship. Good apologetics works the same way. It is argued that apologetics cannot work the same for a believing Latter-day Saint because the conclusions—that God exists, that Jesus is the Christ, that Joseph Smith was a prophet, that the Book of Mormon is the word of God, etc.—are unwavering beliefs that drive the selection of evidence and argument; it doesn't allow for the facts to speak for themselves or to let the evidence lead where it may. While there is some truth to this claim, it is over-stated, misleading, and ultimately reflects what happens in mainstream scholarship.

Not all intelligent people are swayed by the same arguments. Not everyone assigns the same weight to evidence. If they did we wouldn't have the multitude of political parties and religions that we find in the world today. A number of Latter-day Saints have left the faith because they believe that critical claims are stronger than the apologetic responses (or because they were unaware of apologetic responses). I must personally concede that at the time of this writing I could, theoretically, become an unbeliever if I discovered a very powerful piece of LDS-critical evidence which in my mind proved Joseph Smith to be a fraud. Some members, however, would never be swayed by any evidence regardless of how damning.

Interestingly enough, such reactions to evidence are not limited to believers. A number of non-believers or struggling believers have found defensive and affirmative apologetic arguments strong enough to permit room in their hearts for a spiritual witness. In such cases, LDS scholarship has been instrumental in fertilizing the ground for a testimony to sprout, in nourishing a growing witness, or in weeding the garden to keep the testimony alive. Other non-believers, however, take the same approach

---

52. Daniel Little, "Falsifiability," (unpublished paper available on Little's university website, http://www-personal.umd.umich.edu/~delittle/resources/falsifiability.pdf), 1–2.

as some unwavering believers. They claim that *no* evidence could ever persuade them to accept Mormonism or even to believe in God.[53] Even Michael Shermer, the renowned skeptic, admits as much:

> If sufficient evidence did emerge that God is real, atheists should—at least in principle—assent to his existence. Would they? What evidence would be sufficient that both theists and atheists would agree to settle the issue once and for all? I contend that there is none.[54]

Different interpretations of the evidence always exist. There is no evidence that *must* be interpreted in a way that would definitively prove the Church to be true or false to the satisfaction of all intelligent people. Neither the pro-LDS nor contra-LDS apologist is forced to concede their initial assumption that drives their paradigm regarding the truth of Mormonism.

Excluding what can happen to personal testimonies, on a universal scale the worst that could happen if an affirmative apologetic falls is that we lose an evidence that helps support belief—it wouldn't automatically cause belief to collapse. The worst-case scenario for the fall of a defensive apologetic argument (for most truth-seeking people) would be a paradigm shift that might understand the scriptures or prophets in ways previously not understood. There are a number of faithful Latter-day Saints, for example, who do *not* believe that the Book of Mormon is based on real historical people or events. Personally I find such a position illogical[55] but I fully recognize that our commitment to an historical Book of Mormon is not among the questions that Latter-day Saints are asked to determine worthiness to participate in sacred temple worship.

Instead, most high-profile LDS apologists take the same approach that we find in mainstream scholarship when a theory has been shown to be invalid—it is discarded. A belief in the existence of God and that He communicates with His children is not dependent on any defensive or affirmative apologetic argument. LDS scholars and apologists are just as likely as critics or any other mainstream scholars to let the facts speak for themselves and to follow the evidence where it leads (which, as shown above, is actually a ridiculous claim because facts don't speak for themselves—they must

---

53. See Michael R. Ash, "Rational Belief and Rationalization," *FairMormon* (blog), October 7, 2008, http://blog.fairmormon.org/2008/10/07/rational-belief-and-rationalization/.

54. Shermer, *Believing Brain*, 178.

55. See Stephen O. Smoot, "The Imperative for a Historical Book of Mormon," *Interpreter: A Journal of Mormon Scripture* (blog), October 20, 2013, http://www.mormoninterpreter.com/the-imperative-for-a-historical-book-of-mormon/.

be interpreted—and evidence can lead in many directions). Evidence leading to belief is just as logical as evidence leading to non-belief.

As Henry Eyring, father of LDS Apostle Henry B. Eyring, once explained, religious truth comes forth "'line upon line, precept upon precept' in a process of sifting and winnowing similar to the one I know so well in science."[56] Most early Latter-day Saints, for example, believed in a hemispheric model for Book of Mormon geography. Apologetic arguments were employed to defend the historicity of the Book of Mormon based on a hemispheric model. Today, LDS scholars almost universally reject the hemispheric model and favor a limited geographic model. The previous apologetic arguments were rejected and replaced with superior arguments.

Many Latter-day Saints believe that the Quetzalcoatl legends of a white God who visited ancient America manifest affirmative apologetic support for the Book of Mormon. Brant Gardner, an LDS apologist and scholar of ancient America, conducted a thorough investigation of Quetzalcoatl myths and came to a different conclusion. Gardner explains,

> When I began working on Quetzalcoatl mythology, I started with the assumption that I would confirm the standard LDS interpretation. I soon found that the evidence was quite complicated and that in the end it did not confirm the standard LDS interpretation. . . . That required me to restructure the way I saw the Book of Mormon relative to that particular issue (and to understand that it has nothing to do with the Book of Mormon, so it was a restructuring of folklore more than scripture).[57]

Gardner approached this LDS apologetic in the same manner as anyone in mainstream scholarship approaches secular topics. He found serious weaknesses in the argument for Quetzalcoatl as a Book of Mormon evidence and rejected it. His belief in the Book of Mormon as scripture and a text based on a real ancient American record did not impact his ability to employ the fundamental tools of mainstream scholarship to uniquely LDS themes. As Apostle Henry B. Eyring's father told him when he left for college, "[i]n this Church you don't have to believe anything that isn't true."[58]

---

56. Henry Eyring, *Reflections of a Scientist* (Salt Lake City: Deseret Book, 1983), 47.

57. Brant Gardner, as quoted by Blair Hodges, "Method and Skepticism (and Quetzalcoatl.)," *Life on Gold Plates* (blog), September 29, 2008, http://lifeongoldplates.blogspot.com/2008/09/method-and-skepticism-and-quetzalcoatl.html.

58. Henry B. Eyring, "My Father's Formula," *Ensign*, October 1978, available at https://www.lds.org/ensign/1978/10/my-fathers-formula.

Duffy—certainly not someone who would identify as a Mormon apologist—apparently would disagree with those who claim that LDS apologetic arguments are the antithesis of real scholarship. Citing critics of apologetics, Duffy explains that revisionist Mormons are critical of orthodox LDS scholarship because they believe a

> true scholar is "dedicated to pursuing the truth, regardless of where it leads," [whereas] an apologist "knows the conclusions at the start and sifts the facts and evidence to find support." Revisionists therefore dismiss orthodox scholarship as "pseudo-scholarship," mere "rationalizations" to shore up LDS faith claims against contrary evidence.[59]

This view of scholarship, however, is "naïve" notes Duffy. Citing non-Mormon observer Massimo Introvigne, Duffy points out that "there is no scholarship without an agenda; there is no such thing as simply following the evidence to its logical conclusions." Favoring facts that support one's conclusion, notes Duffy, is "what all scholars do."

> In the face of contrary evidence, all scholars invent hypotheses that will preserve the paradigm to which they are committed, unless extra-scientific forces prompt them to convert to a different paradigm. All scholars assign the greatest relevance to those facts for which their paradigm accounts; facts they cannot explain, they set aside as problems for which solutions will later have to be found. As Kuhn says, scholarship is "a strenuous and devoted attempt to force nature into the conceptual boxes supplied by" one's paradigm. This is as true for orthodox scholars as it is for revisionists.[60]

Study after study demonstrates that we are all apologists for our personal worldviews and that holding worldviews doesn't vitiate scholarly discourse. At times, all people seek data for an interpretation rather than an interpretation for the data. Like mainstream scholarship, apologetics may start with a preconceived assumption but will invariably apply scholarly tools to defend or affirm a position. Because careful investigation demonstrates that the distinction between "scholarship" and "apologetics" is often multiple shades of gray rather than black or white, it's just not accurate to describe apologetics as the antithesis of scholarship. Ironically the very act of demarcating apologetics outside the scholarly arena is based on assumptions about the perceived boundaries between apologetics and scholarship and is, in itself, an exercise in apologetics.

---

59. Duffy, "Defending the Kingdom," 34.
60. Ibid., 35.

FIVE

A Wall Between Church and Academy

Benjamin E. Park

I'd like to begin this essay in the most logical place for any paper on Mormon scholarship and apologetics: Thomas Jefferson's political theology. It is quite well-known that Jefferson, author of the Declaration of Independence and America's third president, held unorthodox beliefs. His dismissal of the Trinity as "Abracadabra" and "hocus pocus," his hatred of ministers for "pervert[ing] the purest religion ever preached to man," and the excising of miraculous passages from the New Testament in his creation of the "Jefferson Bible" are only the most prominent examples. But it was his quest to legally protect these unorthodox views—his famous formulation of a "wall between church and state"—that I want to draw upon.[1] Jefferson's "wall" is notorious for protecting the government from religion, but to Jefferson it was just as important for the preservation and development of religious belief itself. He believed that the merging of the two spheres, religion and government, had led to one half of the "world [becoming] fools, and the other half hypocrites," due to conflicting allegiances and ceaseless in-fighting. Only in the free marketplace of religious belief, where a clear demarcation of duties and obligations is instilled, could religion actually flourish. This required a complete ideological separation between the ecclesiastical and civic worlds. "Harmony is unparalleled," he wrote of Pennsylvania's experiment in religious liberty, "and can be ascribed to nothing but their unbounded tolerance." Once this wall was in place,

---

1. "Abracadabra" is from Thomas Jefferson to Francis Adrian Van der Kemp, July 30, 1816. "Purest religion" is from Thomas Jefferson to Horatio G. Spafford, March 17, 1814. "Church and state" is from Thomas Jefferson to the Danbury Baptist Association, December 31, 1801. All letters are found at https://founders.archives.gov/.

the "shackles" of false religion would finally fall away and the two entities, Church and State, could flourish independently of each other.[2]

There are a number of connections between Thomas Jefferson and Mormonism, both serious and playful. Both are embodiments of lofty ideals and gritty realities, both had radical origins and conservative endings, and both have recently been remixed on Broadway—Mormonism as naïve missionary hucksters sent to Africa, and Jefferson as the Afroed, hip, and line-spitting nemesis to Alexander Hamilton.[3] In the scholarly world, one historian of religion devoted individual chapters to Jefferson and the Mormons in tracing America's Jesus imagination.[4] But in this essay, I want to talk about how the development of Mormon studies relates to Jefferson's desire to separate Church and State for the purpose of saving both. Just as Jefferson's disestablishment inaugurated a flowering of religious expression in the early republic, I argue that a split between Mormon studies and Mormon apologetics will lead to better relations and a more robust community. To do so, I will provide a general overview of the development of Mormon scholarship as an academic field, and demonstrate that its logical progression required an evolution from the world of insider, parochial, and, indeed, apologetic work; in turn, apologetics are then left to address the significant questions within a devotional and ecclesiastical setting. In the end, the split between Mormon studies and Mormon apologetics was both necessary and beneficial to both sides, an example of a no-fault divorce where the two parties are much better friends than spouses.

The seeds of Mormon scholarship were planted by forerunners in the 1940s and 1950s by authors like Fawn Brodie, Hugh Nibley, and Juanita Brooks, but they did not reach full bloom until a few decades later when academics like Leonard Arrington and Eugene England helped develop a rich intellectual community based in the Wasatch region. Both Arrington and England were academically trained, institutionally committed, and

---

2. Thomas Jefferson, *Notes on the State of Virginia* (1784), in *The Portable Thomas Jefferson*, ed. Merrill D. Peterson (New York: Penguin Press, 1977), 212. For Jefferson's views on Church and State, see Daniel Dreisbach, *Thomas Jefferson and the Wall of Separation Between Church and State* (New York: New York University Press, 2003); John Ragosta, *Religious Freedom: Jefferson's Legacy, America's Creed* (Charlottesville: University of Virginia Press, 2013).

3. *The Book of Mormon*, Eugene O'Neill Theater, New York, 2011–; *Hamilton: An American Musical*, Richard Rodgers Theatre, New York, 2015–.

4. Stephen Prothero, *American Jesus: How the Son of God Became an American Icon* (New York: Farrar, Straus, and Giroux, 2003), chapters 1 and 5.

respected among scholars. They eventually became martyrs for the cause when they suffered reversals at the hands of ecclesiastical retrenchment and, indeed, were not able to live long enough to witness the full flowering of the gardens they helped cultivate. But they were also products of their time and prone to cultural entanglements. The very decades that witnessed the most innovative and prolific scholarship were also eras of immense conflict. Understanding the development of the field is a key element for understanding the birth of modern Mormonism.[5]

The academic accomplishments from this generation are impressive. The advent of Mormon scholarship, represented by but in no way exclusively found in New Mormon History, was a successful attempt to use the tools of the broader academy to help understand the Mormon tradition. Steeped in the social history movement of the 1960s and 1970s, scholars invoked sophisticated methodologies, drew from rich contextual sources, and appropriated provocative cultural theories in order to explain the LDS Church's past and present. While some were explicitly devoted to challenging traditional narratives and embraced the title of "revisionist," most who were part of the movement were primarily interested in formulating a more flesh-and-blood narrative of the faith's history. The multiple accounts of the First Vision, the origins of the Church's racial restriction, the evolving understanding of the Word of Wisdom—these were merely some of the issues addressed through academic means. These works brought new rigor and insight to the Mormon tradition.[6]

But that is a key element that defines this era of Mormon scholarship: the primary focus remained the Mormon tradition. The primary subjects were Mormon, the primary practitioners were either Mormon or attached to the Mormon culture, the primary venues were tethered to Mormon communities, and the primary audience was Mormon as well. Questions were often dictated by concerns within the Mormon tradition,

---

5. A general overview of the development of Mormon history as a field is found in Ronald W. Walker, David J. Whittaker, and James B. Allen, *Mormon History* (Urbana: University of Illinois Press, 2003); Gregory A. Prince, *Leonard Arrington and the Writing of Mormon History* (Salt Lake City: University of Utah Press, 2016).

6. See James B. Allen, "The Significance of the 'First Vision' in Mormon Thought," *Dialogue: A Journal of Mormon Thought* 1, no. 3 (Autumn 1966): 29–46; Lester E. Bush Jr., "Mormonism's Negro Doctrine: An Historical Overview," *Dialogue: A Journal of Mormon Thought* 8, no. 1 (Spring 1993): 229–71; Thomas G. Alexander, "The Word of Wisdom: From Principle to Requirement," *Dialogue: A Journal of Mormon Thought* 14, no. 3 (Autumn 1981): 78–88.

and arguments were often meant to address a modern Mormon anxiety. That is, in the phrase "Mormon scholarship," the latter was meant as a tool to understand the former, rather than the other way around. Because insider discourse often perpetuates institutional policies, the field replicated broader cultural issues, most especially with regard to gender. And as the academic quality of work on Mormonism garnered more respect and attention due to these developments, much of the resulting corpus remained of peripheral interest to the non-Mormon academy. The field was still a largely Mormon operation, even when committed to challenging its narratives and myths.[7]

While the non-Mormon community was somewhat hesitant with this new body of work, Mormon audiences were all the more intrigued. Because Mormon scholarship was focused on Mormon topics and primarily consumed by a Mormon audience, it fell under the scope of divisive internal Mormon politics. Critics of the movement denounced it as naturalist, positivist, and revisionist, often because they believed it challenged foundational truths and stories. As long as it perpetuated an insider discourse it remained an insider battle. This inevitably led to the turf battles over historical memory and the Book of Mormon. Many not used to academic dialogue chafed at the scholarly discourse, and those protective of the faith's history and tradition worried about the implications. New institutions cropped up, armed with support from ecclesiastical leaders, focused on defending the Church. In return, revisionists only grew bolder. These tensions cultivated a culture based in combat and division. In the academic sphere, books and articles were dedicated to challenging the other side; in the ecclesiastical sphere, prominent intellectuals were excommunicated for, at least in part, their scholarly projects.[8]

---

7. See Jan Shipps, "Richard Lyman Bushman, the Story of Joseph Smith and Mormonism, and the New Mormon History," *Journal of American History* 94, no. 2 (September 2007): 498–516. I chart some of this development in Benjamin E. Park, "Camelot's Crucible: The Historiographical Context for *Refiner's Fire*," *Journal of Mormon History* 41, no. 4 (October 2015): 178–87.

8. See John G. Turner, "'All The Truth Does Not Always Need to Be Told': The LDS Church, Mormon History, and Religious Authority," in *Out of Obscurity: Mormonism Since 1945*, ed. Patrick Q. Mason and John G. Turner (New York: Oxford University Press, 2016), 318–40. These conflicts are exhaustively covered in John-Charles Duffy, "Faithful Scholarship: The Mainstreaming of Mormon Studies and the Politics of Insider Discourse" (MA Thesis: University of North Carolina at Chapel Hill, 2006).

In such a setting, Mormon scholarship was performing an impossible balancing act. Academic work devoted to answering Mormon questions often resulted in the failure to satisfy either side: non-Mormon academics struggled to understand the broader meaning, and Mormon audiences wrestled with devotional significance. In an attempt to address both audiences, many works reached neither. This anxiety was perhaps best embodied in Richard Bushman's reflections after the publication of his biography of Joseph Smith:

> Even though I wrote for a diverse audience, as the reviews came in I realized, that I had not kept everyone with me. As was probably inevitable, readers who came to the book with their own strong notions of Smith found my account wanting. Those on the Mormon side thought I failed to describe his noble character and supernatural gifts; non-Mormons said I painted too rosy a picture and failed to acknowledge the obvious fraud. At both ends of the spectrum, I lost readers.[9]

This anxiety and result was a common theme during the period.

The success of New Mormon History and these first few decades of Mormon scholarship cannot be overlooked, of course. One of their greatest accomplishments was setting a foundation for the next generation of scholars who were prepared to build on their work and prove the relevance of Mormonism to the broader academy. In the wake of the cultural wars that dominated the field in the 1980s and early 1990s, the new millennium brought a new generation of work. Not as an exceptionalist narrative that makes the movement and its various facets unique, however, but as an embodiment for broader cultural and religious tensions. Mormons became the objects, rather than the subjects, of studies to interpret much larger interpretive themes. Scholars like Sarah Barringer Gordon and Kathleen Flake used common topics in Mormonism's past—polygamy during the territorial period and during Reed Smoot's congressional hearings, respectively—to tell larger stories of America's religious history. Rather than just telling these stories from Mormonism's polygamous past for Mormonism's historical sake, these books used the characters and events as case studies to understand America's legal and political boundaries. A wave of other books accomplished similar feats, and an eager academic marketplace was anxious to digest the new literature. Non-Mormon scholars no longer saw Mormonism as a peripheral quixodity, but rather an integral part to broader narratives. A wide range

---

9. Richard Lyman Bushman, *On the Road with Joseph Smith: An Author's Diary* (Salt Lake City: Greg Kofford Books, 2007), 127.

of academic journals and books quickly adopted Mormon topics as a prominent feature in their publications.[10]

Once Mormon scholarship shed its insider discourse and focus, it became Mormon *Studies*, an interdisciplinary conglomerate that integrated Mormonism into the academic community. Soon, thanks to the quality work and the requisite funding base, Mormon studies programs and chairs were established in secular locations like Utah State University, Claremont Graduate University, Utah Valley University, and the University of Virginia, with other schools like University of Southern California and Graduate Theological Union still in the development stage. This should hardly be surprising for a nation that simultaneously provided *The Book of Mormon* musical as well as countless conversations concerning Mitt Romney's presidential run—America has long found cultural power and fascination in the Mormon tradition, and the Mormon Studies community has finally developed the intellectual resources and discursive tools required to quench that thirst. In an important way, Mormon studies has helped to bridge the loch in which the previously mythic "Mormon Monster" used to lurk.

This has meant an obvious boon for the academic study of Mormonism. Whereas previously the geographic location for the field was in the Mountain West, with practitioners representing the faculties of Utah schools, the employment of the LDS Church, or the vast armies of amateur scholars, participants in the field are now spread across the academy. Not only are young scholars who do their dissertations on Mormon topics landing jobs—as much as can be expected in the notoriously fickle job market, anyway—but established scholars are choosing Mormonism for their second or third book projects, institutions are hosting Mormon-themed conferences, and elite publication venues are seeking Mormon content. Mormon studies as a field has never been more integrated into the broader academic world.

But I would argue that, barring the occasional dust-ups, this separation from insider discourse should also be a boon for apologetic, devotional, and otherwise Mormon-centric work. If good fences make good neighbors, firm disciplinary boundaries make congenial colleagues. Freed from the expectations to satisfy both camps, authors can be more pious to their various audiences, whether academic, public, or apologetic. As recent generations have

---

10. For this shift in focus and methodology, see Keith A. Erekson et al., "What We Will Do Now That New Mormon History is Old: A Roundtable," *Journal of Mormon History* 35, no. 3 (Summer 2009): 190–233; "Roundtable: The State of Mormon Studies," *Mormon Studies Review* 1 (2014): 53–102.

demonstrated, attempts to address two audiences often leave both unsatisfied and, at times, even angry. But by clearly separating the purposes and arguments—the separation of Church and Academia—there is less risk for topical overlap. Works of Mormon studies can address the broader academy without fear of upsetting Mormon apologists, and Mormon apologists can address a Mormon audience without worry of satisfying the non-Mormon academy. Greater attention to audience and discourse can only help hone scholarship on either end of the spectrum. The more rigorous the boundary, the less turf crossed, the less offense given, and the fewer battles invoked.

Perhaps the most poignant example of these divided purposes is Paul Reeve's book on Mormon race relations in the nineteenth century, *Religion of a Different Color*. While the origins of the LDS Church's racial restrictions have received plenty of attention, Reeve uses the topic to address one of the larger questions most relevant to the broader academy: What does this story reveal about ideas concerning "race" and "whiteness" in nineteenth-century America? So while the book adds new insight into Mormonism's perplexing practice of racial in/exclusivity, its primary purpose is to add to broader historiographical narratives concerning racial ideas. As a result, it was simultaneously embraced by the non-Mormon academy and seen as less of a threat to Mormon audiences. Yet that is only half of Reeve's accomplishment. Though the book was directed to a non-Mormon audience, he was also willing to explain—or, to use a Mormon term, *translate*—the story's lessons to Mormon audiences, through venues such as the Maxwell Institute podcast as well as the FairMormon Conference. Different audiences, different approaches, different sides satisfied. As we've learned, no book can serve two masters. Another example is the work of Patrick Mason, currently the Howard W. Hunter Chair of Mormon Studies at Claremont Graduate University, whose academic books—like *The Mormon Menace*—are directed to the academy, while his more devotional work—like *Planted*—is directed to an explicitly Mormon readership.[11]

---

11. W. Paul Reeve, *Religion of a Different Color: Race and the Mormon Struggle for Whiteness* (New York: Oxford University Press, 2015); W. Paul Reeve, "From Not White Enough, to Too White: Rethinking the Mormon Racial Story," paper presented at the 2015 annual FairMormon conference on August 7, 2015 in Provo, Utah, available at https://www.fairmormon.org/conference/august-2015/rethinking-the-mormon-racial-story; "Race and Mormonism in the Nineteenth Century," *Maxwell Institute Podcast* no. 23, https://mi.byu.edu/mip-23-mormonism-race-reeve-parshall-p2/; Patrick Q. Mason, *Planted: Belief and Belonging in an Age of Doubt* (Salt Lake City: Deseret Book, 2015).

Which brings the essay back to Thomas Jefferson's "wall" metaphor. Just as Jefferson believed a firm separation between government and organized religion was necessary for both to flourish, so it is that Mormon scholarship is much healthier when there is a clear separation between Mormon studies and Mormon apologetics. Forced integration leads to unnecessary complications, turf wars, and general unpleasantness. But by establishing a wall between Church and State, both fields can flourish uninterrupted. If modern Mormonism's primary challenge is to address the reality of heterogeneity and divergent interests, then Mormon scholarship's attempt to learn coexistence is just part of a larger story.

SIX

Mormon Apologetics and Mormon Studies: Truth, History, and Love

Ralph C. Hancock

There is no inherent contradiction in principle between the aims and the practice of "Mormon apologetics" and those of "Mormon Studies." This should be obvious, but the relationship between these two enterprises has been obscured by events and controversies. Questions of principle have become so mingled with circumstantial judgments and personal interests that it is easy to lose sight of just what is at stake.

So here is the simple and unoriginal truth of the matter: Mormon apologetics seeks to explain and defend Mormon claims, historical as well as doctrinal. (The historical and the doctrinal cannot really be separated for Mormons any more than for Christians generally: if Christ is not risen, then our preaching and our faith are in vain.) We should note that the word *apologia* is found in the New Testament nine times. The most famous instance is Peter's letter where he admonishes the Saints to be ready to set out the faith that they have. Hence, we have clear New Testament authority for defending the faith with reasons. In any case, anyone who holds any opinion will, if she is rational (actually able to articulate reasons), defend her opinion—that is, we are all apologists for whatever we believe that matters to us. And this is especially true of academic professionals whose business it is to do just that. So no one—or at least no one involved in the business of reasoning—can avoid being an apologist for something.

Mormon Studies, for its part, is a domain within the more general area of "religious studies" that applies to Mormon scripture, history, belief, and practice. It thus involves looking at Mormon things from the outside—or, let us say, not necessarily from the inside—and employs frames of reference used by academics who study religious things. These frames must be explained and defended, and so the resort to "apologetics" is inevitable on the one hand as on the other.

This description of Mormon Studies is quite general and abstract, and therein lies the central problem in coming to terms with the apologetics/Mormon studies question. For just what are these "frames of reference" through which it is proposed to study Mormon things? Needless to say, they are many. They might go under names (still pretty vague) such as comparative, historical, sociological, literary, etc. Now, there is no reason why a good Mormon apologist, or just a good Mormon, should necessarily fear having a look at Mormon things from one or more such scholarly perspectives. For example, I'm interested in Aristotle's (not a Mormon) understanding of virtue—in fact, I find much to like in it—and I wonder if such an understanding has or could have a place within Mormonism. (Article of Faith 13 suggests it might.) At the same time, I am more than open to the possibility that some Mormon truth that I glimpse might shed some light on the partial truth of Aristotle's teaching. In comparing Mormonism with Aristotle, I step out of my present understanding of Mormonism to see whether it might be enlarged or enriched by such a juxtaposition. This seems innocent enough—even faithful—doesn't it? By rubbing Aristotle and Mormonism against each other I am demonstrating faith in the depth and scope of Mormonism by seeing what truths uncovered by others it might encompass, or what partial truths it might refine and enlarge.

It is important to note that, in this example, I have very deliberately stepped outside of Mormonism in order to enrich my understanding of Truth, which remains a Mormon understanding. This is what it means to think: to prove all things and to hold fast to that which is good. To be sure, my understanding of my own Mormonism is never complete and final, so it is to be expected—it is to be hoped—that my reflections on Aristotle will enrich, and therefore will modify, my understanding of the religious essentials that I remain committed to. Of course, in the abstract, there is the possibility that I will become so enamored of Aristotle's philosophy that I will embrace it in such a way as to require my leaving Mormonism behind. But this possibility is indeed abstract for me, because I have tested the Mormon Truth over many years by study and by faith, have received many witnesses, both intellectual and spiritual, and have, moreover, made covenants that define and ground my life—none of which are conditional on anything to do with Aristotle.

So naturally I have no problem with other Mormons faithfully exploring Mormonism with the help of non-Mormon frameworks. But the oft-overlooked problem is that the academic disciplines that supply our alternative frameworks have reductive and imperialist tendencies: historians tend to reduce Truth to or replace Truth by History, sociologists by Society, etc. And professors and other professionals get paid (in money and prestige) to impose their frameworks and to publish the results to the applause of others who have an interest in those frameworks. And they are naturally inclined to recruit others to their methods and to the frames of reference they imply. And so it would be not at all intellectually rigorous, but on the contrary rather naïve, to imagine that there is not an inherent tension in practice between the cultivation and enrichment of Mormon Truth and the adoption of the various perspectives employed and deployed in the non-Mormon field of Mormon Studies. There is always the possibility that the adoption of these perspectives will be enriching, but the tendency of a wholesale, uncritical, or unapologetic adoption will always be intellectually and spiritually impoverishing. And it is important to add that such uncritical embrace of academic frameworks will often have implications for our understanding of basic moral principles that are essential to our beliefs and to our covenants. These risks are all the greater because the academic disciplines tend to hide their distinctive frames of reference behind a façade of neutral "methodology." This is why, I would suggest, Mormon engagements with other bodies of thought that involve frank and straightforward Truth-claims—Aristotle or Hegel, Mohammed or Martin Luther—are surer sources of spiritual and intellectual enrichment than "methodological" exercises in the hidden or disguised frameworks of the contemporary specialized disciplines.

"Fact" vs. "Faith"?

A common obstacle to fruitful discussions of the relation between Mormon apologetics and Mormon studies is a simplistic dichotomy between "objective facts" on the one hand and "faith" on the other. It is comforting to suppose that there is an unproblematic world of facts, untroubled by any problems of verification or interpretation and untouched by bottomless questions of human meaning. This would be the world of "secular scholarship," a field of neutral, scientific, or quasi-scientific observation, where honest scholars with no particular "dog in the race," religiously, morally, or politically, just apply their universally accepted methods to bring to light and present things the way they are. This is a simple and appealing way to imagine the realm of "Mormon Studies."

Over against this neutral, objective, and secular field of unbiased scholarship we often posit some realm governed by "faith," which has all the characteristics supposedly eliminated from the first: it is biased, subjective, and determined by personal prejudices, with no ascertainable rational content. One may choose to respect this realm of "faith," but it has nothing to do with rational and objective truth, nothing to do with learning or intellectual enrichment. This is supposed to be the domain of "apologetics."

Where this dichotomy between "fact" and "faith" is presumed at the outset, the prospects for a fruitful engagement between Mormon Studies and Mormon apologetics are not promising. Whereas Mormon Studies scholars are presumed to be purely open to all possible outcomes of research, apologists are known to have prior commitments that limit their rationality; for example, the latter cannot be expected to be open to the possibility that the Restoration is false. But are we to imagine that, unlike the mere "apologist," the "secular" student of Mormonism wakes up every morning ready to cast all inherited and habitual elements of his worldview aside and to start afresh to discover the meaning of life—including his own scholarly activity—with not the slightest prejudice in favor of, say, what he has already been doing, what people expect him to do, what others praise and pay him to do, etc.? That seems a lot to ask. But if the apologist is blamed for not demonstrating awareness in every moment of his writing of the potential that the Church is false, would it be too much to ask that every practitioner of secular Mormon Studies similarly demonstrates openness to the possibility *that the LDS Church is true*? Well, of course, in practice, this would be too much to expect. And so we ought to keep this limitation of secular Mormon Studies in mind.

As soon as we thus turn the tables on the claims of objectivity in this way, we begin to see that the simple dichotomy between scholarship and faith represents a rather thin view of apologetics and a rather idealized view of the academic enterprise in general, and thus of Mormon Studies. To divide up the world between "faith" and "fact" leaves little room for qualitative differences in understanding, both spiritual and intellectual, or for a kind of learning that is both spiritual and intellectual at the same time. In particular, to compare the academic student of Mormonism to some kind of natural scientist dispassionately examining a world of inert facts seems completely to dismiss the problem inherent in the scientific or academic study of religion: the scientist is not examining a human being, or at least a human being *as such*, in his or her humanity; despite the pretensions or aspirations of neuroscientists, for example, there is no simply objective way to put a human soul under the microscope, if only because the observer himself has a soul that cannot be indifferent to the question at hand. The natural scientist may be guided by an understanding of "fact" completely indifferent to questions of human meaning, but this can never be the case with the study of religion. It is impossible to approach the study of religion or of any fundamental dimension of human existence (politics, the family, literature, history) from a simply objective standpoint, since the object of research (humanity) cannot be divorced from the very being of the human researcher. In other words, the student of Mormonism, whether she acknowledges it or not, is necessarily invested as a human being in the central questions to which Mormonism is a response: What is a human being? What is the meaning or purpose of human existence? These are by no means questions peculiar to Mormons or to Christians or to any class of believers; they are the same kinds of questions that Socrates introduced into the heart of philosophy when he proposed that the unexamined life was not worth living. Any pretense of some inhuman, scientific objectivity can be nothing but a mask serving to evade Socrates's imperative to "know thyself," a device for hiding the scholar's point of view (even from herself) and to intimidate readers who might be tempted to contest this point of view.

Some suggest resolving the tension between Mormon apologetics and Mormon studies by respecting a kind of Jeffersonian "wall of separation" between the two activities. On the homely principle that "good fences make good neighbors," it is proposed that a clean separation between these two approaches to Mormonism will promote congenial relations between colleagues on the two sides of the divide. But such a separation depends upon and reinforces the simplistic dichotomy between objective knowledge and subjective faith laid out above. On the one hand, exclusion of believing voices and the emphasis on one or another scholarly framework that excludes the problem of ultimate meaning can only result in the reduction of Mormonism to a network of explanatory causality that leaves no opening for the question of religious truth. On the other hand, the narrowing of faith to a subjective, non-rational feeling or identity strips Mormonism, or any other religion, of its claim of access to things as they really are. In practice, the "good fence" strategy is transparently a means of rendering the content of religious belief harmless and irrelevant to serious engagements with what is held to be reality.

As we will see, the subtlest mask worn by the would-be objective researcher in religious studies is perhaps the one donned by historians, who see Mormonism, like any other human phenomena, as reducible to a certain historical context—which they, unlike simple believers, or ordinary human beings who are not historians, have the expertise to bring into view. And if we were to ask about the human meaning of this particular context—what view of human existence it proposed, and how we should stand with respect to this view (accept it, reject it, modify it)—well then, the master of historical consciousness will respond by pointing out that this context is embedded in yet another context, and so on ad infinitum. Thus the mastery of historical studies defers the most important questions and seems to escape the imperative to respond to them as a human being. I will argue, however, that the vacuum created by the professed inhuman objectivity of the "objective" historian tends to be filled by some combination of the following: the idea of Progress, the postmodern exultation of play, and a new this-worldly theology of "love."

In any case, to define the apologetics/religious studies debate a priori as between biased apologists and objective scientists does not seem a promising way to invite civil discussion or mutually beneficial engagement; this simplistic dichotomy is better seen as a defensive measure on the part of would-be objective scholars who prefer to believe that they have already won the battle, if not the argument, and wish only to quiet those who would contest their pre-eminence.

It suffices to read Richard Bushman's *On the Road with Joseph Smith* in order to see the problem, from a Mormon point of view, with dividing the field according to the simple fact/faith dichotomy. Bushman reports having learned the hard way that "an epistemological gap yawns between my view of the Prophet [Joseph Smith] and that of most academics. Believing Mormons stand on the other side of a gulf separating us from most educated people."[1] My view of the "epistemological gap" is actually more moderate than Bushman's, perhaps because I deal with political philosophers who often believe in a truth above historical construction, whereas Bushman deals almost exclusively with historians—that is, very largely, I imagine, with historical relativists, or scholars who believe there is no truth above whatever truths define human consciousness in a given historical context. But Bushman seems to believe in the tidy gap I have described between partisan apologetics and scientific scholarship, and he

---

1. Richard Lyman Bushman, *On The Road with Joseph Smith: An Author's Diary* (Salt Lake City: Greg Kofford Books, 2007), 101.

concludes that this gap necessarily cuts off "believing Mormons" from "most educated people"—whose assumptions, I gather, it would be impolite to question. This implies a sadly-narrow view of education, I would say. But if this view were true, what would be the implication for academic Mormon Studies? The answer seems clear: A believing Mormon could not participate in Mormon Studies without shedding (or at least appearing to shed) his Mormon beliefs. Driving a wedge between "faith" and "fact"—as do the "academics" Bushman describes—leaves no space for a higher convergence between apologetics and Mormon Studies.

The Problem of "Tone"

Another question that has been prominent in debates between Mormon apologists and advocates or practitioners of Mormon Studies is the question of "tone." The latter have made the case for their own activity in part by declaiming against the alleged bad manners or uncongenial tone in the writings of the apologists. It is difficult to come to terms with these complaints, because specific cases are rarely cited and the objection is apparently held to apply against inherent features of the very activity of apologetics. Of course it would be surprising if no failures of civility or reasonableness could be found among writers on either side of this debate, and I have no interest in arguing that no lapses could be ever found among those embracing an apologetic viewpoint. But the debate itself has certain general features and presupposes certain assumptions that ought to be examined.

From the point of view of advocates for Mormon Studies, their activity is objective and scientific, whereas apologetics is, well, apologetic—it defends a certain point of view. For those who believe their perspective is dispassionate and in a way neutral, involving no fundamental claims, at least no claims with debatable moral or spiritual implications, it is annoying to be confronted by arguments that raise questions that would be more conveniently left aside. But in fact anyone making an argument is an apologist, a defender of some perspective on the truth; and there is no neutral refuge where questions of human meaning and society are concerned.

There is another complication, moreover, in this self-presentation of Mormon Studies scholars as objective and dispassionate. For at the same time they often distinguish themselves from apologists by touting certain virtues: Whereas apologetics is thought to be proud and mean, Mormon Studies is supposed to be compassionate, empathetic, humble, and nice.

The connection between science and compassion, I note in passing, is not clear. In any case, it should first be noted that the soundness of a defense of any opinion is not determined by matters of style or tone, but by reasoning and evidence. Of course style and tone inevitably play their part in persuasion, but to make these the primary issue is to distract from the main question at hand, to obscure or avoid the issue of truth. One might assume that the apologists for Mormon Studies are more "rationalist" in their mode of argument than the apologists for Mormon scripture or doctrine, but in fact the opposite is more commonly true—it is the supposed rationalists who end up appealing to warm feelings. It is the critics of apologetics who make a big point of calling for, not so much calm and deliberate reason, or even simple civility, but such expansive emotional dispositions as "empathy," "compassion," "forgiveness"—and of course, "humility." Humility, it should be noted, is not a natural but a distinctively Christian virtue, and would seem to require its own apologetics and would be a particularly awkward characteristic to recommend to others—and especially to claim for oneself—in an intellectual debate. There is considerable risk of brandishing one's supposed humility in order to gain advantage over another in argument. "More humble than thou" is not a promising posture in an intellectual discussion. The classic warning about motes and beams ought to be kept in mind when the sublime virtue of humility becomes a stake in a debate.

The application of the Christian virtue of humility to intellectual debates is a complex question. Here I would simply ask whether on occasion some sharpness of tone, some irony and even some measured indignation would not be inherent in the task of rigorous intellectual engagement. An example, external to the intra-Mormon debate, that happens to fall before my eyes at this moment is this comment on the New Atheism from the fine Aquinas scholar Edward Feser: "Their books stand out for their manifest ignorance" of the Western religious tradition, he says, "and for the breathtaking shallowness of their philosophical analysis of religious matters."[2] Now, that seems harsh, you might well say. But is not the important question: Is it true, or largely true, and therefore substantially justified? Will truth be served by such verve and clarity rather than by diplomatic dodging? Transposing this question into the field of Mormon apologetics, I would simply ask: Have there been no writings by critics of Mormonism or by quasi-Mormon dissidents that merit the same kind of liveliness and directness that Feser applies to the New Atheists?

---

2. Edward Feser, *The Last Superstition* (South Bend, Ind.: St. Augustine Press, 2008), i.

If we had the space and the stomach for it, we might revisit the question of the Neal A. Maxwell Institute for Religious Scholarship's decision to not publish Gregory L. Smith's clear, direct, and factual exposé of John Dehlin and his Mormon Stories Podcast—a question that was a kind of occasion for the Maxwell Institute's transformation in the direction of a supposedly more irenic commitment to "Mormon Studies." So I would just ask: In hindsight (now that there can be no questions about Dehlin's very active and influential efforts to encourage apostasy from the LDS Church), would both reason and faith not have been served by the Institute's publishing the exposé before Dehlin had attained a larger following and influence?[3] Was it really a responsible exercise of Christian love, either towards Dehlin or towards those seducible by his fairly crude but specious arts, to suppress publication? I grant that there are likely some costs in terms of reputation among non-Mormon scholars associated with such—shall we say—"negative" apologetics. But the costs involved in ignoring and thereby seeming to grant the legitimacy of attacks on the Church are not negligible.

Rational, critical argument is a coherent practice with its own inherent purpose and corresponding rules, modes, and manners. Certain rhetorical devices may be essential in bringing to light the true character of the matter under discussion. Consider another example, this from Roger Scruton's lively critique of certain Parisian philosophies associated with the "events" of May 1968, when a student revolt beginning in Paris came close to toppling the Republic:

> The resulting nonsense, although it cannot easily be deciphered intellectually, can be deciphered politically. It is directed nonsense, and it is directed at the enemy. We are to discard the old hierarchies, the binary structures, the "trees" of the bourgeois family and the capitalist machine, and to reform ourselves as rhizomes, grass-roots communities of underground activists, who will achieve the revolution through the reterritorialization of desire, and the deterritorialization of the existing hierarchies. . . . The privileges previously enjoyed by truth, validity and rational argument are cancelled at a blow, and the materials

---

3. It would eventually be published by The Interpreter Foundation, the spiritual successor of the earlier Foundation for Ancient Research and Mormon Studies (FARMS) and Maxwell Institute. See Gregory L. Smith, "Gregory L. Smith's Review of 'Mormon Stories,'" *Interpreter: A Journal of Mormon Scripture*, February 23, 2013, http://www.mormoninterpreter.com/gregory-l-smiths-review-of-mormon-stories/. For one perspective on this event, see Mike Parker, "Changes at the Maxwell Institute, and 'controlling the narrative,'" *FairMormon* (blog), June 23, 2012, https://www.fairmormon.org/blog/2012/06/23/changes-at-the-maxwell-institute-and-controlling-the-narrative.

now exist with which to build an impressive scholarly career on a foundation of nothing. Moreover, howsoever you build your career, one thing will be certain, you are "on the left" politically, vindicated by all the righteous causes (whatever they might be) of the day, and therefore immune from serious criticism.[4]

"Directed nonsense"—that's a pretty bold critique, and Scruton compounds the offense against delicate academic manners by more than suggesting defects of character (opportunistic careerism) behind the defects of argument. Is the author's tone appropriate? Well, if he's right, then it is! Scruton is writing from outside a hermetic academic consensus whose very foundations he is criticizing, and his emphatic rhetoric is part of the truth he needs to tell. To suppress the word "nonsense" and leave the matter at some cool, technical critique would be to miss the point. To forbid such vigorous rhetoric by appeal to some standard of "humility" or "charity" would be to undermine the rigor and the energy of the very practice of rational investigation and debate. Real humility would consist, I think, not in trying to oppose limitations on the perhaps emphatic but reasoned discourse of one's opponents, but on accepting the rules of the intellectual game one is playing—while privately offering one's heart and motives to God for His inspection and any due chastisement. To attempt to impose the lofty ideal of charity on the intellectual practice of the debate itself would be like expecting a competitor in a race to step aside and say, "after you"; such an appeal to charity and humility makes the names of the most demanding Christian virtues a tool of rhetorical power. Some virtues are better taught by silent practice than by public brandishing.

History and Truth in the New *Journal of Book of Mormon Studies*

Having discussed some basic and general considerations affecting the Mormon studies/apologetics debate, let me now consider certain case studies in the form of articles published by the newly reconstituted Maxwell Institute, which is considered and considers itself a kind of flagship in the promotion of Mormon Studies as compatible with LDS beliefs. My premise, it should be remembered, is the fruitful complementarity, in principle, between the deepening of understanding and defense of Mormon beliefs with the exploration of ideas from other intellectual sources.

---

4. Roger Scruton, *Fools, Frauds and Firebrands: Thinkers of the New Left* (London: Bloomsbury, 2015), 189.

Since its first publication in 1992, the *Journal of Book of Mormon Studies* published articles that explicitly assumed the ancient historicity of the Book of Mormon and its translation from buried plates of gold. This took a striking change with the Maxwell Institute's 2014 publication of the first volume of the *Journal of Book of Mormon Studies* since the Institute's reformation. This volume of the *Journal* stimulated a vigorous online discussion that bears directly on the question of apologetics and Mormon Studies. A particular focus of discussion has been Benjamin E. Park's essay, "The Book of Mormon and Early America's Political and Intellectual Tradition," which reviews two books relating the Book of Mormon to American history.[5]

To get to the heart of the matter, we will first leap over Benjamin Park's review and the criticisms and defenses of it, and proceed directly to his statement posted on the *Times and Seasons* blog, where Park had a chance to explain himself after taking into account the questions and criticisms his review essay had provoked.[6]

Park's review had seemed to many to indicate that he did not believe in, or at least was not willing to defend, the Book of Mormon's own account of its ancient origins. Here at *Times and Seasons* he addresses those concerns directly: "I believe in the Book of Mormon, both its powerful spiritual message and its historical claims." That seems to settle that. And he continues: "It is, in part, because of that belief that I hope to see academic engagement with the Book of Mormon expanded."[7] What will interest us here is precisely the relation between, on the one hand, the belief Park shares with faithful Mormons everywhere in the Book of Mormons's spiritual message as well as its (I would say inseparably connected) historical claims and, on the other hand, his desire to "expand" the academic engagement with this book.

What is interesting is that this expansion seems for Park to depend upon setting aside the very claims that the author says "in part" motivate his interest in the expansion. The "laudable" expansion of Book of Mormon Studies is made possible by certain scholars' setting aside the discussion that "continued to circle around the nature of Joseph Smith's authorship, a question which, while important, has only a limited audience." Now, while Park has no objection to those earlier, less-expansive discussions, he notes that

---

5. Benjamin E. Park, "The Book of Mormon and Early America's Political and Intellectual Tradition," *Journal of Book of Mormon Studies* 23 (2014): 167–75.

6. Benjamin E. Park, "A Statement Regarding a Recent Review Essay," *Times and Seasons*, December 15, 2014, http://www.timesandseasons.org/harchive/2014/12/from-benjamin-park-a-statement-regarding-a-recent-review-essay/.

7. Ibid.

they "fail to explain what made the Book of Mormon such a potent artifact in antebellum America." Park does not explain why the question of miraculous authorship should be considered less expansive than that of antebellum influences, nor even whether it makes sense to sever these questions. What seems to be decisive for Park is what might "be of greater interest to historians of the nineteenth century, including those that are otherwise uninterested in Mormonism and perhaps even religion in general."[8]

What is not clear, then, is why it is more expansive, intellectually exciting, or even intellectually rigorous to attend to nineteenth-century influence, or perhaps more generally to historical context, than to inquire into authorship. What is clear is that some people we are supposed to consider very important are interested in the former and not in the latter. Apparently it detracts nothing from the importance of these people that they are uninterested not only in Mormonism but even maybe in religion itself. So the people we should consider most important for determining the meaning of intellectual expansion are those who are not interested in religion in itself, that is, in such questions as the meaning (if any) of human existence and of the cosmos, but instead in some nineteenth-century American historical contexts.

To Park it seems self-evidently justifiable to turn away from interest in narrowly "religious" questions in order to participate in the excitement over "historical" questions. He praises the authors under review for seeing that "the Book of Mormon has potential to address many historical issues and engage multiple academic fields," thus moving beyond concerns "of primary interest to those in Mormon circles." Park wants to pay due respect to "an *internal, predominantly Mormon* audience," to questions of vital importance to Mormons, but clearly he sees more value in moving beyond "the typically narrow circles of Mormon studies"—a phrase that does not seem to me to represent a significant shift from the one he now says he regrets, namely, the reference in the article itself to "the parochial boundaries of Mormon-centric discussions."[9]

Let me pause here to clarify the question I am raising. I do not at all object to the suggestion that there can be narrowness in an intra-Mormon discussion, or even in a discussion that focuses somewhat narrowly on certain distinctive Mormon claims. We can all benefit from engaging in unaccustomed conversations. My question is, rather, like Peter's: To whom then shall we go? What interlocutors should we seek in trying to expand our minds to more fully appreciate, as Park says, "the Book's power and

---

8. Ibid.
9. Ibid.

promise"? His answer to Mormon narrowness is a turn towards a majority or critical mass of a certain group of historians, a group that is interested in "history" *as opposed to* Mormonism or even religion in general. Why exactly the conversation with historians uninterested in religion ought to be considered a "broader scholarly conversation" than that involving people, including Mormons, interested in truths that might guide our lives, even change our lives, is far from obvious. I suppose "broader" here expresses more a certain quantitative than a qualitative judgment: there are more historians who will talk with us if we talk a certain way and set aside questions they have set aside. (No matter that there are more *people* interested in the meaning of life than in nineteenth-century cultural influences—and not only the legendary Relief Society sister from Parowan.[10]) I am simply asking, is this "breadth" worth the cost of such a dismissal? Note that I am questioning, not so much Benjamin Park's readiness to distance himself provisionally from a certain Mormon conversation, but rather the nature of the alternative he embraces as more "exciting" and "broader"—that is, a historical approach or method that consists in, or that at least results in, setting aside the profound human concerns (such as are expressed in religion) that have always moved people and, I would venture, made "history," in order to study a "history" detached from these concerns. Interest in religion was likely fundamental in the lives of Joseph Smith and others who made nineteenth-century American history, but for the historians who excite Park and promise intellectual expansion, well, not so much.

Turning now directly to the review by Park in the *Journal of Book of Mormon Studies* that sparked this wave of discussion of "Mormon Studies," we see that it is indeed thoroughly informed by a rhetoric that promises an exciting "breadth" as an alternative to a "narrow" or "parochial" past. Of course every reasonable person will prefer the broad to the narrow. But our question is just what it means to be "broad" where the study of the Restoration is concerned.

Park's answer is not immediately easy to track. His first example of narrowness or of the "parochial" is that of academic Mormon Studies that have focused on Mormon things: Mormon approaches to scripture and to the

---

10. Concerning the establishment of FARMS, Daniel Peterson recalls being counseled by a senior Church leader to "Never . . . forget the Relief Society in Parowan"—that is, to produce work that "would be both scholarly and, for a particular kind of interested Latter-day Saint, practical, even inspiring." See Daniel C. Peterson, "Interpreter: A Journal of Mormon Scripture," *Meridian Magazine*, September 12, 2012, http://ldsmag.com/article-1-11431/.

Book of Mormon in particular, or Joseph Smith's "religious genius." Park recommends taking a cue from Mormon and Moroni themselves by placing "the narrative's importance on a much broader scale—demographically, geographically, and chronologically," as opposed, it is said, to the more "familial and tribal" perspective of "the Nephite record."[11] So here "broader" means something like "addressed to the salvation of all mankind," which seems a fair understanding of breadth. But then Park turns immediately to touting the two books under review for "using the Book of Mormon as a crucial text in their broader narrative of American intellectual and social history during the early republic"; these are the "larger historiographical concerns" that can lift us above the parochial fixation on narrowly Mormon things.[12] Now, I can see how both a concern for the salvation of all mankind and an interest in early American history can be seen as "broader" in one sense or another than the more focused academic study of Mormonism, but the reader is left to wonder just what kind of "breadth" the reviewer is finally recommending.

Park does not delay in giving his answer, though, and it seems to have little to do with the salvation of all humankind. In fact, we see that "breadth" will require that some "chop away at Mormonism's distinct message" concerning salvation in order to add another kind of "significance to the particulars of Mormonism's revelatory claims."[13] Here the move to "breadth" is a move to a certain historical context, a move from revelation to history: it is "broader" to see the Mormon prophet "as the climax of a profound cultural tradition" than it is to take seriously his claim to be a prophet (and not just a literary "prophet" like, say, Emerson or Blake).

> Indeed, approaching the Book of Mormon as a way to examine an American problem, rather than merely a Mormon problem, makes the text much more relevant to students of American religious and intellectual history.[14]

To be broader is to go from prophecy to History, and thus to embrace "the important lesson that the Book of Mormon is *best seen* as one of many examples that embody the same cultural strains and that its importance for American intellectual historians is *best seen* as part of a tapestry of scriptural voices that speak to a culture's anxieties, hopes, and fears."[15]

---

11. Park, "The Book of Mormon," 167, 167 n. 1.
12. Ibid., 168.
13. Ibid.
14. Ibid., 171.
15. Ibid., 173; emphasis added.

Park thus seems to accept that what is best for "American intellectual historians" is simply what is considered "broad" in the sense explained.

To his credit, Park goes on to note, in a friendly critique of Shalev's book, that there are "elements found within the Book of Mormon" that "dissent" from nineteenth-century American cultural trends.[16] But the purpose of Park's critique is not to point beyond the historian's framework of cultural context, but rather to enlarge that context beyond "the chronological narratives and cultural compartmentalization invoked by historians of American religion," to invite a more "nuanced and complex" understanding of the way "religious innovation ebbs and flows . . . [as it] relates to cultural evolution." Thus Benjamin Park praises "the broad narratives and sophisticated analysis" of the two works under review, but seems to see these "new vistas" as opening up onto a still broader perspective.[17]

What is this still greater breadth? Of course it remains to be explored, and Park is not to be faulted for not specifying just what the "real work of contextualization and interpretation" that the future seems to promise will look like.[18] What does seem clear is that the work of the "interpretation" of prophetic claims will remain the historian's work of "contextualization." To understand religion is to understand the particular history, the cultural context that produces it. It is not clear that this is what Mormon and Moroni had in mind, but this is, it seems, what "breadth" must mean for us today, at least for us academics, in our cultural and intellectual context. And while some who are excited by the new vistas of historical-cultural-contextual explanation are no doubt very sincere in their tolerance of old-fashioned apologetics, it surely must be considered hopelessly naïve—or at least a little out of step with the progress of contextualization—to study Mormonism or any religion with a view to something as "narrow" as, say, the salvation of the human family.

Turning now to editor Brian M. Hauglid's Introduction to this updated expression of the new Maxwell Institute's *Journal of Book of Mormon Studies*,[19] we are pleased to find a candid confrontation with the challenge of working at the interface of apologetics and Mormon Studies:

---

16. Ibid.
17. Ibid., 174.
18. Ibid., 175.
19. For several years, the *Journal of Book of Mormon Studies* was oriented toward a faithful, non-scholarly audience and printed magazine-style with full-color images and art. With this volume, the *Journal* returned to its earlier focus on scholarly articles for an academically-inclined audience.

We are aware that the approach to Book of Mormon studies on which we have settled may not please both believers and nonbelievers at the same time. It is, of course, inevitable that both will be coming to the Book of Mormon with differing assumptions and expectations, especially in light of the way that discussion of this volume of scripture has traditionally been governed by debates about the volume's claims to describe ancient American history. We expect that both some believers and some nonbelievers will therefore experience some discomfort in joining the conversation. In the long run, however, we feel strongly that this is the best way to gather into one place serious research that will speak both to believers interested in investigating their own sacred text with genuine rigor and to nonbelievers interested in investigating how the Book of Mormon works as a religious volume meant to speak to the modern world.[20]

All this strikes me, in principle, as very good: I have no quarrel with the tactic of provisionally bracketing historical claims (although such claims are clearly essential to the very meaning of the Book of Mormon and of Mormonism) in order to engage a conversation that includes believers and nonbelievers. However, it becomes clear at some points in the volume, as I have shown elsewhere, that this provisional tactic of bracketing clearly gives way to a viewpoint, like that of Park's, in which the question of Truth itself is bracketed—and by no means provisionally—in favor of an ostensibly "broader" perspective in which all religious questions and concerns are but grist for the mills of the historian's mania for "contextualization."[21] According to contributor Paul Owen, this "broader" historicizing approach is qualified as "conservative" and contrasted with the "genuine rigor" of an account that "would allow the Book of Mormon to be taken as simultaneously modern and fictional, on the one hand, and miraculous and inclusive of authentic ancient material on the other."[22] The tactical bracketing of Truth thus issues pretty quickly into the liquidation of the very problem of Truth in the name of historical relativity.

---

20. "Editors' Introduction," *Journal of Book of Mormon Studies* 23 (2014): vi–vii.

21. Ralph C. Hancock, "To Whom Shall We Go? From 'Apologetics' to 'Mormon Studies,'" *Meridian Magazine*, December 21, 2014, http://ldsmag.com/to-whom-shall-we-go-from-apologetics-to-mormon-studies/.

22. Paul Owen, "Theological Apostasy and the Role of Canonical Scripture: A Thematic Analysis of 1 Nephi 13–14," *Journal of Book of Mormon Studies* 23 (2014): 98.

Asymmetrical "Friendship"

Some of the costs of this academic broadening by means of intellectual narrowing can be seen in early attempts by the new Maxwell Institute to articulate its new mission. Similar to the inclusion of skeptical voices to the *Journal of Book of Mormon Studies*, the first volume of the new Institute's *Mormon Studies Review* (suitably numbered Volume 1, so as to clearly indicate the rupture with the *Review*'s apologetically-oriented approach) wrestles with the problem of being a BYU-produced journal engaging non-LDS scholars on their own terrain.

In his Introduction to this new journal, editor Spencer Fluhman acknowledges what is problematic in the procedure of bracketing out one's own religious beliefs, and promises only to provide a kind of clearing-house of scholarly work relating to Mormonism. Such a characterization of the *Review*'s editorial policy seems successfully to sidestep the hard religious and intellectual issues. The move beyond a firmly LDS standpoint is clear, however, in the editor's commitment to becoming "less parochial"[23] and to repudiating the "navel-gazing questions and answers that resonate with Latter-day Saints only."[24] To make this step "across boundaries" will require a "'multiplex subjectivity' . . . a messier comingling of one's intellectual and religious commitments" in which the very question "what is Mormon?" is held open.[25] The only principle that can be taken as normative from the outset in this new enterprise is the idea of "friendship . . . a very Mormon ideal indeed."[26]

The gesture of friendship across religious and philosophical boundaries is welcome, but the question remains of the character of this friendship, or of the conception of the activity to be shared. Just what common purpose, or at least common activity, is supposed to bring these Mormon and non-Mormon (and often non-religious) friends together? This question is very much at stake in a roundtable on "The State of Mormon Studies" published in this inaugural volume.

Two of the six participants in the roundtable propose a "strong pluralist" conception of the project of Mormon Studies. Daniel Peterson argues

---

23. "Mormon Studies in the Academy: A Conversation between Ann Taves and Spencer Fluhman," *Mormon Studies Review* 1 (2014): 6.
24. Spencer Fluhman, "Friendship: An Editor's Introduction," *Mormon Studies Review* 1 (2014): 6.
25. Ibid., 4, 6–7.
26. Ibid., 6–7.

against indifference to the question of religious truth or falsity, and thus for the continuing role of apologetics, including "negative apologetics," or the task of answering critics.[27] Kristine Haglund, for her part, cogently doubts the notion of a "clean space" defined only by a commitment to "scholarly excellence" and free of commitments defined by faith or academic ambitions, and she argues against checking religious beliefs at the door of Mormon studies.[28] She does, however, appeal to some shared and presumably unbiased "rigorous standards of evidence and argument" (which Peterson surely embraces as warmly as she does) and, finally, reaches out for some emerging common language of "ultimate concern."[29] Haglund here touches, I think, on the key problem that advocates of a secularizing Mormon Studies would prefer to avoid.

The risks involved in this quest for some standards and understandings common to religious studies scholars but distinct from a religious community's particular religious beliefs, or, for that matter, for any shared "ultimate concern," become apparent in examining other contributions to the roundtable. Brian Birch wants to give apologetic scholarship a place at the Mormon Studies table—but only on condition that the apologists accept answering to the authority of academic standards: their positions must be "publicly sustainable" and "objectively correctable," meaning that "they need to be publicly accessible to criticism and *potential* defeat."[30] Only in this way, he thinks, can the "conversation stopper" of appeal to authoritative revelation be avoided.[31]

Birch is certainly right that a flat and final appeal to revealed authority is hardly conducive to conversation. But the resort to some supposedly settled and authoritatively public standards of objectivity is another way of defining in advance what modes of persuasion and conviction are to be considered legitimate. Birch trusts implicitly in the standard of "publicity" operating within a self-authorized academic community as the ultimate horizon of truth-seeking discourse. But exactly what is the "public" understanding of truth among academic scholars in religious studies? What

---

27. Daniel C. Peterson, "'Let a Hundred Flowers Blossom': Some Observations on Mormon Studies," *Mormon Studies Review* 1 (2014): 84.

28. Kristine Haglund, "We'll Find the Place: Situating Mormon Studies," *Mormon Studies Review* 1 (2014): 97.

29. Ibid., 101.

30. Brian D. Birch, "In Defense of Methodological Pluralism: Theology, Apologetics, and the Critical Study of Mormonism," *Mormon Studies Review* 1 (2014): 58, 66.

31. Ibid., 61.

counts as "objective"? Is historical contextualization, for example, the gold standard, whether implicit or explicit, in defining "objectivity"?

The appeal to the ultimacy of History is inseparable, finally, from a certain secular humanism. The phrase, I know, is loaded, but the argument is not complicated: if there is no truth above History, then, short of a serious appeal to Providence or to some Hegelian argument for History as the unfolding of a divine Absolute (an argument that only makes sense from the standpoint of Hegel's End of History), then to explain religion finally in terms of historical context is to explain it as a variable and finally accidental human construction. The implications of such a secular academic faith are apparent in Stephen Taysom's call for a new "maturity" in Mormon Studies.[32] To be regarded as a mature discipline "that is held in esteem by the larger academic community," he argues,[33] will require that we distinguish "the rules of scholarly inquiry" from "those that govern eternal truth."[34] Implicit in these standards is the premise that Mormonism is "a cultural phenomenon . . . a human construct. . . . Like it or not, this is what the academic study of religion is about."[35] These are the assumptions Mormons must accept if Mormon Studies is "to find a place in the broader academic world."[36]

It should be emphasized that, although Taysom's argument was featured in this inaugural volume, it would be wrong to conclude that he is speaking for the Maxwell Institute. Still, it is hard to see how the Institute's repudiation of a "narrowly" LDS standpoint in favor of a new project of "friendship" across boundaries could fail to lead it in the direction of such "maturity" as measured by the esteem of a "public" defined by its distance from any "parochial" religious commitments.

From History to Sex

A further perusal of this volume yields further signs that this process of maturation is underway. Steps along the path to public scholarly esteem can best be discerned by first noting that there are two main ways in which

---

32. Stephen C. Taysom, "Mormon Studies and Method: The Rigors of the Academic Study of Religion and the Maturity of Mormon Studies," *Mormon Studies Review* 1 (2014): 89.
33. Ibid., 90.
34. Ibid., 96.
35. Ibid., 91.
36. Ibid., 93.

distinctively LDS views normally run afoul of respectable scholarly opinion: let's call them 1) history and 2) sex. Mormonism, in its own self-understanding, stands or falls with its claims to the historicity of its founding events. The most concrete of these is surely the translation of the Book of Mormon from ancient golden plates, the existence of which was testified to by at least eleven eyewitnesses. As Elder Jeffrey R. Holland has written, "everything in the Church—everything—rises or falls on the truthfulness of the Book of Mormon and, by implication, the Prophet Joseph Smith's account of how it came forth."[37] To deny the founding events thus would be and has been grounds for disqualification as a member of BYU's faculty. Certainly the old Maxwell Institute was firmly committed to defending this historicity. But already in the first volume produced by the new Institute, a softening of this position is perceptible. In a conversation between *Mormon Studies Review* editor Spencer Fluhman and prominent non-Mormon scholar of Mormon Studies Ann Taves, the latter states flatly her view "that there were no ancient golden plates."[38] In the spirit of friendship among mature and "cosmopolitan" scholars, Fluhman holds his silence on this question. What is a little question of gold plates among friends?

This inaugural issue of the new *Review* is thus very helpful in seeing what is at stake in the terms of toleration of the "conservative" view of scripture. Despite their own skepticism, Taves and other prestigious scholars may well be prepared to admit into the company of scholars some LDS academics who hold traditional Mormon beliefs on the question of historicity. Such picturesque "conservative" beliefs neither pick anyone's pocket nor break his bones, as Jefferson would say. But other forms of conservatism are less amenable to the strategy of peace by bracketing; beliefs surrounding sexuality have an immediate personal and political resonance that makes it hard to seem to split the difference on discomfort. In the contemporary academy, a belief in the angelic delivery of golden plates may be tolerated, but a belief in the moral norm of heterosexual marriage will place an aspiring scholar beyond the pale of respectability. Elder Neal A. Maxwell himself clearly saw this coming: "This new irreligious imperialism," he wrote, "seeks to disallow certain opinions simply because those opinions grow out of religious convictions. Resistance to abortion will

---

37. Jeffrey R. Holland, "True or False," *Ensign*, June 1995, available at https://www.lds.org/new-era/1995/06/true-or-false.

38. "Mormon Studies in the Academy," 14.

be seen as primitive. Concern over the institution of the family will be viewed as untrendy and unenlightened."[39]

The maturation of LDS scholars on questions of sex and family is not trumpeted by the new Maxwell Institute, and perhaps not deliberately intended by its editors, but it is plainly enough indicated to the attentive reader of the new incarnation of the *Mormon Studies Review*. Begun in 1989 as the *Review of Books on the Book of Mormon* (and later renamed *FARMS Review of Books* in 1996 before becoming the *Mormon Studies Review* in 2011), the *Review* had a long history of focusing on detailed apologetic responses to books critical of the Church of Jesus Christ of Latter-day Saints and its founding narratives. The departure of this focus in the name of more openness towards the academic mainstream of religious studies—regardless of the positions and doctrines of the LDS Church—is readily apparent in the reviews published in the *Review*'s 2014 rebranding. For example, in Jana Reiss's review of the anthology *Mormon Women Have Their Say* (a volume examining hundreds of oral histories taken of Mormon women), Reiss leaves an author's discussion of the existence of "patriarchal oppression" and recommended moderate means of resistance assumed and unanswered.[40] Similarly, Reiss fails to defend the LDS Church when a quote from a woman's oral history claims that the Church's defense of traditional marriage against efforts to redefine it in the name of rights of homosexuals is a sign of the fallibility of Church leaders.

Most tellingly, perhaps, there is a warmly favorable review by Zina Petersen of Joanna Brooks's *Book of Mormon Girl*—wherein Brooks has a chapter dedicated to her opposition to the Church's stance against same-sex marriage.[41] Rather than defending the Church, Petersen's review only notices approvingly that Brooks "does not abandon her stance on marriage

---

39. Neal A. Maxwell, "Meeting the Challenges of Today," BYU Speeches, October 10, 1978, https://speeches.byu.edu/talks/neal-a-maxwell_meeting-challenges-today/.

40. Jana Riess, "Review of Claudia L. Bushman and Caroline Kline, eds. *Mormon Women Have Their Say: Essays from the Claremont Oral History Collection*," *Mormon Studies Review* 1 (2014): 198–99.

41. Joanna Brooks, *The Book of Mormon Girl: A Memoir of an American Faith* (New York: Free Press, 2012), 161–80. In her original, independently-published edition, Brooks refers to the efforts to prevent same-sex marriage as being rooted in "a millenia's worth of homophobia." See Joanna Brooks, *The Book of Mormon Girl: Stories From an American Faith* (Somerset, Engl.: Queen Bee Press, 2012), 179. While this explicit description was removed from the nationally-distributed Free Press edition that Petersen reviewed, the general sentiment nevertheless remains.

equality" and welcomes her call for "room at the table for every brand of Mormon, non-Mormon, or Other she can think of"—except, to be sure, those who oppose same-sex marriage and others who share Brooks's childhood "shadowless good/evil distinctions."[42] (For comparison, see the *Review*'s 2011 defense of the Church's positions in Gregory L. Smith's "Shattered Glass: The Traditions of Mormon Same-Sex Marriage Advocates Encounter Boyd K. Packer," published under the previous Maxwell Institute's editorial philosophy.) Here, I suppose, is a kind of answer to the question the editor left open in his introduction: "What is Mormon?" At least it seems clear to me what kind of Mormon is not welcome at this table—just the kind, that is, that once defined the Maxwell Institute.[43]

---

42. Zina Petersen, "Review of Joanna Brooks, *The Book of Mormon Girl: A Memoir of an American Faith*," *Mormon Studies Review* 1 (2014): 209.

43. The *Mormon Studies Review*'s apparent willingness to overlook Joanna Brooks's position against clear and emphatic Church teachings is not alone. A review posted on the popular Mormon Studies blog *By Common Consent* does not seem to discern or acknowledge any *necessary* tension between Brooks's militant feminism, her pro-gay marriage positions, and her Mormon faith: "If Brooks is an uncommon Mormon in her support of marriage equality for gays, she is perhaps an uncommon social activist, with her love of and activity within the Mormon tradition. Her faith and politics don't simply clash, however—they intertwine. . . . Her morality is directed toward the sort of equality she believes God wishes—even commands—for humankind: '*All are alike unto God*' is her constant mantra." To be sure, the reviewer speaks of a "tension between personal and institutional revelation," but finally it seems that this tension is resolved in favor of a view of Mormonism that includes and even commends "a variety of Mormon voices . . . broadcast in the public square, *each negotiating their own understanding of what it means to be Mormon*, each telling their Mormon story." See Blair Hodges, "Review: Joanna Brooks, *The Book of Mormon Girl: Stories From an American Faith*," *By Common Consent*, May 17, 2012, https://bycommonconsent.com/2012/05/17/review-joanna-brooks-the-book-of-mormon-girl-stories-from-an-american-faith-2/; emphasis added.

BYU Studies also failed to subject Brooks's ideas to any remotely rigorous examination; its gentle review on *Book of Mormon Girl* concludes approvingly: "For Joanna Brooks, faith and striving are the bedrock of her journey, but she appears to have found personal peace on a different path than many others in her faith community." Jacqueline S. Thursby, "Review of Joanna Brooks, *The Book of Mormon Girl: A Memoir of an American Faith*," *BYU Studies Quarterly* 54, no. 2 (2015): 195.

So, I suppose I must claim the honor of publishing the only known critical review of the famous Mormon Girl, at least in an LDS publication addressed to academics and intellectuals. See Ralph C. Hancock, "Confessions of Joanna

From Playfulness to Love

My point in examining the assumptions underlying the conception of "Mormon Studies" that have informed a number of articles published by the new Maxwell Institute is not to discredit everything published in these or later volumes, or to suggest some deliberate conspiracy against Mormon orthodoxy. My argument rather is that the much-touted "openness" to non-Mormon perspectives on Mormonism involves certain risks that have not been fully appreciated—and I am concerned here not so much with risks to orthodoxy but with the tendency to succumb to professional pressures towards a narrowing of the intellectual field itself, the bracketing not only of specific Mormon beliefs but of the very problem of a truth that transcends reductionist methodologies. And I have given textual evidence that this intellectual narrowing has implications for moral principles associated with religious faith; the intellectual narrowing of historical relativism tends to serve or to issue into a broadly "progressive" counter-orthodoxy concerning the institution of the family and sexual morality.

Space will allow only a brief consideration of these methodological and moral tendencies in Volume 2 of the new *Mormon Studies Review*. (I leave aside for now various articles and reviews that I might be inclined to praise.)[44]

Scott Hales reviews two novels by BYU's Steven L. Peck. He situates Peck's work in the line of Levi Peterson's landmark *The Backslider*, in which

> Peterson's Cowboy Jesus preaches a gospel that offers an alternative standard of righteousness from the one Frank gleaned from the more dogmatic members of his southern Utah community—particularly his mother, whose narrow views on keeping the commandments would make even the most orthodox Mormon squirm.... This alternative standard ... seeks actually to improve it by redefining our understanding of what it means to be a faithful Mormon.[45]

And the new meaning of faithful Mormon involves replacing "hard-line, dogmatic approaches to Mormon living with greater attention to faith instead of works, compassion instead of judgment, and grace instead of

---

or Towards a Mormonism Lite," *Meridian Magazine*, March 13, 2012, http://ldsmag.com/article-1-9497/.

44. Only the first two years of publications by the new Maxwell Institute have been evaluated in my analysis; more recent publications may or may not reflect the same ideological tendencies that I have highlighted here.

45. Scott Hales, "Review of Steven L. Peck, *The Scholar of Moab* and *Short Stay in Hell*," *Mormon Studies Review* 2 (2015): 179.

condemnation."⁴⁶ Now, to be clear, Hales's Peck is not a reformer in the way of Peterson. He does not offer "pat conclusion on questions of ethics and morality" but rather proposes to "explore other avenues of meaning—and meaning-making—in the Mormon world." Peck "perceives the whole of Mormon cosmology as a kind of playground where one can tell offbeat and fanciful stories that revel in the chaotic now of an information-age Mormonism."⁴⁷ Thus, while there may remain an element of Peterson-style "artistic preaching" in Peck's work, he is among those who preach "in a manner that often raises more questions than they answer." Peck "asks readers to imagine how they would react . . . to the collapse of the assumptions that govern their lives and their worldviews."⁴⁸ Thus Peck avoids the "tidy heresies" of writers such as Peterson.⁴⁹

I am struck by the parallels between Patrick Mason's description of his own classroom in this volume of the *Review* and Hales's account of Peck's chaotic cosmic playground.⁵⁰ Both celebrate the playfulness of the collapse of authoritative worldviews. Both, I would say, thereby open themselves to the alternative authorities that dominate the academy. There is something to be said, perhaps, for Levi Peterson's more candid heretical preaching.

The attitude of postmodern playfulness towards historical and, especially, moral questions in fact masks a sympathy for a "progressive" understanding of the family and of sexual morality. The moral seriousness associated with the postmodern playfulness celebrated earlier in this volume in Patrick Mason's classroom as in Steven Peck's fiction (according to Hales at least) comes into perfectly clear focus in the work of Craig Harline (*Conversions: Two Family Stories from the Reformation*), as reviewed by Randall Balmer of Dartmouth's religion department. Harline, a professor in BYU's History department and an accomplished historian of religion in early modern Europe, is gifted with a literary flair that broadens the appeal and the influence of his scholarly writing. In this book Harline skillfully juxtaposes two wrenching tales, separated by three and a half centuries, of the conflict between religious conviction and familial loyalty. It is, unsurprisingly, in the contemporary tale that Harline's very clear moral and theological lesson comes into focus. Michael Sundbloom (the modern protagonist) tried

---

46. Ibid.
47. Ibid., 180.
48. Ibid., 183.
49. Ibid., 184.
50. See Patrick Q. Mason, "The Graduate Mormon Studies Classroom," *Mormon Studies Review* 2 (2015): 11–18.

his Evangelical parents' love and loyalty, first by becoming a Mormon, and then by leaving Mormonism in favor of his newly announced identity as a homosexual. Fortunately, from Harline's and Balmer's point of view, the apparent conflict between being Evangelical and being Mormon, as well as that between being Mormon and being a proudly practicing homosexual (and so, it seems to follow, the tension between being Evangelical and being homosexual) can be happily resolved. This resolution draws on two worldviews that one might have thought quite distinct but that Balmer's Harline now forges into a very powerful alliance: First, the reconciliation of former religious and moral tensions "has something to do with cultural diversity or the Enlightenment or the postmodern validation of an infinite variety of experiences."[51] Second, there is the theological discovery of the "New Testament teaching that love trumps law," a "capacious" teaching that enables the overcoming of "the premise of dogma." This alliance of postmodern Diversity with the new Love produces a miracle of reconciliation, which saves Michael's parents from having to choose between "their conservative evangelical beliefs or affiliations" and their loyalty to their son. Postmodern love thus allows Evangelicals (and Mormons) to move beyond mere tolerance to "a willing embrace of the Other,"[52] that is, an embrace (I infer) that abandons all reference to a demanding code of sexual morality and thus to the need for repentance from sexual sin.

History, Diversity, and Love

My premise has been that we can all agree that LDS engagement with perspectives external to Mormonism can be fruitful spiritually as well as intellectually. At the same time, I have argued, temptations are rife that tend to induce the faithful Mormon scholar to set aside his Mormon questions and to relativize authoritative moral teachings in order to "play the game" of scholarship as this is defined and incentivized in the contemporary academy, including the moral laxity that is praised and incentivized in the contemporary world more generally. The Latter-day Saint's faithful but venturesome dialogue with an "external" point of view can easily yield to pressure to modify the "internal" point of view so as to reduce the tension between the two. This is the oldest story in the world where human actions and institutions are concerned: means become ends. Forays

---

51. Randall Balmer, "Review of Craig Harline, *Conversions: Two Family Stories from the Reformation and Modern America*," *Mormon Studies Review* 2 (2015): 132.
52. Ibid., 133.

into the realm of diverse and playful scholarship that might have enriched understandings and commitments of the Restored Gospel evolve, under professional and social pressures, into quite a different orientation that now looks back at the original religious viewpoint with some disdain.

The supposedly "objective" viewpoint of the master of historical contexts is the leading edge of an orientation dismissive of authoritative truths. The "objective" mastery of history constructs a multiplicity of interpretive frameworks, each of which defers the most important questions and seems to escape the imperative to respond to them as a human being. But in fact a kind of answer is implicit in the perpetual deferral of an answer. One such implicit answer is the assumed perspective of Progress: human affairs have a meaningful direction, and we (expert historians) are further along in this direction than the human types we study, classify, embed in their contexts, etc. But of course this is another kind of masking or deferral, for what exactly is the meaning of this supposed "progressive" direction of history? We have seen that a certain literary sensibility helps to supply this meaning, and that the "objective" historian and the literary connoisseur of subjectivity are partners in the surpassing of traditional, "non-scholarly" propositions about human meaning and purpose. Finally, a counter-traditional morality of love as boundless tolerance in the realm of sexual morality supplies the positive content to replace the old morality that has been relativized by History and by postmodern playfulness or Diversity.

Harline's tale, or Balmer's review of it, thus reveals in vivid colors (rainbow colors, if you like) the core of the dominant version of such a new orientation. This core—which, we have seen, enjoys pride of place, if not complete dominance, in the new *Mormon Studies Review*—is composed of three main elements, or moments: Objective History, postmodern literary playfulness or Diversity, and a New Morality presented as a new Theology of Love. Objective History reduces moral and religious claims to historical contexts; a postmodern literary sensibility of "play" and "diversity" celebrates the relativism produced by the historical reduction; and finally, a New Theology of Love is proposed to provide religious sanction to the relativistic morality.

Please observe that this critique of powerful tendencies in the secular religious studies in no way implies that sincere Latter-day Saint scholars and their readers cannot benefit from dialogue with scholars (including historians, literary critics, and theologians) who do not share their beliefs or their moral commitments. Still, I believe I have given clear evidence, drawn right from the pages of BYU's new Maxwell Institute's publications, that, given the pronounced tendencies of today's larger academic environment, the clear momentum of "Mormon Studies" as it is actually practiced, the default orientation or path of least resistance (which will always be a crowded path), is towards precisely the relativist compassion of the postmodern "village love-in" that Elder Jeffrey R. Holland so eloquently and pointedly derided (yes, derided—points off for tone!) in his landmark April 2014 General Conference address:

> Talk about man creating God in his own image! Sometimes—and this seems the greatest irony of all—these folks invoke the name of Jesus as one who was this kind of "comfortable" God. Really? He who said not only should we not break commandments, but we should not even think about breaking them. And if we do think about breaking them, we have already broken them in our heart. Does that sound like "comfortable" doctrine, easy on the ear and popular down at the village love-in? . . .
>
> At the zenith of His mortal ministry, Jesus said, "Love one another, as I have loved you." To make certain they understood exactly what kind of love that was, He said, "If ye love me, keep my commandments" and "whosoever . . . shall break one of [the] least commandments, and shall teach men so, he shall be . . . the least in the kingdom of heaven." Christlike love is the greatest need we have on this planet in part because righteousness was always supposed to accompany it. So if love is to be our watchword, as it must be, then by the word of Him who is love personified, we must forsake transgression and any hint of advocacy for it in others. Jesus clearly understood what many in our modern culture seem to forget: that there is a crucial difference between the commandment to forgive sin (which He had an infinite capacity to do) and the warning against condoning it (which He never ever did even once).[53]

In the powerful synthesis of Objectivity, Diversity, and Love that defines the mainstream of the contemporary academy, the moral theology of relativistic Love (compassion, empathy, openness to the Other, etc.) is clearly the powerful driving force. Holland has warned pointedly (no doubt forfeiting some "tone" points) of a "village love-in" style of belief that depreciates commandments.[54] The dominant tendency, the practical truth of the "broadening" of Mormon Studies is the embrace, only more or less deliberate to be sure, of a new Love-In Mormonism. The question of the status of commandments (or what the academy might call the "lifestyle" question) is in the end more fundamental than the historical questions that often seem to frame the debate between "apologists" and

---

53. Jeffrey R. Holland, "The Cost—and Blessings—of Discipleship," *Ensign*, May 2014, available at https://www.lds.org/ensign/2014/05/saturday-morning-session/the-cost-and-blessings-of-discipleship; emphasis added.

54. Ibid.

"Mormon Studies" scholars. In fact, the very ideology of "diversity," the vogue of celebration of the "infinite variety of experiences," the playful postmodern exploration of reason's limits, may actually tend to promote a good-natured if somewhat condescending indulgence in Mormon beliefs in golden plates, and sometimes even in the "diversity" of earlier LDS marital practices. But where the commandment of the New Love is clear, there no deviance is allowed. A Latter-day Saint who clings to the belief in a historical Nephi may succeed in a PhD program or earn tenure in a major university, but a Latter-day Saint who openly flouts the new morality supporting homosexual "marriage" will almost certainly find himself or herself considering another line of work.

Under these circumstances, it is misleading, to say the least, to portray the question we have been considering as one between apologists (who are supposedly biased because they know their conclusions before they start) and the supposedly infinitely open-minded and purely objective practitioners of Mormon Studies. Latter-day Saints who engage the academic world are engaging a society, even a tribe, with its own definite moral theology. This does not imply that such engagement cannot yield good fruit, but it does mean that any who venture into the academic world should keep in mind the cautions of scripture and of modern prophets concerning the influence of the world. President Thomas S. Monson, quoting J. Reuben Clark Jr., expressed this caution very plainly:

> "Not unknown are cases where [those] of presumed faith . . . have felt that, since by affirming their full faith they might call down upon themselves the ridicule of their unbelieving colleagues, they must either modify or explain away their faith or destructively dilute it, or even pretend to cast it away. Such are hypocrites." None of us would wish to wear such a label, and yet are we reluctant to declare our faith in some circumstances? . . .
>
> We will all face fear, experience ridicule, and meet opposition. Let us—all of us—have the courage to defy the consensus, the courage to stand for principle. Courage, not compromise, brings the smile of God's approval.[55]

---

55. Thomas S. Monson, "Be Strong and of Good Courage," *Ensign*, May 2014, available at https://www.lds.org/ensign/2014/05/priesthood-session/be-strong-and-of-a-good-courage.

SEVEN

The Intellectual Cultures of Mormonism: Faith, Reason, and the Apologetic Enterprise

Brian D. Birch

In 1912, the fiery evangelical preacher Billy Sunday delivered a sermon in which he famously declared that "when the consensus of scholarship says one thing and the Word of God another, the consensus of scholarship can go plumb to hell for all I care."[1] Sunday was preaching during turbulent times in American religious history. Among other concerns, Christian denominations were fiercely divided over the extent to which critical scholarship could have anything valuable to say about the Bible, the origins of human life, or the nature of God. Charles Darwin's *Origin of Species* and Julius Wellhausen's *Prolegomena to the History of Israel* were two examples of scholarship that upended traditional orthodoxy and helped lead to the Fundamentalist/Modernist divide beginning in late-nineteenth-century America. Contrary to Sunday, the Modernists argued that the discoveries of scientific analysis and literary criticism could not be set aside in favor of traditional dogma. On their view, religious traditions needed to be more healthily engaged in scientific discovery—even if this meant revising longstanding and deeply held beliefs. This is just one example among scores in the history of Christianity, Judaism, and Islam in which the contemporary findings of science and scholarship clashed with the received teachings of a religious tradition.

---

1. Billy Sunday, quoted in "Looking 'Em Over," *The International Socialist Review* 16, no. 8 (February 1916): 465.

Mormonism is no different in this regard. Despite its relative youth, the tradition has experienced its share of provocative episodes highlighting the tensions between faith, reason, science, and revelation. Examples include the very public debates between B. H. Roberts and Joseph Fielding Smith, the debates surrounding the New Mormon History, and the more recent tensions surrounding reorientation of the Neal A. Maxwell Institute for Religious Scholarship at Brigham Young University. This paper is an effort to address competing sensibilities within Mormonism regarding the relationship between secular scholarship and traditional LDS teachings—and to reflect on their implications for contemporary apologetic discourse. As others have effectively argued, diverse sensibilities have been present within Mormonism throughout the bulk of its history. They have, however, taken different forms depending on the issues at hand, the personalities involved, and broader societal trends and tendencies. Armand Mauss's account of Mormon *assimilation* and *retrenchment* is especially resonant for our purposes. These concepts emerge out of his sociological investigation of twentieth-century Mormonism—and in particular from the dynamic relationship between Latter-day Saints and the institutions of American society.[2] Mauss features education and academic culture as among the key examples and employs the terms *reconciliation* and *indoctrination* to describe the "push and pull" of the forces at work within institutionally-sponsored educational programs. I would like to employ the spirit of this distinction for the purposes of this paper, and orient it in ways more specifically related to the theoretical debates surrounding Mormon apologetics.

A useful point of departure lies in reference to the scriptural command to "seek learning, even by study and also by faith" (D&C 88:118). This maxim is inscribed on LDS universities and libraries, and it has a pervasive presence throughout Church curriculum and institutional discourse. Latter-day Saints are proud of their commitment to education and understand the acquisition of knowledge to be a fundamental form of spiritual growth. For

---

2. See Armand L. Mauss, *The Angel and the Beehive: The Mormon Struggle with Assimilation* (Urbana: University of Illinois Press, 1994). See especially chapter 6, "The Official Response to Assimilation" (pp. 95–99). Other related accounts include Terryl L. Givens, *People of Paradox: A History of Mormon Culture* (New York: Oxford University Press, 2007); Leonard Arrington, "The Intellectual Tradition of the Latter-day Saints," *Dialogue: A Journal of Mormon Thought* 4, no. 1 (Spring 1969): 13–26; Davis Bitton, "Anti-Intellectualism in Mormon History," *Dialogue: A Journal of Mormon Thought* 1, no. 3 (1966): 111–34; and Davis Bitton, "Mormon Anti-Intellectualism: A Reply," *FARMS Review of Books* 13, no. 2 (2001): 59–62.

this reason, secular knowledge has never been a problem in principle for the Latter-day Saints. The challenges, rather, lie in certain key areas of intellectual inquiry and in the particular forms these inquiries have taken within academic culture. Though the appeal to both "study" and "faith" works to advance the *idea* of a complementary relationship, it does not provide specific guidance as to how to navigate this relationship in cases of perceived conflict. Only by exploring concrete applications of these concepts can the divergent sensibilities within Mormonism be brought into relief.

The Historical Backdrop

A critical moment in the intellectual life of Mormonism came in the summer of 1938. As part of a symposium for Church educators, President J. Reuben Clark addressed the group and laid out the agenda that would dramatically alter the direction and culture of Mormon education. His remarks were entitled "The Charted Course of the Church in Education," and Clark took the occasion to introduce a definitive educational philosophy for the Church. Among the speech's key elements was the injunction to teach the gospel

> using as your sources and authorities the standard works of the Church and the words of those whom God has called to lead his people in these last days. You are not, whether high or low, to intrude into your work your own peculiar philosophy, *no matter what its source or how pleasing or rational it seems to you to be.*[3]

The core teachings of the Church, Clark explained, are "matters of faith, not to be explained or understood by any process of human reason." Latter-day Saints were hungry for spiritual truth in a clear, simple and undiluted form, and his emphasis on simplicity and common sense resonated with fundamentalist Christian discourse that had, by that time, become commonplace among the leadership of the LDS Church. The purpose of Church education was now exclusively centered on building faith and testimonies. All other aims were to be regarded as secondary and, in some cases, detrimental. Drawing from Paul's distinctions in the second chapter of Corinthians, Clark declared that the young people of the Church "are prepared to understand and to believe that there is a natural world and there

---

3. J. Reuben Clark, "The Charted Course of the Church in Education," August 8, 1938, available at https://www.lds.org/manual/the-charted-course-of-the-church-in-education/the-charted-course-of-the-church-in-education; emphasis added.

is a spiritual world; that the things of the natural world will not explain the things of the spiritual world; that the things of the spiritual world cannot be understood or comprehended by the things of the natural world."[4]

In the years prior to this address, the Church had invested in an effort to send select educators to the University of Chicago Divinity School. Despite its status as being among the most liberal seminaries in the country, LDS students were warmly received there and most returned to Utah with the aim of strengthening Church curriculum and applying their academic knowledge to LDS scripture and doctrine. Armed with the tools of critical scholarship, some began to engage scripture using the categories and vocabulary of their disciplines. This situation increasingly worried local Church leaders whose complaints eventually made their way to Clark and his fellow apostles.

With antecedent concerns regarding the influence of secularism in the Church, Clark determined to act decisively, and the summer seminar was his venue of choice. Clearly hinting at the "Chicago experiment," he stated that

> [o]n one or more occasion our Church members have gone to other places for special training in particular lines. They have had the training which was supposedly the last word, the most modern view, . . . then they have brought it back and dosed it upon us without any thought as to whether we needed it or not.[5]

---

4. Ibid., 5. 1 Corinthians 2:11–13 (NRSV) reads "For what human being knows what is truly human except the human spirit that is within. So also no one comprehends what is truly God's except the Spirit of God. . . . And we speak of these things in words not taught by human wisdom but taught by the Spirit, interpreting spiritual things to those who are spiritual." For more on the connection between LDS and fundamentalist leaders, see Ronald L. Numbers, *The Creationists: From Scientific Creationism to Intelligent Design* (Cambridge: Harvard University Press, 2006), 339–45; and Philip L. Barlow, *Mormons and the Bible: The Place of the Latter-day Saints in American Religion* (New York: Oxford University Press, 2013), 133–40.

5. Clark, "The Charted Course," 8. For more on the Chicago Divinity School experiment, see Casey Paul Griffiths, "The Chicago Experiment: Finding the Voice and Charting the Course of Religious Education," *BYU Studies* 49, no. 4 (2010): 91–130; Russel Swenson, "Mormons at the University of Chicago Divinity School: A Personal Reminiscence," *Dialogue: A Journal of Mormon Thought* 7, no. 2 (Summer 1972): 37–47; and Thomas W. Simpson, *American Universities and the Birth of Modern Mormonism* (Chapel Hill: University of North Carolina Press, 2016), 98–121.

From this moment forward, the course was indeed firmly charted, and Church educators were strongly discouraged from integrating secular learning into the curriculum. A stark division of labor was established, and LDS religious education became increasingly isolated from broader academic currents. By the time of Clark's address in 1938, the groundwork had been sufficiently laid for this shift. In response to a dispute among Church leaders related to the theory of evolution, the LDS First Presidency released a statement in 1931 that instructed leaders to, "Leave Geology, Biology, Archaeology, and Anthropology, no one of which has to do with the salvation of souls of mankind, to scientific research, while we magnify our calling in the realm of the Church."[6]

Among Clark's successors in shepherding the Church Educational System was Boyd K. Packer, a longtime teacher and administrator in the system prior to his service in the Quorum of the Twelve Apostles. In 1981 Packer delivered another landmark address to Church educators that channeled the spirit of Clark in response to a new intellectual challenge—one which came to be known as the "New Mormon History." In the ten years prior to Packer's address, the Church had named Leonard Arrington as Church Historian. This was the first time in the Church's history that someone other than a general authority had been called to that position. Arrington was anxious to help move the Church toward greater transparency and to demonstrate the value of employing critical methodologies as they relate to LDS history. His efforts, however, were met with resistance from the very beginning. Among Arrington's chief critics was Packer, who

---

6. First Presidency memorandum to general authorities, April 1931. The issue at hand for the First Presidency involved an extended public dispute between apostle Joseph Fielding Smith and B. H. Roberts, who was then serving in the Quorum of the Seventy. Roberts was advocating a view of the Creation and Fall that allowed for death prior to Adam, and which took account of evidence of human life prior to the traditional dating of the Creation narrative. Smith strongly opposed Robert's position and argued that organic evolution is incompatible with the core doctrines of the Fall and the Atonement: "If there was no 'Fall' consequently there could be no Atonement, for if there had been no Fall there had been no need of Jesus Christ who came into the world to be its Redeemer from a fallen state." See Joseph Fielding Smith, *Man: His Origin and Destiny* (Salt Lake City: Deseret Book Co., 1954), 264. Smith's rhetoric during this period was similar to fundamentalist preaching on the age of the earth and to the relative value of science overall. See Richard Sherlock, "'We Can See No Advantage to a Continuation of the Discussion': The Roberts/Smith/Talmage Affair," *Dialogue: A Journal of Mormon Thought* 13, no. 3 (Fall 1980): 67–68.

believed Arrington's approach posed the same kinds of dangers as the "divinity school experiment" and would result in more naturalized accounts of Mormon history and scripture—the primary arenas in which the sensibilities of LDS intellectual life have played themselves out. In the end, LDS Church leadership judged that Arrington's vision posed too much of a danger, and his tenure came to an abrupt end in 1982—whereupon he was transferred to Brigham Young University.[7]

These dangers were specified in Packer's 1981 address entitled "The Mantle is Far, Far Greater than the Intellect," in which he identifies "cautions" for Church educators. "It is an easy thing," he says,

> for a man with extensive academic training to measure the Church using the principles he has been taught in his professional training as his standard. In my mind it ought to be the other way around. A member of the Church ought always, particularly if he is pursuing extensive academic studies, to judge the professions of man against the revealed word of the Lord.

Though echoing much of Clark's message in "The Charted Course," Packer goes further and frames the issue in terms of spiritual warfare. "In the Church we are not neutral," he stated. "We are one-sided. There is a war going on, and we are engaged in it. It is the war between good and evil, and we are belligerents defending the good."[8] These two addresses continue to be among the core references in the Seminaries & Institutes of Religion of the Church; and they serve as a bulwark against the corrosive forces of secular scholarship.

---

7. See Leonard J. Arrington, *Adventures of a Church Historian* (Urbana: University of Illinois Press, 1998); Lavina Fielding Anderson, *Doves and Serpents: The Activities of Leonard Arrington as Church Historian* (privately published and circulated, 1982); and Gregory A. Prince, *Leonard Arrington and the Writing of Mormon History* (Salt Lake City: University of Utah Press, 2016). For contrasting perspectives on the New Mormon History, see Thomas Alexander, "Historiography and the New Mormon History: A Historian's Perspective," *Dialogue: A Journal of Mormon Thought* 19, no. 3 (Fall 1986): 25–49; David Earl Bohn, "Unfounded Claims and Impossible Expectations: A Critique of the New Mormon History," in *Faithful History: Essays on Writing Mormon History*, ed. George D. Smith (Salt Lake City: Signature Books, 1992), 227–61.

8. Boyd K. Packer, "The Mantle is Far, Far Greater than the Intellect," *BYU Studies* 21, no. 3 (1981): 1, 8.

"Gone are the Days"

The decades following Packer's address proved especially challenging for the LDS Church as controversies surrounding Mormon history became the stuff of national headlines. From the Mark Hoffman forgeries and murders to high-profile excommunications, the politics of Mormon scholarship was no longer a purely parochial debate. A surge of popular interest followed that carried with it further complexities related to intellectual boundary maintenance. It is one thing to dismantle an institutionally supported Church History Division, but quite another to regulate independent scholarship being produced by a growing cadre of LDS historians, philosophers, literary critics, and social scientists. In 1991, the Church issued a "Statement on Symposia" that discouraged Latter-day Saints from participating in "independent" forums—including, most notably, the increasingly popular Sunstone Symposium. Finally, in the fall of 1993, Church leaders excommunicated (or otherwise disciplined) six LDS scholars for reasons relating to their academic writings and subsequent refusal to avoid public discussion of their views.[9]

With this background in mind, no one could have anticipated that within a decade the vagaries of Mormon history would be laid bare for the world to access, interpret, dissect, and challenge. The internet revolution hampered the ability of the institutional Church to regulate its own narrative and was the means by which many Latter-day Saints were first exposed to unsettling episodes in the Mormon past. The Foundation for Apologetic Information and Research was created in 1997 in large measure to respond to the torrent of online criticisms. Renamed "FairMormon" in 2013, the organization is an independent group of self-described "defenders of the faith" who manage an extensive website, organize an annual conference, and host a wealth of apologetic resources and responses. The leadership and participants come from a variety of professional back-

---

9. For more on this, see Dallin H. Oaks, "Alternate Voices," *Ensign*, May 1989, 27–30; "Statement on Symposia," *Ensign*, November 1991, available at www.lds.org/ensign/1991/11/news-of-the-church/statement-on-symposia; Philip Lindholm, ed., *Latter-day Dissent: At the Crossroads of Intellectual Inquiry and Ecclesiastical Authority* (Salt Lake City: Greg Kofford Books, 2010); D. Michael Quinn, "On Being a Mormon Historian (and Its Aftermath)," in *Faithful History: Essays on Writing Mormon History*, ed. George D. Smith (Salt Lake City: Signature Books, 1992), 69–111; Lavina Fielding Anderson, "The LDS Intellectual Community and Church Leadership: A Contemporary Chronology," *Dialogue: A Journal of Mormon Thought* 26, no. 1 (Spring 1993): 7–64.

grounds and, given the more open platform, the quality of the content can vary widely depending on author or topic.

The internet revolution has coincided with the development of academic Mormon Studies programs at a handful of public and private universities. Since 2001, Utah Valley University has hosted annual Mormon Studies conferences and lectures on topics related to Mormon history, theology, social issues, and comparative religion.[10] The first endowed chair in Mormon Studies was established in 2008 at Claremont Graduate University (CGU) in Southern California. Claremont is a private secular university with a close working relationship with the Claremont School of Theology. In addition to a faculty appointment at the university, the Howard W. Hunter Chair in Mormon Studies operates in relation to a council and foundation that helps support and publicize the activities of the chair. This feature is important because Claremont has been explicit in its efforts to engage religious communities and to promote the study of these traditions in partnership with religious leaders and practitioners. The first occupant of the chair was Richard Bushman, a former endowed chair in history at Columbia University and longtime champion of the academic study of Mormonism. Other Mormon Studies programs include the Leonard Arrington Chair of Mormon History and Culture at Utah State University, and the Richard Lyman Bushman Chair in Mormon Studies at the University of Virginia—along with Utah Valley University's and the University of Utah's Mormon Studies initiatives. Finally, the American Academy of Religion recognized the first Mormon Studies Group in 2007—a designation given to areas of study that show promise and which are supported by a critical mass of scholars willing to advance the field.

The formation of these chairs has been the scene of careful, and at times awkward, negotiations between the LDS fundraising councils and the academic departments in which these chairs are housed. The idea that their resources will be used to dissect their faith at a secular university, and in support of a scholar of the university's choosing, is new territory within the LDS donor community. In the case of Claremont, it took extended discussions to settle on an arrangement whereby the occupant would need to have access to "have a satisfactory enough relationship that he or she

---

10. For a full list of annual conferences, see "Mormon Studies Conference," UVU Religious Studies, https://www.uvu.edu/religiousstudies/archives/mormonstudiesconference.html.

will have access to the LDS Church Archives.[11] Since the archives are managed under the direction of an LDS general authority, the institutional Church could have at least an indirect influence in the hiring process. Though arduous in their formation, these academic programs have emerged as important spaces in which institutional and apologetic voices can engage more freely with scholars from a variety of disciplines and perspectives. LDS leaders and representatives find themselves able participate in Mormon Studies conferences and lectures in ways heretofore unseen. These selective forms of engagement have, on the whole, been a resounding success despite a few awkward moments along the way.[12]

Another form of institutional rapprochement can be seen in a recent series of "Gospel Topics Essays" designed to address the more controversial aspects of the Church's history and theology—including the use of seer stones in the translation of the Book of Mormon, Joseph Smith's plural marriage practices, and issues surrounding the historicity of the Book of Abraham. Recognizing that its members are awash in a sea of information (and misinformation), these documents are presented by the

---

11. Armand Mauss, quoted in Carrie Moore, "Funding of LDS Post Starts," *Deseret News*, April 28, 2006, available at http://www.deseretnews.com/article/635203177/Funding-of-LDS-post-starts.html. In addition to teaching Mormon Studies classes at Claremont Graduate University (CGU), Mauss was among the original council members and has been an instrumental voice in the development of the CGU program. For a candid account in his own voice, see *Shifting Borders and a Tattered Passport: Intellectual Journeys of a Mormon Academic* (Salt Lake City: University of Utah Press, 2012), 144–69.

12. Among the more rewarding moments of my career was co-organizing a conference at Utah Valley University with both Michael Quinn and Elder John Carmack on the program. It was remarkable because just six years prior, Yale Divinity School hosted a symposium entitled "God, Humanity, and Revelation: Perspectives from Mormon Philosophy and History" in partnership with BYU and other universities. It was quietly but widely reported that institutional pressure was brought to forestall an invitation for Quinn to speak. Coincidentally (and ironically), Quinn was a scholar in residence that year at the Beineke Library at Yale. Despite being snubbed as a presenter, Quinn agreed to attend the conference and introduce one of the speakers. For a less sanguine perspective on the rise of Mormon Studies, see John-Charles Duffy, "Defending the Kingdom, Rethinking the Faith: How Apologetics is Reshaping Mormon Orthodoxy," *Sunstone* (May 2004): 23–55. See also Duffy, "Faithful Scholarship: The Mainstreaming of Mormon Studies and the Politics of Insider Discourse," (master's thesis, University of North Carolina at Chapel Hill, 2006).

Church as reliable sources to help Latter-day Saints navigate these increasingly turbulent waters. "The purpose of these essays, which have been approved by the First Presidency and Quorum of the Twelve Apostles, has been to gather accurate information from many different sources and publications."[13] Upon their release (beginning in 2013), the essays received little fanfare and were featured less prominently on the LDS Church's website. This was curious given the implications of their content and the inevitability of widespread media coverage. Over time, however, the Church has not only taken steps to elevate their profile, but has begun the effort to incorporate their content into institutional curriculum. This should prove to be a delicate process given the longstanding practice of publishing idealized and hagiographic curriculum.

The importance of this integrative effort can be observed in Elder M. Russell Ballard's address to Church educators in February 2016. The speech contains some startling admissions and makes it clear that Church educators need to be better prepared to answer difficult questions. "It was only a generation ago," he says,

> that our young people's access to information about our history, doctrine, and practices was basically limited to materials printed by the Church. Few students came in contact with alternative interpretations. Mostly, our young people lived a sheltered life. Our curriculum at that time, though well-meaning, did not prepare students for today—a day when students have instant access to virtually everything about the Church from every possible point of view.[14]

In addition to the narrow range of resources, seminary and institute instructors had been trained to redirect challenging questions and avoid discussion of their implications. In the face of these practices, Ballard responds sharply:

> Gone are the days when a student asked an honest question and a teacher responded, "Don't worry about it!" Gone are the days when a student raised a sincere concern and a teacher bore his or her testimony as a response in-

---

13. "Gospel Topics Essays," The Church of Jesus Christ of Latter-day Saints, http://www.lds.org/topics/essays.

14. M. Russell Ballard, "The Opportunities and Responsibilities of CES Teachers in the 21st Century," (address to CES Religious Educators in the Salt Lake Tabernacle on February 26, 2016), available at https://www.lds.org/broadcasts/article/evening-with-a-general-authority/2016/02/the-opportunities-and-responsibilities-of-ces-teachers-in-the-21st-century.

tended to avoid the issue. Gone are the days when students were protected from people who attacked the Church.[15]

With specific reference to the Gospel Topics Essays, he stresses the need for educators to fully absorb these documents and utilize them in teaching and discussion. As an aid in this endeavor, he encourages them to extend their studies to include "the best LDS scholarship available." By inoculating students prior to their exposure to "incorrect interpretations of doctrine, history, and practices," Ballard hopes the Church can help stem the tide of young Latter-day Saints leaving the organization. Among the practical challenges posed by this imperative lies the effort to identify the "best" scholarly sources outside the self-enclosed orbit of seminary and institute materials. It remains to be seen the extent to which scholarly sources outside the scope of centralized correlation will be sought out and recommended. Some of the research that informed the Gospel Topics Essays comes from sources that have been viewed with a degree of caution or suspicion—or have been largely unknown within Church educational circles.[16] For Ballard's vision to be realized, cultural barriers between institutional and independent scholarship will need to be overcome.

Mormon Apologetics

As our discussion turns toward contemporary apologetics, it makes sense to begin with the legacy of Hugh Nibley, whose prodigious output and forty-plus year presence at Brigham Young University helped set the tone and direction for the discourse that followed. Though specifically

---

15. Ibid.
16. Examples include Richard Lyman Bushman, *Joseph Smith: Rough Stone Rolling* (New York: Alfred A. Knopf, 2005); Lester E. Bush Jr., "Mormonism's Negro Doctrine: A Historical Overview," *Dialogue: A Journal of Mormon Thought* 8, no. 1 (Spring 1973): 11–69; W. Paul Reeve, *Religion of a Different Color: Race and the Struggle for Mormon Whiteness* (New York: Oxford University Press, 2015); Armand L. Mauss, *All Abraham's Children: Changing Mormon Conceptions of Race and Lineage* (Urbana: University of Illinois Press, 2003); Kathryn M. Daynes, *More Wives than One: Transformation of the Mormon Marriage System, 1840–1910* (Urbana: University of Illinois Press, 2001); and D. Michael Quinn, "LDS Church Authority and New Plural Marriages, 1890–1904," *Dialogue: A Journal of Mormon Thought* 18, no. 1 (Spring 1985), 9–105. This is not to say that these sources were cited by the essays. It is to say, however, that the influence of this research pushed the conversation forward toward more explicit recognition.

trained in classics and Near Eastern studies, Nibley's essays covered a wide range of topics and provided ample raw material from which subsequent work was constructed. His engaging and acerbic style influenced a generation of scholars for whom there was no intellectual equal in Mormonism. Of interest for our purposes, Nibley's persistent attacks on the hubris and pretensions of intellectual culture coincided with the institutional Church's efforts in the direction of academic retrenchment.[17]

A second generation of LDS apologists extended and applied Nibley's approach; though these works retained much of his tone and style, they provided more sustained arguments and analysis. Important among these efforts were the attempts to connect Mormon apologetics more explicitly to the broader landscape of Christian thought. These voices included the Anglican theologian Austin Farrer who famously stated that, "Though argument does not create conviction, lack of it destroys belief."[18] Farrer and others are referenced favorably in the works of Mormon apologists including Daniel Peterson, the longtime editor of the influential *FARMS Review* and fierce LDS defender of the faith. Peterson compares apologetics to a buttress in a building. As neither the building nor its foundation, the buttress serves, rather, to provide support and reinforcement.[19] He is quick to point out that argument and evidence should not *replace* faith and testimony. A form of "studied conviction," he says, "can help a believer through spiritual dry spells, when God seems distant and spiritual experiences are distant memories."[20] This approach resonates with the approach described in the literature as *negative apologetics*, which seeks to *neutralize* criticisms rather than *establish* religious truth claims solely on the basis

---

17. See Hugh Nibley, "Prophets and Scholars," in *The World and the Prophets*, ed. John W. Welch, Gary P. Gillum, and Don E. Norton, Volume 3 of the *Collected Works of Hugh Nibley* (Provo, Utah: Foundation for Ancient Research and Mormon Studies, 1987), 26–32; and Hugh Nibley, "Three Shrines: Mantic, Sophic, and Sophistic," in *The Ancient State*, ed. Stephen D. Ricks and Donald W. Parry (Provo, Utah: Foundation for Ancient Research and Mormon Studies, 1981), 311–79. See also Boyd Jay Petersen, *Hugh Nibley: A Consecrated Life* (Salt Lake City: Greg Kofford Books, 2002).

18. Austin Farrer, "Grete Clerk," in *Light on C. S. Lewis*, ed. Jocelyn Gibb (New York: Harcourt and Brace, 1965), 26.

19. Daniel C. Peterson, "The Role of Apologetics in Mormon Studies," *The Mormon Interpreter: A Journal of Mormon Scripture* 2 (2012): xix. See also Peterson, "An Unapologetic Apology for Apologetics," *FARMS Review of Books* 22, no. 2 (2010): xi–xlviii.

20. Peterson, "The Role of Apologetics," xviii.

of reason and argument. Much of LDS literature can be characterized as negative apologetics—with relatively fewer attempts to provide actual proofs for the key claims of the LDS gospel.[21]

A recent manifestation of the "push and pull" of these issues in Mormon intellectual life can be found in the ever-evolving Neal A. Maxwell Institute for Religious Scholarship. As the traditional epicenter of Mormon apologetics, the Institute had historically defined its mission as an effort to "defend the Restoration" and "provide an anchor of faith in a sea of LDS Studies."[22] Their most influential publication was the *FARMS Review* under the leadership of Daniel Peterson. Though oriented primarily toward scholarship on the Book of Mormon, a portion of the *FARMS Review* was devoted to lengthy review essays in response to a variety of Mormonism's critics. Included among these were some penetrating and effective critiques. Others, however, were manifestly caustic and dismissive. Whether deserved or not, the publication developed a reputation for supporting ill-mannered scholarship, and Peterson was unceremoniously dismissed. The *FARMS Review* was dissolved in favor of a new publication entitled the *Mormon Studies Review*; under the leadership of its new editor, Spencer Fluhman, the publication sought almost immediately to expand its reach toward the broader religious studies community. It was also during this period that the Maxwell Institute revised its mission statement to express a broader orientation to "deepen understanding and nurture discipleship among Latter-day Saints while promoting mutual respect and goodwill among people of all faiths."[23] Though apologetic work remained a part of the Maxwell Institute's new direction, their leadership made it

---

21. See Daniel C. Peterson, "'Let a Hundred Flowers Blossom': Some Observations on Mormon Studies," *Mormon Studies Review* 1 (2014), 80–88.

22. "Neal A. Maxwell Institute for Religious Scholarship Mission Statement," Neal A. Maxwell Institute for Religious Scholarship, http://maxwellinstitute.byu.edu/about/missionstatement.php. See Loyd Isao Ericson, "Where is the 'Mormon' in Mormon Studies?" *Claremont Journal of Mormon Studies* 1, no. 1 (April 2011): 7; and Peterson, "The Role of Apologetics," iii.

23. "About the Maxwell Institute," Neal A. Maxwell Institute for Religious Scholarship, https://mi.byu.edu/about/. It should be noted that one issue of the *Mormon Studies Review* first appeared under the editorship of Daniel Peterson prior to his dismissal. The name change reflected the desire on the part of the Institute's leadership to begin expanding the scope of the publication. Nevertheless, it was determined that the first issue of the *Mormon Studies Review* under Fluhman's editorial tenure would be designated as Volume 1 to provide a fresh start to the new enterprise.

clear that apologetics would not play a dominant role to the exclusion of other methodological approaches. In his inaugural essay, Fluhman states that the *Mormon Studies Review* aspires to provide a forum in which "underlying assumptions *can* be assessed, and where comparative possibilities can be explored."[24] In an apparent effort to build upon this momentum, BYU hired Fluhman in 2016 to replace the retiring Gerald Bradford as the Institute's new executive director. For purposes of our discussion, the significance of these changes lies in the degree to which they allow for openness and reciprocity heretofore unseen among LDS educational affiliates. The dialogical space created by other universities has been met in kind by the Maxwell Institute, and the effects have been immediately felt among those working to advance the academic study of Mormonism. Nevertheless, questions remain. As the Church continues to wrestle with the implications of secular scholarship, to what extent might this inclusiveness be seen as a corrosive force to traditional faith? How deeply can the "underlying assumptions" of Mormonism be assessed before Church leadership senses the need for a corrective? If a corrective is ultimately undertaken, what form would it take?

These are not hypothetical questions. The events surrounding Peterson's dismissal ignited a range war over the appropriate mission of the Maxwell Institute and the extent to which its new direction remains consistent with the vision of its namesake, Elder Neal A. Maxwell. Some longtime affiliates of the *FARMS Review* expressed alarm that these changes were further evidence of BYU abandoning its spiritual vocation in favor of accommodation to the secular academy. These traditionalists have continued to argue that the quest for academic legitimacy has led to a requisite compromise of spiritual values. Among the most vociferous has been BYU political science professor Ralph Hancock, who openly worries that his institution is "succumbing to a secular paradigm" and losing the distinctiveness of its institutional mission.

Pursuing a national audience to call out his own university, Hancock published a 2014 article in the Christian Magazine *First Things* under the subtitle "Warning of the Dangers of Secularism for Brigham Young University." Hancock's concerns centered on the stark division of labor he observes between the specific demands of a faculty member's field of study

---

24. J. Spencer Fluhman, "Friendship: An Editor's Introduction," *Mormon Studies Review* 1 (2014), 3; emphasis added. See also Blair Dee Hodges, "Apologetics at the Maxwell Institute? No *and Yes*," Neal A. Maxwell Institute for Religious Scholarship (blog), November 11, 2015, https://mi.byu.edu/miapologetics.

and the university's self-conscious religious identity. The demands of secular academic culture, he argues, have led the university to at least implicitly accept the norms and values embedded in the academy. BYU faculty are encouraged to publish exclusively within their field and discouraged from the public pursuit of connecting their discipline with the scriptures and teachings of the LDS Church. The "reductionist assumptions" demanded within specialized disciplines, according to Hancock, have led to a culture at BYU of increasing acceptance of secular paradigms—and have done so at the expense of efforts to "articulate and defend good and principles fundamental to a Christian and Latter-day Saint view of the world."[25] The danger for Hancock lies in the extent to which these principles are being set aside in the very institution devoted to providing students ways of applying their faith to their learning and ultimately to their experiences outside the university. "Without engaging the ideas underlying the moral and political forces of secular progressivism, BYU can only cooperate by default with the dominant movement. To acquiesce to the authority of the secular academic establishment is effectively to endorse it and to bolster it, even if most do not intend this effect."[26]

---

25. Ralph Hancock, "Keeping Faith in Provo: Warning of the Dangers of Secularism for Brigham Young University," *First Things* (March 2014): https://www.firstthings.com/article/2014/03/keeping-faith-in-provo. Hancock has published a handful of essays and blog posts that address common themes. These include "To Whom Shall We Go? From 'Apologetics' to 'Mormon Studies,'" *Meridian Magazine*, December 21, 2014, http://ldsmag.com/to-whom-shall-we-go-from-apologetics-to-mormon-studies/; "Who's Afraid of Secularism?" *Meridian Magazine*, March 3, 2015, http://ldsmag.com/whos-afraid-of-secularism/; "The Moral Convictions of Secularism," *Meridian Magazine*, March 5, 2015, http://ldsmag.com/the-moral-convictions-of-secularism/; "Nothing to Apologize For – Part I," *Times and Seasons*, July 20, 2012, http://www.timesandseasons.org/harchive/2012/07/nothing-to-apologize-for-part-i/; "Nothing to Apologize For – Part II," *Times and Seasons*, July 25, 2012, http://www.timesandseasons.org/harchive/2012/07/nothing-to-apologize-for-part-ii/; and "Faith, Reason, and the Critical Study of Mormon Apologetics," *Meridian Magazine*, November 10, 2015, http://ldsmag.com/faith-reason-and-the-critical-study-of-mormon-apologetics/.

26. Hancock, "Keeping the Faith." For more on the debates over secularism and higher education, see George Marsden, *The Soul of the American University: From Protestant Establishment to Established Nonbelief* (New York: Oxford University Press, 1994); *The University Gets Religion: Religious Studies in American Higher Education* (Baltimore: The Johns Hopkins University Press, 1999); Douglas Jacabsen and Rhonda Hustedt Jacobsen, eds., *The American*

To help frame his arguments, Hancock employs former LDS Church president Spencer W. Kimball's statement that "[g]ospel methodology, concepts, and insights can help us to do what the world cannot do in its own frame of reference." Because BYU maintains what Kimball calls a "double heritage," faculty must be bilingual. "As LDS scholars you must speak with authority and excellence to your professional colleagues in the language of scholarship, and you must also be literate in the language of spiritual things."[27] Though practical necessities have forced BYU to navigate the straits between the demands of the academy and the teachings of the Church, it was "generally stipulated or assumed," Hancock says, "that the language of faith would be the primary idiom that reflected a scholar's deepest understanding." Nevertheless, he adds, "the risk was always present that the language associated with academic prestige would, often quite surreptitiously, become the dominant or default language."[28] And this is precisely what Hancock believes has taken place. The absence of accounts that challenge prevailing intellectual paradigms leaves students feeling as if they must choose between being thoughtful and well-informed *or* being loyal to LDS teachings. The changes at the Maxwell Institute are, for Hancock, yet another manifestation of the university falling short of its own precepts—among which is to "be in the world, but not of the world."

Hancock's account here raises penetrating and relevant questions that go to the very heart of our discussion. Though his style is captious (excessively so for my tastes), the issues he probes are critical and require thoughtful and productive responses. The very idea of a double heritage—and the bilingualism that follows—invites continual reflection on the meaning of this distinction and how it is to be applied at institutions such as BYU. Though Hancock makes a fair point about the avoidance of BYU faculty in addressing the implications of their fields of study for the truth claims of Mormonism, he leaves unexamined important considerations regarding how this compartmentalization reflects the Church's *own* understanding of how these truth claims ought to be approached—or avoided as the case

---

University in a Postsecular Age (New York: Oxford University Press, 2008); Julie A. Reuben, *The Making of the Modern University: Intellectual Transformation and the Marginalization of Morality* (Chicago: University of Chicago Press, 1996); and Jon H. Roberts and James Turner, *The Sacred and the Secular University* (Princeton: Princeton University Press, 2000).

27. Spencer W. Kimball, "Second Century Address," *BYU Studies Quarterly* 16, no. 4 (Winter 1976): 454, 446.

28. Hancock, "Keeping Faith."

may be. I would argue that particular norms and sensibilities *within* LDS institutional culture inform this contented divide far more strongly than secularizing forces at work in the academy. The language of segregation between the "natural world" and the "spiritual world" has penetrated the Mormon psyche in ways that accommodate a tidy compartmentalization of the findings of science, historical studies, biblical criticism, etc., on the one hand, and the current teachings of the Church on the other. Hancock rightly points out that "large integrating questions" are not being robustly engaged by capable and talented BYU scholars. But this situation applies well beyond the confines of BYU—and is better explained as the predictable outgrowth of norms and attitudes present in the Church since J. Reuben Clark laid out "The Charted Course."[29]

For example, the secularizing forces of the academy cannot account for BYU's longstanding reluctance to support an academic program in religious studies—despite its status as the largest religiously affiliated university in the country. When compared to universities like Catholic University of America, Notre Dame, or Baylor, relatively few BYU professors have academic training in religious studies, theology, or religious history despite having an exceptionally large department of Church History and Doctrine—which operates in closer alignment with the devotional norms of LDS Seminaries and Institutes than to the expectations of related academic disciplines. Again, none of this can be reasonably attributed to the stifling demands of the secular academy. This is a situation, rather, in which LDS educational institutions have *self-selected* out of these academic conversations—and in the very disciplines most accommodating to, and integrative of, religious voices.

The changes at the Maxwell Institute represent a cautious effort to enter the religious studies arena and to help facilitate conversations across disciplinary and methodological lines. The term "facilitate" is important in this context because Fluhman takes pains to emphasize that the *Mormon*

---

29. These observations are intended to be purely descriptive and are specifically related to institutional realities. There are, of course, strong *theological* reasons within Mormonism to support a more adventurous and integrative approach to religious education. See Chapters 1, 2, 5, and 11 of Terryl Givens, *People of Paradox*; Philip L. Barlow, "Mind and Spirit in Mormon Thought," in *The Oxford Handbook of Mormonism*, ed. Terryl L. Givens and Philip L. Barlow (New York: Oxford University Press, 2015), 227–45; and Sterling M. McMurrin, *The Theological Foundations of the Mormon Religion* (Salt Lake City: University of Utah Press, 1965).

Studies Review is designed as a *forum* to help "chronicle and assess" the field. It does not attempt to normatively define Mormonism, nor does it seek to advance a specific methodology. This turn toward inclusion will help, in Fluhman's view, to keep the discussion sharp and "intellectually honest."[30] One challenge in moving this direction involves accepting the implications of dialogue with scholars critical of the Church or publishing academic works that contravene institutionally established teachings. Though the free exchange of ideas is a deeply held principle in American higher education, creating dialogical space to discuss controversial issues in Mormon history, scripture, or theology will test longstanding institutional aversions toward the appearance of complicity or guilt by association. The LDS Church and its affiliates have been loath to present the claims of its tradition in a way that deviates from a simple and monolithic narrative. Elder Packer went so far as to say that the effort by its educators to present Mormon history in an *impartial* manner "may unwittingly be giving equal time to the adversary."[31] In the attempt to balance inclusion and complicity, the extended reach of the Maxwell Institute serves as an important test case in determining how the intellectual cultures of Mormonism will be negotiated as the Church moves forward in the Information Age.

Fideism and Apologetics

Our concluding section leads us to consider the place of LDS apologetics in the academic landscape and its openness to the critical give and take of academic discourse. If apologetics is defined as a *reasoned* defense of faith, then the extent to which its practitioners employ arguments, they are (presumably) engaging in a form of discourse that is, by its nature, subject to rational scrutiny and evaluation. This appears straightforward; but a careful examination of apologetic methodologies paints a more complicated picture. The Anglican theologian David Ford defines apologetics as the branch of Christian theology that is "concerned with defense of orthodox Christian doctrine in the face of criticism and alternative points of view, usually attempting to meet critics' questions and objections by *looking for shared grounds or criteria for what is reasonable and true*."[32] There

---

30. J. Spencer Fluhman, "Friendship: An Editor's Introduction," *Mormon Studies Review* 1 (2014): 5.

31. Packer, "Mantle Is Far, Far Greater," 8.

32. David F. Ford, ed., *The Modern Theologians: An Introduction to Christian Theology Since 1918*, 3rd ed. (Oxford: Wiley-Blackwell Publishing, 2005), 764;

are, however, a considerable number of Christian apologists who argue that rational arguments *could never* serve to threaten the claims of faith. In one such example, it is argued that "the inner witness of the Holy Spirit gives us an immediate and veridical assurance of the truth of our Christian faith." The implications are such that "rational argument and evidence *may properly confirm but not defeat* that assurance."[33] Recalling Daniel Peterson's account, he maintains that a key function of apologetic arguments is to provide *support*. "Someone who has been confused and bewildered by antagonists," he says, "might well justly regard apologetic arguments as a vital lifeline permitting the exercise of faith."[34] But does the reverse hold? In the event such an argument fails, what is the appropriate response? If no skeptical implications follow from failed arguments, what role does this exercise play in advancing our knowledge of the world?

This takes us to the challenges associated with *fideism*. Taken from Latin root for faith (*fide*), this approach maintains that religious belief is sufficiently grounded in faith—such that it is independent of the rational arguments and empirical evidence. Fideism sits on the opposite side of the spectrum from *rationalism*, which holds that religious belief must be justified by appeal to arguments that meet commonly accepted standards of rationality. In cases of perceived conflict between the claims of faith and claims of reason, fideism subsumes rational arguments and classifies them in accordance with religious concepts and narratives. From this perspective, failed apologetic arguments would have no bearing on religious belief and could be dismissed as aberrations, spiritual tests, or the work of demonic forces. Philosopher Nicholas Wolterstorff offers up one such possibility: "Sometimes suffering is a trial. May it not also be that sometimes the nonrationality of one's conviction that God exists is a trial, to be endured?"[35] The implications here are profound. If faith claims can *always*

---

emphasis added. See also John G. Stackhouse Jr., *Humble Apologetics: Defending the Christian Faith Today* (New York: Oxford University Press, 2006); and Maurice Wiles, *Reason to Believe* (London: Bloomsbury T&T Clark, 2000).

33. William Lane Craig, "Classical Apologetics," in *Five Views of Apologetics*, ed. Steven B. Cowan (Grand Rapids: Zondervan, 2000), 28; emphasis added. For a probing treatment of defeaters, see Alvin Plantinga, *Warranted Christian Belief* (New York: Oxford University Press, 2000), 357–73.

34. Peterson, "The Role of Apologetics in Mormon Studies," xviii.

35. Nicholas Wolterstorff, "Can Belief in God Be Rational?" in *Faith and Rationality: Reason and Belief in God*, ed. Alvin Plantinga and Nicholas Wolterstorff (South Bend, Ind.: University of Notre Dame Press, 1983), 177.

trump evidence and argument, then apologetic dialogue runs the risk of being a pretense.

It is partly for this reason that apologetics has been marginalized from the main currents of religious studies. Because apologetics is said to serve spiritual rather than academic ends, it is viewed with immediate suspicion—and occasional disdain. I consider this to be an unfortunate split because it is part of the task of the philosophy of religion and theological studies to ferret out that which apologists recognize as being open to critical scrutiny and that which is not—and this can be an extraordinarily difficult enterprise. These disciplines were designed, in part, to study the structure of apologetic arguments, to examine the coherence and consistency of their reasoning, to identify the ways in which evidence is utilized, and finally to examine how this relates to questions of faith and religious authority. In these cases, apologetics serves as important data for scholars interested in the thought-world of a given religious community and how its practitioners negotiate the dynamics of faith and reason.

In the case of the Latter-day Saints, we have seen the ways in which this relationship tilts decidedly in one direction. This sentiment is summarized well by former Church president Harold B. Lee: "The revelations of God," he declared, "are the standards by which we measure all learning, and if anything squares not with the revelations, then we may be certain it is not truth."[36] Though presented in far more genteel language, the implications return us to Billy Sunday's opening salvo, namely that "the consensus of scholarship can plumb go to hell."

---

36. Harold B. Lee, *Stand Ye in Holy Places* (Salt Lake City: Deseret Book Co., 1974), 143.

EIGHT

The Role of Women in Apologetics

Juliann Reynolds

The Church of Jesus Christ of Latter-day Saints has a venerable tradition of accomplished women who have maneuvered through a maze of competing voices, disapproval, and even disdain to defend their rights, beliefs, and church.

Mormons are justly proud of our nineteenth-century women suffragists and Church mothers who are lauded as an important part of first-wave feminism. What is sometimes overlooked is that they were also first-wave apologists. As they fought for the right to vote they vigorously defended the Church, including their lives as polygamous wives. Mormon suffragists' ability to work with notables Susan B. Anthony and Elizabeth Cady Stanton, despite fundamental differences, provides an exemplar for modern Mormon women defending or promoting their beliefs.

Like Mormon women defenders of the Church today, these women saw the Church as a means to achieve their goals rather than viewing it as an obstacle. Lola Van Wagenen, author of *Sister-Wives and Suffragists*, states that "loyalty to the Church did not outweigh their individual interests or take precedence over their women's rights concerns; rather, they saw no dichotomy between their interests and those of the Church. . . . Mormon women were not asserting individualism through the vote, they were reinforcing community."[1]

Today it is difficult to escape the division over political ideologies, cultural mores, gender identity, sexual orientation, and women's rights. Mormon women are being thrust into a conversation that would have been hard to imagine a mere decade ago.

As rifts appear in the community of Saints, Elder M. Russell Ballard in the 2015 BYU Women's Conference acknowledged that "strong feelings

---

1. As quoted in Ethan R. Yorgason, *Transformation of the Mormon Culture Region* (Urbana and Chicago: University of Illinois Press, 2003), 36.

and deep differences" may exist. It is noteworthy that he was speaking to women when he urged them "to make sure that no schism or division exists within your families or your Church congregations, even with regards to such potentially divisive subjects as the current conversation regarding women and the priesthood."[2]

Ballard spoke to every woman and affirmed her role as a defender: "Righteous and faithful women have always played an essential role in saving souls and in defending the kingdom of God." Mormon women defending the kingdom of God are, by definition, apologists.

Confusion in the Definition

In Mormon culture, the word "apologist" can cause confusion. In an informal Sunday survey, I asked the Relief Society sisters to mark yes or no on a slip of paper in response to two questions: Did she consider herself an apologist, and did she consider herself a defender of the Church. Although all twenty-eight of the women thought of themselves as defenders, only six self-identified as apologists. They either didn't know what the word meant or didn't want the label. These results illustrate the difficulty in trying to count apologists in anything but selective situations that give them visibility. There is no Mormon equivalent of the International Society of Women in Apologetics that can be surveyed.

Mormonism does not have a tradition of college-trained professional apologists found in other religions, but the latter does offer a useful comparison as they struggle with similar problems. *Christianity Today* celebrated five prominent women apologists for its April 2015 cover story, "The Unexpected Defenders."[3] The women hold positions such as Program Director of the Oxford Centre for Christian Apologetics and Director of the Master's in Apologetics program at Houston Baptist University.

Melissa Cain Travis, a professor of Christian apologetics, defines apologetics as telling people the Good News and equipping them to "give the reason for the hope that you have." She thinks that women have a misperception that "theology and apologetics is something men do." Apologist Nancy Pearcey says that empathy, whether innate or socialized, sets women

---

2. Marianne Holman Prescott, "Righteous Women Essential to God's Work, Elder Ballard Says," *LDS Church News*, May 4, 2015, https://www.lds.org/church/news/righteous-women-essential-to-gods-work-elder-ballard-says.

3. Andrea Palpant Dilley, "The Unexpected Defenders," *Christianity Today* (April 2015): 36.

apologists apart from men.[4] There is also an acknowledgement of the impact of mothering; one apologist is described as having "the heart of a mother and the mind of a theologian."[5] These apologists take advantage of the unique perspectives women bring into what has been considered a male bastion. Some have created their own specialties such as cultural or conversational apologetics that emphasize the person and relationships in interactions.

In contrast, Mormons who self-identify as apologists typically consider it only one of the many other activities they engage in which makes it extremely difficult to quantify. Women who consider themselves apologists or who produce apologetic content may gather in academic circles or they may congregate on Facebook. Mormon women apologists are not likely to appear in commanding poses on the *Ensign* cover, nor do we teach our children to grow up wanting to be full-time apologists. We do not award degrees and certificates in apologetics at BYU or create ministries. The rewards in defending our beliefs are gratifying but less public.

Women's Voices

Many of the same characteristics and diversity of opinion shown by our suffragists can be seen in today's women apologists. How do they define what they do? Why and where do they participate and what motivates them?

Cassandra Hedelious, a FairMormon member and writer, envisions apologetics as concentric layers of activity surrounding a core:

> There is a core of apologetics that involves analyzing huge bodies of data, recognizing what's relevant and helpful, and doing the brainwork of showing how it explains issues that members struggle with. It's a fairly bloodless exercise—compile, analyze, explain. And it *must* be done—without that basis of helpfully-presented data, there's no point to anything else. The next layer, tightly surrounding the core, is narrative-building. Then there's a hazy penumbra of apologetics that involves blogging, yakking, understanding, outreaching, psychologizing, etc.[6]

Women have been successful in these activities while also contributing their technological, administrative, and media skills. When she discovered apologetics, Julianne Dehlin Hatton decided to use her broadcasting skills to create podcasts that discussed difficult issues. She explains, "I

---

4. Ibid., 40–41.
5. Katelyn Beaty, "The Oxford Revivalist," *Christianity Today* (April 2015): 46.
6. Comments cited throughout this chapter are from interviews by the author through email or personal conversation between March and September 2015.

wanted to clarify misconceptions about Joseph Smith, and church history. Examining the difficult aspects of my faith was a refiner's fire that made me stronger. Now I try to help others who are struggling."

With the encouragement of the Church, Twitter and Facebook have become important carriers of women's voices and assist in an important function of apologetics, supporting members and explaining the Church and its tenets.

Mary Jane Olhasso is an influential businesswoman with a Twitter account that has accumulated 909 followers (as of June 2017). She said that she shares the gospel so that others can have the blessings of exaltation.

Christy Alfrey, a busy young mother, writes witty and informative "Mormon Awareness" entries on Facebook. She was inspired to begin after a friend's baby was born with a rare syndrome. Alfrey was worried she might offend her friend by asking questions. Her friend then began posting Apert Awareness entries on Facebook. "She talked about all of her baby's symptoms, surgeries and her feelings as a mother," Alfrey recalls. "She answered all the questions I was too afraid to ask." That caused her to wonder if she had Facebook friends with questions about the Church who were also too afraid to ask. And that inspired Alfrey to begin writing her own awareness series explaining Mormon practices and beliefs.

Women find apologetics in various ways. Maya Åsenes, a Norwegian volunteer, was introduced to apologetics through a friend. "I was asked by my best friend to come and help on a website which was full of weird accusations about Mormonism," she recounted. "After a while I found FairMormon and started asking them questions. Scott Gordon, the president, asked if I would like to be a member and I said yes."

Jen Hildebrant discovered apologetics because she was a stay-at-home mom to a two-year old and was desperate for adult conversation. She first started her own Mormon discussion group on Oprah's website in 2002 and has maintained friendships she established back then. Later she found a popular Mormon message board and now contributes there. She says, "I love discussing religion and enjoy a good debate. So, the message board was perfect for me." Hildebrant is typical of women who can change the tenor of a discussion by promoting respectful interactions.

She explains the benefits that apologetics affords women: "It has definitely made me more knowledgeable in the gospel. It's also helped me to be less shy and to feel like I can hold my own in some gospel conversations." Few apologists remain unchanged or unchallenged. "It has also helped me to change the way that I see the gospel," Hildebrant says. "My testimony and my beliefs have become a lot more nuanced than they once were."

Ellen Fehr, a FairMormon volunteer who coordinates transcriptions of FairMormon conference talks said, "I am a member because I love defense of the faith. I have been confronted with a lot of opposition from people I care about and found FairMormon in my research." Hedelius shares this sentiment, adding that she embraced apologetics because of "intellectual curiosity about something very personally important to me."

Tasha Bates is working towards a graduate degree in marriage and family therapy. She is active on message boards and blogs, and she sees her motivation as being fairly simple: "I wanted answers. The critical voices at the time were extreme and dominated multiple boards and websites. I wanted to be able to respond to these concerns. In short, I wanted the truth."

She first became acquainted with critics of the Church when she moved into the Bible Belt as a teen. Bates explains that like any good Millennial, her need for answers led her to the internet where she found a hundred voices, mostly extremely negative or suspicious of Mormonism. She described her first few jumps into it as pretty nasty. "I got banned from one site and frankly deserved it," she admits. Bates is another who views her online activity as a part of her spiritual growth while not self-identifying as an apologist: "Though I would technically fit the definition of an apologist, I don't feel like one," she says. "This is probably because several other labels come before that one on my list of descriptions. But by definition, I do write or make reasoned arguments in defense for my faith and have been doing so since I was fourteen."

Hatton speaks for apologists when she says,

> I am drawn to the community of saints who strive to live as Jesus Christ lived on the earth. I believe God is my Heavenly Father, and Jesus Christ is my Savior, both resurrected beings with bodies of flesh and bone. I believe that the human family is connected as brothers and sisters, who will someday live peacefully in their father's kingdom. My marriage and family will not dissolve after death, but will be celebrated and enhanced in the next life.

Although her faith has never wavered, Hatton has had questions over the years about the doctrines and history of the Church. "I am a journalist," she explains. "We are taught to examine both sides of the issue. As I researched those questions, I found that many books and websites purporting to answer questions about the Mormon faith were designed to cause doubt and confusion over LDS history and practices."

Time constraints are probably the most frequently mentioned impediment to more involvement in apologetics. Fehr says:

> Even though I am a FairMormon member, by the time I get around to even checking the questions, other more scholarly types have already answered. And what I feel even slightly competent to answer tends to be the people who are hurting. I hope that by making the transcripts of FM conference talks more available, I support the scholarly types who have the knowledge I lack.

Hedelius thinks that "Mormon women tend to have a lot of commitments to children, family, church, and neighborhoods that make it unpalatable to spend the time it takes to contribute to apologetics." FairMormon volunteer DeeAnn Cheatham wants to do more but explained, "I know I could gain expertise if I took the time but I am back to not having time. I did a lot more before I had kids, mostly on message boards but not now."

The internet has been a boon for members who are homebound or disabled. Cal Robinson got her start on a once popular but combative message board in 2001. Before that she obtained books on religion from the library and read voraciously. Robinson's first reaction isn't uncommon when posting on contentious forums for the first time. She says, "I was reduced to tears of frustration within the first week." She remembered asking a scholar who dabbled in Mormon apologetics how he could stand "knocking his head against the wall and being told he was a liar." Robinson recalls, "He was so kind and supportive in his reply. I was starving for conversation so I would have stuck around, but I think that post was the first time I felt like I had somehow come home." The online accessibility of experts willing to share and mentor along with ready information is remarkable in Mormon forums. Robinson says she saved every thread and put it on a disk so she "could search for topics and learn, learn, learn."

As a woman of color, Bates speaks to the need for members to be more aware and inclusive of one another's culture. She says, "I don't know how to explain it, but it's apparent at times that a bunch of white people are discussing race issues—even when they're positive about it." She described one message board participant who dismissed her experiences by equating them to his as a missionary in a foreign land without understanding that she sometimes felt treated as a foreigner in her own land. One of the needed tasks of apologetics crosses geographical, ethnic, and cultural boundaries to ensure that all faithful voices are understood as well as heard.

Women frequently look for connection, and most consider talking, understanding, and outreach as critical elements of apologetics. Where women gather, community building is usually not far behind. Apologetics can be proactive or reactive: some women prefer explaining the gospel and Church while others feel called to defend their beliefs against inaccurate or unfair accusations. An unexpected adverse encounter involving Mormonism is a prime motivator for activism. Women may be restricted by time limits or the fear of not knowing enough to counter criticisms, but a love of learning and discovery propels them as the love of community and gospel binds them.

Pioneering the Internet

Apologetics came of age with the internet and provided opportunities for women to become involved on a scale that was previously unimaginable. Chatrooms, message boards, and blogs brought together a mix of eager participants with a newfound ability to bypass barriers of degrees, religious authority, and gender to join a conversation.

Websites continue to grow exponentially. The 1997 book *Mormons on the Internet* is now a time capsule with its ratings of hundreds of LDS websites.[7] Today such an undertaking might require an encyclopedia. FairMormon, *Meridian Magazine*, and Mormon Women Stand are only three of many approaches women have actualized through the World Wide Web.

I co-founded FairMormon in 1997. It offers an expansive website to provide faithful answers to critical questions and hosts yearly conferences that address current apologetic interests and needs.[8] Following my husband's death, I was consumed with a desire to know more about religion and made my way from Sunday school to Claremont Graduate University's School of Religion, where I studied the New Testament and early Christian history.

The next stop on my journey was the internet, primitive by today's standards, but a captivating virtual city that presented exceptional opportunities to connect with others. I found like-minded travelers who were eager to talk about religion.

As I made my way through America Online (AOL) offerings, it became apparent that Mormons who defended their faith were not welcome in the popular religion forum hosted by Christianity Online, a division of

---

7. Lauramaery Gold, *Mormons on the Internet* (Rocklin, Calif.: Prima Pub., 1997).

8. FairMormon maintains BlackLDS.org and selectively provides translations in Portuguese, Italian, Spanish, German, and Finnish. It has also provided several European conferences.

Christianity Today. Their message board folders about Mormons were meant for them to talk about us, not with us. AOL had other message boards, but all their subscribers could post on them, ensuring that any area with "Mormon" in the title would be filled with hostile critics whom we labeled as anti-Mormon. Christian countercultists were significantly ahead of us and even the Church in establishing online websites and ministries.[9] Repeated and well-packaged attacks against Mormonism, some approaching the level of hate speech, were no further away than the click of their mouse.

The idea for the Foundation for Apologetic Information and Research (FAIR), now FairMormon, grew from a desire to provide easily accessible resources for Mormons who were also being barraged with inflammatory cut-and-pasted information. Within a year of my arrival on AOL, I joined a few beleaguered defenders in assembling responses. I wanted a clearinghouse of information culled from authoritative Church sources and up-to-date scholarship that could assist those who were answering questions or countering attacks on their faith.

There were a few notable exceptions, but the average countercultist armed only with biblical proof texts and out-of-context quotes could not respond in kind to scholarship or successfully defend their own beliefs when held to the same standard of scrutiny. Evangelical scholars Carl Mosser and Paul Owen warned they were losing the battle against Mormonism because of the failure to read or address what Mormon scholars were producing:

> Mormon scholars and apologists (not all apologists are scholars) have, with varying degrees of success, answered most of the usual evangelical criticisms. Often these answers adequately diffuse particular (minor) criticisms. When the criticism has not been diffused the issue has usually been made much more complex.[10]

This was an explosive admission, but perhaps the most significant observation was tucked away in the last sentence. As Mosser and Owen warned, countercultists did not rise to the challenge and they no longer overrun all LDS sites. The bar had been raised by the demands of scholar-

---

9. Because nontraditional religious expression threatens the Christian countercult's worldview, so-called cults and sects are considered a social danger. See Douglas E. Cowan, *Bearing False Witness?: An Introduction to the Christian Countercult* (Westport, Conn.: Praeger, 2003), 16–28.

10. Paul Owen and Carl Mosser, "Mormon Apologetic, Scholarship and Evangelical Neglect: Losing the Battle and Not Knowing It," *Trinity Journal* 19, no. 2 (1998): 180.

ship, and it continues to rise as controversy branches into increasingly abstruse and pedantic excursions made possible by an expanding pool of information. This makes it more taxing for all participants—but particularly for women who have internalized cultural expectations of men being more knowledgeable or competent in matters of religion.

Meridian Magazine (ldsmag.org), a leading online Mormon publication, also had its start on the internet. It identifies as a values-based publication, drawing upon the beliefs and teachings of the LDS Church. Harvard-educated Maurine Proctor doesn't consider herself to be an apologist, although she is an ardent supporter and defender of the Church.

Proctor co-founded *Meridian* because of her disappointment over the treatment of LDS delegates at the 1977 International Women's Year conference and its failure to represent all viewpoints. What she saw from the media about this conference looked completely different from what she experienced on the ground. She said, "I suppose I had been an idealist before, the female counterpart of *Mr. Smith Goes to Washington*, but I had assumed that the press was objective, that both sides of an argument were given fair play, that truth won out in the short run as it will in the long." Proctor considered this one of those pivotal experiences that forever changes one's thinking. She continued:

> For years these thoughts lingered with me. Because of this, as well as other reasons, my husband Scot and I began to formulate the idea for *Meridian*, an LDS magazine that would cut through the myths of our world and convey a truer view based on eternal realities. It would feature a buffet of articles and topics for Latter-day Saints, but also have its finger on the pulse of ideas in the public square that are important to us as Church members.

Proctor and her husband also began their journey in the mid-nineties "when the internet wasn't even a twinkle on the horizon of our daily lives." After five years of what she described as beating their heads against a wall because of financing repeatedly falling through, they turned to the internet. Proctor observed that because of that choice, they saw the influence of a publication that comes into a reader's life every day to educate and empower them. Her goal is to be one of the voices in the secular wilderness that articulates important ideas that help people stay grounded in their faith.

Mormon Women Stand (mormonwomenstand.com) was launched on Facebook in 2014 with twelve women from around the world who demonstrate the collective reach of determined women. Kathryn Skaggs, a popular Mormon blogger, says she is frequently asked not only why she initially launched Mormon Women Stand (MWS) but also how they gathered so many LDS women to stand with them in record time. She explains, "MWS came about because of an urgent impression I had to gather like-minded women and to provide an online collective voice reflective of mainstream female members of the Church. I chose to use Facebook (we launched a website/blog a few months later) because of my love for social media as the Lord's 'power tool.'"

Co-founder Angela Fallentine is a researcher and analyst for a policy institute that focuses on current social issues, religious liberty, and international policy affecting the family at the United Nations. She saw a tremendous need for LDS women "to unite in a place where they could engage in conversations about the gospel and social issues in an atmosphere of loyalty to Jesus Christ and His appointed prophets, seers and revelators."

By September 2015, Mormon Women Stand had nearly 40,000 members, and in some weeks, a Facebook reach of 1.2 million people. Fallentine thinks that one of the reasons MWS has been successful is because "it uses a collaborative group of writers from various backgrounds while simultaneously enabling the average LDS woman (who may not necessarily be a blogger) to have a visible presence and voice online." The founders of Mormon Women Stand's efforts have been rewarded through seeing "so many meaningful discussions that help foster connectivity among women on a global scale." Fallentine believes that MWS will continue to fill a much-needed space online and that "the strength that comes from large numbers of faithful women standing together and rallying in defense of truth is undeniable."

Mormon apologetics has had to adapt to challenges such as rising secularism, new technology, the needs of new generations, and the increased availability of information. What has remained constant is the strong community that is created when women gather together to defend and protect that which is dear to them. That community, thanks to the internet, is expanding throughout the world.

Cultural Influences

Mormon online apologetics has rightfully come under more scrutiny as it matures. We know why women do engage in apologetics but also need to understand why they don't. In introducing the podcast topic, "Discussing Gender and Mormon Apologetics," host J. Nelson-Seawright observed:

> Apologetic discourse has taken on new importance in Mormon culture in recent years with the emergence of an apologetic approach to difficult Mormon

problems in the *Ensign*, and more recently on LDS.org., taking the work that . . . FAIR [FairMormon] and the Maxwell Institute have been doing for years to a new place of prominence and importance in Mormonism. At the same time Mormon apologetics remains a very gendered activity. Nearly all prominent Mormon apologists are male. There are some important exceptions. But the statistics bear out a differentiation.[11]

Nelson-Seawright referred to the number of articles by women in two Mormon-themed publications—with *Dialogue: A Journal of Mormon Thought* close to parity, and female contributors to *BYU Studies* making up 21 percent of its content. FairMormon does not produce equivalent journals, but women were 18 percent of its volunteers at the time of the podcast. These numbers, however, do not take into consideration how many women were unavailable or were asked and declined.

It also doesn't account for the influence of less prominent apologetic activity spread throughout the internet, which increased dramatically in the last decade: "[LDS] Church members have long been encouraged to master technology and use it to spread the gospel message, and they have responded in recent years by setting up personal websites and blogs," said *Forbes* contributor Joshua Steimle. They are "flooding walls, streams, and boards with gospel-related content."[12] There are many manifestations of apologetics and some may attract more women than others. Women, of course, have diverse interests, politics, and worldviews. However, those differences are brought together by a shared theology.[13]

Nelson-Seawright presented a compelling point, because it raises the question of why Mormon women would be expected to enter a male-dominated space in greater numbers than women in general typically do. But the ratio of women in apologetics echoes the proportion of those visible in the American hierarchal system and there may be something useful to be learned from that.

---

11. "517: Discussing Gender and Mormon Apologetics – With Nancy Ross, Kevin Barney, and Jessica Finnigan," episode hosted by J. Nelson-Seawright, *Mormon Stories Podcast*, January 8, 2015, http://www.mormonstories.org/discussing-gender-mormon-apologetics-nancy-ross-kevin-barney-jessica-finnigan/.

12. Joshua Steimle, "How Mormons Use the Internet to Spread the Good News," *Forbes*, April 24, 2015, http://www.forbes.com/sites/joshsteimle/2015/04/24/how-mormons-use-the-internet-to-spread-the-good-word/.

13. See Robert D. Putnam and David E. Campbell, *American Grace: How Religion Divides and Unites Us* (New York: Simon Schuster Paperbacks, 2010), 355.

For instance, in the United States 29 percent of the science and engineering workforce are women, yet they make up half of the total college-educated workforce.[14] Less than 25 percent of women occupy statewide and state legislative offices, and less than 20 percent hold congressional seats in the United States.[15] 98 percent of high-tech degrees are held by men. Even though women are now graduating from college at higher rates than men, this is not reflected in appointments as full professors or university president positions.[16]

Most damaging is that women are often held to higher standards in male dominated spaces. In a survey of workplace reviews, "58.9% of men's reviews contained critical feedback, while an overwhelming 87.9% of the reviews received by women did." Furthermore, women's negative critiques were far more likely to be personal and less constructive, such as being told they were too abrasive.[17] Particularly applicable to apologetics, feminist author Deborah Rhode disclosed that "[a]n overview of more than a hundred studies finds that women are rated lower as leaders when they adopt authoritative masculine styles, particularly when the evaluators are men, or when the role is one typically occupied by men."[18]

It should be no surprise that these cultural patterns reach into the Mormon community at every level, even amongst those who consider themselves more progressive or intellectual than the average member. In the words of Neylan McBaine, author of the best-selling Mormon book *Women at Church,* "There can be a perception that we Mormons are wrestling with these challenges in backward isolation and that the rest of the world has figured this all out already. Let me assure you: nobody has figured it out."[19]

Not every woman and man fits neatly into categories, of course, but statistically significant findings paint a discouraging picture for women. In

---

14. "Statistics: State of Girls and Women in STEM," National Girls Collaborative Project, 2016, https://ngcproject.org/statistics.

15. Steven Hill, "Why Does the US Still Have So Few Women in Office?" *The Nation,* March 24, 2014, http://www.thenation.com/article/178736/why-does-us-still-have-so-few-women-office

16. Deborah L. Rhode, *What Women Want: An Agenda for the Women's Movement* (New York: Oxford University Press, 2014), 26, 31.

17. Kathleen Davis, "The One Word Men Never See in Their Performance Reviews," *Fast Company,* August 27, 2014, http://www.fastcompany.com/3034895/strong-female-lead/the-one-word-men-never-see-in-their-performance-reviews.

18. Rhode, *What Women Want,* 32.

19. Neylan McBaine, *Women at Church: Magnifying LDS Women's Local Impact* (Salt Lake City: Greg Kofford Books, 2004), 173.

an expansive study that evaluated the optimal conditions in which women can achieve an effective voice, political scientists Christopher F. Karpowitz and Tali Mendelberg conclude:

> Settings that equalize participation and representation do so in part by elevating women's status in the group. Because women occupy a lower status in society by virtue of their gender, women tend to enter into discussion with less confidence than men and to be more affected by low confidence. Even more important, they are more sensitive to discussion dynamics that fail to provide positive reinforcement and to negative feedback about their competence. Women's lower confidence comes into play more powerfully when they interact with men, and all the more so when there are many men.[20]

It is not conflict itself that is problematic for women; it is that conflict indicates to them that they are of low value to the group. Where more educated women might typically be thought of as most likely to persevere, they are the least likely to participate under these conditions.[21] Those conditions are often found in online discussions regardless of which side of a position a woman represents. This is particularly consequential when her opponents who devalue her, which can include other women, are part of the Mormon community.

Men, of course, can receive similar treatment but they do not enter male space already holding less value and authority because of their gender. Nor does a man's lack of confidence restrict him from reaching equality in communication as it does with women. In a classic double bind, when women respond to signals that assign them lower status by speaking less, they are then perceived as less authoritative and exercise less influence.[22] This is not to say that gendered communication is intentional. But statistics are ubiquitous in confirming that men negatively interrupt women at a significantly higher rate than they interrupt other men. Women also receive less positive feedback and significantly more negative feedback. Anyone who has spent time on the internet discussing religion can confirm that it can be a hotbed of negativity. Women face the same gender gap inequality online.[23]

---

20. Christopher F. Karpowitz and Tali Mendelberg, *The Silent Sex: Gender, Deliberation & Institutions* (Princeton, N.J.: Princeton University Press, 2014), 322.
21. Ibid., 313–14.
22. Ibid., 158, 308.
23. Before using an online screenname that identified me as a woman, I was consistently thought to be male because I was conversant with biblical scholarship.

There may be a simpler explanation as well. Apologetics is a form of activism, and nationally the majority of women are satisfied with their lives. As Rhode explained, there needs to be a sense of relative deprivation to fuel activism.[24] The 2011 Pew poll finding that 90 percent of Mormon women are satisfied with the priesthood policy is not an anomaly.[25] Those women who say they do not think the Church oppresses them or considers them second class need to be taken at their word to enable understanding of the Church from the inside out. Research confirms that women do tend towards the gendered attributes the Church promotes as a woman's role. Women tend to be more moralistic, religious, pro-social, and oriented toward community.[26] "A group where members function as an integrated unit is a group in which women are likely to feel comfortable and content" Karpowitz and Mendleberg conclude. Mormons experience their religion in localized congregations that provide that integrated unit.

Future Implications

Faithful women have been defending the Church since its beginning and the internet has magnified opportunities and extended the reach of their voices. The state of being female, however, does not automatically translate into an interest in women's studies and it certainly does not guarantee agreement with the messages and methods used by all women who speak about their religion. But regardless of the social, religious, or political philosophy Mormon women align with, their lives converge in the Mormon community. *Mormon Feminism: Essential Writings*, edited by Joanna Brooks, Rachel Hunt Steenblik, and Hannah Wheelwright, includes the writings of two FairMormon speakers: Neylan BcBaine and Valerie Hudson Cassler. The first focuses on expanding women's visibility in the Church. The second is a theological treatise on reciprocal female and male roles in our eternal journey. Both make the Church a partner in advancing innovative thinking.

---

24. Rhode, *What Women Want*, 20.

25. Micheal Lipka, "Big Majority of Mormons (including women) Oppose Women in Priesthood," Pew Research Center, October 8, 2011, http://www.pewresearch.org/fact-tank/2013/10/08/big-majority-of-mormons-oppose-women-in-priesthood-including-women/. See also, Putnam and Campbell, *American Grace*, 244–45.

26. Karpowitz and Mendelberg, *The Silent Sex*, 320–21.

The belief that the Church can be a vehicle for enhancing women's voices rather than an obstacle preventing them determines how many in the pews will be listening to those advocating for change. Local congregations give girls exceptional training in skills necessary for future success, such as speaking in front of audiences, developing presentations, and planning activities in a safe and familiar situation. The Church's growing interest in councils provides an ideal situation for women even if they are a minority in numbers. An appropriately run council requires women to contribute rather than silencing them. Women apologists can begin to heal divisions by coming together on points of agreement. They should be leaders in restoring our foremothers to their place in history by ensuring that the recent outpouring of information is found and liberally used along with modern role models. One woman in one ward can enrich hundreds of members.

In cyberspace, it isn't always about numbers. It is about a compelling response or position that ripples throughout the internet and spreads by word of mouth or social media. Carolina Allen, founder of Big Ocean Women (bigoceanwomen.org) eloquently sums it up: "Change doesn't have to be torrential, giant tsunami waves that obliterate landscapes. It can be something subtle, quiet and small. I'm like this small little wave. I'm not insignificant. I'm part of a vast collective that makes up the ocean. That's what womanhood is about." [27]

Mormon women will continue to rise to the challenge of defending their faith. They will continue to pioneer effective approaches to difficult problems. They will continue to push through barriers and create community. Women will change the future of apologetics, one small wave at a time.

---

27. Kelsey Schwab, "Big Ocean Women Healing This World 'One Wave at a Time,'" *Deseret News*, August. 20, 2015, available at http://www.deseretnews.com/article/865634999/Big-Ocean-Women-healing-this-world-one-wave-at-a-time.html.

NINE

Avoiding Collateral Damage: Creating a Woman-Friendly Mormon Apologetics

Julie M. Smith

Introduction

Once when Jesus was teaching in the temple, the scribes and Pharisees approached him, dragging along a woman who they claimed had been adulterous (John 8:1–11). Jesus did not permit them to treat this woman as an object, useful only to trap him in his words; instead, he pivoted the conversation to the accusers' own moral failings. He wasn't willing to let the woman's personal life, status, and sense of self be deployed to make a larger theological point—no matter how important that point might be. He put her human dignity and infinite worth as a daughter of God above all other concerns. In some cases, Mormon apologetics does not follow this pattern of prioritizing people over policies, especially when it comes to women.

I have no reason to believe that any Mormon apologetic deliberately sets out to denigrate women and yet, at the same time, some of Mormon apologetics has this unfortunate effect. So I conclude that women are collateral damage in the world of Mormon apologetics: in the zeal to defend the Church, many apologists are unaware of the detrimental implications of their arguments for women's concerns. I propose four standards which, if used, would largely alleviate this problem.

Inversion

Attentive readers have wondered what happened to the man involved in the alleged adultery in the story recounted in John 8; he's nowhere to be seen since the scribes and Pharisees didn't bring him to Jesus. When we recognize the absence of the man, it becomes obvious that these religious leaders were not primarily concerned with the punishment of sinners but rather with the entrapment of Jesus. It's the realization that the man is missing which makes this observation possible; careful attention to gender parity and inversion can be very revealing. This is why the first idea I recommend to weigh apologetic arguments is that of inversion.

This principle requires the apologist to invert the position of the genders and determine if the argument being proposed is still logical and palatable. Applying the inversion test shows flaws in many common apologetic arguments. For example, apologists for the male-only priesthood sometimes argue that women are naturally nurturing and therefore better suited to motherhood instead of priesthood, but would these apologists feel equally comfortable arguing that men are naturally good leaders and thus uniquely suited to holding the priesthood? The fact that this argument is virtually never made suggests, through an exercise in inversion, that it is illegitimate to argue that women's natural abilities fit them for motherhood unless one is willing to make the same types of claims regarding men's nature. Similarly, one sometimes hears that nothing has been revealed about God the Mother because God the Father does not want Her name profaned through casual use. But why should profaning Her name be categorically worse than profaning His? The inversion test shows that this line of reasoning makes little sense.

Likewise, a common apologetic response to questions about the male-only priesthood is that polls suggest that most Mormon women are content with their exclusion from the priesthood and Church leadership. But this apologetic tactic fails the inversion test: Would we ever discuss a policy affecting men in terms of whether they were happy about it? Would one argue that the age for young male missionaries should not have been lowered because most elders were content with serving at age nineteen? Similarly, recent discussions about female ordination frequently focus on whether the status of women in the Church causes women pain, but we would not consider male suffering a key factor in evaluating policies affecting them; certainly male distress could be substantially reduced by normalizing pornography use, but no one would dare propose such a thing. When it comes to any other issue, we recognize that (temporary) human happiness or pain pales as a metric; the focus is rather on discerning God's will.

Apologetic discussions of polygamy frequently fail the inversion test. It is often taken as a given that polyandry is the most troubling aspect of Mormon polygamy. But why exactly should polyandry be any more troubling than polygyny? Is it because the emotional turmoil which the thought of polygyny creates for (most) women is being experienced by a man? Is it because the thought of being someone's "third husband" requires a man to reconsider everything from his identity and nature to his understanding of what marital faithfulness entails, as polygyny does for women?

The distress that men might feel regarding polyandry might be a useful window for helping them understand how many women feel about polygyny, especially since the Church still permits men to be sealed to more than one woman (assuming, of course, than only one of the women is alive). Most Mormons believe that all of these marriages will last into the next life, so assurances that the Church does not currently practice polygamy can seem disingenuous. Hence, many Mormon women believe that they may—possibly against their will, or at least without their approval, as happened historically—find themselves in a polygamous relationship. Further, the common understanding that the manifesto ending polygamy was a response to government pressure suggests to many people that polygamy might very well return to the Church if it was legalized, which, in the wake of the recent advance of gay marriage, seems plausible.

All of these stresses related to polygamy—not as some arcane historical matter, but rather with very real implications for a woman's current understanding of herself and her roles and her future reality—can perhaps be more easily understood by men when they consider themselves in the role of "third husband." I suggest, and only partially in jest, that the purpose for Joseph Smith's polyandrous marriages may have been to give Mormon men an opportunity to understand why the idea of polygamy is so very troubling to so many women. Ironically, awareness of polyandry decreases the sting of polygyny for many women. And yet current apologetics—even in its most recent iterations—still normally treats polyandry as uniquely troublesome when, for many women, it is precisely the opposite.

Application of the inversion test to polyandry can also be revealing in another way; most commenters do not apply the usual defenses marshaled for polygyny to polyandry. No one suggests that polyandry was a necessary outlet for the excessive sexual desires of some women, or to raise up righteous seed, or to link families together. The fact that polyandry is usually met with raw bewilderment instead of these classic apologetic approaches is telling. Further, most Mormons believe that, in modern times, a man who is sealed to more than one woman will be polygamist in the next life but that a woman who is sealed to more than one man will be forced to choose one husband in the next life; these beliefs fail the inversion test as well.

The inversion test can also be revealingly applied to another apologetic stance: the idea that polygamy will be required in the eternities due to the fact that more women than men will be saved in the highest degree of heaven. To those who are steeped in the rhetoric that women are naturally more spiritual than men or who over-generalize from current disparities in activity rates,[1] it might seem self-evident that there would be a surplus of women, but the most plausible evidence indicates that there will be an excess of men in need of wives in the celestial kingdom.[2] Where are the earnest announcements that polyandry is necessary and will be willingly embraced by men who should not selfishly clinging to their exclusive relationships with their wives and thus cost another man his only chance for exaltation? Our unwillingness to apply the standard apologetic responses to men is very revealing of an unwillingness to hold men and women to the same expectations.

But polyandry is not the only aspect of polygamy which is sometimes justified by apologetics that fail the inversion test. It is frequently argued that in the next life, a woman would not mind sharing her husband because she will be free of the sin of jealousy. But consider the inversion: Would a man believe that in the next life, he would no longer be troubled by the thought of his wife having sex with another man? Thus, apologetic techniques which respond to women's concerns over polygamy by telling them that it will all be acceptable in the hereafter fail the inversion test.

In the past, it was often argued that polygamy was necessary to increase the birthrate. The appeal of this line of reasoning likely stems from the fact that it appears to comport with Jacob 2, one of the few, if not only, scriptural explanations for polygamy. But when data showed that polygamy actually lowered the birthrate of women in pioneer Utah,[3] this apologetic

---

1. While it is generally true that there are more active women than men in the Church, this is not universally true: in Africa, for example, "there are substantially more men than women who are members of the Church." See Tim B. Heaton, "Vital Statistics," in *Encyclopedia of Mormonism*, ed. Daniel H. Ludlow, 4 vols. (New York: Macmillan, 1992), 2:1528.

2. See "'In the Heavens, Are Parents Single?': Report No. 1," *Dialogue: A Journal of Mormon Thought* 17, no. 1 (March 1, 1984): 84–86.

3. See Jacob A. Moorad et al., "Mating System Change Reduces the Strength of Sexual Selection in an American Frontier Population of the 19th Century," *Evolution and Human Behavior* 32, no. 2 (March 2011): 147–55.

morphed slightly to emphasize not the total number of children ("raise up seed") but rather their spiritual quality ("raise up *righteous* seed"), despite the fact that the word "righteous" does not appear in the explanation for polygamy in Jacob 2, but only elsewhere in the chapter, where it explains why they left Jerusalem and were *not* to practice polygamy. Note that the idea of raising up "righteous seed" relies on the belief that the father determines the "spiritual quality" of the children, to the extent that it is better for a woman to have fewer children as the third wife to a "spiritually superior" man than to have more children with an "average" man. This is a troubling argument because it prioritizes the father's contribution to the child's spiritual fitness above the mother's contribution—this runs counter to most of modern Mormon thinking about the crucial contribution of women to their children's spiritual development, and so it is exceedingly difficult to reconcile this thinking with the importance placed on motherhood in the LDS tradition. The inversion test is revealing here: if we were to invert the argument and presume that the mother's contribution to the children's spiritual development was far more important than the father's, we'd be much closer to current Mormon teachings about parental contributions. Thus, the inversion test shows how problematic it is to argue that polygamy was justified in order to raise up "righteous seed."

Recently, the secrecy practiced in relation to Joseph Smith's polygamy—especially in relation to the marriages which he kept secret from his own wife—has been defended as justifiable. But under what conditions could we imagine defending Emma Smith, or any woman, in the keeping secret of anything of significance (let alone an eternal marriage) from her own husband? The fact that this kind of secret-keeping is seen as incompatible with a healthy marriage when done by a woman should raise red flags for its justification when done by a man.

To sum, applying the inversion test to potential apologetic arguments—particularly those related to polygamy—can reveal weaknesses and flaws in the arguments.

"On Earth as It Is in Heaven"

In John 8, the religious leaders attempt to entrap Jesus by treating the Law of Moses as if it held unquestioned primacy. But Jesus operates according to a different, higher standard. Similarly, an apologist's argument must not only support current Mormon practice but also comport well with Mormon beliefs about the nature of God. For example, if one argues that women are naturally nurturing, does that imply that God the Father is deficient in nurturing ability? Likewise, the traditional conception of gender roles as requiring a mother who spends most of her time nurturing her children and a father who attends to other concerns does not map well onto Mormon beliefs of a Heavenly Mother, who does not seem to be primarily involved in the nurture of Her children. Rather, it might be more accurate (if a bit tongue-in-cheek) to describe God the Father as a "stay-at-home dad" and God the Mother as otherwise occupied. Traditional beliefs about gender roles do not correlate very well with what we know of our Heavenly Parents. This means that traditional gender roles, as usually understood, fail to reflect on earth what is in heaven, as we now understand it. This also means that the usual apologetic trope comparing motherhood and priesthood fails the "on earth as it is in heaven" test since earthly motherhood appears to bear little relationship to divine motherhood.

Similarly, apologetics needs to take into account the relationship between women and the priesthood in the temple. As Elder Dallin H. Oaks has explained recently, in the temple women officiate in priesthood ordinances.[4] Given that Latter-day Saints take the temple as a template for the eternities, this teaching has important implications for thinking about women and priesthood: the equation of motherhood and priesthood becomes very difficult to defend if women officiate in priesthood ordinances in our holiest rituals. All of the standard apologetic theories—that women are more spiritual than men, that men lack something for which the priesthood compensates, that men and women have different essential attributes, that the eternal or scriptural order prohibits women from exercising priesthood—require re-examination in light of the fact that they do not apply within the walls of the temple. So we can sharpen our apologetic approaches by ensuring that they reflect not just a defense of the status quo on earth but also accurately reflect our knowledge of eternal realities.

Strict Scrutiny of the Culturally Conforming

The scribes' and Pharisees' complaint about the woman is consonant with their cultural beliefs, reflecting the complete abhorrence for female unchastity and a desire to enforce the letter of the Law of Moses. But Jesus's vision is different. Beliefs which align nicely with the larger culture

---

4. See Dallin H. Oaks, "The Keys and Authority of the Priesthood," *Ensign*, May 2014, available at https://www.lds.org/ensign/2014/05/priesthood-session/the-keys-and-authority-of-the-priesthood.

can seem so self-evident that it may be very difficult to question them but this story shows Jesus doing precisely that. We, too, need to engage in a strict scrutiny of the culturally conforming.

In 1973, the *Ensign* featured an article on the proper roles of husbands and wives; they also published a similar article in 2013.[5] Each article was written by faithful Church members with substantive academic credentials; each passed the correlation requirements of the Church. Both articles describe marital roles as matters of crucial eternal doctrine—not just cultural norm or personal preference. Both substantiate their arguments with reference to statements made by high-ranking Church leaders and scriptures, including Genesis 3:16. Both claim that families which follow these roles will be happier than those that do not and that children raised in homes where these roles are not followed will have behavior problems and other negative life outcomes. The only substantive difference between the articles is that the 1973 iteration argued for male-dominant marriages[6] while the 2013 version advocated for egalitarian ones.[7]

Each of these articles fits comfortably into the beliefs of the larger culture at the time the articles were written. This alone should make us suspicious of *both* articles. As the (possibly apocryphal) proverb claims, to a worm in horseradish, the entire world is horseradish. When the larger culture sees male-dominant marriage as the norm, it seems obvious that Genesis 3:16 supports such a notion; forty years later, finding precisely the opposite idea in Genesis 3:16 seems equally obvious. But a strict scrutiny of the culturally conforming should give the reader of both of these articles pause.

If an apologetic argument is well-aligned with the beliefs of the larger culture, then it deserves extra scrutiny since it may reflect the customs of the interpreter more than it reflects eternal truth. For example, since belief that women are better nurturers fits well in western culture, it deserves close examination to determine whether it is an eternal principle or a cultural artifact. Note that this standard does not demand the abandonment of this belief simply because it conforms to the culture. It deserves

---

5. See MMiles, "Truth for Our Times," *By Common Consent*, March 21, 2013, http://bycommonconsent.com/2013/03/21/truth-for-our-times/.

6. See Brent A. Barlow, "Strengthening the Patriarchal Order in the Home," *Ensign*, February 1973, available at https://www.lds.org/ensign/1973/02/strengthening-the-patriarchal-order-in-the-home.

7. See Valerie M. Hudson and Richard B. Miller, "Equal Partnership in Marriage," *Ensign*, April 2013, available at https://www.lds.org/ensign/2013/04/equal-partnership-in-marriage.

extra analysis because of its cultural conformity, but it may well be that the result of this scrutiny is ultimately acceptance since surely not everything which aligns with the larger culture is necessarily contrary to the gospel.

One of the key benefits of scripture is that it can help us to see around cultural blinders since it contains a record of the gospel as lived in other times and places. Thus an important element of the strict scrutiny of the culturally conforming is to compare the apologetic argument to the canonized record. So, for example, the belief that women are naturally nurturing deserves strict scrutiny as culturally conforming; when we compare it to the scriptural record, we find that the only references to nurturing refer to fathers as nurturers.[8] Because Latter-day Saints accept continuing revelation, there is not necessarily a problem with believing in something that does not contain a scriptural warrant but, at the same time, it is important to be clear on what precisely the record states.

In an interview, Church spokeswoman Ally Isom was asked where in Mormon doctrine it states that women cannot hold the priesthood, she responded that "it doesn't."[9] This recognition is important. The canon of the LDS Church includes female prophets, judges, and witnesses as well as likely references to female deacons and apostles.[10] It contains Jesus's correction of someone who praised a woman for her mothering abilities;[11] it contains multiple stories of Jesus being anointed by a woman.[12] It includes a story where the king went not to a high priest, a scribe, or a male prophet but rather to a female one in order to get the authoritative word of the Lord for the community.[13] More than one in ten of the named prophets in the Old Testament are women. In this dispensation, Joseph Smith told the Relief Society that he "was going to make of this Society

---

8. See Ephesians 6:4 and Enos 1:1. Of course, there are other instances of nurturing behavior which do not use the word "nurture" or "nurturing" and do include women, but to that count should be added instances of the nurturing behavior of males, including especially references to Jesus as a mother hen gathering her chicks under her wings (see Matthew 23:37//Luke 13:34; 3 Nephi 10:4–6; and D&C 10:65, 29:2, and 43:24).

9. Ally Isom interviewed by Doug Fabrizio, "Latter-day Saints and Excommunication, Part II," Radio West, June 16, 2014, available at http://radiowest.kuer.org/post/latter-day-saints-and-excommunication-part-ii.

10. See Luke 2:36, Judges 4–5, Mark 16:1–8, Romans 16:1, and Romans 16:7.

11. See Luke 11:27–28.

12. See Matthew 26:6–13, Mark 14:3–9, Luke 7:36–50, and John 12:1–8.

13. See 2 Kings 22.

a kingdom of priests as in Enoch's day—as in Paul[']s day."[14] Through most of Mormon history, women gave healing blessings.[15] This record must be balanced against uses of the scripture which argue that women cannot exercise the priesthood. This is especially true in a church which believes in an open canon and continuing revelation: while Joseph Smith said that women were organized as a kingdom of priests in Enoch's time, there is not one word about this in the Bible or even when more information is given about Enoch in modern revelation.[16] So absence of evidence in the canonized accounts is not, per the teachings of the prophet Joseph Smith, a reliable indicator of a lack of female priests. This is why apologetic arguments for Mormonism's gendered priesthood based on the lack of evidence of Jesus ordaining women are suspect.

So our analysis of scripture and history can help us remove cultural blinders, but at the same time, we are not entirely reliant on the record of scripture. Thus, scripture and history need to be weighed before we decide what is scriptural, doctrinal, eternal, or unchanging regarding women's roles. Considering these aspects of our tradition may help us see around our cultural blinders regarding women. As General Relief Society President Linda K. Burton explained, benefits will accrue to the Church as "men's vision of the capacity of women becomes more complete."[17]

Paradox Maintenance

There is something of a paradox in Jesus's treatment of the woman in John 8: on the one hand, he does not permit others to condemn her and he does not condemn her himself. At the same time, he tells her not to sin any more. Similarly, it is no secret that Mormon theology is a tapestry woven of paradoxical strands, which means an apologetics which privileges certain threads will not do it justice. Thus, the strands of Mormon

---

14. See March 31, 1842, entry for the Nauvoo Relief Society Minute Book, available at http://www.josephsmithpapers.org/paper-summary/nauvoo-relief-society-minute-book/19.

15. See Jonathan A. Stapley and Kristine Wright, "Female Ritual Healing in Mormonism," *Journal of Mormon History* 37, no. 1 (Winter 2011): 1–85.

16. See D&C 107:48–57 and Moses 6–7; note the promise that more information about Enoch will be forthcoming.

17. See Jodi Kantor and Laurie Goodstein, "Missions Signal a Growing Role for Mormon Women," *New York Times*, March 1, 2014, available at https://www.nytimes.com/2014/03/02/us/a-growing-role-for-mormon-women.html.

thought which have historically viewed women as priests and as potential gods must be interwoven with the strands which have been clearly patriarchal and have restricted women's sphere; neither can be ignored in Mormon apologetics. Commenters, both more traditional and more progressive, are often guilty of simply ignoring the parts of Mormon history and theology that do not align with their vision.

One paradox which ought to be maintained in apologetic discussions is the varied reactions of plural wives themselves to polygamy: "Eugenia Washburn Larsen, fearing the worst, reported feeling 'dense darkness' when she imagined herself and other wives and children being 'turned adrift' by husbands. Other plural wives, however, reacted to the Manifesto with 'great relief.'"[18] So explorations of polygamy should not ignore the happy wives or the disgruntled ones.

One can, of course, point to plenty of *Ensign* articles which advocate for stereotypical gender roles. But one must also acknowledge the articles which celebrated—even a generation ago—an equal partnership with a division of duties so atypical that "Mother Killed the Rattlesnakes."[19] So it is neither appropriate for traditionalists to claim that the Church has always and completely advocated for strict gender division of labor nor for progressives to mourn the same. There has been a demonstrable tension in the Church's teachings; in order to be faithful to the entire Mormon tradition, apologetics needs to maintain that tension—not smooth it out.

There is, obviously, extensive history, comment, teaching, and policy in Mormonism which cleanly separates women from the priesthood. But at the same time, there has been an opposite impulse creating a paradox which must not be ignored. Because of the way Joseph Smith's statement was edited by a later redactor, the idea of the Relief Society as a "kingdom of priests" was not a feature of LDS thought throughout the history of

---

18. "The Manifesto and the End of Plural Marriage," The Church of Jesus Christ of Latter-day Saints, https://www.lds.org/topics/the-manifesto-and-the-end-of-plural-marriage.

19. See Emma Lou Thayne, "Mother Killed the Rattlesnakes," *Ensign*, April 1975, available at https://www.lds.org/ensign/1975/04/mother-killed-the-rattlesnakes. As President Boyd K. Packer said, "There is no task, however menial, connected with the care of babies, the nurturing of children, or with the maintenance of the home that is not his equal obligation. The tasks which come with parenthood, which many consider to be below other tasks, are simply above them." See Boyd K. Packer, "A Tribute to Women," *Ensign*, July 1989, available at https://www.lds.org/ensign/1989/07/a-tribute-to-women.

the Church. But even so, the association of women and priesthood was not foreign to Mormonism during most of its history; Brigham Young preached, "Now, brethren, the man that honors his Priesthood, the woman that honors her Priesthood, will receive an everlasting inheritance in the kingdom of God."[20] And in 1979, Camilla Kimball, the prophet's wife, was invited by Elder Bruce R. McConkie of the Quorum of the Twelve to join him in placing her hands on the prophet's head to give him a blessing.[21]

This complicated history—with all of its eddies and cross currents—needs to be recognized, even by modern apologists. The paradoxes of Mormon history and theology must be defended with at least as much vigor as the status quo. There is an inherent danger related to the enterprise of apologetics: it privileges the status quo and reifies it. To the extent that our discussions focus on apologetics rather than theology, we become more concerned with fossilizing the current historical moment than we are with continuing the ongoing work of the restoration. Apologetics by its nature tends toward dismissing the strands of tradition that do not mesh well with current practice. Therefore, apologetics can inhibit the ongoing nature of the restoration if we are not careful to acknowledge the various strands of Mormonism.

Conclusions

In general, apologetic stances have prioritized defense of the status quo over their impact on women's concerns. So in some cases, these entirely well-meaning apologetic approaches have been detrimental to women. But it is important to note that this is *not* because the policies, doctrines, and history in question cannot or should not be defended; rather, it is because the primary concern was the defense of the status quo and not a consideration of how the arguments marshaled shape perceptions of women. Polygamy, for example, can be defended in ways which respect the dignity and autonomy of women: it could be argued that polygamy was necessary to create a culture of independence among Mormon women. This independence was noticed by a nineteenth-century Gentile woman, Elizabeth Cane, when she visited Utah.[22] Similarly, the *Encyclopedia of Mormonism*

---

20. Brigham Young, June 28, 1874, *Journal of Discourses*, 26 vols. (London and Liverpool: LDS Booksellers Depot, 1854–86), 17:119.
21. See Stapley and Wright, "Female Ritual Healing in Mormonism," 84.
22. See Claudia L. Bushman, "Mormon Domestic Life in the 1870s: Pandemonium or Arcadia?" *Leonard J. Arrington Mormon History Lecture Series,*

noted that "Plural marriage also aided many wives. The flexibility of plural households contributed to the large number of accomplished LDS women who were pioneers in medicine, politics and other public careers. In fact, plural marriage made it possible for wives to have professional careers that would not otherwise have been available to them." In recent years, as more women have engaged in the academic study of Mormonism in general and apologetics in particular, it has been proposed that polygamy may have served to allow women to control their reproductive health,[23] as women's liberation,[24] as a spur to stronger relationships between women,[25] or as a mechanism to make it simpler for women to leave abusive husbands. Nineteenth-century Mormon polygamy also seems to have allowed Mormon women a role in the public and political sphere because they were needed to defend polygamy. In the "Revelations in Context" series on the LDS Church's website, the discussion of Doctrine and Covenants 132 focuses on the experience and perspectives of a woman, Mercy Thompson.[26] This is the kind of approach which will make apologetics more woman-friendly. One can perhaps imagine a world where the actual practice of polygamy was overall beneficial for women, but the rhetoric used to defend it was detrimental. Similarly, there are ways to defend a gendered priesthood which do not run afoul of the criteria proposed in this essay.

It is likely the case that those who want to defend the history, doctrines, and policies of the Church do so not primarily for logical or intellectual reasons but because of a spiritual witness and a commitment to obedience and authority. One frequently hears, for example, that a commenter is not opposed per se to the ordination of women but believes in following

---

October 7, 1999 (Logan, Utah: Utah State University Press, 1999), 26; available at http://digitalcommons.usu.edu/cgi/viewcontent.cgi?article=1003&context=arrington_lecture.

23. See Hannah Wheelwright, "What If Polygamy Was for Birth Control? Part 1," *Young Mormon Feminists*, May 11, 2013, http://youngmormonfeminists.org/2013/05/11/what-if-polygamy-was-for-birth-control-part-1/.

24. See Linda Witt, "A Feminist Studies Mormon Polygamy And, Remarkably, Finds That It Liberated the Wives," *People*, July 10, 1978, available at http://people.com/archive/a-feminist-studies-mormon-polygamy-and-remarkably-finds-that-it-liberated-the-wives-vol-10-no-2/.

25. See Joan Smyth Iverson, "Feminist Implications of Mormon Polygamy," *Feminist Studies* 10 (Fall 1984): 505–22.

26. See Jed Woodworth, "Mercy Thompson and the Revelation on Marriage," *Revelations in Context*, January 2, 2015, available at https://history.lds.org/article/doctrine-and-covenants-eternal-marriage.

Avoiding Collateral Damage

the lead of the Brethren on this matter as opposed to agitating for change in the Church. It is then perhaps no surprise that the arguments against women's ordination offered by someone in such a position may not be persuasive to others; after all, it is not those logical (or historical or doctrinal or scriptural) arguments which led to the stance against women's ordination in the first place—it is her or his commitment to Church leadership. It may be advisable in that case not to offer logical arguments in which one is not fully invested. Sometimes, these poorly-reasoned arguments end up doing more harm than good. While racial restrictions on the priesthood do not perfectly parallel gender restrictions, Elder Oaks's comment about the rationales offered for the racial restriction are still relevant:

> It's not the pattern of the Lord to give reasons. We can put reasons to commandments. When we do we're on our own. Some people put reasons to [the ban] and they turned out to be spectacularly wrong. There is a lesson in that. . . . The lesson I've drawn from that, I decided a long time ago that I had faith in the command and I had no faith in the reasons that had been suggested for it. . . . I'm referring to reasons given by general authorities and reasons elaborated upon [those reasons] by others. The whole set of reasons seemed to me to be unnecessary risk taking. . . . Let's [not] make the mistake that's been made in the past, here and in other areas, trying to put reasons to revelation. The reasons turn out to be man-made to a great extent. The revelations are what we sustain as the will of the Lord and that's where safety lies.[27]

So, in short, if the root of one's commitment to current Church policy is a spiritual witness or the support of Church leaders, then inventing logical, historical, and scriptural arguments ex post facto is not only not likely to persuade but may constitute what Elder Oaks called "unnecessary risk taking." Further, the Mormon tendency to develop theology from policy—not the other way around—amplifies the potential for damage to occur if we are inventing reasons for a policy and then those reasons become our theology.

While it would be a difficult phenomenon to measure, I suspect that within the population of people who have become disaffected from the Church regarding gender issues, there is a fairly large group who have left not because of Church policy per se, but rather because they found the apologetics offered for the policy to be unbearable. I am sure there are some people who have left the Church because they believe that women should be ordained, but I suspect that there are many who have left because they found

---

27. See "Apostles Talk about Reasons for Lifting Ban," *Provo Daily Herald*, June 5, 1988, 21.

the explanations for the gendered priesthood more troubling than the policy itself (or the explanations for polygamy more troubling than the practice of polygamy itself, etc.). In other words, we may be able to keep some sheep within the flock by changing the ways in which we explain and defend those policies. But because androcentric perspectives have constituted an overwhelming proportion of Mormon discourse, the stances and rationales offered have often had a post hoc flavor to them. They have often been incoherent and contradictory. As historian Andrea Radke-Moss explained, most Mormon women have heard all of the following at some point:

> Women don't have the Priesthood. Women have always had the Priesthood. Women have the Priesthood in the temple. Women have the Priesthood through their husbands. Women will never have the Priesthood. Women don't have the Priesthood because they are spiritually *inferior* to men. Women don't have the Priesthood because they are spiritually *superior* to men. Women will have the Priesthood in the next life. Women don't have the Priesthood because they have motherhood. Not all women are mothers (literally). All women are mothers (symbolically). Mormons practice polygamy. Mormons don't practice polygamy. Traditional marriage is between one man and one woman. Men can be sealed to more than one woman. Members will be required to practice plural marriage in the next life. Members won't be required to practice plural marriage in the next life. Women might exercise the spiritual gift of healing by the laying on of hands. Women cannot heal because it is an exercise of priesthood. Women can heal together with their husbands. A woman's prayer of faith is just as effective as a priesthood blessing. (But then why the need for priesthood blessings?)[28]

This kind of contradiction and incoherence would have almost certainly been noticed and addressed if it were to arise in any other aspect of Mormon theology. But because most of these beliefs have been articulated by men (who, not being personally affected by them, perhaps do not consider their implications as much as they should) or created as post-hoc rationales for something the apologist already believed for other compelling reasons. Since women's voices have not generally been part of the conversation, the contradictions and implications that they might have pointed out have largely remained unnoticed, at least until rather recently. To use one historical example, women's voices and perspectives were

---

28. Andrea Radke-Moss, "Mormon Women, Traditionalists and Feminists: An Evolving Conversation," *Patheos*, July 10, 2014, http://www.patheos.com/Topics/2014-Religious-Trends/Mormon/Mormon-Women-Traditionalists-and-Feminists-Andrea-Radke-Moss-071014.

largely absent from the discussion (apologetic or otherwise) surrounding racial restrictions in the Church before 1978. One result of this is that the policy became framed as "the priesthood ban," when it was actually far more than that: it also kept women and men of African descent out of the temple. And yet very few discussions—either when the ban was in place or since 1978—even mention the impact that the policy had on women with African ancestry, let alone grapple with the fact that, since temple ordinances are required for exaltation, women and men of African descent were denied the promise of exaltation. But the androcentric focus on priesthood denial elided this reality. Not only that, but many apologetic moves that were raised in defense of the policy would have been instantly recognized as illegitimate had more attention been paid to the situation of women. We ignore women at our peril.

As Eugene England wrote, we cannot simply ignore questions concerning women by taking an attitude that they will be resolved later because "the devaluation of women inherent in the expectation of polygyny is destructive of their sense of identity and worth now."[29] I would extend his sentiment so that it applies not only to polygyny but to other issues that affect women as well: it may be less important whether women do or do not exercise the priesthood and more important as to how we think about that fact. It certainly makes a difference to a woman's conception of herself, her world, and her God if she thinks that she does not hold the priesthood because she is *more* righteous than men or because she is *less* righteous than they are.

To sum, it is not my position that apologetic efforts are inherently anti-woman, nor that any apologetic effort on behalf of Mormonism's distinct history, doctrine, and practice is necessarily anti-woman, even when it comes to defending such practices as polygamy or a male-only priesthood. Rather, my contention is that the way in which apologetics has traditionally been practiced in the LDS tradition tends to harm women—not intentionally, but as collateral damage, orthogonal to the main goal of defending the Church. This can be avoided by applying a few simple tests to proposed apologetic arguments: What happens when we invert the genders? Does the argument reflect what we know about heaven as well as earth? Are we strictly scrutinizing beliefs that conform with our culture? And are we honoring the paradoxes at the core of Mormon belief? If these tests are met, the mission of apologetics can proceed in a way that does not inadvertently harm women.

---

29. Eugene England, "On Fidelity, Polygamy, and Celestial Marriage," *Dialogue: A Journal of Mormon Thought* 20, no. 4 (Winter 1987): 152.

TEN

"The Perfect Union of Man and Woman": Reclamation and Collaboration in Joseph Smith's Theology Making

Fiona Givens

Churches that are more than a generation old face the same challenges that confronted early Christianity: how to preach and teach their gospel to myriad peoples, nationalities, ethnic groups, and societies, without accumulating the cultural trappings of their initial geographical locus. As Joseph Milner has pointed out, the rescue of the "precious ore" of the original theological deposit is made particularly onerous, threatened as it is by rapidly growing mounds of accumulating cultural and "ecclesiastical rubbish."[1] This includes social accretions, shifting sensibilities and priorities, and the inevitable hand of human intermediaries.

For Joseph Smith, the rescue of the precious ore upon which he embarked was not just the reclamation of the kerygma of Christ's original Gospel. Rather, he was attempting to restore the Ur-Evangelium itself—the gospel preached to and by the couple Adam and Eve (Moses 6:9). In the present essay, I wish to recapitulate a common thread in Joseph's early vision, one that may already be too obscure and in need of excavation and celebration. Central to Joseph's creative energies was a profound commitment to an ideal of cosmic as well as human collaboration. His personal mode of leadership increasingly shifted from autocratic to collaborative—and that mode infused both his most radical theologizing and his hopes for Church comity itself.

---

1. Joseph Milner, *The History of the Church of Christ*, 3 vols. (Boston: Farrand, Mallory, and Co., 1809), 1:v, 3:221.

His manner of producing scripture, his re-conceived doctrine of the Trinity, and his hopes for the Nauvoo Women's Relief Society all attest to Joseph's proclivity for collaborative scriptural, theological, and ecclesiastical restoration. Although Smith was without Mormon parallel in his revelatory capacities (by one count he experienced seventy-six documented visions),[2] he increasingly insisted on democratizing that gift. As one scholar remarked, "Joseph Smith was the Henry Ford of revelation. He wanted every home to have one, and the revelation he had in mind was the revelation he'd had, which was seeing God."[3] Richard Bushman has noted how "Smith did not attempt to monopolize the prophetic office. It was as if he intended to reduce his own role and infuse the church bureaucracy with his charismatic powers."[4] This he principally effected through the formation of councils and quorums equal in authority—and revelatory responsibility—to that which he and his presidency possessed.[5] Most remarkable of all, perhaps, was Smith's readiness to turn what revelations he did receive and record into cooperative editing projects. With his full sanction and participation, the "Revelation Books," in which his divine dictations were recorded, bear the evidence of half a dozen editors' handwriting—including his own—engaged in the revision of his pronouncements.[6]

It was in the work of this scriptural production that Joseph recognized that theological reclamation necessarily entailed fracturing the Christian canon to allow for excision, emendation, and addition. Arguably, the most important work of reclamation and re-conceptualization is Joseph's under-

---

2. They are treated in Alexander L. Baugh, "Parting the Veil: Joseph Smith's Seventy-Six Documented Visionary Experiences," in *Opening the Heavens: Accounts of Divine Manifestations 1820–1844*, ed. John W. Welch and Erick B. Carlson (Provo, Utah, and Salt Lake City: Brigham Young University and Deseret Book, 2005), 265–326.

3. Interview of Kathleen Flake, *The Mormons*, PBS Frontline/American Experience, April 30, 2007, http://www.pbs.org/mormons/interviews/flake.html.

4. Richard Bushman, "Joseph Smith and His Visions," in *The Oxford Handbook of Mormonism*, ed. Terryl L. Givens and Philip L. Barlow (Oxford: Oxford University Press, 2015), 118.

5. This practice is most clearly evident in his revelation on priesthood, Doctrine and Covenants 107.

6. See Robin Scott Jensen, Robert J. Woodford, and Steven C. Harper, eds., *Revelations and Translations, Volume 1: Manuscript Revelation Books*, vol. 1 of the Revelations and Translations series of *The Joseph Smith Papers*, ed. Dean C. Jessee, Ronald K. Esplin, and Richard Lyman Bushman (Salt Lake City: Church Historian's Press, 2011).

standing of the nature and attributes of the three members of the Godhead whose own collaborative work and glory are "to bring to pass the immortality and eternal life of man" (Moses 1:39). Smith believed that the true nature and attributes of the Trinity, the truly "plain and precious things," were either buried, revised, camouflaged, or expunged from the biblical text (1 Ne. 13). Part of his reclamation entailed a restoration of the Divine Feminine together with a revision of contemporary conceptions of priesthood power and authority in conjunction with "keys" Joseph believed had been lost following the advent of Christianity. Joseph saw himself as midwife in the restoration of the priesthood of the Ur-Evangelium. Within this framework, he envisioned collaborative roles for women and men within the ecclesiastical structure and ministry of the nascent LDS Church, evidenced in partial form in the initiatory, endowment, and sealing rites of the LDS temple.

Reclamation of Divine Collaboration

In answer to William Dever's question "Did God have a Wife?" the LDS faith responds with a resounding affirmative.[7] Relatively recent excavation of the symbols and modes of worship attributed to the Divine Feminine both within and outside the ancient Hebrew tradition, together with salient clues within the biblical text, are helping to support Joseph's reclamation of God, the Mother, from the textual absence to which She has been consigned. As Joseph's theology never emerged ex nihilo, neither is it reasonable to infer his re-introduction of the doctrine of Heavenly Mother to be without canonical and, given Joseph's penchant for rupturing boundaries, extra-canonical precedent. Joseph showed himself to be quite happy trawling through every possible resource in order to reclaim what he considered was most "plain and precious" (D&C 91:1).[8]

Joseph's theology was Trinitarian, but in a radically re-conceptualized way. A conventional Trinity, in its thrice-reiterated maleness, could never have produced the collaborative vision of priesthood that Joseph developed. It is, therefore, crucial, both for historical context and theological rationale, to recognize that Joseph reconstitutes the Godhead of Christendom as a

---

7. William Dever, *Did God Have a Wife? Archaeology and Folk Religion in Ancient Israel* (Grand Rapids, Mich.: Eerdmans, 2005).

8. Among Joseph's reading material is Willam Hone, ed., *The Apocryphal New Testament* (London: Hone, 1821). For Smith's library, see Kenneth W. Godfrey, "A Note on the Nauvoo Library and Literary Institute," *BYU Studies* 14 (Spring 1974): 386–89.

Heavenly Father who co-presides with a Heavenly Mother. In 1878, Apostle Erastus Snow stated:

> "What," says one, "do you mean we should understand that Deity consists of man and woman?" Most certainly I do. If I believe anything that God has ever said about himself . . . I must believe that deity consists of man and woman. . . . There can be no God except he is composed of man and woman *united*, and there is not in all the eternities that exist, or ever will be a God in any other way, . . . except they be made of these two component parts: a man and a woman; the male and the female.[9]

In his 1876 general conference address, Brigham Young suggested a striking equality within that Godhead when he talked of "eternal mothers" and "eternal daughters . . . prepared to frame earths like unto ours."[10]

Prescient but not surprising, therefore, is the merging of Smith's reconstituted Godhead with the traditional Trinity. Elder Charles W. Penrose drew an unexpected inference from Joseph's new theology when he suggested an identification of the Holy Spirit with Heavenly Mother. He responded to a Mr. Kinsman's assertion that "the members of the Trinity are . . . men" by stating that the third member of the Godhead—the Holy Spirit—was the feminine member of the Trinity: "If the divine image, to be complete, had to reflect a female as well as a male element, it is self-evident that both must be contained in the Deity. And they are. For the divine Spirit that in the morning of creation 'moved upon the face of the waters,' bringing forth life and order, is . . . the feminine gender, whatever modern theology may think of it."[11] Penrose may have been relying upon Joseph's re-working of the creation narrative in the book of Abraham, where "movement" is replaced with "brooding" so that "the Spirt of the Gods was brooding upon the face of the waters" (Abr. 4:2)—a striking image of a mother bird during the incubation period of her offspring. (One remembers in this context Gerard Manley Hopkins's lovely allusion to the Holy Spirit who, "over the bent/World broods with warm breast and with ah! bright wings.")[12]

---

9. Erastus Snow, March 3, 1878, *Journal of Discourses,* 26 vols. (London and Liverpool: LDS Booksellers Depot, 1854–86), 19:269–70; emphasis added.

10. Richard S. Van Wagoner, ed., *Complete Discourses of Brigham Young* (Salt Lake City: Smith-Petit Foundation, 2009), 5:3092.

11. "Women in Heaven," *Millennial Star* 64 (June 26, 1902): 410. Penrose, who was editor at the time this editorial was written, is likely the author.

12. Gerard Manley Hopkins, "God's Grandeur," *Poems* (New York: Oxford University Press, 1961), 70.

Even though recorded third-hand, the following account suggests that the prophet Joseph, while not expressing the same identification as Penrose, was projecting the same reconstituted heavenly family:

> One day the Prophet, Joseph, asked [Zebedee Coltrin] and Sidney Rigdon to accompany him into the Woods to pray. When they had reached a secluded spot Joseph laid down on his back and stretched out his arms. He told the brethren to lie one on each arm, and then shut their eyes. After they had prayed he told them to open their eyes. They did so and saw a brilliant light surrounding a pedestal which seemed to rest on the earth. They closed their eyes and again prayed. They then saw, on opening them, the Father seated upon a throne; they prayed again and on looking saw the Mother also; after praying and looking the fourth time they saw the Savior added to the group.[13]

V. H. Cassler has written, "What we have taken as absence was presence all along, but we did not have the eyes to see it."[14] Even within the LDS tradition, glimpses of Smith's radical innovation have neither been sufficiently recognized nor appreciated. One such unrecognized symbol resides on the threshold of the celestial room in the Salt Lake Temple. Just above the veil on the west wall stands a remarkable, six-foot statue of a woman, holding what looks very much like a palm frond. She is flanked by two easily discernible cherubs to whom she is linked by garlands of colorful, open flowers. While chubby cherubs are ubiquitous in Renaissance art and could, therefore, be mistaken as merely decorative, the number and placement of the cherubs in the celestial room of the temple draw one back to the majestic, fearful Cherubim—guardians of the Mercy Seat in the Holy of Holies of the First Temple. The Lady of the Temple is positioned at the portal of the veil—the representation of the torn body of the Lord, Jesus Christ—through which all kindred, nations, tongues, and people shall pass into the celestial kingdom (Heb. 10:20, Matt. 27:50–51).

The original statue was purchased by Joseph Don Carlos Young, who was called by the Church Presidency to succeed Truman O. Angell

---

13. Abraham H. Cannon, Journal, August 25, 1880, LDS archives, quoted in Linda P. Wilcox, "The Mormon Concept of a Mother in Heaven," in *Sisters in Spirit: Mormon Women in Historical and Cultural Perspective*, ed. Maureen Ursenbach Beecher and Lavina Fielding Anderson (Urbana: University of Illinois Press, 1992), 66; see also Maxine Hanks, *Women and Authority: Re-Emerging Mormon Feminism* (Salt Lake City: Signature, 1992).

14. V. H. Cassler, "Plato's Son, Augustine's Heir: 'A Post-Heterosexual Mormon Theology'?" *Square Two* 5, no. 2 (Summer 2012): http://squaretwo.org/Sq2ArticleCasslerPlatosSon.html.

as decorator of the temple interior. Young purchased the winged statue named the "Angel of Peace" and two cherubs on a visit to New York in 1877. However, during a dream vision one night Young recorded: "I felt impelled to remove the wings. Now I saw a smile and expression that I never saw before and I can now allow this . . . to be placed there."[15] The enigmatic lady's station at the veil of the temple, replete with crucifixion imagery, makes it unlikely that she represents Eve. Mary, the mortal mother of the Lord, is a possibility, given her maternal relationship to the Messiah. However, the Lady's presence at the entrance to the celestial room, representing the celestial kingdom, suggests someone else. There are several key clues as to her possible identity.

Of note is the palm frond the Lady is holding. Anciently, trees were a potent symbol of Asherah, God the Mother.[16] In fact, the Menorah—the seven-branched lamp—that is reputed to have given light in the original Holy of Holies is fashioned after an almond tree, covered in gold—representing the Tree of Life spoken of at the beginning and end of the biblical text.[17] Not only are flowers fashioned into the Menorah: open flowers are one of the temple's primary decorative motifs.[18] Palm trees also were closely associated with the First Temple with which the interior was liberally decorated together with cherubim: "And it was made with cherubims and palm trees, so that a palm tree was between a cherub and a cherub; and every cherub had two faces" (Ezek. 41:18).[19]

Of interest to this discussion is that palm fronds also play a conspicuous role in Jesus's Passion—in particular his dramatic entry into Jerusalem on Palm Sunday, the day that begins the week ending in the crucifixion and resurrection of the Lord. The thronging crowds, waving and throwing palm fronds beneath the hooves of the donkey carrying the Messiah,

---

15. Joseph Don Carlos Young, Private Notebook (no date; no pagination), currently in the possession of Richard Wright Young, grandson of Joseph Don Carlos Young, quoted in Alonzo L. Gaskill and Seth G. Soha, "The Woman at the Veil," in *An Eye of Faith: Essays in Honor of Richard O. Cowan*, ed. Kenneth L. Alford and Richard. E. Bennett (Provo, Utah: Religious Studies Center, 2015), 91–111.

16. Daniel Peterson, "Nephi and His Asherah: A Note on 1 Nephi 11:8–23," *Journal of Book of Mormon Studies* 9, no. 2 (2000): 16–25, 80–81.

17. See Exodus 25:31–37, 37:17–22; Zechariah 4:1–3; Genesis 2:9; Revelation 22:2. See also Margaret Barker, *King of the Jews: Temple Theology in John's Gospel* (London: SPCK, 2014), 34–38. Biblical quotations in this essay are from the NRSV unless otherwise noted.

18. See 1 Kings 6:18, 29, 33.

19. See also Ezekiel 40:16, 31.

"chant a Hoshi'ahnna" (Hebrew "Save Us")—a clear indication that many, if not all, of the Jews present understood that the man astride the donkey was the promised Messiah.[20] The palm fronds together with the chant suggest a recognition on the part of the thronging masses of the presence of the goddess—the Mother of the Lord—whose primary symbol is the Tree of Life. The Goddess Asherah, to whom the Tree of Life is inextricably linked, figured prominently in Hebrew worship from the time Israel first settled in Canaan until King Josiah's attempt to purge Her from religious life just prior to the Babylonian captivity.[21]

Asherah is referred to in Proverbs by her dominant symbol, "Tree of Life" (3:18), the "fruit [of which] is better than gold, even fine gold" (8:19). Those who hold Her fast are called happy (a word play on the Hebrew *ashr*). It can be assumed, therefore, that Asherah and Wisdom (Sophia in the Greek) are different names for the same deity.[22] According to Proverbs, Wisdom is the name of the deity with whom "the Lord founded the earth" (3:19–20). Before the world was, She was. "Long life is in her right hand; /in her left hand are riches and honor. Her ways are ways of pleasantness and all her paths are peace. She is a tree of life" (3:16–18). Latter-day Saints are enjoined to search for Her in the opening chapters of the Doctrine and Covenants as Wisdom holds the keys not only to the mysteries of God but to eternal life (D&C 6:7, 11:7).

Interestingly, the biblical association of Sophia with the Tree of Life finds a powerful echo in the Book of Mormon narrative. Nephi begins the account of his vision by expressing an ardent desire to "see, and hear, and know of these things, by the power of the Holy Ghost, which is the gift of God unto all those who diligently seek him [God]" (1 Ne. 10:17, 19). Nephi's narrative starts in the company of the Spirit, who immediately draws his attention to the Tree of Life—"the whiteness [of which] did exceed the whiteness of the driven snow . . . the tree which is precious above all." Mary, the mortal mother of the Messiah, whom Nephi sees following the vision of the tree (the Asherah), is similarly described as "exceedingly fair and white" (11:13, 15, 18). After Mary is "carried away in the Spirit for the space of a time," she is seen bearing the Christ child (vv. 19–20). This association of Christ's birth with the Tree of Life, with its echoes of a Divine Feminine, is

---

20. See John 12:12–13. The Hebrew for "Hosanna" is *Hoshi'ahnna* meaning "Save us" as noted in Margaret Barker, *The Gate of Heaven* (Sheffield: SPCK, 2008), 84.
21. William Dever, *Did God Have a Wife?* 101.
22. E.g., Proverbs 1:20.

not unique to the Book of Mormon. The oldest known visual representation of the Madonna and Child effects the same conjunction. In the Roman catacombs of St. Priscilla, a fresco dated to the second century depicts the mother and child, with a magnificent Tree of Life overarching both.[23]

Immediately following Nephi's vision of Mary and the Christ child, he watches "the heavens open, and the Holy [Spirit] come down out of heaven and abide upon [Christ] in the form of a dove" (1 Ne. 11:25–27). In his book *The Hebrew Goddess* Raphael Patai suggests that the Shekhina, the Cloud of Glory, which dwelt in the Holy of Holies of the First Temple is also the Holy Spirit: "When, therefore, a Talmudic teacher speaks of the Holy Spirit, he may as well have used the term Shekhina...[because] the 'Holy Spirit,' like the Shekhina is feminine [and is] considered to have an opinion, a mind, a will, and a personality of her own."[24] It does not, therefore, appear to be coincidental that both "Spirit" and "dove" are gendered female in Hebrew, Syriac, and Aramaic. In Semitic languages verbs adopt either the feminine or masculine form. Therefore, the verb used to describe the activity of the Shekhina or Holy Spirit would (and does) emphasize the femininity of both epithets.

Augustine also finds his theological heartstrings pulled by the provocative power and logic of the Holy Spirit as the Wife of the Father and Mother of the Son: "For I omit such a thing as to regard the Holy Spirit as the Mother of the Son and the Spouse of the Father; [because] it will perhaps be answered that these things offend us in carnal matters by arousing thoughts of corporeal conception and birth."[25] At about the same time, the early church Father, Jerome, interpreting Isaiah 11:9 in light of the Gospel of the Hebrews, noted that Jesus spoke of "My mother the holy spirit."[26]

Even though Jews returning from the Babylonian captivity were essentially monotheistic, there is evidence that their belief in a deity that comprised the Father (El), the Mother (Asherah), and the Son (Yahweh)

---

23. See photographs of the fresco at Catacombe Di Priscilla, http://www.catacombepriscilla.com/visita_catacomba_en.html.

24. Raphael Patai, *The Hebrew Goddess*, 3rd ed. (Detroit: Wayne State University Press, 1990), 105–6.

25. Augustine, *The Trinity*, Book XII, ch. 5. Translation by Stephen McKenna, in Augustine, *On the Trinity: Books 8–15*, ed. Gareth B. Matthews (Cambridge: Cambridge University Press, 2002), 85. My gratitude to Rachael Givens Johnson for alerting me to this passage.

26. Margaret Barker, *The Mother of the Lord, Volume 1: The Lady in the Temple* (London: Bloomsbury, 2012), 104.

from the First Temple tradition and before persisted. For example, in 1449 Toledo some "conversos" (Jewish converts to Christianity) were alarming their ecclesiastical leaders by refusing to relinquish certain tenets of their previous faith:

> In as much as it has been shown that a large portion of the city's conversos descending from the Jewish line are persons very suspect in the holy Catholic faith; that they hold and believe great errors against the articles of the holy Catholic faith; that they keep the rites and ceremonies of the old law; that they say and affirm that our Savior and Redeemer Jesus Christ was [a] man of their lineage who was killed and whom the Christians worship as God; that they say that there is both a god and a goddess in heaven.[27]

As Margaret Barker has stated:

> It has become customary to translate and read the Hebrew Scriptures as an account of one male deity, and the feminine presence is not made clear. Had it been the custom to read of a female Spirit or to find Wisdom capitalized, it would have been easier to make the link between the older faith . . . and later developments outside the stream represented by the canonical texts.[28]

Reclamation of Ecclesiastical Collaboration

The reciprocal synergy of the Godhead was a catalyst—or at least precursor—to Joseph's quest for a universal collaboration of male and female. On March 17, 1842, he took another momentous step in that direction. At that time both male and female members of the Church were actively engaged in the construction of the Nauvoo temple. Women collaborated in the enterprise primarily by contributing financially and by providing the masons with clothing. In addition, they saw to the needs of impoverished members arriving daily seeking refuge. As the number of women engaged in support of temple construction and relief efforts grew, a group of them, at the instigation of Sarah Kimball, formed the Ladies' Society of Nauvoo. Eliza R. Snow drafted the constitution and bylaws and then took them to Joseph, who, while applauding the enterprise, suggested the ladies might prefer something other than a benevolent or sewing society. He invited the sisters to "meet me and a few of the brethren in the Masonic

---

27. "*Sentencia-Estatuto* de Toledo, 1449," trans. Kenneth Baxter Wolf, *Texts in Translation*, 2008, https://sites.google.com/site/canilup/toledo1449. My gratitude to Rachael Givens Johnson for this reference.

28. Barker, *Mother of the Lord*, 331.

Hall over my store next Thursday afternoon, and I will organize the sisters under the priesthood after the pattern of the priesthood."[29] In other words, just as the male society had been organized after the pattern of the priesthood, the women of the Church would form a female society, with Joseph's sanction and blessing, after the same pattern.

Like the men before them, the women were to be organized under the umbrella of the priesthood "without beginning of days or end of years" (Moses 1:3). Joseph further stipulated: "the keys of the kingdom are about to be given to them [the sisters], that they may be able to detect every thing false—as well as to the Elders."[30] While it has been argued that the expression "keys of the kingdom" in regard to women refers solely to their initiation into the ordinances of the "greater [or] Holy Priesthood" in the temple, Joseph seemed to attribute to women a priestly standing. In other words, he acted on the assumption that in order to access the priesthood that "holdeth the key of the mysteries of the kingdom, even the key of the knowledge of God" together with the temple ordinances in which "the power of godliness is manifest," one would already need to be a priest (D&C 84:19–22). At least, there is evidence that this is how Joseph understood access to priesthood power and authority.

On March 31, 1842, Joseph announced to the inchoate Female Relief Society of Nauvoo, first, his recognition that collaboration between men and women was key to spiritual and ecclesiastical progress—"All must act in concert or nothing can be done," he said. Second, "the Society should move according to the ancient Priesthood" as delineated in Doctrine and Covenants 84 (given in Kirtland on September 22 and 23, 1832). And, third, in order to accomplish the above, "the Society was to become a kingdom of priests as in Enoch's day—as in Paul's day." Eliza R. Snow understood that the women's Society or priesthood would enable women to become "Queens of Queens, and Priestesses unto the Most High God."[31]

Joseph's conception of female authority may have been tied to his understanding of the New Testament. That women as well as men held church offices in "Paul's day" has become apparent with the recent, more accurate translations of the Greek New Testament and research into early Christian ecclesiology. In his letter to the Ephesians Paul enumerates the gifts of the

---

29. Sarah M. Kimball, "Auto-Biography," *Woman's Exponent* 12, no. 7 (September 1, 1883): 51.

30. *Nauvoo Relief Society Minute Book*, April 28, 1842, 38.

31. Eliza R. Snow, "An Address," *Woman's Exponent* 2, no. 8 (September 15, 1873): 63.

Spirit imparted by the Lord before His ascension: "[S]ome would be apostles, some prophets, some evangelists, some pastors and teachers, to equip the saints for the work of ministry, for building up the body of Christ, until all of us come to the unity of the faith and of the knowledge of the Son of God to maturity" (Eph. 4:11–13). Women as well as men were to be found in possession of each of these "gifts." Peter Brown demonstrates that, unlike pagans and Jews, Christians "welcomed women as patrons and . . . offered women roles in which they could act as *collaborators.*"[32]

In his letter to the Romans, Paul sends greetings to Andronicus and Junia (perhaps Julia), commending them for their faith and stating that "they are prominent among the apostles" (Rom. 16:7). Later writers would masculinize the name, but John Chrysostom in the late fourth century had no problem praising "the devotion of this woman" who was "worthy to be called an apostle."[33] In Acts, Luke records Peter quoting the prophet Joel: "I will pour out my Spirit upon all flesh, and your sons and your daughters shall prophesy" (Acts 2:17–18). The apostle Paul considered the gift of prophecy one of the greatest spiritual gifts: "Pursue love and strive for the spiritual gifts," he said, "and especially that you may prophesy [for] those who prophesy speak to other people for their upbuilding and encouragement and consolation" (1 Cor. 14:1, 3). Indeed, Orson Pratt stated in 1876 that "there never was a genuine Christian Church unless it had Prophets and Prophetesses."[34] It is, therefore, not surprising to find them mentioned in the New Testament. In Acts 21, we learn that the four unmarried daughters of Philip the evangelist possessed "the gift of prophecy" (Acts 21:8–9).

The primary role of evangelists was to teach the death and resurrection of Jesus Christ. Raymond Brown has noted that in the Gospel of John the Samaritan woman serves "a real missionary function," while the women at Christ's tomb are given "a quasi-apostolic role."[35] As Kevin Giles puts it,

> the Synoptic authors agree that it was women who first found the empty tomb. And Matthew and John record that Jesus first appeared to women.

---

32. Peter Brown, *The Body and Society: Men, Women, and Sexual Renunciation in Early Christianity* (New York: Columbia University Press, 2008), 145; emphasis added.

33. John Chrysostom, "Homilies on Romans 31," in *Ancient Christian Commentary on Scripture: New Testament, VI: Romans*, ed. Gerald Bray (Downers Grove, Ill.: InterVarsity Press, 1998), 358.

34. Orson Pratt, March 26, 1876, *Journal of Discourses,* 26 vols. (London and Liverpool: LDS Booksellers Depot, 1854–86), 18:171.

35. Raymond Brown, "Roles of Women in the Fourth Gospel," *Theological Studies* 36 (1975): 691–92.

The encounter between the risen Christ and the women is drawn as a commissioning scene. The Lord says, "Go and tell my brethren" (Matt. 28:10, cf. John 20:17). The women are chosen and commissioned by the risen Christ to be the first to proclaim, "He is risen."[36]

Deacons are also listed among the offices in the nascent Christian Church, and women are included. Thus, in his letter to the Romans, Paul commends Phoebe, "a deacon or minister of the church at Cenchreae" (Rom. 16:1). The terms "pastors" and "teachers" are joined grammatically in Ephesians 4:11. It appears that the term "pastor" in the New Testament was the universal term referring to spiritual leadership. Among the female pastor-teachers, Priscilla is singled out for her theological acumen, instructing (together with—possibly her husband—Aquila) the erudite and eloquent Apollos of Alexandria "more accurately . . . in the way of God" (Acts 18:18, 24–26). Significantly, of the six times this couple is mentioned, Priscilla precedes Aquila in four of them, according her prominence over Aquila either in ministry or social status—or both. As Rodney Stark states in his book *The Rise of Christianity,* "It is well known that the early Church attracted an unusual number of high status women. . . . Some [of whom] lived in relatively spacious homes," to which they welcomed parishioners.[37] Priscilla is not the only woman mentioned in connection with church leadership. In addition to Priscilla we learn of Mark's mother (Acts 12:12), Lydia from Philippi (Acts 16:14–15, 40), and Nympha in Paul's letter to the Colossians (Col. 4:15). The apostle John addresses a letter to the Elect or Chosen Lady and her children (congregation) in 2 John 1:1. All apparently function as leaders of the church.

The title translated as "Lady" in the New Testament is the equivalent to the title "Lord," generally denoting social standing but possibly, in an ecclesiastical sense, denoting someone in a position of church leadership.[38] According to Stanley Grenz, the nascent Christian Church "radically altered the position of women, elevating them to a partnership with men unparalleled in first-century society."[39] It appears that Joseph was engaged

---

36. Kevin Giles, *Patterns of Ministry among the First Christians* (Victoria: Collins Dove, 1989), 167.

37. Rodney Stark, *The Rise of Christianity: How the Obscure, Marginal Jesus Movement Became the Dominant Religious Force in the Western World in a Few Centuries* (San Francisco: Harper San Francisco, 1997), 107.

38. For example, 2 John 1:1, 4, 13; 3 John 1:4; 2.

39. Stanley R. Grenz and Denise Muir Kjebo, *Women in the Church: A Biblical Theology of Women in Ministry* (Downers Grove, Ill.: InterVarsity Press, 1995), 78.

in the same endeavor in mid-nineteenth-century America. During the inaugural meeting of the Relief Society, after reading 2 John 1:1 Joseph stated that "this is why she [Emma] was called an Elect Lady . . . because [she was] elected to preside."[40] While it can be argued that the aforementioned are all gifts of the Spirit that do not necessarily involve priesthood, there is evidence that Joseph saw the Spirit as directing the implementation of these gifts into specific priesthood offices.

I mention these historical precedents because it is clear that Joseph Smith was aware of them and that they influenced his directive to Emma that "If any Officers are wanted to carry out the designs of the Institution, let them be appointed and set apart, as Deacons, Teachers &c. are among us."[41] On April 28, 1842, after reading 1 Corinthians 12 to the Society, he gave "instructions respecting the different offices, and the necessity of every individual acting in the sphere allotted him or her; and filling the several offices to which they were appointed."[42]

And so we find that the striking degree of collaboration between men and women in the early Christian Church is replicated in the founding of the LDS Church. In this regard, Bishop Newel K. Whitney's words are significant: "It takes all to restore the Priesthood . . . without the female all things cannot be restor'd to the earth."[43] This implies a much broader role for women in the Church structure than temple service alone. In Joseph's journal account following the Female Relief Society meeting of Thursday, April 28, 1842, he writes: "Gave a lecture on the pries[t]hood shewing how the Sisters would come in possession of the priviliges & blessings & gifts of the priesthood—&c that the signs should follow them. such as healing the sick casting out devils &c."[44] Commenting on Doctrine and Covenants 25, which Joseph read at the inaugural meeting of the Female Relief Society of Nauvoo, he stated that Emma "was ordain'd at the time, the Revelation was given"—that is, Emma was ordained not by man but

---

40. *Nauvoo Relief Society Minute Book*, March 17, 1842, 9.
41. Ibid., 8.
42. Andrew F. Ehat and Lyndon W. Cook, eds., *The Words of Joseph Smith* (Orem, Utah: Grandin Book Company, 1991), 115.
43. *Nauvoo Relief Society Minute Book*, May 27, 1842, 58.
44. Joseph Smith, Journal, April 28, 1842, in Andrew H. Hedges, Alex D. Smith, and Richard Lloyd Anderson, eds., *Journals, Volume 2: December 1841–April 1843*, vol. 2 of the Journals series of *The Joseph Smith Papers*, ed. Dean C. Jessee, Ronald K. Esplin, and Richard Lyman Bushman (Salt Lake City: Church Historian's Press, 2011), 52.

by God to the position of Elect Lady ("and thou art an elect lady, whom I have called [or chosen]" [D&C 25:3]) as Joseph was ordained/chosen by God to the position of First Elder. It is clear from Emma's remarks two years later at the Female Relief Society meeting of March 16, 1844, that she recognized that her ordination to the position of Elect Lady with its attendant power, privileges, and authority were divinely bestowed: "if thier ever was any authourity on the Earth [I] had it—and had [it] yet."[45]

The second Relief Society president, Eliza R. Snow, who gained and retained possession of the Nauvoo Relief Society minutes, also recognized that Emma's authority to preside over the Female Relief Society gave the women's organization independence:

> The Relief Society is designed to be a self-governing organization: to relieve the Bishops as well as to relieve the poor, to deal with its members, correct abuses, etc. If difficulties arise between members of a branch which they cannot settle between the members themselves, aided by the teachers, instead of troubling the Bishop, the matter should be referred to their president and her counselors.[46]

Reynolds Cahoon, a close affiliate of Joseph, understood "that the inclusion of women within the [ecclesiastical] structure of the church organization reflected the divine pattern of the perfect union of man and woman." Indeed, Cahoon continued, "the Order of the Priesthood . . . which encompasses powers, keys, ordinances, offices, duties, organizations, and attitudes . . . is not complete without it [the Relief Society]".[47]

The source of women's ordination, Joseph suggested, was the Holy Spirit. He understood the women to belong to an order comparable to or pertaining to the priesthood, based on the ordinance of confirmation and receipt of the Holy Spirit. To the Nauvoo women, he suggested that the gift of the Holy Spirit enabled them to "administer in that authority which is conferr'd on them."[48] The idea that priesthood power and authority were

---

45. *Nauvoo Relief Society Minute Book*, May 16, 1877, 126.

46. E. R. Snow Smith, "To Branches of the Relief Society (republished by request, and permission of President Lorenzo Snow)," *The Woman's Exponent* 27, no. 23 (September 15, 1884): 140.

47. Quoted in Jill Mulvay Derr, Janath Russell Cannon, and Maureen Ursenbach Beecher, *Women of Covenant: The Story of Relief Society* (Salt Lake City: Deseret Book Company, 1992), 39, 50.

48. Ehat and Cook, *Words*, 115. As Ehat and Cook point out, there seems little alternative to reading the "confirmation" in his expression as a reference to the gift of the Holy Ghost (p. 141).

bestowed through the medium of the Holy Spirit was commonly accepted among both Protestants and Catholics at that time. The nineteenth-century Quaker William Gibbons articulated the broadly accepted view that "[t]here is but one source from which ministerial power and authority, ever was, is, or can be derived, and that is the Holy Spirit."[49] For, "it was by and through this holy unction, that all the prophets spake from Moses to Malachi."[50] The *Reformed Presbyterian Magazine* cites this "holy unction" as "not only the fact but the origin of our priesthood" claiming to be made "priests by the Great High Priest Himself . . . transmitted through the consecration and seal of the Holy Spirit."[51]

Such a link between the priesthood and the gift of the Holy Spirit is traced back to the early Christian Church, based on two New Testament passages. In John 20, the resurrected Christ commissions his disciples to go into the world proclaiming the Gospel, working miracles, and remitting sins in the same manner he was sent by his Father—through the bestowal of the Holy Spirit: "As my Father has sent me, so send I you. When he had said this, he breathed on them, and said to them, 'Receive the Holy Spirit'" (John 20:21–23). Peter preached that "God anointed Jesus of Nazareth with the Holy Spirit and with power" (Acts 10:38). And so to the Relief Society sisters Joseph "ask'd . . . if they could not see by this sweeping stroke, that wherein they are ordained, it is the privilege of those set apart to administer in that authority which is confer'd on them . . . and let every thing roll on."[52] He called this authority "the power of the Holy Priesthood & the Holy Ghost," in a

---

49. William Gibbons, *Truth Advocated in Letters Addressed to the Presbyterians* (Philadelphia: Joseph Rakenstraw, 1822), 107, quoted in Benjamin Keogh, "The Holy Priesthood, The Holy Ghost, and the Holy Community," (paper presented at the Mormon Scholars Foundation Summer Seminar at Brigham Young University on July 23, 2015).

50. Gibbons, *Truth*, 85.

51. "Hours With Holy Scripture," *The Reformed Presbyterian Magazine* (Edinburgh: Johnstone, Hunter & Co., 1866), 45, quoted in Keogh, "The Holy Priesthood."

52. On April 28 Joseph again visited the Relief Society meeting and discoursed on the topic of "different offices, and the necessity of every individual acting in the sphere allotted to him or her." Given what follows it is evident that Joseph is addressing the different spiritual gifts allotted to each member of the community. For, he continues that "the disposition of man [is] to look with jealous eyes upon the standing of others" and "the reason these remarks were being made, was that some little thing was circulating in the Society," complaints that "some [women] were not going right in laying hands on the sick &c," instead of rejoicing that "the sick could be heal'd." *Nauvoo Relief Society Minute Book*, April 28, 1842, 35–36.

unified expression.⁵³ Elsewhere he stated that "[t]here is a prist-Hood with the Holy Ghost and a key."⁵⁴ Indeed, Joseph presses the point even further. In a *Times and Seasons* article, he wrote that the gift of the Holy Ghost "was necessary both to 'make' and 'to organize the priesthood.'"⁵⁵ It was under the direction of the Holy Spirit that Joseph was helping to organize—or, more accurately, re-organize—women in the priesthood.

For Joseph, the organization of the Female Relief Society was fundamental to the successful collaboration of the male and female quorums: "I have desired to organize the Sisters in the order of the Priesthood. I now have the key by which I can do it. The organization of the Church of Christ was never perfect until the women were organized."⁵⁶ It was this key Joseph "turned" to the Elect Lady, Emma, with which the gates to the priesthood powers and privileges promised to the Female Relief Society could now be opened. The injunction given to recipients of priesthood privileges in Doctrine and Covenants 27 could, therefore, also apply equally to the nascent Female Relief Society to whom the keys of the kingdom were also promised.⁵⁷

The fact that the Female Relief Society was inaugurated during the same period and setting as the founding of the Nauvoo Masonic Lodge is helpful in understanding its intended purpose. Joseph had been raised to the Third Degree of Freemasonry (Master Mason) the day before this auspicious meeting.⁵⁸ And a plausible argument has been made that the prophet considered the principal tenets of Masonry—Truth, Friendship (or Brotherly Love), and Relief—to be in complete harmony with the reclamation of the Ur-Evangelium.⁵⁹ It can, therefore, be argued that

---

53. Ehat and Cook, *Words*, 7.

54. Ibid., 64.

55. Joseph Smith, "Gift of the Holy Ghost," *Times and Seasons*, June 15, 1842, quoted in Keogh, "The Holy Priesthood."

56. Sarah Kimball, "Reminiscence, March 17, 1882," in *The First Fifty Years of Relief Society: Key Documents in Latter-day Saint Women's History*, ed. Jill Mulvay Derr et al. (Salt Lake City: Church Historian's Press, 2016), 495.

57. *Nauvoo Relief Society Minute Book*, April 28, 1842, 40; Doctrine and Covenants 27:13–18.

58. Cheryl L. Bruno, "Keeping a Secret: Freemasonry, Polygamy, and the Nauvoo Relief Society, 1842–44," *Journal of Mormon History* 39, no. 4 (Fall 2013): 159.

59. Don Bradley has illuminated these connections in "The Grand Fundamental Principles of Mormonism: Joseph Smith's Unfinished Reformation," *Sunstone* (April 2006): 32–41.

Friendship, "the grand fundamental principle of Mormonism," formed the sacred bond between the male and female priesthood quorums in their efforts to proclaim truth, bless the afflicted, and alleviate suffering by providing relief as they worked side by side on their united goal to build the Nauvoo temple, assist those in need, preach the Gospel, excavate truth, and establish Zion.[60]

The organization of the female society also finds instructive parallels with the creation story in the books of Genesis and Abraham. Abraham states that "the Gods took counsel among themselves and said: Let us go down and form man in our image, after our likeness; and we will give them dominion. . . . So the Gods went down to organize man[kind] in their own image, in the image of the Gods to form they him, male and female to form they them" (Abr. 4:26–27). In the second biblical creation narrative, Eve is created after Adam when it was decided by the Gods that "it was not good for man to be [act] alone" (Gen. 2:18). After Adam and Eve were organized they were given the family name of Adam. He "called their name Adam" (Gen. 5:2, Moses 6:9). Adam is the family name, the couple's surname. (One can note here the precedent set by "God" as a family name evidenced in the appellation: God, the Father; God, the Son; and God, the Holy Spirit). Erastus Snow's remark bears repeating here: "Deity consists of man and woman. . . . There never was a God, and there never will be in all eternities, except they are made of these two component parts; a man and a woman; the male and the female."[61]

The divinely decreed identity of the couple, Adam, is one of complementarity, two beings separated by a creative act and then reconstituted as one by divine sacrament. Only later does the name Adam come to denote the individual male rather than the couple. It is, perhaps, in this context of Adam as the family name that the following scripture from the Book of Moses should be read:

> And thus [they were] baptized, and the Spirit of God descended upon [them], and . . . [they were] born of the Spirit, and became quickened. . . . And they heard a voice out of heaven, saying: [ye are] baptized with fire, and with the Holy Ghost. This is the record of the Father, and the Son, from henceforth and forever; And [ye are] after the order of him who was without beginning of days or end of years, from all eternity to all eternity. Behold, [ye are] one in me, [children] of God; and thus may all become my children. (Moses 6:65–68)

---

60. Ehat and Cook, *Words*, 234.
61. Snow, *Journal of Discourses*, 19:266.

In the Book of Moses, we learn that Eve labored with Adam. They worship together. They pray together. They grieve the loss of Cain together. Together they preach the gospel to their children (Moses 5:12). The right to preside over the human family was given jointly to Eve and Adam, as were the sacred rights of the temple: "And thus all things were confirmed unto [the couple] Adam, by an holy ordinance" (Moses 5:59). The sacerdotal nature of "ordinance" implies that Adam and Eve were also to collaborate in the powers inherent in priesthood. They were both clothed in holy garments representing the male and female images of the Creator Gods.

Adam and Eve, therefore, represent the divine union of the God, El, and His Wife, variously known as Asherah (The Tree of Life), El Shaddai (God Almighty),[62] Shekhina (The Holy Spirit), and Sophia (Wisdom). As Heber C. Kimball said, "'What a strange doctrine,' says one 'that we should be taught to be one!' I tell you there is no way for us to prosper and prevail in the last day only to learn to act in Union."[63]

It is this union that Joseph appears to be attempting to restore with the organization of the Female Relief Society. The Nauvoo Relief Society minutes indicate that Joseph considered himself to be authorizing the women of the Church to form an institution fully commensurate with the male institutions he had organized earlier. The name the founding mothers chose for their organization was the Female Relief Society of Nauvoo, possibly suggesting their recognition that what was being organized was the full and equal counterpart to the already operating male priesthood quorums.[64] John Taylor's suggestion to name the female quorum "The Nauvoo Female Benevolent Society" in lieu of the Relief Society presidency's proposal "The Nauvoo Female Relief Society" was rejected outright by the female presidency. "The popularity of the word benevolent is one great objection," adding that we "do not wish to have it call'd after other

---

62. For example, Exodus 6:3. For a discussion of Shaddai/Shadday as a female name, see Harriet Lutzky, "Shadday as a Goddess Epithet" in *Vetus Testamentum* 48, Fasc. 1 (January 1998): 15–16.

63. Heber C. Kimball, November 29, 1857, *Journal of Discourses*, 26 vols. (London and Liverpool: LDS Booksellers Depot, 1854–86), 6:102.

64. Considering the male priesthood to be the "Male Relief Society" is no stretch. The profound influence of Masonry on Smith, his choice of the Masonic Lodge for organizational purposes, the association of Masonic thought with "Relief," and the women's choice to employ that term explicitly in their organization's name, all suggest that the male organization was effectively in Smith's conception a "male Relief Society."

Societies in the world" for "we design to act in the name of the Lord—to relieve the wants of the distressed, and do all the good we can."[65]

It appears likely that the second president of the Female Relief Society recognized exactly that. As Eliza R. Snow reminded a gathering of sisters from the Salt Lake City Eighth Ward: the Relief Society "was no trifling thing, but an organization after the order of Heaven."[66] In her article entitled "The Female Relief Society" that appeared in the *Deseret Evening News* on April 18 and 20, 1868, Eliza wrote:

> Although the name may be of modern date, the institution is of ancient origin. We were told by our martyred prophet, that the same organization existed in the church anciently, allusions to which are made in some of the epistles recorded in the New Testament, making use of the title, "elect lady". . . . This is an organization that cannot exist without the priesthood, from the fact that it derives all its authority and influence from that source. When the Priesthood was taken from the earth, this institution as well as every other appendage to the true order of the church of Jesus Christ on the earth, became extinct, and had never been restored until the time referred to above.[67]

In her poem "The Female Relief Society: What is it?" Eliza expresses her understanding that the Female Relief Society of Nauvoo is the legitimate counterpart to the male organization by emphasizing the word "order" in the sixth and last stanza. She does so by enlarging the word in such a way that it immediately draws attention to itself, implying that she understands the "Relief Society" to be an order of the priesthood.[68] The "Chosen Lady," Emma, is so called "because [she was] elected to preside" as Joseph, the First Elder, was also elected to preside.[69] In the words of President John Taylor, "this Institution was organiz'd according to the law of Heaven—according to a revelation previously given to Mrs. E. Smith, appointing her to this important calling—[with] . . . all things moving forward in . . . a glorious manner."[70]

---

65. *Nauvoo Relief Society Minute Book*, March 17, 1842, 11–12.

66. Eighth Ward, Liberty Stake, Relief Society Minutes and Records, 1867–1969, vol. 1, May 12, 1868, in Derr, *First Fifty Years*, 270.

67. Eliza R. Snow, "Female Relief Society," April 18 and 20, 1868, in Derr, *First Fifty Years*, 271.

68. Eliza R. Snow, "Female Relief Society of Nauvoo: What is it?" in Derr, *First Fifty Years*, 135.

69. *Nauvoo Relief Society Minute Book*, March 17, 1842, 9.

70. Ibid.

The female counterpart of the male priesthood would be linked to that of the male order in the appropriated grand fundamental of Masonry: friendship. One could construe that the name for the women's organization, "The Female Relief Society," was chosen with the Masonic fundamentals of "truth," "friendship," and "relief" in mind—therefore empowering the female and male organizations to work together in mutual support, encouraging each other and meeting together in council—patterned after the Divine Council presided over by El, Asherah/El Shaddai, and Yehovah. If that collaborative vision did not yet come to fruition, it did not go unnoticed by those who constituted the second generation of Relief Society sisters who were very familiar with the founding events of their organization. Susa Young Gates wrote that "the privileges and powers outlined by the Prophet in those first meetings [of the Relief Society] have never been granted to women in full even yet."[71]

In turning "the key" to Emma as president of the Female Relief Society, Joseph encouraged Emma to "be a pattern of virtue; and possess all the qualifications necessary for her to *stand and preside* and dignify her Office."[72] In her article for the *Young Woman's Journal*, Susa Young Gates, in her recapitulation of Doctrine and Covenants 25, reminds her young, female readership that Emma was not only called to be a scribe but a "counselor" to the prophet and that she was "ordained to expound the scriptures. Not only set apart but ordained!"[73] With Emma in possession of the keys to preside over the Female Relief Society, it was now possible to create a "kingdom of priests as in Enoch's day—as in Paul's day."[74] As in the ancient church of Adam and Eve envisioned by Joseph and as in the early Christian Church, women would share the burdens of administering the affairs of the kingdom together with ministering to their congregations, the sick, the poor and the needy, and proclaiming the Gospel of Jesus Christ.[75]

Indeed, Relief Society sisters performed a vital role in their ministrations to the poor and the sick—including the pronouncement of blessings of healing. For example, Helen Mar Kimball Whitney records being blessed at the hands of Sister Persis Young, Brigham's niece, who "had been impressed by the Spirit to come and administer to me. . . . She rebuked

---

71. Susa Young Gates, "The Open Door for Women," *Young Woman's Journal* 16 (March 3, 1905): 117.
72. *Nauvoo Relief Society Minute Book*, March 17, 1842, 9; emphasis added.
73. Gates, "Open Door," 116.
74. *Nauvoo Relief Society Minute Book*, March 24, 1842, 22.
75. Ehat and Cook, *Words*, 110.

my weakness . . . and commanded me to be made whole, pronouncing health and many other blessings upon me. . . . From that morning I went to work as though nothing had been the matter."[76] At the Nauvoo Relief Society meeting of April 28, 1842, Joseph Smith had promised that "if the sisters should have faith to heal the sick, let all hold their tongues, and let every thing roll on."[77] Women and men would also be endowed to perform the saving ordinances performed initially in the Masonic Lodge and then in the newly constructed Nauvoo Temple in order to redeem "all nations, kindreds, tongues and people" culminating in the sealing of the human family to each other and to the Divine Family, thereby fulfilling their collaborative roles as "Saviours on Mount Zion."

As Susa Young Gates noted, "there were mighty things wrought in those long-ago days in this Church. Every great and gracious principle of the Gospel—every truth and force for good—all these were conceived and born in the mighty brain and great heart of that master-mind of the nineteenth century, Joseph Smith, the development and expansion of these truths he left to others." Susa then added that Joseph "was never jealous or grudging in his attitude to woman. . . . He brought from the Heavenly store-house that bread of life which should feed her soul, if she would eat and lift her from the low estate of centuries of servitude and ignominy into equal partnership and equal liberty with man."[78]

Author's Note: This essay is based on an article previously published as Fioana Givens, "'The Perfect Union of Man and Woman': Reclamation and Collaboration in Joseph Smith's Theology Making," *Dialogue: A Journal of Mormon Thought* (Spring 2016): 1–26.

---

76. Helen Mar Whitney, "Scenes and Incidents at Winter Quarters," *Woman's Exponent* 14, no. 14 (December 15, 1885), 106.

77. *Nauvoo Relief Society Minute Book*, April 28, 1842, 36.

78. Gates, "Open Door," 116.

ELEVEN

Lamanites, Apologetics, and Tensions in Mormon Anthropology

David Knowlton

Lamanites and Anthropology

The Book of Mormon introduced categories speaking to types of people, of which Lamanites may well have been the most widely used. Both rejected and embraced, the term *Lamanite* is often at the heart of discussions about the Book of Mormon. It resides in a space of tension and argument and yet, for us, it also serves as a window into Latter-day Saint anthropology.

By this term, I do not mean the social science discipline of anthropology. Instead, I mean the assertions of people's nature such that they might become objects of thought and discussion. This anthropology is a set of ideas about humanity and the cosmos that varies among different societies and among different religious bodies. While at the root of what we social-scientific anthropologists do, this is more a theological or philosophical concern.

In other words, I am interested in what the concept of Lamanite tells me about itself, about other concepts concerning people, and about Latter-day Saint notions of humans, divinity, and life.

Nevertheless, this chapter is not a disquisition of the Book of Mormon to learn about those issues. Instead, it is concerned with the writings of Mormon apologists who use the concept of Lamanite in their discussions about the Book of Mormon and the people it describes.

I shall specifically look at writings on the FairMormon website (what used to be called the Foundation for Apologetic Information and Research). This organization defines itself with the following slogan: "[D]edicated to providing well-documented answers to criticisms of LDS doctrine, belief and practice."[1] It further defines itself with words from Brigham Young: "Every time they persecute and try to overcome this people, they elevate us, weaken their own hands, and strengthen the hands and arms of this people. And every time they undertake to lessen our number, they increase it."[2]

My concern is neither to challenge their apologetics nor to make an argument in favor of them. Those concerns simply do not interest me in this essay. Instead, my questions are: How is the word Lamanite used and defined by FairMormon's writers? What is the universe of concepts in which they place the word and the issues which they see it answering? What are the key concerns in it for their vision of LDS theology and cosmology? What importance might this have for both kinds of anthropology that I am practicing here, the theological and philosophical anthropology and the social science discipline?

Book of Mormon Historicity, Lamanites, and Indexicality

At the root of many issues discussed on the FairMormon site using the term Lamanite we find the question of the authorship of the Book of Mormon. John Tvedtnes writes that the concern is whether the text of the Book of Mormon demonstrates Joseph Smith was its author or whether it shows the Book of Mormon to be a translation of an ancient text.[3] This issue is certainly an intriguing one and one on which FairMormon and others have expended much effort. Whatever the final results of this argument it is not one that interests me here, other than for the fact that Lamanites as category have been elicited as evidence. For this essay, the qualities given to the term Lamanite that make it elicit-able for the purposes of arguments about the Book of Mormon's historicity are important while the issue of ancient or modern origin is not.

As an example we can return to the Tvedtnes article mentioned above. He discusses whether accusations of racism against the Book of Mormon can challenge the historicity of the Book of Mormon:

---

1. Homepage, http://fairmormon.org.
2. "About FairMormon," FairMormon, http://www.faimormon.org/about.
3. John A. Tvedtnes, "The Charge of Racism in the Book of Mormon," FairMormon, https://www.fairmormon.org/conference/august-2003/the-charge-of-racism-in-the-book-of-mormon. The article is also hosted at BlackLDS.org, which operates under the umbrella of FairMormon, http://www.blacklds.org/tvedtnes.

Determined to read the Book of Mormon in purely naturalistic nineteenth-century terms, rather than as an ancient text, recent criticisms of that volume of scripture are offended by some descriptions of Lamanites in the text. This is particularly true when the Nephites describe the Lamanites in pejorative terms, such as blood-thirsty, idolatrous, ferocious, idle, lazy, and filthy. The question is whether these terms can be considered "racist," and whether supposed "racist" attitudes of the Nephites are evidence against the authenticity of the Book of Mormon.[4]

What makes Lamanite elicit-able here is that Tvedtnes is responding to how some people have seen in the negative descriptors attached to Lamanite signs of what people today label racism. It is not the category per se but how its use speaks to modern audiences. Though I wish to look at the substance of the category to grasp it as anthropology, I must first recognize it is an index in a chain of indices, where the point is not what it is but what it can remit to. I could throw my hands in the air and turn to another quote or article to find substance, but instead let me argue that this has anthropological meaning and creates a kind of substance for Lamanite as an index.

I should explain what I mean by "index." I draw the word from C. S. Peirce where it is one of three kinds of signs defined in terms of the relationship between that which carries meaning and that which is meant.[5] The index is defined by a spatio-temporal contiguity, perhaps most easily explained with the notion of where there is smoke there is fire; smoke is an index of fire. Indices not only contain that logic of co-association, they also can remit out of a chain of signification to something outside. They connect to other concerns and arguments beyond their own immediacy.[6] Indeed, this connection provides the basic meaning for an index.

Therefore we shall make our first claim about the anthropology of Lamanites. The term is often less relevant for what Lamanites are by themselves than for what they remit to. They are indices, which have also been called shifters. While Tvedtnes's text alone is not sufficient to make this statement, other than as example, we do find Lamanites operating as shifters in many parts of FairMormon's corpus.

---

4. Ibid.

5. C. S. Peirce, "Logic as Semiotic," in *Philosophical Writings of Peirce*, ed. Justus Butler (Mineola, N.Y.: Dover Publications, 2011), 98–119.

6. Michael Silverstein, "Shifters, Linguistic Description, and Cultural Categories," in *Meaning in Anthropology*, ed. Keith Basso and Henry Selby (Albuquerque: University of New Mexico Press, 1976), 11–55.

The shifters, or indices, we refer to here are similar to the signature in Foucault and Medieval semiotics. It is not surprising at all to find signatures in Christian semiotics or, in this case, apologetics. They are common rhetorical and structural devices within historic Christianity where their value is less what they appear to be than what they ultimately remit to.

Religious Value of Lamanites

Tvedtnes specifically addresses the issue of historicity—whether a nineteenth-century set of concepts drives the Book of Mormon text or whether it is an ancient production—but there is much more here than a simple argument around the production of a book. The question is whether the Book of Mormon qualifies as scripture and as a result is covered with sacrality, what Latter-day Saints would call "true." This concern drives much of the FairMormon writing about Lamanites: How can critiques that might challenge the sacred sanction of the Book of Mormon be reverted, rebutted, or themselves critiqued in such a way that the door is left open so that the Book of Mormon can be considered holy?

As a result, their argument and discussion proceeds as if based on three things: close textual reading, claims to logic and evidence, as well as an almost unspoken commitment to positivism, i.e., that concepts refer to a positive reality in the world. Strangely, specific claims to the sacred outside of this are scarce.

This means a weight hangs over their discussions of Lamanite. They carry this problem of the sacred and how it is known (which includes the role of language, logic, and evidence, against a tacit positivism) in relation to other modes of knowing—for example, what Latter-day Saints call spiritual experiences or witnesses such that the Book of Mormon can be considered sacred and hence true, or true and therefore sacred—even if that is not the direct material of their arguments.[7]

To this list of religious modes of knowing haunting their texts we can add authority, following FairMormon writings on Lamanites. The words of religiously-sanctioned leaders carry sacred force which Mormons reference as authority. FairMormon's understanding of authority moves us out of logical or religious epistemology and creates a set of sociological

---

7. The religious epistemology of this in relationship with secular epistemologies is undeveloped in the literature I focus on, despite the existence of gifted LDS philosophers and social theorists. As a result, we can label this a literature guided by a naïve epistemological stance.

categories in FairMormon.org's pages, a division of Mormonism into authorities proper (the Church's General Authorities), scholars, and ordinary Mormons. They also contrast faithful Mormons with cultural Mormons.[8]

To this sociology is added a distinction separating textual analysis—which they call scholarship—from the un-analytical and un-scholarly religious words and ideas of General Authorities and especially of folk Mormons. It biases in favor of the ways and styles of scholars above those of other Mormons, although the scholars must also recognize and pay homage to General Authorities and to scriptures.

Let us look at a non-attributed article on understanding the "Lamanite curse" and whether it was a "red skin" or a "mark" to grasp more on this point. The article explains that writers who understand the "Lamanite curse" as a "red skin" are following Fawn Brodie, a kind of scholar. Nevertheless, the article dismisses Brodie's scholarship, and hence authority, by saying she makes the claim "without attribution of evidence" and as a "critical author"—that is, as a doubly inappropriate authority, evidence-free and critical (i.e., not "faithful").[9]

This word—"critical"—is fascinating. Even when the scholar shows good scholarship, their motive—criticism—can be contrasted with scholarship whose telos is faith. Thus FairMormon has two kinds of scholars who work with texts, study them, and interpret them: the critic and the faithful. These depend on contrasting a telos of faith and one of critique.

On one side are what we can call "faithful exegetes," the group of people that are part of the FairMormon set and people who agree with them. They contrast themselves with what they take as critical writers, those whose analyses threaten faith.

In articles following the dismissal of Brodie, the FairMormon writers deny status to what they call Mormon folklore: "It is claimed by some that the Church believed that Lamanites who accepted the Gospel would become light-skinned, and that 'Mormon folklore' claims that Native Americans and Polynesians carry a curse based upon 'misdeeds on the part

---

8. For example, see "A FairMormon Analysis of: *No Man Knows My History: The Life of Joseph Smith*," FairMormon, http://fairmormon.org/Criticism_of_Mormonism/Books/No_Man_Knows_My_History:_The_Life_of_Joseph_Smith.

9. "Question: Does the Book of Mormon describe the Lamanites as being 'cursed' with a 'red skin'?" FairMormon, https://www.fairmormon.org/answers/Question:_Does_the_Book_of_Mormon_describe_the_Lamanites_as_being_%22cursed%22_with_a_%22red_skin%22%3F.

of their ancestors.'"[10] They also reject, by implication, how Brodie may have drawn this notion from ordinary Mormonism or from her General Authority family of the time. As a result they create a field of illegitimate Mormonism (folklore) distinct from what they accept as legitimate, even if the category has no specific name.

The exegetes of FairMormon then seek teachings by Latter-day Saint General Authorities that they can read and interpret through the application of their hermeneutic and praxis—logic and readings based on their understandings of technical, academic terms in order to read faithfully and to demonstrate their faithfulness.[11] These texts by Mormon authorities are not simply taken at face value, but must themselves be submitted to "faithful" readings by the FairMormon community.

In this we find a sociology of Mormonism that goes beyond a simple dual contrast of legitimate and illegitimate. It classifies Mormonism as a community divided among faithful exegetes, followers of folklore (i.e., those not carefully guided by Mormon scripture and textual interpretations of the General Authorities' words supported by FairMormon but by Mormon verbal and social practice), and cultural Mormons (i.e., people who are Mormon in culture but without having a necessary faith in Mormonism). Culture and faith are thus contrasted as poles against the intermediate term of the Mormon folk. This produces the key contrast we saw above between the telos of faith and that of critique among scholars with other Mormons and General Authorities as seen through the ways they use texts.

Inevitably, discussions of what Lamanite means get caught up in the sociological struggle of FairMormon to claim an orthodox or legitimate space of authority and to dismiss other claimants, or to interpret them if they are General Authority or Mormon scriptural sources. Theirs is a push for exegetical power and authority, and hence a preemptive claim to the holy as faith and as assistance to other Mormons. The term Lamanite, as a result, has more value in their writing for what it enables in justifying this sociology and the religious worlds the sociology allows than it does in its own terms, or than it does as something with empirical or strictly spiritual referents.

---

10. "The Lamanite Curse," FairMormon, https://www.fairmormon.org/answers/Book_of_Mormon/Lamanites/Curse.

11. Ibid.

Lamanite and Interpretive Authority

As we have seen in passing, Lamanites have been argued to be cursed, to be describable in pejorative terms "as blood-thirsty, idolatrous, ferocious, idle, lazy, and filthy," and to have been held to have a red skin. The reader might ask, why we did not explore these and other descriptors of the Lamanites first instead of roaming through the religious sociology espoused by FairMormon. To explain this, let us look at the first paragraph of a FairMormon article (this one with a cited author, Michael R. Ash) entitled "Who are the Lamanites?" Ash also gets to the issue slowly, by locating it in other concerns.

> Many Latter-day Saints have taken seriously the admonition to study the Book of Mormon. Such study and research has lead [sic] to a greater understanding of the book—not only spiritually, but also from an historical perspective. This greater knowledge has led to the discovery that some of our traditional ideas about the Book of Mormon are not supported by the text.[12]

Ash then goes on to explore these "traditional assumptions that do not conform to an enlarged understanding of the text." These include ideas such as that the Lamanites and Nephites, subsumed as Lehites, inhabited the whole New World and that we do not find "Lehite DNA." Now he gets to his key concern:

> [S]ome members have wondered if an acknowledgement of non-Lehite populations runs counter to the many statements by LDS scriptures, prophets, and general authorities who have referred to American, Central American, and South American natives as "Lamanites."[13]

In other words, his Ur concern is that textual study may lead to an understanding that General Authorities may have been wrong. The term Lamanite may not have a stable empirical referent outside the Book of Mormon, hence the need to faithfully interpret General Authority statements to save them from readings that lead to an attribution of error, whether those are traditionally Mormon or not.

This implicit recognition of LDS General Authority fallibility creates the primary sources of hierarchical authority in Mormonism as a problem desperately needing resolution, and that resolution authorizes faithful exegetes to replace General Authority stances with their understandings.

---

12. Michael Ash, "Who are the Lamanites?" FairMormon, 2004, https://www.fairmormon.org/wp-content/uploads/2011/12/ash-Who_Are_the_Lamanites.pdf.

13. Ibid.

These faithful interpreters are further authorized by claiming to be learned and scholars; they perform faithful scholarship although that is not well defined other than in the negative (people who have fallen into the category of critical authors) or in the teleology of intent.

Ash goes on to describe the first Lamanites not as a kind of people, despite the sense that the word should lead to such a conclusion, but as a "cultural organization"; they were not simply composed of the children of Laman. Instead they included anyone from their kin group and other people who "joined the Lamanites," who fell into that cultural category.

By doing this bit of casuistry, Ash implicitly recognizes an anthropological problem: there might not be empirical referents for the term Lamanites yet the faithful exegetes are working in a scholarly positivist world which requires terms to have empirical referents if they are to be real and hence true in a religious context.

The Lamanites may have been defined as descendants of Laman and other kin, but not all Native Americans (since the Americas is where traditional Mormons see the Book of Mormon taking place) can be proven to be descendants of Laman's father in the Book of Mormon, Lehi. Nevertheless, the term Lamanite must demonstrate the sacred value—truth—of Mormon teaching. In other words, Lamanite is not simply a statement about the nature of a kind of human being; rather, it is also a truth claim of Mormonism and the two cannot be separated easily.

This could simply be the slippage of an anthropological category into one of demonstrating a key theological premise: what God sanctions is true. It can also, at the same time, be an anthropological concern—i.e., that human categories such as Lamanite are not only things such as descendants of Father Lehi, they are also shifters which remit to the relationship of God to humanity.

This idea raises an intriguing concern with Ash's position. In his desire to stabilize his crisis of faith in the General Authorities' words, he changes Lamanites from an aggregate of people who are descended from Lehi (or followers of a descendant) into a "culture." In other words, what is anthropologically relevant here for him is that they have a culture and what the nature of that culture is rather than the nature of the Lamanites per se.

As a professional anthropologist I must say he is not using the word "culture" with the precision I would require in my discipline where humans are often understood to be culture-bearing beings. He is confusing "culture" with "group," or "society." He also lacks a clear idea of the content of the term "culture" as we understand it. Nevertheless, his argument is important because he makes the culture of Lamanites the potential problem, and not their being.

Ash separates culture from being in the same way FairMormon separates culture from being in the case of Latter-day Saints who are called cultural Mormons. In other words, a sociology built around acts of culture (as they understand it)—such as not accepting key tenets of Mormon belief while doing Mormon practice or holding Mormon identity—is contrasted with one of responding to that crisis of faith by performing exegesis in ways that can support the sacrality of Mormonism even while denying its traditional form. Both of these contrast with a naïve, believing Mormonism in which faith is uncritical and whose possessors, as a result, do not suffer the crisis that is foundational to these exegetes' sociology and hence to their anthropology.

This crisis of faith and an intellectual response is necessary for their definition of a proper human being. It is not a choice to believe or to practice no matter what, but one that relies on the intellect and the choices made in terms of exegesis, i.e., critical or faithful.

Lamanite Defined by Opposition

Not surprisingly, FairMormon seizes on a definition such that Lamanites refers to dissension:

> Although the term "Lamanite" was first applied to the literal family of Laman, the name "Lamanite" later referred to a religious/political faction whose distinguishing feature was its opposition to the church (Jacob 1:13–14). The concept of Lamanites being associated with lineage "became an increasingly minor factor."[14]

Opposition to the Church is joined here with the notion of dissension, although the two terms need not be so connected. The issues of Native Americans, skin, race, and color that FairMormon's authors work hard to argue their way around—because they are troublesome for them and provoke crises of faith (given contemporary intellectual Mormon understandings of racism, race, color, and of aboriginal Americans)—are diminished in the face of this emphasis on opposition and dissension.[15]

---

14. "Who can be called 'Lamanites'?" FairMormon, https://www.fairmormon.org/answers/Question:_Who_can_be_called_%22Lamanites%22%3F.

15. One sees in FairMormon's corpus I consulted no discussion of indigenous peoples' or Latin Americans' and Polynesians' feelings and critiques, readings of the Book of Mormon and the category of Lamanites, nor of the basic hierarchical

As an aside, it is worth noting that there is more motivation for this than simple textual reading gives, as important as that is. FAIR, which became FairMormon, was founded in the fall of 1997 in a particular and relevant context. It was just after Brigham Young University, where many of its scholars find employment and a home, was censored by the American Association of University Professors following an investigation into the firing of Professor Gail Turley as well as other faculty.[16] As the AAUP noted, BYU had argued that Turley (and others) showed a "pattern of publicly contradicting fundamental Church doctrine and deliberately attacking the Church."[17]

As a result, dissension and opposition were defined as typifying the scholars fired from the Provo university and, by implication, were seen as typifying much extra-mural Mormon intellectuality. Arguably, FAIR created its sociology of Mormon types in reference to this context and reified them in the contrast we have described as cultural Mormons and critics versus faithful exegetes. In either case, the bulk of Latter-day Saints are on exegetical ground here whether they are considered General Authorities or folk Mormons.

The main difference between Lamanites and Nephites appears akin to that between cultural Mormons and faithful exegetes. It is not whether they have faced crises of faith and even disbelief, but it is rather how they have arguably responded to that, whether with dissent and opposition, or faithful exegesis, in the rendering of FairMormon.

Notice how "faithful" here replaces an earlier term with great resonance in folk Mormonism: "righteousness." I suspect this is because of the focus of the scholars of FairMormon on the act of faith in performance of exegesis instead of the orthopraxy implied in much of ordinary Mormonism, where issues of proper belief are far less important although not completely irrelevant.

Whiteness following critical race theory, in relation to the apologists' stance and arguments.

16. Bryan Waterman and Brian Kagel, *The Lord's University: Freedom and Authority at BYU* (Salt Lake City: Signature Books, 1998). American Association of University Professors (AAUP), "Academic Freedom and Tenure and Brigham Young University," *Academe* (September–October 1997): 52–71, available at http://www.aaup.org/file/Academic-Freedom-and-Tenure-Brigham-Young-University.pdf.

17. AAUP, "Academic Freedom," 52. I must include a note that I was one of the people fired from BYU on third-year review who found themselves in the AAUP report and in Waterman and Kagel, *The Lord's University*. While that did not consciously motivate my analysis, I expect some will argue it is a critical factor. I let the analysis speak for itself, whatever the nature of the analyst. This nexus brings us back together only momentarily, both in this essay and in life.

But this paper is not about those categories of cultural Mormon and faithful exegete. It is about Lamanites, a term which seems to constantly remit within the work of FairMormon to external issues.

Dissent and Human Type

The focus on dissent—an action—might seem to remove Lamanite from a notion of anthropological type; it creates instead a basic dyadic category of humanity: the dissident and opponent versus the faithful person. At the root of these are devotional attitudes that become key to the typology. In the rendering above they were critical exegesis (even if one stays within the community and participates in Mormon religious life) versus faithful exegesis (despite crises of textual sacrality). However, let us look more closely at discussions of Lamanite to better understand the anthropological issues here.

FairMormon's articles show that a contrasting anthropology sees Lamanite dissension and opposition as defined far more broadly than in the above contrast such that they include murder, violence, and rejection, as well as disagreement and crises of faith. Disobedience, per se, is less the issue because even the Nephites, the contrasting type in the Book of Mormon, did not always follow the preachings that composed the gospel, the word of God.

This is demonstrated in FairMormon's discussion of "curse" and "mark." For this, FairMormon relies on an article by the aforementioned John Tvedtnes distinguishing the two. They draw the distinction from a rhetorical repetition of curse and mark as parallel in Alma 3:14 in the Book of Mormon. While recognizing that the Book of Mormon will not support a distinction consistently, they split the text's parallelistic structure of repetition to make twin, distinguishable categories. They define "curse" as being cut off from the presence of God, while "mark"—a tangible token of the curse—was something else and potentially varied.

They argue that while the curse was a separation from God the mark was something to distinguish people from each other and impede interaction between members of the two groups. After noting the Book of Mormon language in which God caused "a skin of blackness" to fall on them and that "the most typical reading is that there was some type of dramatic change that turned white skin into black skin,"[18] FairMormon hastens to see this change as symbolic or as some other kind of mark, rather than one of skin.[19]

In this they reject a racialist anthropology that sees skin color as separating people into different types and replace it with a metaphoric reading of skin that emphasizes the mark as something—anything—symbolic of a cursed status that can keep people separated from one another. The skin color, in other words, was not just to create different types but to distinguish and separate people just as the metaphoric skin should do. Out of the fear of race as something which would create dissonance and perhaps dissidence in the minds of modern Latter-day Saints, FairMormon strains at the racial gnat while maintaining typological separation of humankind.

This is a major anthropological issue: people come in distinguishable types and they should be separate from one another. In FairMormon's read of this anthropology, the types stem from a joining of human action (separation, disobedience, dissidence, opposition, or faith) with that of God (blessing or cursing). The basic typology of human kind, then, is created by this interaction of things humanity can do (which take precedence over all the rest of their possible activities) with the divine and its repertoire of actions in which two are key, the blessing or cursing we have already mentioned.

Earlier in this essay we mentioned the hypothesis that categories such as Lamanite may be fundamentally indexical, in that they constantly remit to something more than themselves or outside the immediate context in which they are. We see here a confirmation of this notion; however, the indexicality depends on something foundational in human nature, which is to say that the status of being arguably depends on a relationship of two sets of actions, the human and the divine. The human is not sufficient in itself; its being depends on its choices and actions as well as those of God, although these latter are often posed in a reactionary form—they react to human action and do not set form in and of themselves.

---

18. Brant A. Gardner, "What Does the Book of Mormon Mean by 'Skin of Blackness'?" FairMormon, https://www.fairmormon.org/archive/publications/what-does-the-book-of-mormon-mean-by-skin-of-blackness. See also, Brant A. Gardner, *Traditions of the Fathers: The Book of Mormon as History* (Salt Lake City: Greg Kofford Books, 2015), 159–64.

19. For example, see "What is the difference between the 'curse' and the 'mark' of the Lamanites?" FairMormon, https://www.fairmormon.org/answers/Question:_What_is_the_difference_between_the_%22curse%22_and_the_%22mark%22_of_the_Lamanites%3F.

Therefore, this human reality depends on the separation of humanity into kinds which ideally should be visible. Furthermore, though perhaps related in origin, as the Nephites and Lamanites were as groups grounded in lineages descended from Lehi, the types become different enough in sacred implications that they must be kept separate.

On the one hand, this is a powerful negation of racialist arguments of separate evolutionary origins or separate geographical origins for races such that they form clearly different kinds of people. On the other hand, it is an argument for a divine sociology building on this anthropology in which different kinds of people, akin to the racialist notion, should be kept separate and distinct classificatorily if not socially.

Visible Difference and America

In its focus on skin, whether literal or metaphorical, FairMormon.org flirts with, though it never develops as far as I can see, a notion that what is key to people—their sacred typological status—is visible in that it is a covering, their skin. I am drawn to this observation not just by reading FairMormon.org but by Eduardo Viveiros de Castro's discussions on naturalism versus perspectivism.[20] His ideas are quite involved, but among other things he argues that Amerindians reject the classic Western notion that the core or the universal is found on the inside (in nature) in favor of notions that see them in sociality and in the skin. FairMormon does not go that far on either side of the Viveiros duality. Unlike Viveiros and the Amerindian life he narrates, Mormonism is not perspectivist. It does, however, deemphasize interiors for exteriors, for the visible, as a matter of sacred sociology if not anthropology. And, it justifies that visible as a necessity for anthropology (i.e., maintaining one's own status) and for the construction of social groups. The skin—the surface and hence the visible—is a key site of social attraction and interaction (i.e., sociality) rather than people's depths per se, although it has implications for those depths and may arguably be caused by them.

Another means of visibility lies in claiming place, especially if places can be argued to be discrete and differentiated, such that they can give concrete observability to anthropological types. FairMormon.org expends considerable effort in considering this taking place. It is far from a neutral subject.

---

20. Eduardo Viveiros de Castro, *Cosmological Perspectivism in Amazonia and Elsewhere,* Hau Book Series, available at http://haubooks.org/cosmological-perspectivism-in-amazonia/.

Locating the Book of Mormon in place can have considerable implications for issues of the historicity of the Book of Mormon, especially since that idea of the engagement of God and human action for creating kinds of people is key to their understanding of the book. Place, like race, then is troublesome. If the Book of Mormon is located in too small or too large a part of the Americas it runs into evidentiary contradictions from the work of textual scholars and archaeologists, not to mention a host of other specialists from ethnohistorians to geneticists.

Place is more than simple ground. It becomes a proxy for distributions of known peoples, and hence genes, as well as different American Indian groups—Maya, Inca, Iroquois, Goshute, etc. Place also ties into the problematic assumptions of race as they played themselves out in American history and still have purchase today. In other words, it is not simply locating oneself on a piece of earth but in the history and social differentiation that place entails. It also runs into the clear traditional association in General Authority and folk Mormonism of the Book of Mormon with the American Indians and with America, North and South.

Nevertheless, as a book that makes sacred claims to being historical, the Book of Mormon must have a place unless its emplacement is to be defined as a fictional device and hence call into question the empirical sacredness of the book itself, in FairMormon's rendering.

This concern about place and its relationship to sacred history is not just an issue of the Book of Mormon but also of the broader Mormon notion of Zion. The opening of Zion to allow worlds beyond the classic Deseret in the Mountain West as a land of gathering such that it became a place wherever Latter-day Saints come to live parallels the issue the faithful exegetes of FairMormon face. However, that notion of emplacement proved solvable by transforming it to include any place Saints lived and a holy territory to be one without consistent and concise boundaries but one defined by the presence of temples, stakes, wards, families, buildings, groups, and persons organized around them. It is the emplacement of the buildings, now, that creates a land for Latter-day Saint life as it increasingly encompasses the whole world while being permeable in ways that recognize the coexistent non-Holy and keeps it out.

For the Book of Mormon the problem of emplacement is simply not so easily solvable, given the textual claiming of place within the book and more than a century and a half of General Authority and Mormon scholarly writing about it in a world with very active scholarship about the same places and peoples, even if some would like to find a way to de-localize the book and make it more easily universal or localizable in a less troublesome place.

Lamanites Continue to Stimulate and Trouble

The concept of Lamanite presents many problems for students of Mormonism and, especially, for people who insist on notions of sacred truth that require congruence between statements and empirical referents. Perhaps, as a result of this and of how it plays itself out within a complex and differentiated community of Latter-day Saints, we see that a key anthropological aspect (in the social science sense) of Lamanite is to provide means of distinguishing categories of Mormons, including unscholarly ones (folk and General Authorities) from scholarly ones among which there is a divide of critical or cultural from faithful.

Apologists gathered in FairMormon.org similarly interpret the issues of curse, mark, and skin referring to Lamanites to define them as being like the exegetes' opponents as defined by dissension and opposition to the gospel, a proxy for how the FairMormon people understand what they exegetically protect as an act of faith.

At the heart of their quest lies a crisis of faith: that the Book of Mormon and the statements of General Authorities might not be empirically sustainable and so must be made able through exegesis to sustain sacrality (truth) at the same time the exegetes do not take seriously the thought and ways of Mormons who, not being scholars and intellectuals, manage to create lives of faith and obedience without falling into the textual crisis of faith. The apologists allow themselves no out except exegesis.

In the apologist's writings we find not only a sociology of Mormonism and a hierarchical understanding of kinds of religious life, we also find notions of the human—an anthropology—that are worth further consideration in other bodies of Mormon writings, as well as in the lives of ordinary Mormons.

Lamanite is more a shifter, a kind of index, than a category of substance. It and the issues around it remit to the cosmogonic drama of faith as found in scholarship, faithful or otherwise. But humans are also shifters, in that they remit to cosmogony and the relationship of God to humanity. Whatever separations and distinctions that may exist among people otherwise lose relevance in the face of the ways in which sacred sanction comes on people and distinguishes them from other people.

However, the direction of this is curious. The universe we have seen in the texts we looked at saw the key in the decisions and actions of people to be faithful or dissident, with the latter the type of Lamanites. God, in this narrative, becomes a reactive marker or acknowledger of how human actions separate people into types.

It is a principle of this anthropology that people fall into distinguishable types and that both their action and God's response to it separates them into groups that not only are divided in some non-visible way, but become visibly different.

This visibility relates to taking place, where the nature of place and its relationship to history and to the divine reciprocally makes human difference all the more seeable and builds tangible barriers to interaction between the groups. Made in the interaction of people and the divine, these groups should be separate as a basis of their nature.

In closing, since I am a social-scientific anthropologist, I wish to return to the issue of culture. As I mentioned above, this term is not used by the apologists, as they describe cultural Mormons, in the same way it is used by my discipline. For them, it defines a kind of Mormonism in which faithfulness is separable from being a member of the religious community or society with any degree of activity, from full to none. This notion motivates as well the apologist's use of the term "folklore" as something appropriate to this kind of Mormon where Mormonism is a culture and not a faith.

I find this notion intriguing for analysis and suspect it developed in the seventies with the growth of an international Church and, as a consequence, a need for an analytical separation of Deseret Mormonism, with its deep historical and devotional roots and ties to the complex teachings of General Authorities over more than a century, from a purified Mormonism. It also grows in the development of a caste of defenders of the faith at BYU and their professional and ideological need to separate and legitimate themselves from other Mormons, scholarly and non-scholarly

Of course, purification requires an argument and a procrustean bed on which to base classifications of what must go and what can stay. For the faithful exegetes we have looked at here, that basis is one of loyalty as a meaning of "faithful"; one of performing exegetical scholarship to defend against the inherent problems of a historical faith in a scholarly and perhaps social world of naïve positivism; and one in which "faithful" is contradictorily in intent and result since the one may not result in the other.

The Book of Mormon with its story of Lamanites and their sacred drama remains confusing, troubling, and demanding even after all the effort of the writers gathered in FairMormon.org. Lamanite remains as a prototype and challenge for Mormon thought and Mormon life.

TWELVE

Conceptual Confusion and the Building of Stumbling Blocks of Faith

Loyd Isao Ericson

When discussing the role of apologetics in Mormon Studies the discourse usually turns into a debate concerning the *quality* of the scholarship used or the *tone* in which apologetics are done. Criticisms of apologetics generally then involve accusing apologists of lacking academic rigor or engaging in unbecoming polemics. Such accusations may certainly describe some, or even much, of Mormon apologetics—especially when done by novices or those without academic training. On the flip side, however, there are also many apologetic works that involve the highest quality of rigorous scholarship and are models of charitable dialogue. Departing from this standard debate over apologetics, the criticism that concerns me here is not one of quality of scholarship or tone; rather, it is my contention that the very act of participation in apologetics involves a confusion of what is being defended. That is, it affirms a mistaken conceptual assumption that religious claims are the sort of thing that can be defended or proven through fundamentally nonreligious, secular scholarship. Thus, I argue that rather than defending any religious claims, apologetics actually establishes or affirms the false criterion by which those religious beliefs may be unfortunately lost. In other words, instead of tearing down potential stumbling blocks to faith, Mormon apologetics actually and unknowingly engages in building and establishing those blocks—blocks that may be tripped upon by others who have accepted the conceptual confusion.

As the preeminent Mormon apologist, Daniel C. Peterson correctly notes that, broadly speaking, "every argument defending any position . . .

is an apology."[1] Thus, before going further, allow me to narrowly define a few terms. First, by "apologetics" I am specifically referring to *religious* apologetics—what Peterson defines as "attempts to prove or defend religious claims."[2] To be even more specific, I am here defining "religious apologetics" as the "attempt to *utilize scholarship* to prove or defend religious claims." Under this definition, an appeal to Mesoamerican scholarship in defense of the divinity of the Book of Mormon would fall under the definition of apologetics. However, a missionary testifying or witnessing to a skeptic in defense of the same would not be an example of apologetics.

Second, by "scholarship" I am referring broadly to secular studies exemplified in academia.[3] Thus, "scholarship" may include studies in fields such as historical research and methodology, philosophy, biblical and textual studies, ancient languages, genetics, anthropology, and archaeology. It would not include whispers of the Spirit, burning bosoms, visions, or other subjective religious experiences.

What then is a "religious claim"? It is the final term that this essay will largely focus on. Returning to my definition, what does it mean to "utilize scholarship to prove or defend *religious claims*"? Why is doing so a result of confusion? And how does it contribute to building stumbling blocks of faith?

In his book *Religion and Friendly Fire*, D. Z. Phillips criticizes Christian apologists like Alvin Plantinga, William Lane Craig, and others who use philosophy to defend traditional Christian beliefs and Western theology in general. His primary contention, as he explains in his preface, is that "apologetics is guilty of friendly fire when it says more than it knows."[4] What apologetics *say*, according to Phillips, is that religious beliefs can be

---

1. Daniel C. Peterson, "The Role of Apologetics in Mormon Studies," *Interpreter: A Journal of Mormon Scripture* 2 (2012): http://www.mormoninterpreter.com/the-role-of-apologetics-in-mormon-studies/. Peterson's article was originally presented at the 2012 annual FairMormon Conference. A portion of his article is a response to what I believe is an unintentional misreading of my "Where Is the 'Mormon' in Mormon Studies?" *The Claremont Journal of Mormon Studies* 1, no. 1 (April 2011): 5–13.

2. Peterson, "Role of Apologetics."

3. For the inherently secular nature of apologetics, see Joseph M. Spencer, "Apologetics Again—But This Time with Feeling," *Peculiar People*, November 13, 2013, http://www.patheos.com/blogs/peculiarpeople/2013/11/apologetics-again-but-this-time-with-feeling/.

4. D. Z. Phillips, *Religion and Friendly Fire* (Burlington, Vt.: Ashgate Publishing Co., 2004), xii.

Conceptual Confusion and the Building of Stumbling Blocks of Faith 211

proven or defended using the tools of philosophy and scholarship. What it fails to *know*, though, is that religious claims are not the sort of thing that can be proven or defended with those tools. Mormon apologetics, no matter how rigorous its scholarship may be, or no matter how civilly it may be presented, suffers from this same problem. While apologists may believe they are defending the prophetic calling of Joseph Smith, the divinity of Restoration scripture, and so on, in doing so they are saying more than they know. They are, as Phillips puts it, contributing to fantasy. He writes,

> I have suggested that fantasies have been sustained by the philosophical friends of religions [the apologists]. If such fantasies are then attacked by religion's despisers, it means that the defense and attack of religious beliefs alike become a kind of shadow-play that misses the reality. *There could not be such play, however, if the friends of religion had not determined the agenda that makes it possible.*[5]

He later adds,

> It cannot be denied, of course, that the pervasive confusion I am referring to has been attacked by the enemies of religion. But the enemies see no alternative to it. *The friends of religion are the authors of what is attacked.* It is in that way . . . that religion becomes the victim of friendly fire.[6]

To better understand Phillips's point, let me turn to a couple of Mormon apologetic examples. In a 2014 internet exchange on apologetics, Blake Ostler defended its role, writing: "Apologetics is providing a defense—for instance, explaining that it is likely that Joseph Smith did not have sexual relations with any of his polyandrous wives or that there is evidence for the Book of Mormon (or arguments against it are unsound) and so forth." He later adds, "Some of the best apologetics in my view are like good scholarship and does its best to take an objective look at the issues."[7]

While Ostler does not make it explicit here, I believe it is safe to assume that his use of "apologetics" is, like Peterson's above, concerned with religious claims and not with simple brute facts of history and such. Thus, for apologists like Peterson and Ostler, a debate over Joseph Smith's sexual life is different than a debate over Thomas Jefferson's, and a debate over

---

5. Ibid., 2; emphasis added.
6. Ibid., 5; emphasis added.
7. See Ostler's comments in response to the pseudonymously authored "An Apologetics of Care," *Faith Promoting Rumor*, July 29, 2014, http://www.patheos.com/blogs/faithpromotingrumor/2014/07/an-apologetics-of-care/. I concur with Ostler's view that the pseudonymous author's "'care apologetics' is not apologetics, it is just empathetic listening."

evidence of the Book of Mormon is different than a debate over Homer's *Odyssey*. While the pair of latter claims may be loosely construed as apologetics of scholarly theses, the former claims are religious apologetics of religious claims; that is, they are defending Joseph Smith as *a prophet of God* and the Book of Mormon as *the word of God*.

The problem with defending religious claims using the tools of scholarship is that claims such as "The Book of Mormon is the word of God" and "Joseph Smith is a prophet of God" are of a religious nature and are conceptually unrelated to claims about the Book of Mormon's historicity and Joseph Smith's sexual morality. By joining or establishing the assumption that these religious claims can be proven or defended by scholarly means, they are creating or adding to the "fantasy," as Phillips calls it, that religious claims can be disproven and attacked by the very same means. They are joining hands with the critics they are opposing in their misguided understanding that religious claims stand or fall on secular historical, philosophical, or scientific argumentation.

By agreeing with their critics that scholarship can have something to say about the truthfulness of religious claims, apologetics is establishing (or at least supporting) potential, unnecessary, and misguided stumbling blocks to faith. It does this in two primary ways. First, given the ever-changing status of what is known through scholarship, by linking the supposed truth of a claim of scholarship to the truth of a religious claim (such as the Arabian peninsula place-name NHM being evidence of the divinity of the Book of Mormon[8] or Eliza Snow's testimony of Smith's marriage to Fanny Alger as a defense of his prophethood[9]) they implicitly raise doubts of the latter if the former is disproven. An example of this is Thomas Ferguson, one of

---

8. See, for example, Neal Rappleye and Stephen O. Smoot, "Book of Mormon Minimalists and the NHM Inscriptions: A Response to Dan Vogel," *Interpreter: A Journal of Mormon Scripture* 8 (2014): http://www.mormoninterpreter.com/book-of-mormon-minimalists-and-the-nhm-inscriptions-a-response-to-dan-vogel/. Their abstract conclusion that "the NHM inscriptions still stand as impressive evidence for the historicity of the Book of Mormon" is especially pertinent in light of Stephen O. Smoot, "The Imperative for a Historical Book of Mormon," *The Interpreter* (blog), http://www.mormoninterpreter.com/the-imperative-for-a-historical-book-of-mormon/.

9. See, for example, Brian C. Hales and Gregory L. Smith, "A Response to Grant Palmer's 'Sexual Allegations against Joseph Smith and the Beginnings of Polygamy in Nauvoo,'" *Interpreter: A Journal of Mormon Scripture* 12 (2014): http://www.mormoninterpreter.com/a-response-to-grant-palmers-sexual-allegations-against-joseph-smith-and-the-beginnings-of-polygamy-in-nauvoo/.

the fathers of modern Book of Mormon apologetics, who once argued that archaeological evidence in Mesoamerica would one day "constitute [a] final and complete vindication of the American prophet, Joseph Smith."[10] After publishing multiple titles defending the historicity of the Book of Mormon (some of which are still in circulation today), Ferguson failed to discover the evidence he hoped, causing him to stumble over his own criterion he had established and privately lose his faith.

Second, regardless of whether or not any particular work of secular scholarship in defense of religious claims withstands the rigorous debates of time, it wrongly establishes secular scholarship in general as an ever-present potential defeater for religious belief. Religious claims thus survive at the mercy of scholarship, and apologists must stand ready to defend them against any and all new threats. Thus, Peterson writes in defense of apologetics:

> [E]vidence and logic are [not] wholly irrelevant to religious questions. Apologetics is no mere luxury or game. Someone who has been confused and bewildered by the sophistry of antagonists . . . might well justly regard apologetic arguments as a vital lifeline permitting the exercise of faith.[11]

By failing to realize the unnecessary affirmation of scholarships' relevance to religious claims, apologetics continues its luxurious shadow play with religious critics in a continuing cycle of argumentation that fails to recognize the stumbling blocks it has scattered about.

The obvious apologetic to this criticism of apologetics is the rejoinder that it is not trying to *definitively* prove or defend religious claims but is rather attempting to prove or defend the *possibility* of the truthfulness of those claims. For example, it is common for a Mormon apologist to say that she is not trying to defend the divinity of the Book of Mormon by *proving* its ancient historicity but is merely trying to defend it by showing that its historicity is *possible*. As Peterson puts it, "Moreover, most would agree—I certainly would—that it is impossible, using empirical methods, to prove the divine." However, he later adds, "It's the duty of the apologist . . . to clear the ground in order to make it *possible* for the seed to grow. Faith is still

---

10. Thomas Ferguson, "The World's Strangest Book: The Book of Mormon," *The Millennial Star* 118 (February 1956): 42–46; quoted in Stan Larson, *Quest for the Gold Plates: Thomas Stuart Ferguson's Archaeological Search for the Book of Mormon* (Herriman, Utah: Freethinker Press, 2004), 56. Thomas Ferguson was one of the co-founders of the New World Archaeological Foundation (NWAF). The NWAF received funding at times from the LDS Church to search for proof for the Book of Mormon in Mesoamerica.

11. Peterson, "Role of Apologetics."

necessary. . . . Apologetics is simply a useful tool that . . . helps to preserve an environment that *permits* such faith to take root and flourish."[12]

Far from avoiding the conceptual problem inherent to apologetics, this nuance actually exacerbates the apologetic building of stumbling blocks of faith. This is because not only does such rhetoric imply that secular argumentation has something to say about particular religious claims, it implies that religious claims are only possible or may only be permitted if certain secular claims are in fact true.[13]

What then is a religious claim? Endless pages have been written attempting to define religion. While no clear, agreed-upon definition might be available, we can readily see how religious claims are understood in the religious expressions and practices of believers. When faithful Latter-day Saints study the Book of Mormon *as scripture*, they are not trying to identify where in the Western Hemisphere the events took place nor do they find salvation in the assurance that the text does not explicitly mention coins. They are looking for inspiration on how to raise their families, deal ethically in their community, strengthen their relationship with the divine, situate themselves in a world of suffering, and to "know to what source they may look for a remission of their sins" (2 Ne. 25:26). They are seeking for God to speak to them through the text. In a typical fast and testimony meeting, Mormons bear witness of the Book of Mormon by echoing the eighth Article of Faith's declaration that they "believe the Book of Mormon to be the word of God." The Book of Mormon is truly the word of God to them because of the spiritual feelings it elicits as they read its words, because of the answers to prayers they discover in its many messages, and the fruits they see and feel in their lives that they believe are the results of reading and living its instructions. We do not hear—or at least I have never heard—testimony born of its brute historicity. And why would we? We would find it odd if someone got up to the pulpit and bore testimony of the truthfulness of a history textbook, the ratio of teaspoons to a tablespoon, or translation of a Japanese poem. While these things may be true, these secular claims are not the sort of thing that testimonies are concerned with.

---

12. Ibid.; emphasis added.

13. I suppose that one could counter this by claiming that the possibility of belief defended by apologetics is one of a psychological and emotional freedom of mind and not one of logical contingence on the validity of scholarship. But this would then beg the question of the integrity of the whole apologetic endeavor and support the criticism I am making here.

But isn't an assertion about the Book of Mormon's historicity an assertion about its being the word of God? While the traditional understanding of the miraculous coming forth of the Book of Mormon may seem to imply as much, a closer examination reveals that such a line of thinking still falls into the same confusion. If Joseph Smith's translation of the buried Nephite record had revealed that the plates of gold consisted of a daily log of Mormon's grocery lists and losing lottery ticket numbers (or some other mundane record), few testimonies would be given of the Book of Mormon, and it would have hardly ever gained any traction as containing the word of God. Or to pull directly from the Book of Mormon, imagine that the entire writings on the plates consisted of only Alma 11:5–19:

> Now the reckoning is thus—a senine of gold, a seon of gold, a shum of gold, and a limnah of gold. A senum of silver, an amnor of silver, an ezrom of silver, and an onti of silver. A senum of silver was equal to a senine of gold, and either for a measure of barley, and also for a measure of every kind of grain. Now the amount of a seon of gold was twice the value of a senine. And a shum of gold was twice the value of a seon. And a limnah of gold was the value of them all. And an amnor of silver was as great as two senums. And an ezrom of silver was as great as four senums. And an onti was as great as them all.
>
> Now this is the value of the lesser numbers of their reckoning—A shiblon is half of a senum; therefore, a shiblon for half a measure of barley. And a shiblum is a half of a shiblon. And a leah is the half of a shiblum. Now this is their number, according to their reckoning. Now an antion of gold is equal to three shiblons.

Now imagine that it could be undeniably proven that this text was a supernatural translation of an ancient record. In what sense would it be the word of God? Would religious testimony be shared of an onti of silver being the greatest of all? While such an undeniable proof of a miracle might shatter the wider, modern understanding of ontological reality, the text would still just be an ancient list of measurements with the religious importance of an English measurements conversion table between teaspoons and tablespoons.

What this hypothetical exploration reveals is that the religious claims that apologetics seeks to defend or prove using secular scholarship are conceptually different from that which scholarship can show. They, borrowing from Ludwig Wittgenstein's philosophy, are both participating in different language games—that is, the rules by which they are used are different and do not bear on one another. These attempts to defend religious claims are akin to attempts to announce the winner of a baseball game by the total number of touchdowns, trying to assess the beauty of a painting by licking it, or determining that two people are in love based on a list of each person's separate personality traits.

Making this similar point, Phillips points to the Gospels' accounts of Jesus's questioning of Peter concerning his messiahship. Phillips writes,

> It is in this context that the question "Whom do you say that I am?" has to be faced. It makes no sense to speak of "right," "wrong," or "the truth of the matter" here outside matters of the spirit. Spiritual matters can only be resolved spiritually, and the search for some extra-spiritual guarantee is misguided, distorting the kind of importance spiritual matters have.[14]

Peter's answer, "You are the Christ," is something very different than someone at an earlier time possibly saying, "You are a carpenter." As Phillips puts it,

> If someone had seen the young Jesus at work, was acquainted with his upbringing, and so on, yet denied that he was an apprentice carpenter, we would assume that he did not know what an apprentice carpenter was. But the disputes about the Incarnation are not like this. If they were, we could ask, "We know what we mean by 'the Son of God,' so how could they have made a mistake, or missed it, when Jesus came along?" Others could find out on our behalf that Jesus was an apprentice carpenter, but, if we try this with respect to the Incarnation, the result is a joke: "Have you accepted that Christ is your Redeemer?" "Sure I have. I heard the news about the same time I was told that he was an apprentice carpenter." I hope you agree that this would not count as "acceptance of Christ" at all. For some, "the joke" may become a research project. They hope to find out whether Jesus is the Son of God through the search for the historical Jesus. What if they were successful? It would mean that we could abdicate from answering, "Whom do you say that I am?" and rely on, "Whom do they say that he is?"[15]

The parallels between Phillips's argument and Book of Mormon apologetics should be obvious. Jesus's response to Peter's answer was that "flesh and blood hath not revealed it unto thee" (Matt. 16:17). This religious truth was not something that could be taught and argued through research. It cannot be proven or defended by another. In fact, this was not even something that Peter had deduced through his own research and study. He had, after all, been a witness and recipient of multiple miracles performed by Jesus—for a brief moment he had even walked on water with him!—but those could only defend or prove that Jesus was a miracle worker; they could not defend or prove that Jesus was the Messiah. Even

---

14. Ibid., 98.
15. Ibid., 94–95.

Jesus's own flesh and blood did not reveal this truth. Rather, such a truth could only come from the "Father which is in heaven."

So it is with the truths of the Book of Mormon. As declared in its title page, the primary truth of this book of scripture is that "Jesus is the Christ, the Eternal God"—the same religious claim declared by Peter that cannot be learned through the works of flesh and blood. And as traditionally directed by Moroni in the final chapter, this truth found in the Book of Mormon is not to be gained through scholarly study, but through reflection of the mercy of God and prayer, whereby the truth would be revealed "by the power of the Holy Ghost" (Moro. 10:5).[16]

An apologetic response to this might be that the traditional narratives surrounding the coming forth of the Book of Mormon are themselves religious claims. While this may be true in a sense, apologetics for these claims still fall under the same conceptual confusion. First, even if it could be shown or defended that the Book of Mormon was a translation of an ancient text, this would say nothing of its being a *divine* translation. Among many things, it could mean that Joseph Smith was inspired by a devil and his angels of hell, that the translation was made by intelligently-advanced extraterrestrials, that Joseph Smith was a linguistic genius, etc.[17] A believer's view of the divine translation of the Book of Mormon is informed by her belief of it being the word of God, not the other way around. It is because of her belief in the Book of Mormon being the word of God that she is able to believe it was translated by the power of God. In the same sense, Peter's belief in the divinity of Jesus's miracles was a result of his belief in Jesus's divinity. Had he not believed the latter, he would have viewed the miracles as works of the devil or of a charlatan.

---

16. More congruent with the thesis of this essay, I believe a closer reading of Moroni's promise in Moroni 10:1–5 reveals that the "these things" that Moroni wants readers to read and know the truth of is not referring to the entire Book of Mormon, but rather the final sermon he gives to readers concerning the gifts of the spirit, i.e., that God does not change and is still is actively involved with His creation.

17. It does not seem to me that other traditional Mormon narratives of the Restoration (such as the First Vision, priesthood restoration, etc.) cannot also be alternatively explained. For example, if one could prove that Joseph Smith was visited by two beings floating above him or by other beings claiming to hold divine authority, it would not be proof that he was visited by God and Jesus or angelic messengers. The claim that those beings were deity or divinely authorized angels and not deceptive demons or extra-terrestrials is a religious belief that could not be proven.

Second, an apologist might respond that while the Book of Mormon's ancient historicity might not demand its divinity, the narratives surrounding its coming forth demand historicity in order to maintain its divinity. In other words, if the Book of Mormon was not a translation of an ancient text, then Joseph Smith was either lying or delusional about its coming forth, and then the Book of Mormon could not possibly be the word of God.[18] The discussion of what makes something scripture could fill volumes and cannot possibly be adequately summed up here. However, logically the same conceptual issue exists—the divinity of the Book of Mormon (and our way of knowing that) is wholly distinct from secular argumentation of its origin. If it could be shown that the Book of Mormon was not a translation of an ancient text, believers of its being the word of God might have to revise their understanding of its coming forth and the narratives surrounding it, but there is no logical necessity to abandon their belief in its divinity.[19] In an analogous fashion, in the last few decades, secular, historical research by faithful Latter-day Saint historians (including the LDS Church History Department) have required revisions to and opened questions of several traditional narratives of the Restoration; however, these scholars would hardly claim that these revisions deny Joseph Smith's divine calling. Similarly, biblical criticism over the last century has revealed that many, if not most, books of the Bible are not actually authored by their explicitly named, implied, or traditional authors; but this has not caused knowledgeable believers to deny the Bible's divine inspiration.[20]

---

18. See Smoot, "The Imperative for a Historical Book of Mormon." Smoot is partly responding to Anthony A. Hutchinson's argument that the Book of Mormon can be authored by Joseph Smith and still be the word of God. See Anthony A. Hutchinson, "The Word of God Is Enough: The Book of Mormon as Nineteenth-Century Scripture," in *New Approaches to the Book of Mormon: Explorations in Critical Methodology*, ed. Brent Lee Metcalfe (Salt Lake City: Signature Books, 1993), 1–19.

19. I agree that a belief in the Book of Mormon's historicity might make it psychologically easier to accept as divinely inspired. However, that is tangential to the argument here.

20. For a faithful LDS discussion on the authorship of the Pentateuch, see David Bokovoy, *Authoring the Old Testament: Genesis–Deuteronomy* (Salt Lake City: Greg Kofford Books, 2014). In chapters seven through nine, Bokovoy discusses challenges biblical criticism present to the authorship of the books of Abraham and Moses and the Book of Mormon. For a faithful LDS discussion of the authorship of Job, see Michael Austin, *Re-reading Job* (Salt Lake City: Greg Kofford Books, 2014).

None of this is to say that Mormon scholars should not attempt to show the ancient historicity of the Book of Mormon. If this is their belief and they have the skills to do so, then they can and perhaps should. Such an activity in and of itself is not engaging in apologetics though—as it is not an attempt to prove or defend a religious claim. Using textual, historical, and archaeological tools to make and defend theses about the past is simply an act of scholarship. While the text of the Book of Mormon may be closely bundled with supernatural claims, attempts to prove its ancient origin are secular activities.

Thus, with Book of Mormon apologetics, confusion arises when the apologist goes beyond the limits of scholarship and argues that such scholarship is making a claim about religious truths of the Book of Mormon. That is, they (like the critics they oppose) tie the religious truthfulness of the scriptures to their historical authenticity. To quote from the past FARMS-produced volume of apologetics arguing for the ancient authorship of the Book of Mormon, the apologists are attempting to defend against "the anti-Mormon arguments against the *divine origin* of the Book of Mormon."[21] By participating in this game, both apologists and critics alike wrongly support the view that the religious value and truths of the Book of Mormon hinge on its historical authenticity.

With this view, the Mormon believer's testimony in the scriptures as "from God" necessarily involves the belief in the scriptures' ancient historical authenticity. To make this connection, however, confuses what it means for something to be religiously true. As illustrated above, when a Mormon gets up in a testimony meeting and says, "I know that the Book of Mormon is true," she is not referring to the historicity of the scriptures, but rather she is testifying about the role that the Book of Mormon plays in her life. When she says it is from God, she is saying that it inspires her, gives her answers to existential questions, gives her hope, comforts her, helps her know that Jesus is the Son of God, etc. Her testimony is about

---

21. Noel B. Reynolds, "Introduction," in *Book of Mormon Authorship Revisited: The Evidence for Ancient Origins*, ed. Noel B. Reynolds and Charles D. Tate (Provo, Utah: FARMS, 1996), 3; emphasis added. FARMS (The Foundation for Ancient Research and Mormon Studies) was once the premier center of Mormon apologetics before it largely abandoned apologetics after its rebranding as the Neal A. Maxwell Institute for Religious Scholarship. For a largely positive review of FARMS's general scholarship by evangelical critics of Mormonism, see Carl Mosser and Paul Owen, "Mormon Scholarship, Apologetics, and Evangelical Neglect: Losing the battle and not knowing it?" *Trinity Journal* 19, no. 2 (Fall 1998): 179–205.

the role of God in her life and how the Book of Mormon helps mediate that role. It is not a simply-stated proposition or statement of fact. She does not get up and say, "I know that Nephi built a boat in the sixth century before Jesus." That says as much about the book's divinity as does her saying "I know that Jesus was crucified by Roman soldiers" says anything about Jesus being the Christ. Returning to Phillips's discussion between Jesus and Peter, Phillips points out:

> I do not think Jesus is saying, "Peter, flesh and blood did not reveal this to *you*, but of course, others may have come to this conclusion by those means." It is not as though, although Peter reached the conclusions by means of what is revealed to him, philosophers may come along later . . . and reach the same conclusion by other means, for example probability theory. Jesus is saying that the *kind* of confession Peter makes *can only be arrived at by God working in us*."[22]

Religious claims are things of the soul and can only be evaluated and known by the experiences of the soul.

Similar problems arise with the other example of apologetics mentioned earlier by Blake Ostler—that of defending Joseph Smith against accusations of sexual immorality. Just as scholarship concerning the ancient historicity of the Book of Mormon can be done *as scholarship* if one believes that is what the evidence shows, historical argumentation can and should be used by historians to show that such accusations are not true if they believe the evidence shows as much. That is just doing good historical scholarship. The problem arises when the scholarship is then used for apologetic purposes, and the apologist believes that they are not just defending Joseph Smith from allegations of sexual impropriety, but are defending his being *a prophet of God*. An example of this is the concluding line of the introduction to Brian C. Hales and Laura H. Hales's book, *Joseph Smith's Polygamy: Toward a Better Understanding*. After briefly discussing charges against Joseph Smith surrounding the practice of polygamy (which I think they adequately address), they conclude, "[O]ur examination of the historical record has *reinforced our convictions* that Joseph was a virtuous man and *a true prophet* of the living God."[23] Like Book of Mormon apologetics, by attempting to defend or prove religious claims the Haleses here are trying to get the scholarship to say more than it can know.

---

22. Phillips, *Religion and Friendly Fire*, 91; emphasis added.

23. Brian C. Hales and Laura H. Hales, *Joseph Smith's Polygamy: Toward a Better Understanding* (Salt Lake City: Greg Kofford Books, 2015), xvii. As the editor for their volume, I am of course biased, but I nevertheless find their scholarship and arguments about Joseph Smith's practice of polygamy to be quite convincing.

While historical research may know whether or not Joseph had sex with this or that woman, it can know nothing of whether Joseph was a prophet of God. What if, despite their excellent research, new and undeniable evidence was discovered that Joseph Smith had, in fact, acted in a way that the Haleses would view as sexually immoral? For example, what if a handwritten note by Joseph Smith was discovered where he explicitly says that his relationship with Fanny Alger had begun as an affair, that he had consummated his marriage with the fourteen-year-old Helen Mar Kimball, or that he participated in sexual polyandry with one of his wives? My guess is that they would say that Joseph was a prophet of God regardless. Why? Because this is a religious claim that had been revealed to them by God and would be true to them regardless of Smith's imperfect morality. Joseph Smith was human and capable of sinning like all the rest of us; after all, some of our most beautiful and religiously poignant scriptures are psalms written by a polygamous adulterer (David) who had another man killed to cover up his affair with (or possible rape of) that man's wife.

By saying that religious claims are not the sort of thing to be affirmed or dismissed using scholarship, and that apologists are incorrect in their confused assumption that they can, I am not proposing a religious fideism whereby religious claims are outside the realm of reason or immune from criticism altogether. Religious claims such as Jesus being the Son of God, the Book of Mormon being the word of God, and Joseph Smith being a prophet of God are of a different kind and participate in a different language game from scholarship that has its own rules and measures. Just as one should not judge a book by its cover or determine the deliciousness of a meal by the china it is served on, religious claims should be evaluated on religious terms and not on tangential secular criteria. Religious claims are things of the soul and can only be evaluated and known by the experiences of the soul.

In his *Death and Immortality,* Phillips writes that religious truths or religious pictures, as he calls them there, are

> not established by means of evidence and cannot be overthrown by means of evidence either. That is not to say that they cannot be overthrown [at all]. . . . In what ways can religious pictures lose their hold on people's lives? Does the undeniable fact that they often lose their hold mean that contrary evidence has been found which shows the picture to have been mistaken? . . . A religious picture loses its hold on a person's life because a rival picture wins his allegiance. A tragic event in a person's life may make him unable to respond in the way the religious belief demands. Or a person may bring moral objections

against the religious picture. In such circumstances, the religious picture may be called senseless, but it is important to recognize that that this has little in common with demonstrating the falsity of an empirical proposition. The situation is far more akin to a radical moral disagreement, where one evaluative judgment is brought to bear against another. Again, a person may understand the force of a religious picture and yet not feel that he could live by it.[24]

Compare this with Alma's metaphor for examining religious claims. Speaking to the poor among the Zoramites, he says,

> Now, we will compare the word unto a seed. Now, if ye give place, that a seed may be planted in your heart, behold, if it be a true seed, or a good seed, if ye do not cast it out by your unbelief, that ye will resist the Spirit of the Lord, behold, it will begin to swell within your breasts; and when you feel these swelling motions, ye will begin to say within yourselves—It must needs be that this is a good seed, or that the word is good, for it beginneth to enlarge my soul; yea, it beginneth to enlighten my understanding, yea, it beginneth to be delicious to me. (Alma 32:28)

For Alma, the measure of a religious claim is its deliciousness to the soul, not the authenticity of the china it is served on or the personal hygiene of the chef. While a meal's presentation or preparer may affect the likelihood that someone will give it a fair taste, the test of its quality is, in the end, how it affects your taste buds, belly, and health. By engaging with critics in defending religious claims through scholarship, and by attempting to prove religious claims through empirical tests, apologists are, in effect, declaring that a meal ought to be judged by things other than the meal itself.

For the believer, the Book of Mormon is the word of God because its fruit nourishes her soul. Joseph Smith is a prophet of God because the fruit of his work brings joy to her life. Jesus is the Son of God because his fruit gives her peace, comfort, and life. These are wholly unconnected to the claims of scholarship and the brute facts of archaeology, history, and biblical criticism. By promoting a conceptual confusion of relevance that does not exist, apologists believe they are demolishing and hacking away at potential stumbling blocks of faith. Instead, they are building and placing those very blocks in the paths of struggling believers who may stumble on them and fall.

---

24. D. Z. Phillips, *Death and Immortality* (London: Macmillan, 1970), 72–73, 75.

THIRTEEN

Shifting Intellectual and Religious Paradigms: One Apologist's Journey into Critical Study

David Bokovoy

This is a different type of essay. It's a personal story—a story about my own journey as an apologist. I have chosen to share it here in the hopes that my experiences might prove beneficial to others. I returned home from serving an LDS mission in October of 1992. As much as I loved my mission, I longed for the days when I could devote more time to LDS scholarship. And so, when I returned home, my free time was spent collecting material on LDS doctrine and history. I had only been back for a couple of months when I experienced my first faith crisis.

One day, while looking through BYU's card catalogue on Bruce R. McConkie, I stumbled across a reference to a letter he had written to Mormon Studies scholar Eugene England. According to the catalogue, this was a letter that discussed Brigham Young's "Adam-God Theory." I had to have it. So I walked up the stairs to BYU's Special Collection's office and asked for a Xerox copy. At first, the woman behind the desk hesitated. "I'm not sure I can give that to you," she said. "Let me check." I wasn't afraid of this letter. I knew everything about the Adam-God Theory. By this time I had read most of Brigham Young's sermons from the *Journal of Discourses* and I had practically memorized what Elder McConkie had said concerning the matter in his book *Mormon Doctrine*. I simply wanted a copy because I was collecting everything I could from Elder McConkie. A few minutes later the woman returned with a copy and a concerned look on her face. "Here you go," she said.

I immediately sat down and began to read. And what I read shocked and upset me. In that now infamous letter, Elder McConkie acknowledged to Professor England that in fact Brigham Young *did* teach the Adam-God Theory, but that President Young was wrong. This was shocking! Not only was I bothered that a prophet of God believed that Adam was our Father in Heaven, I was upset that my hero, Elder McConkie, had officially denied in print that the idea was ever taught—he had gone so far as to call those who said otherwise "cultists" and "enemies of the restored Church." I was deeply upset, and yet, I had enjoyed powerful spiritual experiences through my Mormon faith. As I pondered this newfound reality, I realized that if I was going to continue my passion for scholarship, I would need to constantly shift my paradigms of belief to reconcile with new information.

At this time in my life, I was only interested in Mormon scholarship. In fact, my interests were even more specific. I was only concerned with things that General Authorities of the LDS Church had said about our scriptures, doctrine, and history. The McConkie letter changed all that. I began to read what LDS scholars had said about various topics, and I began to study Hebrew so that I could read the Old Testament in its original languages. By the end of my final year at BYU, I had taken two years of Biblical Hebrew, but I still had never read anything that a non-LDS scholar had ever written about the Bible. Then one day, I was perusing the shelves in the BYU bookstore when I stumbled across a copy of Robert Alter's *The Art of Biblical Narrative*. I picked it up and began to read, and what I read I found captivating. I couldn't put it down. And then I couldn't stop. I would read everything I could get my hands on that explored the topic of biblical studies. This led to a desire to pursue graduate work in the Hebrew Bible (the academic term for the Christian Old Testament) at Brandeis University, a non-sectarian Jewish institution with a famous program in Bible and the Ancient Near East. I had my heart completely set on Brandeis, and so foolishly, it was the only school I applied to.

I remember when the acceptance letter came my wife and I could hardly contain our excitement—jumping up and down together in our little married-student apartment. Studying at Brandeis for my MA and PhD was a life-changing experience—for which I feel truly grateful. But before my wife and I loaded up our moving van with our two young daughters for the trek east, I received some important counsel from two of my BYU professors. One of my teachers pulled me aside and said, "David, you may wish to rethink going to Brandeis." "Well, it's a little late in the game for that," I thought.

Shifting Intellectual and Religious Paradigms 225

Then the professor explained,

> At Brandeis, you'll be studying with an excommunicated Latter-day Saint, the only non-Jew Brandeis has ever had as a full-time faculty member in their Near Eastern and Judaic Studies program. He would never be unkind to you, but the fact that he teaches there is indication of how critical their program in Hebrew Bible must be, and as a believing Latter-day Saint, you simply won't feel comfortable with the academic material you'll be forced to study.

Even though I already knew all of this, I was still surprised to hear him make this assertion. My response was direct: "Thank you for your concern," I said. "I just really want to understand the way biblical scholars interpret the Bible in its historical setting. But don't worry, I'll never buy into a model like the Documentary Hypothesis." (I knew that this was a big concern for the professor.)

Despite the fact that I had majored in history, minored in Near Eastern studies, and had taken every Biblical Hebrew course I could, at that point my knowledge of academic theories concerning the historical development of the Bible was extremely limited. The topic had never been addressed in any of my courses. I had read a couple of articles on my own, and I knew what the Documentary Hypothesis was—that it is an academic theory for how the first five books of the Bible developed—but I didn't believe. Still, I was curious and wanted to pursue a historical analysis of the text and enhance my understanding of Biblical Hebrew, so Brandeis felt like the perfect fit. And it was.

Later, however, another well-meaning professor came to me and said,

> I think it's wonderful that you're going to Brandeis. But don't focus on Bible. Because we've yet to have a Latter-day Saint pass through an academic program on the Bible and retain his or her testimony. Instead, choose an ancillary Near Eastern topic such as Assyriology, Comparative Semitics, Canaanite Languages, or even Egyptology. But whatever you do, don't do Bible.

I've come to realize that my undergraduate alma mater is not unique in encouraging this approach. It's been the one that conservative divinity school programs have adopted for many years. Traditionally-minded scholars will often head off to graduate programs and study Egyptology, Comparative Semitics, Second-Temple Literature, or even the History of Interpretation in order to avoid dealing directly with scripture. They'll then return to their respective faith communities as experts in "Bible." Those like myself who do choose to study Bible often (but not always) lose their faith.

But I dismissed this advice as well. I loved these other topics, but mainly, I wanted to study the Bible. I assumed that I would be able to use my studies as an apologist for the LDS Church. And at first I did.¹ In those early days, I honestly had no intention of personally adopting critical approaches to the development of scriptural sources. I knew enough to know that they were incompatible with the traditional models I embraced. But my quick dismissal expressed through the words, "I'll never buy into a model like the Documentary Hypothesis," didn't last long. In fact, despite my deep religious convictions, it only took a couple of weeks at looking seriously at biblical legal collections for the first time in my life before I realized that if I was going to make sense of this material, I had to allow for separate contradictory scribal traditions. And once I made that allowance, everything—*everything*—began to change. I found that the best way I could make sense of the material in the Pentateuch was allowing for separate documentary sources (in other words, the Documentary Hypothesis).

I'll admit that this was, perhaps, a bit difficult, but not as much as it might seem. I had already come to terms with the fact that in my quest for knowledge I would have to change paradigms in order to make sense of my religious convictions. And the challenge of factoring in my new observations

---

1. Examples include David Bokovoy, "From Distance to Proximity: A Poetic Function of Enallage in the Hebrew Bible and the Book of Mormon," *The Journal of Book of Mormon Studies* 9 (2000); David Bokovoy, "Inverted Quotations in the Book of Mormon," *FARMS: Update* 20, no. 8; David Bokovoy, "Altars as a Place of Deliverance," *FARMS: Update* 21, no. 2; David Bokovoy, "The Calling of Isaiah," *Covenants, Hymns, and Prophecies of the Old Testament* (Salt Lake City: Deseret Book, 2001); David Bokovoy, "Love vs. Hate: Covenant Language in the Book of Mormon," *FARMS: Update* 21, no. 7; David Bokovoy, "Book Review: *Jews and Mormons: Two Houses of Israel*, by Frank L. Johnson and Rabbi William J. Leffler," *BYU Studies* 41, no. 4 (2002), 121–24; David Bokovoy, "Let Us Be Strong," *FARMS: Update* 22, no. 9 (2002); David Bokovoy and John A. Tvedtnes, *Testaments: Links Between the Book of Mormon and the Hebrew Bible* (Tooele, Utah: Heritage Press, 2003); David Bokovoy, "Repetitive Resumption in the Book of Mormon," *FARMS: Update*, no. 182 (2007); David Bokovoy, "The Bible vs. the Book of Mormon: Still Losing the Battle," *FARMS Review* 18, no. 1 (2006): 3–19; David Bokovoy, "Ye Really Are Gods: A Response to Michael Heiser Concerning the LDS Use of Psalm 82 and the Gospel of John," *FARMS Review* 19, no. 1 (2007): 221–66; David Bokovoy, "Zarahemla: Revisiting the Seed of Compassion," *Insights* 30, no. 5 (2010); David Bokovoy, "On Christ and Covenants: An LDS Reading of Isaiah's Prophetic Call," *Studies in the Bible and Antiquity* 3 (2011): 29–49; David Bokovoy, "'Thou Knowest That I Believe': Invoking the Spirit of the Lord as Council Witness in 1 Nephi 11," *Interpreter: A Journal of Mormon Scripture* 1 (2012): 1–23.

into my religious views was countered by the excitement I experienced that for the first time in my life, the Bible was actually making sense. By adopting a critical model, books that I had always struggled to comprehend—books like Isaiah, for instance—were becoming clear, and this, I admit, was *very* exciting. I became, you might say, a true convert to critical analysis.

At this point in my life, I have come to believe that a critical approach to scripture is, in fact, an essential part of a spiritual journey. This perhaps explains my concern with contemporary apologetics, meaning an active attempt to defend a specific religious paradigm or belief system. As religious people, I do not think we should strive to force scripture (or our understanding of LDS doctrine or history for that matter) to match our expectations, whatever they may be. I don't believe that coercing our history and our scriptural texts to fit our traditional beliefs constitutes an act of faith. In fact, from my perspective, doing so is just the opposite.

Apologetics assumes that we *have* the answers. Instead of allowing critical thinking to shape our relationship and understanding with divinity, apologetic defense may simply disguise a fear that God and the universe are much more complex than we would like to believe. It doesn't take too much understanding of history to recognize that religious paradigms (including LDS doctrines and approaches to scripture) exist in a perpetual state of flux—always evolving, always changing.[2] Apologetics, therefore, may be evidence that we don't really trust God's ability to grant further light and knowledge. From this angle, failing to allow critical thinking to enhance our understanding of scripture creates a barrier to true faith.

Today, I'm not entirely opposed to apologetics, but I think we need to recognize that this effort, though no doubt often well intended, can prove stifling to our spiritual journey and pursuit of truth. We must allow room for contradiction, and fortunately for Mormons, our scriptural heritage encourages us to do so.

In his recent Oxford University Press study, David F. Holland shares a profound observation concerning the great scriptural paradox within the Book of Mormon:

> The Book of Mormon itself reinforces the message that when heavenly light mixes with human messengers, God's treasure is to be found in earthly vessels. It repeatedly warns its readers not to discard the things of God because of the flaws of men (Morm. 9:31). . . . The notion that later generations

---

2. For a discussion of changing doctrines, see Charles Harrell, *"This Is My Doctrine": The Development of Mormon Theology* (Salt Lake City: Greg Kofford Books, 2010).

may improve upon the scriptural text—even be "wiser" than its inspired authors—brings the Book of Mormon closer to the most radical elements of America's emerging culture of biblical criticism than to its long tradition of biblical conservatism.

And yet, in contrast to the critical approach, the Mormons' canonical culture did not invite individuals to try to separate the wheat from the chaff, to personally determine what had to be obeyed from what might be discarded. Scripture was to be engaged holistically. The same Book of Mormon prophet who offered three statements of the book's flaws also insisted that "God will shew unto you, that that which I have written is true." The foundational documents of Mormonism taught that God could reveal the divine authority of both flawed men and imperfect scripture.[3]

This is a significant observation. Yet, I have come to the conclusion that I would probably take the same observation Holland makes in a different direction. It seems to me that the Book of Mormon literally begs its readers to adopt a critical approach to scripture by separating the "wheat from the chaff." True, the text should be taken "holistically" as the inspired word of God, but I believe that readers are being invited to judge those words and determine what is divine and what is flesh. The same would be true for doctrines, policies, and historical analysis. It seems Joseph Smith himself models this approach when on the one hand, he identifies the Bible as the "word of God," yet on the other, he seems to have believed that the Song of Solomon is not inspired.

The Book of Mormon repeatedly warns its readers that scripture should not be interpreted unintelligently. Amongst other points, to me, this means that there is simply no need within Mormonism to adopt an anti-intellectual approach to questions of historicity. To be honest, this has from my perspective often been the case with a significant portion of LDS apologetics. And yet, to quote LDS Apostle Russell M. Nelson, when it comes to the Book of Mormon (and no doubt the same could be said for the Bible), "*historical* aspects of the book assume *secondary* significance."[4] They should not distract from the book's spiritual message.

This view accords with the way ancient biblical authors viewed sacred literature, a point that has been well articulated by Marc Brettler, a criti-

---

3. David F. Holland, *Sacred Borders: Continuing Revelation and Canonical Restraint in Early America* (Oxford: Oxford University Press, 2011), 155–56.

4. Russell M. Nelson, "A Testimony of the Book of Mormon," *Ensign*, November 1999, available at https://www.lds.org/ensign/1999/11/a-testimony-of-the-book-of-mormon; emphasis in original.

cal Bible scholar I had the privilege to study with—a man who remains deeply committed to his religious community. Brettler writes:

> Historical traditions, namely, narratives that depict a past, were often treated in the biblical period as "clay in the hands of the potter" (Jer. 18:4, 6). The book of Chronicles is a creative revision of Genesis–Kings, especially Samuel to Kings, and Deuteronomy often revises narratives found in earlier sources in the Torah. This suggests that the earlier historical sources were seen as flexible rather than absolutely true. Similarly, the fact that non-Torah texts disagree with historical traditions found in the Torah—for example, the many disagreements between the plague narrative in Exodus and in Psalms 78 and 105—implies a malleable view of history.
>
> This is because in ancient Israel, as in other premodern societies, the facts themselves or the historical events were not primary—what could be learned from the stories was primary. This explains, in part, why the classical rabbis were so playful in their engagement with the biblical text, rewriting it so extensively and creatively. Even more drastically, this focus on lessons rather than facts may suggest that Job was a character in a parable (*mashal*) rather than a historical figure—as a narrative of the actual past the text was not paramount.[5]

This perspective, that the Bible lacks "historicity," is not a problem within Judaism, and it should never be an issue for Latter-day Saints.

From start to finish, the Book of Mormon presents readers with a fascinating paradox. On the one hand, the book itself is a miracle and is defined by Joseph Smith as "the most correct" book ever written, since a person can "get nearer to God by abiding by its precepts, than by any other book."[6] And yet, Book of Mormon authors constantly refer to the text's inherent weakness. It is as if the Book of Mormon personifies John's New Testament depiction of the Word of God, which is both divine and made flesh.

The Book of Mormon, therefore, presents a profound theological construct concerning scripture and the nature of revelatory text. Human beings have always had an influence on the development of sacred literature. Hence, allowing for human agency in the production of scripture creates an analogy with Jesus Christ himself—i.e., the "Word of God":

---

5. Marc Zvi Brettler, "My Bible: A Jewish Perspective," in *The Bible and the Believer: How to Read the Bible Critically and Religiously*, ed. Marc Zvi Brettler, Peter Enns, and Daniel J. Harrington (Oxford: Oxford University Press, 2012), 52.

6. Joseph Smith, et al., *History of the Church of Jesus Christ of Latter-day Saints*, ed. B. H. Roberts, 7 vols., 2nd ed. rev. (Salt Lake City: Deseret Book, 1948 printing), 4:461.

In the beginning was the Word, and the Word was with God, and the Word was God.... And the Word was made flesh, and dwelt among us, (and we beheld his glory, the glory as of the only begotten of the Father,) full of grace and truth." (John 1:1, 14)

Like Jesus himself, the Book of Mormon seems to teach that scripture is a divine word made flesh among us. Evangelical scholar Peter Enns expresses the analogy this way:

> As Christ is both God and human, so is the Bible. In other words, we are to think of the Bible in the same way that Christians think about Jesus. Christians confess that Jesus is both God and human at the same time. He is not half-God and half-human. He is not sometimes one and other times the other. He is not essentially one and only apparently the other.... Jesus is 100 percent God and 100 percent human—at the same time. This way of thinking of Christ is analogous to thinking about the Bible. In the same way that Jesus is—must be—both God and human the Bible is also a divine and human book.[7]

The traditional LDS understanding of the Bible and scripture takes the metaphor of divine word being made flesh even further. As Joseph Smith once explained, Mormons "believe the Bible to be the word of God as far as it is translated correctly" (A of F 8). Implicit with the belief that the Bible contains errors introduced by humans is the belief that there are portions of the Bible that are fully human and cannot be said to be divine. There is error; there is weakness; there is flesh.

Historical Criticism allows Latter-day Saint readers to identify both attributes in the written word. Sacred words must pass through a human filter; there is therefore no such thing as the pure, unadulterated word of God. It is always both human and divine, and this point seems to be one that the Book of Mormon itself practically begs its readers to recognize.

Book of Mormon narrators constantly attest to the fact that they struggled to put into words their spiritual feelings. Moroni refers to this matter through the expression "my weakness in writing" (Ether 12:23, 25, 40). Moreover, fully aware that revelatory insights must always pass through imperfect human vessels, Nephi informs his readers,

> I do not write anything upon plates save it be that I think it be sacred. And now, if I do err, even did they err of old; not that I would excuse myself because of other men, but because of the weakness which is in me, according to the flesh, I would excuse myself. (1 Ne. 19:6)

---

7. Peter Enns, *Inspiration and Incarnation: Evangelicals and the Problem of the Old Testament* (Grand Rapids, Mich.: Maker Academic, 2005), 17–18.

At the conclusion of his record, Nephi returned to this same theme, testifying that despite the weakness of his written record, Christ approved his words:

> And I know that the Lord God will consecrate my prayers for the gain of my people. And the words which I have written in weakness will be made strong unto them; for it persuadeth them to do good; it maketh known unto them of their fathers; and it speaketh of Jesus, and persuadeth them to believe in him, and to endure to the end, which is life eternal. . . . And if they are not the words of Christ, judge ye—for Christ will show unto you, with power and great glory, that they are his words, at the last day; and you and I shall stand face to face before his bar; and ye shall know that I have been commanded of him to write these things, notwithstanding my weakness. (2 Ne. 33:4, 11)

Revelatory insights, no matter how inspired, must always pass through weak human vessels. In this process, mistakes are inevitably made, notwithstanding the sacred nature of religious texts. For this reason, in the title page of the Book of Mormon, Moroni explicitly recognized the possibility of error: "And now, if there are faults they are the mistakes of men; wherefore, condemn not the things of God, that ye may be found spotless at the judgment-seat of Christ."

I believe that Latter-day Saints must allow room for such error as we seek to expand our understanding through revelatory and scholarly insights. I can see no reason, therefore, that a Latter-day Saint should ever adopt an anti-intellectual approach to the apologetic concern of "historicity" and scripture. In fact, from my perspective, the Book of Mormon begs us not to.

I believe we must read scripture critically, evaluating questions of historicity with the tools of academic inquiry. In the process, as we use this material to access divinity, we should learn to separate the wheat from the chaff as part of that religious quest. In fact, according to the Book of Mormon, that may very well be the key to spiritual growth.

As a critical student of the Bible and Mormonism, I'm not entirely opposed to apologetics. But I am opposed to academic apologetics. Simply put, I do not believe that the tools of scholarship can be used to establish the validity of religious experiences. Take for example, the tools of the historian's craft when applied to the Book of Mormon. The historian seeks to uncover the most likely things that occurred in the past. By definition, a miracle is the most unlikely thing to occur—that's what *makes* it a miracle. If historians are trying to uncover what is *most* likely to have happened in the past, and a miracle is the most unlikely thing to have occurred, historians can never take seriously such miraculous things as golden plates or resurrection. These things may be true, but they are beyond the ability of a historian to address. They are matters of religious belief.

The historicity of scripture is not a matter of faith. It is an issue of critical analysis and academic inquiry. On the other hand, the inspiration of scripture, meaning its ability to assist readers access divinity, can never be a matter of critical analysis and academic inquiry. Instead, much like beauty, inspiration is found in the eye of the beholder. Therefore, while critical analysis and academic investigation can enhance faith, they need not destroy it.

Speaking personally, I strongly resonate with the position articulated by the Jewish scholar of philosophy Samuel Fleischacker in his book *Divine Teaching and the Way of the World: A Defense of Revealed Religion*. Defending revelation, Fleischacker declares:

> There can, accordingly, never be scientific evidence that a revelation has taken place. Scientific evidence establishes empirical facts: facts within nature. Revelation discloses a realm or entity beyond nature. . . . Whether an event or text is revelatory or not depends, rather, on how it appears to those inclined to have faith in it. And it is ethical, not empirical evidence that draws the commitment of religious believers.[8]

Fleischacker also observes:

> To make room for revelation we need to make sense of what it might mean for a truth to come from something more radically outside ourselves, more radically different from any aspect of who we are: "Other" to us, in contemporary jargon.[9]

An apologist who uses empirical facts to create a case for his religious convictions is fighting a losing battle. I believe apologetics, therefore, is best performed by simply demonstrating to others the spiritual benefits to living a religious life. Within the LDS tradition, this is especially necessary for those who encounter critical studies of the Bible and Mormonism. Given the nature of the inquiry, academic arguments in support of Mormonism will never be as strong as their secular counterpoints. Apologetics cannot be used to defend the historicity of LDS scripture.

It's not uncommon for religious believers who engage in critical analysis to feel lost—to question whether they can continue to find spiritual value in texts that do not live up to their traditionally held beliefs. Trying

---

8. Samuel Fleischacker, *Divine Teaching and the Way of the World: A Defense of Revealed Religion* (Oxford: Oxford University Press, 2011), 281.

9. Ibid., 303.

to answer this question when a person's worldview begins to change can be a painful process. The answer is highly personal; it will inevitably differ for each individual. But it is possible to discover great spiritual value in adopting a critical approach to scripture, even when that view requires believers to alter their religious paradigms.

Despite its religious merits, scripture should not be seen as an infallible manual to divinity. Instead, scripture is the textual result of a human effort to reflect the divine. Though inevitably flawed by mortal hands, that endeavor can inspire meaningful spiritual growth. This is true even when a reader encounters a construct in holy writ that she rejects, since that problematic paradigm has caused the reader to define her own spiritual conviction in opposition to the one held by the author. Scripture is not a manual. It is a springboard to enlightenment.

If scripture is the word of God then it is the word of God made flesh. We cannot (nor should we) seek to escape the reality that scripture is a human product that, for believers, contains both human and divine qualities.

As a model for this perspective, we might consider the way the author of Matthew presents Jesus's genealogy. Like much of the Bible, the account is strikingly patriarchal. Even though the author insists that Jesus's conception occurred by a female generating a son without a male, Matthew's genealogy depicts fathers begetting sons without females: "Abraham begot Isaac; and Isaac begot Jacob; and Jacob begot Judah and his brothers;" father, son, father, son, etc. But there are exceptions to this pattern. Matthew's genealogy contains four female names and one female designation:

"Judah begot Perez and Zerah from Tamor" (1:3)
"Salmon begot Boaz from Rahab" (1:5a)
"Boaz begot Obed from Ruth" (1:5b)
"David begot Solomon from the wife of Uriah" (1:6)
"Joseph the husband of Mary, from whom Jesus was begotten" (1:16)

The passive nuance in this final line—"from whom Jesus was begotten"—is significant. It means that Jesus was "begotten" by God.

More to the point, Matthew's genealogy mentions only these five females, even though he could have obviously named a woman with each male. Clearly, the author intended to say something meaningful in referencing these four women from Israel's past.

Who are these women? Well, Tamar deceived her father-in-law by pretending to be a harlot. Rahab was a harlot. Ruth uncovered the "feet" (a euphemism for genitals) of the drunken Boaz, and Bathsheba, the wife of Uriah, was involved with an infamous adulterous affair. A sexual aberration of some sort occurred in each of these women's lives, including Mary's. Yet according to Matthew's genealogy, God controlled the lineage of the Messiah through these unusual unions. The list seems to suggest that divinity can work through less than ideal circumstances—a point powerfully articulated by New Testament scholar and Catholic theologian Raymond Brown:

> These women were held up as examples of how God used the unexpected to triumph over human obstacles and intervenes on behalf of His planned Messiah. It is the combination of the scandalous or irregular union and of divine intervention through the woman that explains best Matthew's choice in the genealogy.[10]

According to this paradigm, God is made manifest through a combination of the scandalous and the divine. This same perspective can be adopted to conceptualize scripture (and in fact, all aspects of Mormonism). When a believer in holy writ adopts a critical interpretive approach, this is precisely what she encounters with the written word of God.

In my own journey as an apologist, I have come to believe that critical studies need not produce a spiritual loss. Defining scripture as a human product that is both scandalous and divine can lead to greater heights of spiritual growth. We must not be afraid to pursue academic knowledge that directly challenges our belief. If we are to be apologists, let us be apologists for critical inquiry and the constant need to shift intellectual and religious paradigms.

---

10. Raymond E. Brown, *The Birth of the Messiah: A Commentary on the Infancy Narratives in the Gospels of Matthew and Luke* (New York: Anchor Bible, 1999), 73–74. For an LDS perspective on these women in Matthew's genealogy of Jesus, see Julie M. Smith's essay, "Why These Women in Jesus's Genealogy?" in her *Search, Ponder, and Pray: A Guide to the Gospels* (Salt Lake City: Greg Kofford Books, 2014), 255–59.

FOURTEEN

Toward a New Vision of Apologetics

Joseph M. Spencer

In an 1831 revelation, the Lord announced his will that the Saints "should overcome the world" (D&C 64:2). The chief evidence that the world was overcoming the Saints rather than vice versa was that, like the Lord's "disciples in days of old," they "sought occasion against one another and forgave not one another in their hearts" (D&C 64:8). To reverse this situation, the Lord pointed out to them a duty and a requirement: "[Y]e ought to forgive one another; . . . of you it is required to forgive all men" (D&C 64:9–10). I take it as granted that this text remains relevant and binding. We share the same obligation to overcome the world, but we likewise fail to do so because we seek occasion against one another; the way forward lies in fulfilling our duty to forgive. As an academic dedicated to the intellectual investigation of Mormonism, I am often struck by how much occasion-seeking and how little forgiving can be said to go on in the corner of the Lord's vineyard where I do so much of my work. I fear that the world overcomes us much more than we ever overcome the world.

The worst of it, I think, grows out of the acrimony between so-called "conservatives" and so-called "liberals." The latter accuse the former of a kind of intellectual backwardness, of using shoddy intellectual tools to protect the borders around an ill-defined orthodoxy in an unnecessarily reactionary way. The former accuse the latter of a kind of intellectual shallowness, of following flighty but fashionable intellectual movements to erase the tried and true boundaries established by divinely called prophets. Both camps seek occasion against each other, too vigilantly on the watch for good opportunities to reveal the failings of their opponents. What strikes me as I watch this war progress, however, is how hard those involved work to convince themselves that their differences are real and important. From where I stand, watching, all involved seem to me not only to agree on more than they realize, but also—somewhat paradoxically, perhaps—to agree on too much. All the most important questions seem to me to go unanswered, unasked even, while a war of remarkable intensity rages over the least interesting and least pressing questions of all.

Among the questions that go unasked is this: *What is apologetics?* Infinitely more has been said among intellectually-inclined Latter-day Saints about *whether* or *why* apologetics should or should not be done—endless conversations about its virtues or its dangers, its valiance or its blindness—than about *what* apologetics actually is. As I watch the fighting, I find myself wanting to shout to everyone involved a line from Plato's *Sophist*, albeit replacing the word "being" with the word "apologetics": "Then clarify this for us, since we're confused about it. What do you want to signify when you say 'apologetics'? Obviously you've known for a long time. We thought we did, but now we're confused about it."[1] In short, I find that the war of words and tumult of opinions concerning the status of apologetics serves the Mormon intellectual community as a means more of avoiding than of answering essential questions.

In the pages that follow, I want to ask and to provide a preliminary answer to at least this one essential question: *What is apologetics?* As a theologian with a prescriptive streak, I aim here to outline what apologetics ought to be, ideally or according to its idea. I certainly take for granted that Latter-day Saints have a real duty to defend the Restoration, and to do so intellectually wherever necessary. I am convinced, however, that most all of our apologetic work fails to achieve the ideal form of executing that duty. If my reflections here contribute in any way to our working collectively to do things better, I would be thrilled. If they serve only to reveal to us what we all need forgiveness for, that too would be a success.

What Is Apologetics?

The same 1831 revelation to Joseph Smith I have already mentioned distinguishes an important passage between the "heart" and the "mind," stating that the Lord requires both from those who would "eat the good of the land of Zion in these last days" (D&C 64:34). The coupling of mind and heart, built on an apparent distinction between them, appears throughout the Doctrine and Covenants. Those who would serve God

---

1. Plato, *Sophist*, 244a. I have taken this translation from John M. Cooper, ed., *Plato: Complete Works* (Indianapolis: Hackett Publishing, 1997), 265.

should do so with both heart and mind (see D&C 4:2); the very "spirit of revelation" comes when the Lord speaks in mind and heart (D&C 8:2–3); truths are to be treasured in the heart as they rest on the mind (see D&C 43:34); the law of consecration requires the Saints to act both "with one mind" and "with one heart" (D&C 45:65); and the Lord prepares the way for the Church by softening the hearts and changing the minds of those who threaten it (see D&C 104:81). This coupling of distinct—if not often opposed—elements of human being seems to lie at the heart of apologetics, however we approach it. Placing herself under the constraints of reason but refusing to abandon the convictions that come through revelation, the apologist attempts to wed mind and heart. More, the apologist aims ultimately to speak to the heart of those she addresses, but her resources for doing so are limited to what can be communicated between minds.

The complex relationship between the mind and the heart, lying at the heart of apologetics, has received an illuminating analysis in a 1978 essay by the Catholic philosopher Jean-Luc Marion.[2] The difficulty experienced by every person who speaks mind to mind in the hope of seeing another's heart touched as one's own is this: "Only the will can allow itself to be convinced, and all constraint of reason by reasons remains totally heterogeneous to it, remains on the threshold and decides nothing."[3] The heart never loves simply because the mind has reasons. The heart loves on its own terms, develops genuine convictions only on its own terms. Even if reason plays some role in softening someone's heart, genuine conviction is of another order. Indeed, conviction comes into its own only when it can continue in conviction despite there being reasons that would constrain it to follow other directions. The heart's convictions can never be equated with the constraints reason imposes on the mind.

This much, it seems to me, every conception of apologetics accounts for. Although one sometimes hears it said that apologists attempt to prove the truth of the Restoration, I see little of that actually on offer in apologetic literature. The vast majority of apologists—even apologists who are bad

---

2. For the full essay, see Jean-Luc Marion, "Evidence and Bedazzlement," in *Prolegomena to Charity*, trans. Stephen Lewis (New York: Fordham University Press, 2002), 53–70. Marion provides what might be the best summary of the debate between "conservatives" and "liberals" in the Mormon intellectual community: "Apologetics . . . attempts to gain Christ's admittance (at the risk of the Christian's being poorly received), while nonapologetics . . . tries to gain the Christian's reception (at the price, sometimes, of Christ's not being admitted)" (p. 54).

3. Ibid., 58.

at what they do—recognize that their intellectual defenses of Mormonism can only go so far, that there remains after every argument a certain leap to be made with one's heart. After all, as James says in the New Testament, "the devils also believe, and tremble" (James 2:19). Signs follow faith, but faith does not follow signs. All this we seem to recognize readily.

Consequently, to answer the question of what exactly apologetics is ideally, one must go beyond just the distinction between mind and heart. To clarify the nature of apologetics, one must say something about *how* heart and mind interact in the apologetic enterprise. If apologetics takes as its aim to produce conviction in the heart of another, even as it universally recognizes that it cannot do so directly, then at issue in every conception of apologetics is a certain account of the *indirection* of promoting nonrational conviction by rational argument. In other words, what distinguishes differing accounts of what ideally constitutes apologetics is the different ways in which they conceive of *the indirect manner in which reason makes for the possibility of revelation*. What are the varieties of indirect relationships one might conceive between the constraints of reason and the convictions of the heart, as these operate in apologetics? And which of these varieties provides us with apologetics in the most proper sense?

Before rendering any judgments, let me begin by outlining two common varieties of apologetics. According to a first, minimalist conception, the good reasons or good reasonings and the apologist serve only to undercut the bad reasons or bad reasonings of Mormonism's critics, criticisms likely offered in bad faith or with malicious intent. This first approach to apologetics, in other words, sees as the apologist's task to reveal the ways in which arguments against the truth of the Restoration begin from faulty evidence, misrepresent history and beliefs, refuse to entertain real possibilities, employ fallacious reasoning, or otherwise unfairly attack Latter-day Saint claims. The aim is to bring the contest regarding the truth of the Restoration back onto an even playing field by insisting that critics be fully honest in their presentation of relevant data. The minimalist aims just at keeping everyone honest so that the sheer *possibility* of the Restoration's faith claims can be recognized. Once that is achieved thanks to reason's constraining power, she ceases her strictly apologetic work, either exchanging the mind for the heart by bearing her own testimony or leaving to the Spirit to do the work of promoting conviction. The indirect work of apologetic reason amounts, on this conception, to clearing the ground so that revelation might be unhindered but in no way forced.

Toward a New Vision of Apologetics

A second variety of apologetics goes further. Here the apologist accomplishes her work by constructing positive rational arguments for the truth of the Restoration, rather than always and only aiming negatively to undercut the arguments of its critics. Happy to have an even playing field or even to get to work without leveling the field, this second sort of apologist joins the actual contest—and she does so eagerly, convinced that there are evidences for Mormonism's truth. She might turn to aspects of Mormon scriptural texts that arguably lay beyond the capacities of a New York farm kid, or she might turn to the philosophical usefulness of Mormonism's most audacious theological claims, or she might turn to moments in Mormon history that suggest a remarkable sense of prophetic insight. Whatever resources she determines to be most useful, she brings them together to make a reason-based case for the likelihood of the truth of the Restoration. Here, then, the aim is to move beyond establishing just the *possibility* of the Restoration's truth to establishing its *plausibility*. In a way, this approach to apologetics assumes that reason can go somewhat further toward promoting conviction than the first approach does, because it presupposes the possibility of predisposing its readers and listeners to the likelihood that Mormonism's claims are true. But apologists of this second sort almost universally recognize that reason still can go only so far. Having established plausibility, they too cease their apologetic efforts and exchange the resources of the mind for the resources of the heart, turning from argument to testimony.

Whatever real differences distinguish these first two conceptions of apologetics, they share an understanding of how the mind operates indirectly in favor of the heart in apologetic work. Although the first aims minimally at establishing possibility and the latter aims more robustly at establishing plausibility, both understand the task of apologetics to be to create, through the resources of the mind, *favorable conditions* for developing conviction in the heart. Largely due to this shared understanding of how the mind and the heart relate to one another in apologetics, these first two varieties often appear together, woven into each other in so-called "traditional" apologetics. As often as not, these first two approaches succeed one another in apologetic efforts: first the clearing of the ground through a counter-critique of criticisms leveled against the Restoration, and then the construction on that cleared ground of a battery of positive arguments for the Restoration; first the establishment of possibility, then the establishment of plausibility. At both levels or in both stages, one understands the apologetic task to achieve its purpose in creating favorable conditions for the development of abiding conviction—without, however, wrongfully attempting to force such conviction.

The picture just presented, it seems to me, adequately portrays the going conception of apologetics. Not only do many apologists seem to embrace or even to promote it (against the evidence of their best work), most critics of apologetics embrace or even promote it. So far as I can tell, too many of those arguing about whether apologetics deserves praise or blame would paint this same picture. It is in this sense that, on my view, those involved in the conversation agree about too much. The debate regarding apologetics overlooks a rather different conception of the task, a rather different conception of what constitutes the aim of the apologetic enterprise, a rather different conception of the indirect relationship therein between mind and heart.

What needs calling into question, it seems to me, is the very idea that the Restoration needs or even wants favorable conditions for the development of genuine conviction regarding its truth. The apostle Paul said that "it pleased God by the foolishness of preaching to save them that believe" (1 Cor. 1:21), arguing that God intervenes in the world by erecting a barrier against belief. The Restoration, like the Gospel it revitalizes and announces anew, is meant to present a kind of scandal or a stumbling block to the world. Whatever makes belief *easier* makes belief *weaker*, suggesting that what faith requires amounts to less and less. Paradoxically, the more reason does to create favorable conditions for the development of conviction, the less forceful and passionate conviction will usually be when revelation has its way. Thus the constant temptation that attends apologetics, its all-too-natural tendency against which it must ideally work, is precisely to minimize the scandalous nature of the Restoration by attempting to create favorable conditions for developing spiritual conviction. But as Marion says in the same essay cited above, the task of apologetics is paradoxically "*to reinforce* the difficulty" of decision in favor of truth.[4]

All this might sound rather ridiculous, as if I were suggesting that the real task of apologetics is to make it impossible for people to believe and then to leave them to wallow in confusion and doubt until God sees fit to fill them with understanding, against all odds. I mean no such thing, however. I fully recognize that there is useful and even necessary work to do in cutting down ridiculous arguments against and misrepresentations of Mormonism, just as there is useful and even necessary work to do in con-

---

4. Ibid., 62; emphasis in original.

structing positive rational arguments for the likelihood of the Restoration's truth claims. What I mean to suggest is that all such apologetic work must aim (in Marion's words once more) at "settling as quickly and as well as possible the theoretical debate" only so as to "*indicate the place where the decision of the will must intervene*, so that the will might know what it must, without avoidance, accept or refuse, and above all that the will might know the One whom it must repudiate or confess."[5] In other words, I have little to criticize in the usual *methods* employed in apologetics, described above. I mean rather to critique the *aim* with which apologists tend to use those methods. The point of clearing away bad arguments and false representations is, ideally, to bring into real clarity what faith in the Restoration requires, not to undercut the credibility of the critics. The point of constructing rational arguments for the truth of Mormonism's faith claims is to reveal the coherence and richness of faith in the Restoration, not to predispose people to actual conviction regarding its truth. Apologetics achieves its ideal when *it wears itself out in making the stakes of the Restoration fully clear*. That ideal can only be compromised where one works only or primarily to make conditions for developing conviction favorable.

Here, then, is a rather different conception of the indirect relationship between the mind and the heart in the work of apologetics. The apologist ideally mobilizes the resources of the intellect in order to make perfectly clear the scandal of the Restoration, cutting away misrepresentations that would make faith into something other than what it is, critiquing arguments that would leave faith emaciated, constructing a rich portrait of the life of faith so that one knows what one is called to, developing in full the remarkable fortitude that genuine conviction requires. Where, instead, one attempts to lessen the burden of belief, to veil the scandal of faith, to widen the road that leads to eternal life, or to remove the stumbling block divinely placed in our paths, one compromises the apologetic task. Apologetics should not resolve crises of faith but provoke them, helping those who stumble to recognize that they are likely stumbling for the first time in their lives on the *real* because of the *robust* faith to which conviction would commit them. Apologetics fails when it instead attempts to solve doubts too quickly. Apologetics ideally poses a problem—the central and *only* problem, that of whether and how God has intervened in history to accomplish a divine work—rather than answers questions. Apologetics

---

5. Ibid.; emphasis added.

ideally seeks, in fact, to reveal that our reasonable questions are usually asked in an attempt to avoid this one problem.

All this might sound fine—or perhaps horrendous!—in the abstract. To make fully concrete what I am here proposing, however, I would like to conclude this essay by using an example of two different approaches to a single—and well-known—objection to Mormonism's truth claims. I hope it helps to make perfectly clear what I am after here.

What Does Apologetics Look Like?

Believers in the Book of Mormon are inevitably acquainted with Revelation 22:18–19:

> For I testify unto every man that heareth the words of the prophecy of this book, If any man shall add unto these things, God shall add unto him the plagues that are written in this book: And if any man shall take away from the words of the book of this prophecy, God shall take away his part out of the book of life, and out of the holy city, and *from* the things which are written in this book.

For as long as the Book of Mormon has been in circulation, this passage has been presented to defenders of the book as biblical warrant for its wholesale rejection. In the very last words of the Christian Bible, a warning sounds: *Do not add anything to God's word—especially a whole volume!*

Most Latter-day Saints are familiar with standard apologetic responses to this objection. Defenders of the faith point out (1) that the author of Revelation clearly had reference, in context, just to his own prophecy—*not* to the Christian Bible as a whole; (2) that Revelation was likely not the last book written among those included in the New Testament, such that the objection would work against parts of the New Testament as much as against the Book of Mormon; or (3) that a similar passage can be found in the Hebrew Bible (see Deuteronomy 4:2), such that Jews might make the very same criticism of the whole of the New Testament that Christians make against Latter-day Saints. These are entirely accurate and largely effective responses. The difficulty, however, is that they serve only to undercut the credibility of the criticism or of the critics who make it. These responses do nothing to reveal the real stakes of believing the Book of Mormon to be true.

Strikingly, canonical Mormon texts arguably take this criticism more seriously than do the apologetic responses provided just above. An early revelation to Joseph Smith—now canonized as Section 20 of the Doctrine and Covenants—contains a lengthy passage concerning what Latter-day Saints "know" thanks to the Book of Mormon (D&C 20:17). As this passage comes to its conclusion, it alludes to Revelation 22:18–19:

> And we know that these things are true and agreeable to the revelations of Jesus Christ which was signified by his angel unto John, neither adding nor diminishing to the prophecy of his book; neither to the holy scriptures; neither to the revelations of God which shall come hereafter by the gift and power of the Holy Ghost, neither by the voice of God, neither by the ministering of angels. And the Lord God hath spoken it—and honor, power, and glory be rendered to his holy name both now and ever.—Amen.[6]

This is a complex passage, but its reference to Revelation 22:18–19 is unmistakable. Apparently, no skeptical outsider is needed to raise the potential objection that the Book of Mormon runs into trouble with Revelation's warning. Mormonism's own scriptures *themselves* note the potential objection and offer a response to it, making clear at the very least the possibility that the scope of Revelation 22:18–19 should be limited to "the prophecy of his [John's] book."

This might sound at first like one of the usual apologetic responses mentioned above. But I hear something more at work here than that. Note how the passage from the Doctrine and Covenants picks up on the language employed in Revelation 22:18–19: "the *prophecy* of this book." This wording, original to the New Testament passage, suggests that what is essential and therefore unrevisable according to Revelation 22:18–19 is not the *biblical text* (whether in general or even with special reference to John's book), but rather *a specific prophecy* the biblical text aims—however imperfectly or perfectly—at promulgating. The Doctrine and Covenants thus arguably claims that there lies behind the written Book of Revelation a prophecy—a specific or specifiable prophecy—that is the real focus of Revelation 22:18–19. It is particularly interesting that this claim appears at the conclusion of a passage outlining what every Latter-day Saint should know from reading the Book of Mormon. It seems clear to me that one of the founding claims of the Book of Mormon concerns just such a prophecy. Developing this point at length will allow for a more strictly ideal apologetic response to the criticism laid out above.

---

6. Michael Hubbard MacKay, et al., eds., *Documents Volume 1: July 1828–June 1831*. Vol. 1 of the Documents series of *The Joseph Smith Papers*, ed. Dean C. Jessee, et al. (Salt Lake City: Church Historian's Press, 2013), 123. This passage, somewhat altered, is now D&C 20:35.

Readers of the Book of Mormon have long recognized that the Revelation to Saint John is relevant to a most remarkable vision contained in Nephi's record (see 1 Nephi 11–14). In that vision, a sweeping historical panorama passes before the young prophet Nephi, stretching from the events surrounding the Messiah's appearance to the final redemption of Israel. At the end of what he records of the vision, Nephi learns that his own experience is entangled with the (then-still-future) Revelation to Saint John. Nephi's angelic guide directs his visionary attention to "one of the twelve apostles of the Lamb" (1 Ne. 14:20), explaining that this person—whose "name . . . was John" (v. 27)—would witness the same vision, but that he would be "ordained" to write out a full account of the experience (v. 25).[7]

But Nephi learns still more about John's written prophecy. The angel tells him this also regarding John and his Book of Revelation:

> The things which he shall write are just and true. And behold, they are written in the book which thou beheld proceeding out of the mouth of the Jew. And at the time they proceeded out of the mouth of the Jew, or at the time the book proceeded out of the mouth of the Jew, the things which were written were plain and pure and most precious and easy to the understanding of all men. (v. 23)

The angel's words here make reference to an earlier sequence in Nephi's apocalyptic vision, a sequence that describes a book "proceeding out of the mouth of the Jew." That earlier sequence presents the book in question (the Christian Bible) as originally containing "the fullness of the gospel of the Lamb, of whom the twelve apostles bare record" (1 Ne. 13:24), appearing at first "in purity" (v. 25). But it *then* presents the same book as having had removed from it (or, more strictly, from "the gospel" it contains) "many parts which are plain and most precious; and also many covenants of the Lord" (v. 26). The phrase the angel uses in describing this perversion of the text is this: "[T]hey have taken away from" (v. 26).

These several pieces might be put together. The Book of Mormon claims (1) that the Revelation to Saint John lies at the heart of the Christian Bible; (2) that the Book of Revelation above all else is what in that Bible goes forth originally in purity—exhibiting the plain and the precious of the covenantal gospel; (3) that the same Book of Revelation above all else is what in that Bible ends up transformed by whatever process is involved

---

7. All quotations from the Book of Mormon are taken from Royal Skousen, ed., *The Book of Mormon: The Earliest Text* (New Haven: Yale University Press, 2009).

in removing the plain, the precious, and the covenantal; and (4) that the process by which that transformation is accomplished is apparently to be described as a taking-away-from.

Assembled into a single picture, we have this: *The Book of Revelation as it has come down to modern Christianity is already the product of the very taking-away-from warned against within that same book.* That proscription is tragically ironic, first because it serves in its canonical form to warn only against what has already happened to the book the integrity of which it is meant to protect, and second because it therefore deceptively seems to warn against restoring to the book what has already devastatingly been removed from it. From the outset, the Book of Mormon seems not only to be aware of the warning in Revelation 22:18–19; it makes an accusation against certain of the transmitters of the book in which that passage appears—namely, that *they* have already transgressed the book's warning, and that they have taken advantage of that warning itself to keep others blind about what they have done in manipulating the book's prophecy!

It is essential, then, to recognize that the same apocalyptic vision of Nephi goes on to claim that the central purpose of the Book of Mormon's emergence in the last days is to *restore* what has been compromised in the Christian Bible's concluding book. Unfortunately, "because of the many plain and precious things which have been taken out of the book, . . . an exceeding great many do stumble" (1 Ne. 13:29). But, the angel tells Nephi, God will not allow people to "forever remain in that state of awful wickedness which . . . they are in because of the plain and most precious parts of the gospel of the Lamb which hath been kept back" (v. 32). And God will overcome the situation by manifesting himself directly to Nephi's children, "that they shall write many things which I shall minister unto them, which shall be plain and precious" (v. 35). The Book of Mormon, by its own account, was prepared in order to bring the prophecy lying behind the Book of Revelation quite fully—and quite purely—to the attention of the world. And it is to do so by restoring what has been—in Revelation 22:18–19's own words—"taken away" from the prophecy of that book.[8]

---

8. The twist, oddly, is that the Book of Mormon does not actually contain the prophecy in question. It contains only dark hints, scattered fragments that cannot be reassembled into a complete prophetic picture. At the same time, the Book of Mormon contains promises of when and how the full prophecy will be given eventually. See 2 Nephi 27:7–8; 3 Nephi 26:11; Ether 4:6–7, 16. These passages deserve close exposition, which will have to await another occasion.

Now, how does what I have outlined here amount to an ideal apologetic response to the criticism that Revelation 22:18–19 warns against accepting something like the Book of Mormon as scripture? Going far beyond merely undercutting the credibility of the critics or their criticism and thereby satisfying itself with having established the possibility of the Restoration's truth, it elaborates at length how much *more* radical the Book of Mormon's claim is than the critics assume. This approach reinforces the difficulty of deciding in favor of the Restoration's truth, since one is now asked not only to believe just that God could and in fact did reveal more than is contained in the Bible, but also and especially to believe that the supposed warning contained in the Bible about adding to it has been manipulated in order to ensure that readers would never attempt to restore to it what has been maliciously taken from it. The conditions for belief are, in a certain way, *less* favorable in light of this apologetic effort—but they are therefore all the more profound and in a certain way all the more inviting. To decide in favor of the Restoration's truth requires much more than it might have seemed to require; one can no longer attempt to embrace the Book of Mormon without at the same time embracing claims regarding the instability of biblical texts. The canon is not *simply* but *radically* open.

Apologetics ideally radicalizes, bringing into the open how much more extreme the faith demanded by the Restoration is than its critics recognize. My own experience has been that the Spirit brings conviction to my heart more powerfully and more lastingly when I encounter the depth of the Restoration, not when I find just that there are reasons to be suspicious about Mormonism's critics or reasons to think Mormonism's claims are rationally defensible. An apologetics fully worthy of the Restoration must be at least as profound as the Restoration itself, and that depth *can* be investigated rationally. To glimpse the richness of the restored gospel is *both* to see the real, reinforced difficulty of developing faith in it *and* to open oneself to the possibility of finding real conviction regarding its truth.

Perhaps the difficulty is not that there has been too much of the apologetic in Mormon intellectual conversations. Perhaps the difficulty is that there has not yet been enough.

FIFTEEN

Apologetics as Theological Praxis

Seth Payne

> The truth is that anyone who keeps being kind is able to soften hearts which are otherwise like iron.
> —John Calvin[1]

Introduction

In 1 Peter 3, the apostle Peter encourages the early Saints to "always be ready to provide a defense to anyone who demands an accounting for the hope that is in you" (1 Pet. 3:15).[2] From this partial verse has sprung a continuous stream of Christian apologetics, beginning with a defense against criticisms of Christianity within Hellenistic culture and early heresies within the early church and continuing through the Reformation, wherein Luther offered various defenses to justify separation from Rome.

Today, Christians face wide-ranging critiques of their faith spawned from science, philosophy, and emerging social trends such as the "New Atheism." Perhaps no other biblical phrase has inspired more books, debates, conferences, and even YouTube videos than this simple admonition.

In light of modern challenges to their faith, Christians have leveraged this biblical phrase to establish what one commenter describes "as a well-paying *industry*, with books, videos, seminars—even academic positions,

---

1. Joseph Haroutunian and Louise Pettibone Smith, eds., *Calvin: Commentaries* (Philadelphia: Westminster Press, 1958), 220.

2. In this essay biblical quotations are from the New Revised Standard Version (NRSV) unless otherwise indicated. There is debate among NT scholars as to whether Peter authored the two epistles that bear his name; however, consideration of authorship is well beyond the scope here. For our purposes, I will refer to Peter as the author.

programs, and institutions."³ And, while I question the characterization of apologetics as "well-paying," there is no doubt that apologetics, in one form or another, has established itself as a feature of modern Christian life. Just as other Christians, Latter-day Saints have also established an apologetic industry meant to counter, defend, and—in some cases—even promote specific truth claims as legitimate, reasonable, or well-supported both by religious and secular authorities.⁴

Given the widespread access to information today afforded to us by technological advances unthinkable a mere twenty-five years (perhaps fewer) ago, LDS apologetic arguments and techniques from years past are being read more widely than ever before and reexamined in light of a fresh context.⁵ Past apologetic efforts from individuals such as Jack Welch,⁶ John Sorenson,⁷ Hugh Nibley,⁸ Daniel Peterson,⁹ and others have contributed to the increasing body of knowledge and literature accompanying the emergence of Mormon Studies in academia. Young LDS scholars continue on in this tradition.¹⁰

But apologetics is not simply an intellectual enterprise. It touches on subjects of incredible importance to many Latter-day Saints, impacting not simply the minds of seeking Mormons, but also their souls. For those Saints who do seek out products of the apologetic industry, two motiva-

---

3. Myron Bradley Penner, *The End of Apologetics: Christian Witness in a Postmodern Context* (Ada, Mich.: Baker Academic, 2013), 62; emphasis in original.

4. For example, the Bible may be considered a religious authority. Among Christians of all varieties the Bible is revered in some form. Thus, it becomes a common starting point from which to establish the veracity of a doctrinal claim.

5. This is purely anecdotal conjecture, but I believe it to be both reasonable and accurate. With easy access to both apologetic and critical arguments and ideas, today's Latter-day Saints are, quite naturally, exploring what was most likely not easily available to them in prior years.

6. John W. Welch, "Chiasmus in the Book of Mormon," *BYU Studies* 10, no. 1 (1969).

7. John L. Sorenson, *An Ancient American Setting for the Book of Mormon* (Salt Lake City and Provo, Utah: Deseret Book Company and Foundation for Ancient Research and Mormon Studies, 1985).

8. Nibley was such a prolific author it is difficult to list just one work. See: "Hugh Nibley," Neal A. Maxwell Institute for Religious Scholarship, https://publications.mi.byu.edu/people/hugh-nibley/.

9. Daniel C. Peterson, "Nephi and His Asherah," *Journal of Book of Mormon Studies* 9, no. 2 (2000).

10. Carl Cranney, "The Deliberate Use of Hebrew Parallelisms in the Book of Mormon," *Journal of Book of Mormon Studies* 23, no. 1 (2014).

tions may exist, either simultaneously or in isolation. First, some Saints are inclined, out of personal interest or curiosity, to study or approach their faith from an academic viewpoint. They read apologetic literature not because of any personal doubts or struggles but because they enjoy considering their faith from the unique vantage point apologetics provides.

Other Saints may seek out apologetics after an encounter with concepts or information that may challenge their existing cherished and foundational assumptions. This can be particularly difficult as much of Christian theology—and especially Mormon theology—is what we would call systematic: a set of beliefs wherein each proposition represents a progression from an idea or notion that came before.[11] A systematic theology need not be creedal; in the LDS tradition, no official creed exists, as opposed to most mainline Christian churches that adhere to various creeds in one form or another. In Mormonism the nearest equivalent of canonical creedal belief would be the thirteen Articles of Faith, but these articles, of course, are far different from the Apostles' Creed or the Nicene Creed, for example. Systematic theology may also be culturally influenced and somewhat fluid—as is the case in Mormonism, where contemporary Church leaders may introduce modified interpretations and clarifications related to past beliefs and practices. Put simply, systematic theology exists when there is significant dependence and interdependence between doctrinal propositions. In other words, meat seems incoherent without first having experienced milk (1 Cor. 3, Heb. 5:12).

The result of this systematic theology is a web of interdependent beliefs supported by a handful of core propositions that provide the context or framework within which these interdependent beliefs become coherent. As a result, when any belief within the system—and especially a core or essential belief—is called into question, the entire *system* or *worldview* may seem threatened. Thus, Saints who have encountered a challenge to their beliefs seek out apologetics as a means not only to answer a given question, but also to reestablish harmony among a broader set of beliefs. To put it another way, Saints who encounter difficult questions or challenges seek solace and comfort in apologetics. Unfortunately, some of these Saints seeking answers have come away dissatisfied—in some cases, with contempt for both Mormonism and its apologists. This is both unfortunate and unnecessary. It is my contention that Latter-day Saints can

---

11. *The Lexham Bible Dictionary*, ed. John D. Barry, et al. (Bellingham, Wash.: Lexham Press, 2016), s.v. "Systematic Theology."

do better by augmenting past efforts with a pastoral mindset well-suited for contemporary criticism, questions, and concerns.

Given our modern context I believe it is not only prudent but necessary to consider the broad devotional, pastoral, and ethical constructs that govern apologetic activity. In this essay I will argue that religious apologetics must be approached as a devotional act—an act not necessarily intended to "rescue" those who question, but rather as an expression of our inner convictions and commitments. Additionally, I will propose that contemporary apologetics should be both formulated and expressed with an awareness of the pastoral theology which motivates all Christian ideals of friendship, empathy, and compassion.

1 Peter as Apologetic Foundation

To begin, we need look no further than 1 Peter 3, the foundational text of apologetics, in order to examine both the cultural, pastoral, and ethical context of Peter's admonition as well as its scope.

According to New Testament scholar John Elliot, 1 Peter is an acknowledgment of a "paradoxical feature of Christian existence; namely, rejoicing despite, or even because of suffering." Shortly after an introduction and praise of rebirth through Christ, "the critical problem of affliction, pain, and suffering is introduced" and is "an issue that dominates the letter as a whole." These early Saints were suffering from "social harassment" in similitude of the "suffering of Christ." Peter attempts to comfort these believers by demonstrating that "suffering affliction for the faith from hostile outsiders . . . is a *potentially* Christian experience" that creates unity and devotion within the church, "since believers share the experience of their suffering Lord."[12] Present trials and challenges are described as a temporary condition that serves to test believers' faith, ultimately culminating in praise and glory upon Christ's return (1 Pet. 1:6–7, 22–24).

In chapter 2, Peter urges the Saints to follow the example of Christ by enduring suffering in love, patience, and kindness. Godly living in the face of unjust persecution "silence[s] the ignorance" of Christian persecutors while glorifying God (2:11–15). The Saints are advised to love each other and give due honor to human institutions and to the Roman emperor. Peter encourages believers to endure unjust suffering, as "when you do right, and suffer for it, you have God's approval" (2:20).

---

12. John H. Elliott, *1 Peter: A New Translation with Introduction and Commentary* (New Haven; London: Yale University Press, 2008), 339.

Chapter 3 is a continuation of this counsel as the Saints are encouraged to "have unity of spirit, sympathy, love for one another, a tender heart, and a humble mind" (3:8). Peter echoes Jesus's teaching by encouraging believers to "not repay evil for evil or abuse for abuse; but, on the contrary, repay with a blessing" (3:9). Saints should be without fear because godly living and doing "what is good" may discourage others from seeking to harm believers. Yet, even if believers do "suffer for doing what is right, [they] are blessed." Additionally, believers are not to "fear what [their enemies] fear" and are "not [to] be intimidated" (3:13–14).

It is at this point, and only after laying out a very specific social and theological framework, that Peter delivers the admonition that motivates all of Christian apologetics:

> [B]ut in your hearts sanctify Christ as Lord. Always be ready to make your defense to anyone who demands from you an accounting for the hope that is in you; yet do it with gentleness and reverence. Keep your conscience clear, so that, when you are maligned, those who abuse you for your good conduct in Christ may be put to shame. For it is better to suffer for doing good, if suffering should be God's will, than to suffer for doing evil. (3:15–17)

The Greek word *apologia* (ἀπολογία), found in verse 15 has been translated into English in several forms. The New Revised Standard Version (quoted above) employs "defense" while The King James Version renders "answer," as does the New International Version. New Testament scholar John Elliott translates apologia in this context as simply "reply."[13]

Regardless of how apologia is translated, however, Peter's intended meaning seems clear given the greater context of the passage and in light of what the apostle had laid out prior to this specific admonition. Simply stated, Peter encourages the Saints to be prepared to explain, defend, or reply to any who demand "an accounting for the hope" within them. Equally important was for believers to do so as a *devotional* act "with gentleness and reverence." The Saints' answer to the question, "Why are you a Christian?" as well as the manner in which they provide such an answer, is to serve as both a testimony and an example of Christ's steadfast love. By responding to their persecutors with "a tender heart and a humble mind," believers ensured that "when [they were] maligned, those who abuse[d] them for [their] good conduct in Christ [would] be put to shame" (1 Pet. 3:8, 16).

While Peter is explicit in *how* such an accounting or answer is to be given, he is not explicit in describing the *expected content* of such an answer.

---

13. Ibid., 618.

This is not surprising, of course, given that the community of early believers understood, due to the pastoral activity of Peter and others, the fundamental doctrine of Christ to be shared with non-believers and persecutors.[14]

"With Gentleness and Reverence"

The counsel given to these early Saints provides us with our first point of reference when considering apologetics as a pastoral act of devotion. The apologetic enterprise, above anything else, must be carried out with gentleness and reverence so that any defense or explanation of our inner hope is carried out or presented in such a way as to clearly demonstrate Christian devotion. Presented otherwise, the apologetic explanation becomes self-defeating and self-contradictory, revealing that our chosen words betray our claimed inner conviction. If we attempt to defend our faith in a way inconsistent with its very foundation, we are better off remaining silent. Writing of modern apologetics, Irish theologian Alister McGrath argues:

> Apologetics is about defending the truth with gentleness and respect. The object of apologetics is not to antagonize or humiliate those outside the church, but to help open their eyes to the reality, reliability, and relevance of the Christian faith. There must be no mismatch or contradiction between the message that is proclaimed and the tone of the messenger's proclamation. We must be winsome, generous, and gracious. If the gospel is to cause difficulty, it must be on account of its intrinsic nature and content, not the manner in which it is proclaimed. It is one thing for the gospel to give offense; it is quite another for its defenders to cause offense by unwise choice of language or an aggressive and dismissive attitude toward outsiders.[15]

Although we live in a modern world quite different from that of the ancient Saints who received Peter's original admonition, our responsibility to defend the faith as a devotional act remains. No longer are we accused of atheism, cannibalism, and sedition; rather, we find ourselves defending the very notion of faith itself in addition to specific doctrinal truth claims

---

14. The New Testament itself can be considered an apologetic text in that it lays out the fundamental reasons, within an OT religious tradition and Hellenistic culture, for accepting Christ. See William Edgar and K. Scott Oliphint, eds., *Christian Apologetics Past and Present: A Primary Source Reader, Volume 1, to 1500* (Wheaton, Ill.: Crossway, 2009), 19–27.

15. Alister E. McGrath, *Mere Apologetics: How to Help Seekers and Skeptics Find Faith* (Grand Rapids: Baker Books, 2012), 16.

Apologetics as Theological Praxis

or beliefs. Yet, our modern position mirrors that of the early Saints in some important respects.

Just as those who received Peter's counsel, we too live within a cultural ethos sometimes at odds with notions of divinity and faith. Within the ancient Hellenistic culture of the first and second centuries, Christianity seemed an absurd departure from Greek and Roman philosophy, which was ubiquitous, part of nearly every aspect of social and civil life, and widely accepted as simply a given truth. Similarly, our talk of God, grace, prayer, meditation, and inspiration appears equally as foolish in light of secularism, modern science, and especially the increasing prevalence of scientism.[16] Our task, then, is fundamentally similar to that of the ancient Saints: we are to provide a defense or explanation of our faith within the context of a seemingly hostile culture.

This is precisely what Justin Martyr did in one of the earliest apologetic texts of which we are aware—*The First Apology of Justin*—addressed to the Roman Emperor and his son, both of whom who were apparently well-versed in Hellenistic philosophy and, of course, Roman religion.[17] Justin's *Apology* is instructive in several respects. First, Justin (not surprisingly) shows great respect for his intended audience. He does so not only with his chosen tone, but also because he shows a deep understanding of the beliefs, traditions, history, and philosophy of the Roman empire. Even in isolation, Justin's show of respect demonstrates that the early Saints approached their faith with seriousness and with an awareness of opposing views. Justin lays out a reasonable defense of Christianity within the context of the assumptions and beliefs of the Emperor and his son. He does so by citing Plato and other philosophers, as well as referencing gods of the Roman cult to illustrate both their similarities and differences with early Christian concepts of the Logos. Ultimately Justin's efforts proved ineffective, and he was eventually tortured and beheaded because he, as well as other Christian believers, refused to sacrifice to idols. Yet, regardless of the ultimate impact on his audience, Justin's *Apology* and his subsequent willingness to confess Christ in the face of terrible earthly consequences stand as examples of Christian virtue and an unwavering commitment to moral principles.[18]

---

16. Huston Smith, *Why Religion Matters* (San Francisco: HarperCollins, 2001).

17. Justin Martyr, "The First Apology of Justin," in *Christian Apologetics Past and Present: A Primary Source Reader, Volume 1, to 1500*, ed. William Edgar and K. Scott Oliphint (Wheaton, Ill.: Crossway, 2009), 42–63.

18. Tertullian also produced an *Apology*. Addressed to "Rulers of the Roman Empire," the work is an elaborate plea for fairness as "Tertullian ask[s] [Roman

Like Justin, we too have a moral responsibility to understand the motivations, assumptions, beliefs, and general worldview of our critics. It is impossible to offer a meaningful defense with little or no knowledge of what motivates our intended audience. Without question Justin is critical of certain Roman cult practices, especially as they related to the veneration of idols, however, he offers respectful criticism and calls upon the Emperor to utilize his reasoning ability to see that idols are nothing more than mere empty vessels devoid of the Logos, or motivating force.

Justin did not set up straw men to be easily knocked down. He did not present a caricature of Roman and Hellenistic thought. Rather, Justin offered up an accurate—albeit critical—portrayal of Roman and Hellenistic culture and belief such that his audience would 1) easily recognize and 2) understand Christianity as being part of this larger cultural milieu. That Justin's *Apology* ultimately proved unpersuasive to the Emperor is of little importance when considering apologetics. Justin knew, understood, and could articulate the reasons for his Christian faith. He spoke *as a Christian* as his words reflected inner conviction and courage. Justin also showed his audience due respect—despite the fact that his Christian brothers and sisters were suffering under tremendous persecution and that Justin, himself, was putting his own life in peril by writing in defense of Christian faith. Justin's *Apology* stands as a microcosmic example of Christian virtue showing patience, understanding, courage, and gentleness—all in accord with the counsel of Peter and the example of Christ.[19]

---

rulers] simply to look closely into the matter of charges brought against Christians, so that the rulers can determine how false the charges are." Throughout his *Apology* Tertullian employs both reason and a polemical edge to demonstrate the moral inconsistency of condemning, torturing, and murdering Christians while supporting certain aspects of the Roman cult and allowing other non-Roman cultists to function without persecution. And, while Tertullian is sharply critical of Roman gods, the criticism is intended to demonstrate the incoherent accusations against Christian believers. See Edgar and Oliphint, *Christian Apologetics . . . to 1500*, 117.

19. Of course, critics of our faith need not be "outsiders"; while Peter does not address this issue specifically in his first epistle, we can see from some of the Christianity's earliest thinkers and scholars that it is sometimes necessary for Christians to address and possibly counter so-called heretical notions that threaten the health and cohesiveness of the community of believers. Those who countered such heresies are known as heresiologists. For information on one of the first centuries' most prominent heretics, Marcion, see John J. Clabeaux, "Marcion," in *The Anchor Yale Bible Dictionary*, ed. David Noel Freedmon, et al. (New York: Doubleday, 1992), 514.

"Come To Me All of You That Are Weary and Are Carrying Heavy Burdens"

Apologetics, of course, is not solely intended for consumption by outside critics. Indeed, apologetics can serve as an effective tool not only for building faith within the flock, but also for providing pastoral care to brothers and sisters in spiritual need. The pastoral letters of Paul—and indeed large portions of the New Testament—can be considered apologetic works intended to strengthen and support the larger flock. We can see from Paul's example and teachings that we need not be weak or timid when we engage in apologetics. Paul was often firm and sharp in both establishing and exerting his apostolic authority, but it is clear that this firmness was born of the deep and abiding love Paul had for the Saints. Yet "even within the stern rhetoric of his letter to the Galatians Paul draws on maternal imagery to woo his readers away from the choices that he fears will put them at risk."[20] Indeed, Paul "frequently draws on family images to describe his pastoral relationship with the churches he [had] established."

Paul stands as an excellent example of courage and boldness, motivated not by a desire to win an argument or prove the validity of his doctrinal views but rather influenced by the love Jesus commanded his disciples to share with on another—the hallmark and very definition of what it means to be a Christian (John 13:34). In his letters Paul is anything but timid, and despite any doctrinal viewpoints he was attempting to correct, his love and concern for the flock is never in question. Paul was able to be bold and confident, yet also humble and compassionate.[21]

As Christians we are called to develop and exercise this same love for fellow members of the flock. The centrality and importance of this calling has been consistently emphasized by modern LDS Church leaders.

During the 1996 October General Conference, Elder Jeffery R. Holland delivered a sermon entitled "The Peaceable Things of the Kingdom." He explains:

> Peace and good tidings; good tidings and peace. These are among the ultimate blessings that the gospel of Jesus Christ brings a troubled world and the trou-

---

20. Jacob W. Elias, *Remember the Future: The Pastoral Theology of Paul the Apostle* (Harrisonburg, Va.: Herald Press, 2006), 50.

21. An example of this can be found in Galatians where it is clear Paul takes issue with certain views and actions embraced by Peter. Yet despite these disagreements, Paul remained focused on the core Gospel message.

bled people who live in it, solutions to personal struggles and human sinfulness, a source of strength for days of weariness and hours of genuine despair.[22]

Holland also observes that there are "people in the broad congregation of this conference or in your local ward or stake—or in your own home—courageous people who are carrying heavy burdens and feeling private pain, who are walking through the dark valleys of this world's tribulation." Such "beloved people seek the Lord and His word with particular urgency, often revealing their true emotions only when the scriptures are opened or when the hymns are sung or when the prayers are offered" and "sometimes only then do the rest of us realize they feel near the end of their strength—they are tired in brain and body and heart, they wonder if they get through another week or another day or sometimes, just another hour."

Latter-day Saints who seek answers from apologetics may be among those who are "tired in brain and body and heart." Holland's sermon reminds us, as Christians and Latter-day Saints, that we are all called to the pastoral role. This duty is universal and independent of gender, priesthood office, or institutional Church responsibilities. According to the Book of Mormon prophet Alma, the acceptance of this call is an outward sign of an inner desire to "come into the fold of God, and to be called his people." Alma further states that to accept Christ is to gladly take upon ourselves the very nature of discipleship; to "bear one another's burdens, that they may be light" (Mosiah 18:8–9). We are to "mourn with those who mourn" and "comfort those that stand in need of comfort." During our own times of mourning and discomfort we become the recipients of much needed solidarity and support. It is this symbiotic relationship of charity, empathy, and kindness that is the very essence of the Gospel of Jesus Christ. Holland's words serve as an invitation to put theology into practice within our families, our wards, and our communities.

A devotional and pastoral approach to apologetics is one way in which to do this as apologetics can play an important role as members struggle with difficult questions and concerns.

Pastoral Theology and Apologetics

I have previously labeled such apologetic efforts "pastoral apologetics," which "may be succinctly defined as a response to doubt that focuses primari-

---

22. Jeffrey R. Holland, "The Peaceable Things of the Kingdom," *Ensign*, November 1996, available at https://www.lds.org/ensign/1996/11/the-peaceable-things-of-the-kingdom.

ly on the spiritual, social, and psychological desire for meaning, purpose, and mysticism."[23] This is not to say that a well-researched, humbly-presented, and rigorous defense of specific doctrinal or historical truth-claims is unnecessary or unimportant. Without question such information can be enlightening, inspiring, and uplifting. However, propping up spiritual doubt with academic answers is unsustainable in the long-term.[24] For this reason, our primary concern when interacting with brothers and sisters who doubt should be to provide pastoral care to "address issues of the heart and the [universal] desire to feel connected to a sense of expansive, or ultimate meaning."[25]

Pastoral apologetics, of course, is motivated by pastoral theology; a field of inquiry focused, primarily, on the practical application of the pastoral call and concerned not just with things eternal, but with the present needs of the flock. Such a theology is, of course, supported by scripture and tradition but, as Christian theologian Wayne Morris has observed, theology is "not simply found in magisterial texts, ancient scriptures or significant theological tomes of the past and present that may emerge out of any contextual position, but it is also found in the lived expression of communities of faith in worship, devotion, relationships, social actions [and] community engagement." Indeed "theology is always practiced and practice itself is a theological resource worthy of interrogation."[26] It is this engagement that defines pastoral care generally, and pastoral apologetics specifically. Such engagement, then, is a natural outgrowth of theological reflection on the moral duties of Christian discipleship.

The truth claims made by pastoral theology are as elegantly simple as they are self-evident. Broadly speaking, pastoral theology asserts two primary truths: suffering exists and all Saints are called to act as the agents of God's love in alleviating that suffering. Such a theology cannot be bogged down by dogma, policy, tradition, or authority. Its claims are motivated by, but completely independent of, other LDS doctrines. No belief in or agreement on any abstract idea or assertion is requisite to feed the hungry

---

23. Seth Payne, "Ex-Mormon Narratives and Pastoral Apologetics," *Dialogue: A Journal of Mormon Thought* 46, no. 4 (Winter 2013): 114.

24. While it is difficult to pin down specific numbers, it is clear from a plethora of anecdotal evidence that some Mormons—even those who were once committed Latter-day Saints involved in apologetics—have completely lost faith after concluding the academic answers they had once promoted were lacking.

25. Payne, "Ex-Mormon Narratives," 115.

26. Wayne Morris, *Salvation as Praxis: A Practical Theology of Salvation for a Multi-Faith World* (New York: Bloomsbury, 2014), 16–17.

or comfort the sick. There is a well-known traditional Zen Buddhist story wherein a student asks his master: "What is enlightenment?" The master replied: "When hungry, eat. When tired, sleep." Pastoral care is just as simple. When you meet the hungry, feed. And when you encounter the sick or afflicted, provide comfort. If we find ourselves giving greater allegiance to abstract ideas or organizational practices more than to those we are called to serve, we have fundamentally misunderstood the beautiful simplicity of pastoral theology and the pastoral approach to apologetics.

As doubting brothers and sisters make up a significant part of our intended apologetic audience, it becomes imperative that our apologetic presentation be pastoral, honest, charitable, respectful, and kind, lest our efforts inadvertently create unnecessary and problematic stumbling blocks for others during their time of spiritual need.

Jesus invited all who struggle and carry heavy burdens to come unto him in order to find "rest for [their] souls" (Matt. 11:29). Thus, an essential element of apologetic ethics and pastoral care is to approach the endeavor with soberness and charity, with an awareness that a defense of the faith may have a very real and lasting impact on those to whom the defense is presented. Regardless of our intended audience, we have absolutely no knowledge of who will encounter and engage our apologetic efforts. Therefore, we must assume our responsibility as apologetic pastors in the manner prescribed by Peter and Paul and underscored by Elder Holland.

Engagement with the Modern World

In the recent past, a plethora of apologetic arguments have been presented in favor of Mormon-specific truth-claims. At times, these arguments have been presented as if they were very well-supported by various lines of scholarly, archaeological, or historical evidence with no recognition of the weaknesses, flaws, or challenges to the proposed argument.[27] Latter-day Saints, of course, are not the only religionists to argue for their views in an overly-confident academic manner. Christian apologists, including William Lane Craig and Dan Story,[28] often marshal academic philosophi-

---

27. Ignoring valid criticism of our position is lazy at best, and dishonest at worst.

28. Dan Story is a case study in how not to do Christian apologetics. Story advocates an aggressive apologetic completely out of line with the counsel of Peter. He also demonstrates very little understanding of the religions and worldviews he condemns. See: Dan Story, *Defending Your Faith* (Grand Rapids: Kregel Publications, 1997), Dan Story, *Christianity on the Offense* (Grand Rapids: Kregel

cal arguments in an effort to show the truth-claims of Christianity to be obvious and well-supported.[29]

Other Christian scholars and theologians oppose this type of approach to apologetics. Søren Kierkegaard, for example, maintained that Christianity itself was absurd and should remain so. According to Kierkegaard scholar Malcolm Diamond, the great Danish theologian "violently rejected the idea that the truth claims of Christianity were demonstrable," maintaining that "trust is a crucial element in the faith" and that "the very effort to establish a 'proof' of the truth of Christianity represented a breach of that trust." Kierkegaard remained rooted in mysticism, believing "that the divine and the human realms could never be joined in rational terms and he rejected traditional apologetics" for attempting to harmonize the two.[30]

Kierkegaard, himself, writes:

> Everyone who lives in Christendom ordinarily has received more than enough information about Christianity (even the government sees to that); many perhaps have received all too much. What is lacking is certainly something entirely different, is the inner transformation of the whole mind, by which a person in life-peril of the spirit comes in earnest in true inwardness, to believe at least something—of the considerable Christianity that he knows.[31]

Theologian Kyle Roberts argues that Kierkegaard did not reject "objective approaches to knowledge . . . so long as objectivity was kept in its proper place and only when the 'object' of knowledge could be adequately known through objective approaches." To Kierkegaard, authentic religious existence is characterized by a continual striving "wherein faith presses on and gains a kind of convictional assurance through praxis and the experience of relatedness to God."[32]

Publications, 1998), and Dan Story, *Engaging the Closed Minded: Presenting Your Faith to the Confirmed Unbeliever* (Grand Rapids: Kregel Publications, 1999).

29. William Lane Craig, *Reasonable Faith: Christian Truth and Apologetics* (Wheaton, Ill.: Crossway Books, 1994).

30. Malcolm L. Diamond, "Kierkegaard and Apologetics," *The Journal of Religion* 44, no. 2 (1964): 122–23.

31. *Kierkegaard's Writings, XVII: Christian Discourses: The Crisis and a Crisis in the Life of an Actress*, trans. Howard V. Hong and Edna H. Hong (Princeton, N.J.: Princeton Universiy Press, 2009), 245–46.

32. Kyle A. Roberts, *Emerging Prophet: Kierkegaard and the Postmodern People of God* (Eugene, Ore.: Cascade Books, 2013), 39.

Embracing Religious Experience

As modern Mormons we may find ourselves falling into the trap of searching for a "correct" understanding of the Gospel in an abstract sense—as if our abstract beliefs or notions are of some great importance in themselves. In truth, we best come to know God and the Gospel through our collective and individual practice of religious ideals: by imitating and following Christ. Reading the twenty-third Psalm is one thing, but *experiencing* God's love as we "walk through the darkest valley" is something else altogether (Ps. 23:4). It is the experience of practiced theology—an experience with God as we strive to follow the example of Jesus—which creates lasting spiritual ties not just to the divine, but to our wards and communities as well.

Seeking direct experience with divinity sits at the very heart of Mormonism. From the earliest converts to those whom the missionaries teach today, all have been invited to not just consider the Book of Mormon cerebrally, but more importantly—and most essentially—to seek out and receive a direct spiritual experience regarding those things which have been pondered with a "sincere heart" and "real intent" (Moro. 10:4). As a result, Mormon faith is not based on a reasoned analysis and careful scrutiny of empirical evidence as this is but one of many methods employed to ponder and consider questions of truth. This is both an individual and collective experience. Neither our own faith, nor our pastoral efforts (apologetic or otherwise), can be based solely on logic and reason; rather, they must be borne of our desire to experience God directly, with our families and ward members, and without mediation.

And yet, Mormon culture drives us towards abstract correctness wherein tremendous value is placed on certain "facts" that may have very little bearing on the direct experience of divinity. It may well be, for example, that God the Father has a body of flesh and bones (D&C 130:22), but this conception is both illusory and fleeting. When we face moments of darkness or difficulty we do not yearn for an abstract or objective idea of God. Rather, we seek an experience with divine and compassionate love. The knowledge or belief that God is an anthropomorphic being who resides in both space and time is no source of comfort; it does not bring peace and, in itself, is certainly no indication of God's steadfast love—a love most often demonstrated by the charity of others.[33] This is not to say, of course, that abstract beliefs are unimportant or hollow. Indeed, our abstract beliefs may

---

33. David Hansen and David L. Goetz, *The Power of Loving Your Church: Leading through Acceptance and Grace* (Minneapolis: Bethany House, 1998), 60–61.

strongly influence both our self-conception and moral choices. But we must not lose sight of the motivating force at work. It is not the belief or conception which motivates our faith; rather, it is *the underlying principle of what that belief represents* which is of ultimate importance. In other words, a belief in the anthropomorphic nature of God has no practical or real-world impact absent its implications. Understanding God as anthropomorphic—an exalted man—helps us to feel more connected to Him and gain confidence in His love and willingness to answer sincere prayers.

Yet, consider that many mainline Christians also feel and experience the love of God, not because God is anthropomorphic, but rather because He is seen as a loving, kind, father figure who in His infinite goodness yearns to comfort those who approach Him in humility and faith. Mainline Christian beliefs about the nature of God are generally Trinitarian and as such stand in stark contrast to beliefs generally held by Latter-day Saints. But both Latter-day Saints and mainline Christians approach God seeking answers and comfort; they are seeking an experience with God and not a list of propositional claims. It becomes clear from this example that abstract spiritual beliefs are largely or primarily meant to imply or convey certain meaning. This is their essential, practical purpose. Therefore, as in the case of the competing LDS and mainline Christian views on the nature of God, two very different beliefs may imply a single deeper, experiential truth. It is for this reason that Latter-day Saints should be *most* concerned with what their beliefs *imply* rather than if these beliefs are abstractly correct in isolation.

As Kierkegaard described, however, to approach belief in this way is to work against our most basic and common modern assumptions. And it is for this very reason that Kierkegaard and others (see below) argue against the attempt to marry modern rationalism and New Testament Christianity. This is not a rejection of Christian truth; rather, it serves as an attempt to place this truth within the proper context and a call to put our beliefs into practice.

Apologetics in a Modern Context

Following Kierkegaard, contemporary theologians such as Myron Penner argue that "the shift to modernity . . . entails a new—and diminished—status for Christian thought" because "modern challenges to Christian faith . . . attack the very sources of belief, not just the content of Christian doctrine." He continues:

Objections to faith are now no longer of the sort that question whether a given belief is true, but much more substantially concern how anyone could believe Christian doctrine at all, given the basis on which it is traditionally believed (e.g., church tradition and Scripture). Issues such as the epistemological reliability of Scripture, the intellectual coherence of theism or miracles, the historicity of the resurrection of Jesus, and so on, take center stage in modern discussions of Christian faith. What is more, given the ethos of modernity, the cultural pressure to provide substantial answers to these questions is enormous.[34]

The "shared aim of all the varieties of modern apologetics is to make Christian belief plausible in this modern situation in which belief in God is not at all obvious or intuitive." And "to accomplish this, modern apologists use arguments, evidence, or a philosophical account of the Christian worldview" together with widely accepted—and unquestionably modern—epistemological and philosophical assumptions. Penner refers to this type of apologetics as "secular apologetics," in that it marshals tools and assumptions from the modern secular world in order to present Christianity as not only plausible, but reasonable.[35]

On the surface these modern approaches to apologetics would seem to appear appropriate and even helpful in our present context. However, there is a significant danger as well. These modern apologetic efforts may imply that "Christians have a moral duty to believe only those aspects of Christian doctrine that have sufficient apologetic basis,"[36] a concept that undermines the centrality of faith in Christian practice. Early Christian apologists acknowledged that theology (and its defense) is more than mere rational exercise. Theology is meant to encourage Christian community and devotion. Devoid of this both theology and apologetics become stale, having little real-world impact on the lives of Christian believers.

This is not to suggest that rationality should not inform apologetic efforts. Indeed, it must. However, by exalting rationality above—or even placing it on equal footing with—the precepts of Christian living and Christian community, apologetics becomes an "appeal to genius (experts)" that can easily transform faith into a rigid ideology. As such, "apologetic debates and dissertations on the relative merits of (dis)believing in God turn to mass media and culture production as the means of spreading [the apologetic/ideological] message" wherein "these exercises of 'reason' seem

---

34. Penner, *The End of Apologetics*, 33.
35. Ibid., 36.
36. Ibid., 45.

to function in a manner that is virtually indistinguishable from ideological power plays."[37] The result is a spiritual milieu in which "believing in God is less about the worship of God disclosed to us through a tradition and a historical community called the church, and more about how theistic belief is rationally predictable within the limits of modern secular reason."[38]

Such approaches make no room for the human soul as, having become an ideology, apologetics becomes an exercise in presenting arguments that are rhetorically clever as well as abstractly and academically "correct." Within our modern context, then, apologetics devoid of a pastoral element or motivation can easily lose any and all devotional aspects, becoming no longer the output of Christian witness and charity but rather an intellectual and academic exercise devoid of spiritual richness and love.

If, as defenders of faith in the modern world, we lose sight of the devotional and soul-centric aspects of apologetics, *we have failed, utterly and absolutely.*

To illustrate some potential problems in engaging apologetics from a modern rationalist view, let's consider the question of Book of Mormon historicity. In the minds of most who have considered the question from an academic or rationalistic perspective, the Book of Mormon is a clear product of the nineteenth century.[39] It is only a minute handful of scholars and intellectuals familiar with ancient America who maintain that the Book of Mormon is an ancient text. So what is a Latter-day Saint to do? When 99% of scholars adhere to the idea of an ahistorical Book of Mormon should we simply throw up our hands and proclaim all of Mormonism fraudulent? Or, do we need to wait for 100% agreement between "experts" before such a conclusion is warranted? My point, of

---

37. Ibid., 61.

38. Ibid., 61–62.

39. While the Book of Mormon is seen as ahistorical by non-LDS scholars, it still manages to be widely read and given serious consideration. While a graduate student, my professors encouraged me to write about the theology of the Book of Mormon and explore how it may inform our understanding of the Atonement and the nature of Christ. More recently, respected physicist and mathematician Freeman Dyson explained that he "treasure[s] it [the Book of Mormon] because some of my best friends are Mormons, and the book tells a dramatic story in a fine biblical style" wherein "the reader has to wait with growing tension almost until the end of the story to reach the final climax, when Jesus arrives in America and founds his second kingdom here." See "Freeman Dyson: By the Book," *The New York Times*, April 16, 2015, available at https://www.nytimes.com/2015/04/19/books/review/19bkr-bythebook_dyson.t.html.

course, is that belief in the divinity of the Book of Mormon is a matter of faith, not fact. It is the experience of the Book of Mormon that brings joy to the lives of Latter-day Saints, not the several evidences offered by LDS scholars to support its plausibility. Clearly, then, our faith must not be based on empirical evidence or arguments for plausibility. To base our faith or apologetic methods on such would be to 1) create the impossible task of defining just how much rational argumentation or empirical evidence is required to retain faith and 2) create expectations which can only serve to erode our faith rather than support it. It is only by acting on our faithful beliefs—or rather, their implications—that that they are stripped of abstraction and become fully substantive.

As pastoral apologists we seek to support others in this type of substantive spiritual engagement and do so through our own faithful praxis. If a ward member or family member is struggling with a particular historical or theological question, we should encourage them to reflect on questions of meaning. In other words, we need not maintain a myopic focus on the particulars of truth claims to gain mutual understanding of their underlying principles or truths. As mentioned above, there is no inherent moral value in abstract correctness. In the pastoral role, if we "win" an apologetic argument through the use of methods that serve to divide or separate us from our fellow Saints—even if this is not our intention—we have served up stones, where bread was required (Matt. 7:9).

We must avoid, however, using this focus on underlying principle, meaning, and practice to avoid directly addressing difficult questions. There are significant challenges to LDS truth-claims, and we ignore the reality of these problems at our own peril. Even if we have personally come to some sort of resolution on a given question, it is unreasonable to expect others to simply accept our view or interpretation. Therefore, it is very important to acknowledge the legitimacy of both the questions themselves and the motivations behind asking such questions. We must allow others the opportunity—as we have allowed ourselves—to work out their own interpretations and draw their own conclusions.

Of course, not all who face challenges or doubts will choose to remain Latter-day Saints. Others will feel a strong connection with the Church and its heritage while at the same time struggling to reconsider some of Mormonism's core doctrines. Some will have arrived at a heterodox position relative to mainstream LDS doctrine but desire to stay connected with the Church and its people regardless.

The practical application of pastoral apologetics within an LDS context, therefore, has two primary goals. First, to ensure that members who choose to leave the fold are treated with kindness and respect, so that we may avoid, in our zealotry or personal dismay, offending the dignity of those we truly care for. Second, to present an approach to Mormonism—appropriate for believers of all stripes—centered on putting Mormonism into practice.

To do so, pastoral apologists must cultivate qualities congruent with the pastoral call. Pastoral engagement is not about solving problems. Our intent is not to "fix" people or situations but rather to provide love, comfort, compassion, empathy, and support to those going through various challenges. We must always recognize that those whom we serve are not means to an end of enhancing our own spiritual status; they are beloved sons and daughters of God worthy of compassion and charity by virtue of their very personhood.

The Pastoral Framework

The discussion here about the nature, scope, and purpose of apologetics provides us with important insights into the devotional and pastoral framework from within which apologetics should be pursued and produced. Focusing on apologetics' intended audience and its devotional aspects, as well as its setting within our modern world, leads us to several broad, but essential, principles that must govern our apologetic efforts. In addition, it is clear that apologetics must be an outward expression of our inward Christian faith; an outgrowth of the gentle virtues demonstrated in the life of Jesus and described by the apostle Peter and demonstrated by Paul.

Apologetics is an act of faith and Christian charity. As such, any defense we present must properly reflect the core aspects of Christian discipleship. An apologetic is to be offered up and presented in a way that is consistent with the love of God, Christlike charity, and the admonition of Peter that we always defend the faith with "gentleness and reverence." If our presentation detracts from the very message we are supposedly trying to defend, we may come across as inconsistent at best, and hypocritical at worst.

We must show due respect to our critics and culture. Our arguments should be substantive, demonstrating our commitment to an honest and accurate representation not only of our own beliefs, but the positions of our critics, as well. If we present our critics or aspects of our culture as caricatures to be set up as straw men and easily knocked down, we betray the Christian faith we purport to proclaim and defend. For Latter-day Saints, "we believe in being honest" (A of F 13) is an overarching concept that informs all aspects of our lives. It takes on special significance when we engage our critics because an honest and accurate portrayal of the issues at hand is often the difference between charitable apologetics and polemical screeching.

As believers we have a responsibility to produce apologetic arguments and explanations that are appropriate for a contemporary setting. Poorly researched or misleading apologetics meant to build faith based on questionable assumptions or evidence will only serve to earn the justified ire of critics and cause disillusionment in those Saints seeking answers. In apologetics, humility and charity must rule the day. As believers who seek to defend faith, we are to be judged not by the effectiveness of our arguments in convincing others of a given position or viewpoint, but rather, our apologetic efforts will be measured by how they align with the principles of faith we work to defend.

Author's Note: Several months after completing this essay I made the difficult decision to resign my membership in the Church of Jesus Christ of Latter-day Saints. And although I may no longer have an institutional affiliation with the LDS Church, I remain a proud apologist.

Contributors

Michael R. Ash is a staff member at FairMormon. He has written for the *Mormon Times* and is a consistent contributor to *Meridian Magazine*. He has published in *FARMS Review*, *Sunstone*, *Dialogue*, and the *Ensign*. Ash is the author of *Shaken Faith Syndrome: Strengthening One's Testimony In the Face of Criticism and Doubt* (FAIR, 2013) and *Of Faith and Reason: 80 Evidences Supporting the Prophet Joseph Smith* (Cedar Fort, 2008).

Brian D. Birch received a PhD in philosophy of religion and theology from Claremont Graduate University and is Director of the Religious Studies Program and the Center for the Study of Ethics at Utah Valley University. His areas of specialization include philosophy of religion, ethics, and interreligious studies. He is the founding editor of *Element: The Journal of the Society for Mormon Philosophy & Theology* and series co-editor of *Perspectives on Mormon Theology* (Greg Kofford Books, 2015–).

David Bokovoy holds a PhD in Hebrew Bible and the Ancient Near East and an M.A. in Near Eastern and Judaic Studies, both from Brandeis University. He has published articles on the Hebrew Bible in the *Journal of Biblical Literature*, *Vetus Tetamentum*, *Studies in the Bible and Antiquity*, and the *FARMS Review*. He is the author of *Authoring the Old Testament Genesis—Deuteronomy* (Greg Kofford Books, 2014). David is the online professor in Bible and Jewish Studies at Utah State University.

Loyd Isao Ericson received his BS in philosophy at Utah Valley University and pursued an MA in philosophy of religion and theology at Claremont Graduate University. He is the co-editor of *Discourses in Mormon Theology: Philosophical and Theological Possibilities* (Greg Kofford Books, 2007) and series co-editor of *Perspectives on Mormon Theology* (Greg Kofford Books, 2015–). Loyd has been published in *Sunstone*, *Element: The Journal of the Society for Mormon Philosophy and Theology*, and the *Claremont Journal of Mormon Studies*, which he helped found. Since 2009 he has been the managing editor of Greg Kofford Books.

Fiona Givens received a double BA in French and German at the University of Richmond, followed by an MA in European History at the same university. She is now an independent scholar who has published in several journals and reviews in Mormon Studies, including *Journal of Mormon History*, *Exponent II*, and *LDS Living*. Along with her husband, Terryl Givens, she is the author of *The God Who Weeps: How Mormonism Makes Sense of Life* (Ensign Peak, 2012), and *The Crucible of Doubt: Reflections On the Quest for Faith* (Deseret Book, 2014).

Ralph C. Hancock holds a PhD from Harvard University in political science and is Professor of Political Science at Brigham Young University and was a J. Reuben Clark fellow. He is the author of *Calvin and the Foundations of Modern Politics* (Saint Augustine's Press, 2011; Cornell University Press, 1989) as well as *The Responsibility of Reason: Theory and Practice in a Liberal-Democratic Age* (Rowman & Littlefield, 2011). He is also the editor of *America, the West, and Liberal Education* (Rowman & Littlefield, 1999), translator of a number of books and articles from French, and has published many journal articles on the intersection of faith, reason and politics. Of interest to readers of this volume will be his "Keeping Faith in Provo," *First Things* (March 2014).

David Knowlton is Professor of Anthropology at Utah Valley University with a long history in the anthropological study of Mormonism. As a teenager Knowlton often attended Society for Early Historic Archeology conferences and board meetings with his father, where he learned many arguments about the Book of Mormon and peoples of the Americas. Undoubtedly that, along with a mission in Bolivia and way too many questions, led him to obtain a Ph.D. in anthropology from the University of Texas with a focus on Latin America and specifically the people of Bolivia and Peru—an interest that continues to claim his summers and much of his falls, winters, and springs.

Seth Payne is an independent scholar living in Seattle, Washington. He received an MA in Religion from Yale University, and an MBA from New York University. At Yale, Seth focussed on theological and political ethics, as well as Mormon Studies. His work on Mormon theology has been published in *The Journal of Catholic Legal Studies* and *Dialogue: A Journal of Mormon Thought*.

Contributors

Benjamin E. Park received his BA in English and History from Brigham Young University, an MSc in Historical Theology from the University of Edinburgh, and both an MPhil and a PhD in Political Thought and Intellectual Historyfrom the University of Cambridge. He is currently an assistant professor of American history at Sam Houston State University. His involvement in Mormon Studies include several articles in *Dialogue: A Journal of Mormon Thought*, the *Journal of Mormon History*, and the *Mormon Studies Review*, of which he is an associate editor. His first book, *American Nationalisms: Imagining Union in an Age of Revolutions*, will appear with Cambridge University Press in 2018.

Daniel C. Peterson earned his PhD in Near Eastern Languages and Cultures from the University of California at Los Angeles. He is a professor of Islamic Studies and Arabic at Brigham Young University. Peterson is the author of several books and numerous articles on Islamic and Latter-day Saint topics–including the biography *Muhammad: Prophet of God* (Eerdmans, 2007). He is the founder of the Interpreter Foundation and the initial editor-in-chief of *Interpreter: A Journal of Mormon Scripture*.

Neal Rappleye is a research project manager at Book of Mormon Central. He also volunteers for FairMormon (since 2011) and The Interpreter Foundation (since 2012). He has published several articles in *Interpreter: A Journal of Mormon Scripture* and blogs about LDS apologetics and scholarship at studioetquoquefide.com.

Juliann Reynolds is a co-founder of FairMormon and served on the Board of Directors for 19 years. She earned a BS and MS in Speech Pathology and Audiology from the University of Utah, followed by a career in teaching communication skills. She later studied New Testament at Claremont Graduate University, where she was able to participate in the newly developed Mormon Studies Program.

Julie M. Smith graduated from the University of Texas at Austin with a BA in English and from the Graduate Theological Union in Berkeley, California, with an MA in Biblical Studies. She is on the executive board of the Mormon Theology Seminar and the steering committee for the *BYU New Testament Commentary*, for which she is writing a commentary on the Gospel of Mark. She is the author of *Search, Ponder, and Pray: A Guide to the Gospels* (Greg Kofford Books, 2014) and editor of *As Iron Sharpens Iron: Listening to the Various Voices of Scripture* (Greg Kofford Books, 2016).

Joseph M. Spencer is a Visiting Assistant Professor of Ancient Scripture at Brigham Young University. He is the author of *An Other Testament: On Typology* (Maxwell Institute, 2016), *For Zion: A Mormon Theology of Hope* (Greg Kofford Books, 2014), and *The Vision of All: Twenty-five Lectures on Isaiah in Nephi's Record* (Greg Kofford Books, 2016). He currently serves as the associate director of the Mormon Theology Seminar and as editor of the *Journal of Book of Mormon Studies*.

Blair G. Van Dyke holds a Doctorate in the Philosophy of Education from Brigham Young University and is an independent scholar that teaches philosophy and religious studies at Utah Valley University. He is a Senior Research Fellow at the Foundation for Religious Diplomacy and is the Custodian of the Mormon Chapter of the Foundation. Van Dyke is the co-author of *Holy Lands, A History of the Latter-day Saints in the Near East* (Covenant, 2005) and co-editor of the forthcoming *The Expanded Canon: Mormonism and Sacred Texts* (Greg Kofford Books, 2017).

Index

A

Abinadi, 53–55, 59–60
academia
   and apologetics, vii, 67
   and liberalism, 111
   secular nature of, 134
Adam, 123n 6, 187–88
Adam–God Theory, 223–24
Alfrey, Christy, 142
Alger, Fanny, 212
Allen, Carolina, 153
Alma, 29, 35–36, 39, 222, 256
Alter, Robert, 224
America Online, 145–46
American Academy of Religion, 126
American Association of University Professors, 202
American Psychological Association, 18–19
anti-intellectualism, 13–15
apologetics
   and academia, vii, 67
   acrimony surrounding, 236
   act of faith, 265
   awareness of, 140
   of Book of Mormon. *See* Book of Mormon.
   civility. *See* tone.
   in Christian tradition, 3, 140, 253–54
   classic method, 64
   counterproductive, 209–22, 240–41
   and critics, 197–98
   cumulative case method, 65
   defense of, 27–41
   definition of, vii, 1, 43–64, 210
   as devotional act, 251–66
   in early Christianity, 27, 253–54
   in early Mormonism, 8, 27–28
   evangelical appraisal of, 146
   evidential method, 64
   and gender roles, 160–63
   harmful to faith, 67
   heart and mind, 236–38
   and Heavenly Mother, 156
   industry, 247–48
   influence on Mormon doctrine and understanding, 61–62, 200
   and inversion test, 155–59
   and the internet, 142–48
   limits of, 29, 211–22, 238
   male dominance, 140
   makes faith possible, 40–41
   methods, 64–65
   and moral responsibility, 262
   and Mormon Studies, 77, 91
   need to do, 37–39, 41
   negative. *See* negative apologetics.
   new visions of, 235–66
   not definitive proof, 213
   and openness, 165
   pastoral, 256–58, 264–66
   as pejorative, 28, 43n 1

personal reasons for doing, 141–45
Peter promotes. *See* Peter.
and plausibility of faith, 239
of polygamy, 156–58, 211. *See also* polygamy.
and possibility of faith, 78, 213–14
and possibility of revelation, 238–39
presuppositional method, 65
and public standards of scholarship, 108
quality of, 27–28, 69, 209
and race, 144
reformed epistemology method, 64
replaces devotional, 263
role of women, 139–53
same methods as critics, 212
and scholarship, vii, 258–59
should complicate rather than answer, 246
and social media, 142–44, 148
spiritual goals of, 138
surety of, 227
as theological praxis, 247–66
tone of. *See* tone.
and trust in God, 227
utility of, 259–60
apologia, 27, 31, 64–65, 91, 251
Apostles' Creed, 249
Aquila, 182
Ariel, Dan, 75
Aristotle, 92
Arrington, Leonard, 84–85, 123–24
Art of Biblical Narrative, The, 224
Åsenes, Maya, 142
Ash, Michael, 64–81
  on Lamanites, 199
Asherah, 48–49, 176–77, 188, 190
Atonement, 123n 6
Augustine, 3
authority, 196–99
  General Authorities, 197–99

B

Backslider, The, 113–14

Ballard, M. Russell, 20, 128–29, 139–40
Ballmer, Randall, 114–15
Barker, Margaret, 44–45, 47, 179
Bates, Tasha, 143–44
Bathsheba, 221, 233–34
Benson, Ezra Taft, 6, 13
Bible, 229
Biblical Studies, 13, 225
Big Ocean Women, 153
Birch, Brian, 119–38
  on apologetics in academia, 23–24, 108
  on reason and orthodoxy, 7
Bitton, Davis, 8
Blakeslee, Sandra, 71
Boaz, 233–34
Bokovoy, David, 223–34
  criticism of apologetics, 69
  on Documentary Hypothesis, 77–78
Book of Abraham, 51
Book of Mormon
  academic study of, 102, 104
  and ancient Israelites, 44–46
  American context, 104–5
  authorship of, 101, 194
  critical approach to, 228
  and deification, 52
  divine origin of, 219
  and DNA. *See* DNA.
  geography of, 4, 59–61, 206
  hemispheric model, 80
  historicity of, 40, 44–61, 66, 79, 110, 196, 206, 211, 219, 228, 231–32, 263
  imperfect, 227–30
  and indigenous peoples, 200, 206
  Isaiah in, 53–57
  Lamanite. *See* Lamanite.
  lineage history, 55
  and Mesoamerica, 57–61, 213
  and Mesoamerican kings, 58–59
  miracle of, 229, 231–32
  nineteenth-century context, 102, 195
  NHM, 65–66, 212

Index 273

other inhabitants, 55–56, 65, 200
and racism, 195, 203–4
and reason, 35–36
and Revelation, 242–43
as scripture, 196, 214
and skin of blackness, 203–4
small plates, 46–47, 51
spiritual message of, 101, 104, 214, 217, 227–28, 230, 263–64
and temple, 50–51
translation of, 215
visitation of Jesus, 60–91
word of God, 78, 212, 214, 217, 221–22
Book of Mormon Girl, 111–12
Book of Moses, 50–51
Booth, Ezra, 37
brain. *See* neuroscience.
Brettler, Marc, 228–29
Brigham Young University, 129–30
  censored by AAUP, 202
  and faithful scholarship, 133–34
  and secular scholarship, 132–35
Brodie, Fawn, 84, 197–98
Brooks, Joanna, 111–12, 152
Brooks, Juanita, 84
Brown, Peter, 181
Brown, Raymond, 181, 233–34
Burton, Linda K., 163
Bush, Lester, 10
Bushman, Richard, 87, 96, 126, 172
BYU Studies, 149

C

Cahoon, Reynolds, 184
Calvin, John, 247
Cane, Elizabeth, 165
Carmack, John, 127n 12
Cassler, Valerie Hudson, 152, 175
change blindness, 73
changing doctrines, 227, 264
Chicago experiment, 13, 122
Christian discipleship, 257

Christianity Online, 145–46
Christianity Today, 140, 146
Chrysostom, John, 181
Church Educational System. *See* Seminaries and Institutes.
Church History Department, 21, 218
Claremont Graduate University, 88–89, 126
Clark, J. Reuben, 13, 118, 121–22
Clark, John, 53
Coltrin, Zebedee, 175
conservativism, 235
Conversions: Two Family Stories from the Reformation, 114–15
Craig, William Lane, 10, 258
Creation, 123n 6, 174, 187
cultural Mormon, 208
culture, 200–201

D

de Castro, Eduardo Viveiros, 205
deacons, 182
Death and Immortality, 221–22
Dehlin, John, 99
deification, 52
Dever, William, 173
Dialogue, 149
Diamond, Malcom, 259
disciple-scholar, 22
dissent, 203–5
Divine Feminine. *See* Heavenly Mother.
Diving Teaching and the Way of the World, 232
DNA, 40, 56, 65, 199
Documentary Hypothesis, 77–78, 225–26
Duffy, John-Charles, 68, 81
Dulles, Avery, 8, 11–12

E

Elliot, John, 250
Encyclopedia of Mormonism, 165–66

England, Eugene, 84–85, 169, 223–24
Enns, Peter, 57–58, 230
Ensign, 5, 161
Ericson, Loyd Isao, 209–22
   on apologetics in academia, 23
Eve, 187–88
evidence, 30, 33–35
evidentialism, 4–6
evidentialist-fideist split, 5–8
Eyring, Henry, 80

F

FairMormon, 67–68, 89, 125, 141, 144
   examination of, 193–208
   female participation, 149
   founding of, 145–46, 202
   slogan, 193–94
faith, 3
   possibility of, 40–41
   vs. facts, 93–97
faith crises, 201, 207, 241
faithfulness, 202, 208
Fall, 123n 6
Fallentine, Angela, 148
"Family: A Proclamation to the World, The," 17–19
FARMS Review. *See Mormon Studies Review*.
FARMS. *See* Neal A. Maxwell Institute for Religious Scholarship.
Farrer, Austin, 31
Fehr, Ellen, 143–44
feminism, 139, 150
Ferguson, Thomas, 212–13
fideism, 5–7, 29, 136–37, 221
   definition of, 137
First Apology of Justin, The, 253–54
First Vision, 85, 217
Flake, Kathleen, 87
Fleishacker, Samuel, 232
Fluhman, Spencer, 107, 110, 131–32, 135–36
Ford, David, 136

Foundation for Ancient Research and Mormon Studies. *See* Neal A. Maxwell Institute for Religious Scholarship.
Foundation for Apologetic Information and Research. *See* FairMormon.
Freemasonry, 50, 186, 190
friendship, 107, 190
fundamentalism, 11–15
   in twentieth-century Mormonism, 12

G

Gardner, Brant, 58–59, 80
Gates, Susan Young, 190–91
Gee, John, 56
General Authorities, 197–99
Gibbons, William, 185
Giles, Kevin, 181
Gilovich, Thomas, 71, 75–76
Givens, Fiona, 171–91
God the Mother. *See* Heavenly Mother.
Gordon, Sarah Barringer, 87
Gordon, Scott, 142
Gospel Topics Essays, 9, 127–29
Graduate Theological Union, 88
Grenz, Stanley, 182
Guthrie, Stewart, 70

H

Haglund, Kristine, 108
Hales, Brian C., 220
Hales, Laura H., 220
Hales, Scott, 113–14
Hamblin, William, 50
Hancock, Ralph, 91–118
   in First Things, 132–33
   on secularism, 23, 132–33
Hardy, Grant, 47
Harline, Craig, 114–15
Hatton, Julianne Dehlin, 141–42
Hauglid, Brian, 105–6
Heavenly Mother
   as Asherah. *See* Asherah.

Index   275

in Book of Mormon, 47–49
and gender roles, 160
inversion test, 156
and Mary, 177–78
tree of life, 48–49
vision of, 175
wife of God, 173–74
as Wisdom, 177
Hebrew Goddess, The, 178
Hedelious, Cassandra, 141, 143–44
Hildebrant, Jen, 142–43
Historical Criticism, 230–31
history
  and important questions, 96
  and miracles, 231–32
Holland, Jeffrey R.
  on caring for others, 255–56
  on God's love, 117
  on truth of Mormonism, 110
Holland, David F., 227–28
Holy Spirit, 188
  feminine, 174, 178
  as Heavenly Mother, 178
homosexuality, 17–19, 111, 114–15
Hopkins, Gerard Manley, 174
Houston Baptist University, 140
Hull, Kerry, 59
humility, 98
Hyde, Orson, 36

I

index (anthropological), 195
indigenous peoples, 206
Interpreter Foundation, 99n 3
Introvigne, Massimo, 81
inversion test, 155–59, 169–70
Isaiah. *See* Book of Mormon, Isaiah in.
Isom, Ally, 162
Israelite religion, 44–46, 178–79

J

Jefferson Bible, 4, 83
Jefferson, Thomas, 83–84, 90, 211

Jesus
  in Book of Mormon, 60–61
  and caring for others, 258
  commissions disciples, 185–86
  and evidence, 33
  genealogy of, 233
  and Peter, 216
  Son of God, 221–22
  source of all truth, 15
  and women, 155
  Word of God, 230
John, 244
Joseph Smith Papers, 21
Joseph Smith's Polygamy, 220
Josiah, 45
Journal of Book of Mormon Studies, 103–6
  changes to, 101
  new mission, 105–7
  original mission, 101
Junia, 181

K

Kahneman, Daniel, 70–71
Karpowitz, Christopher F., 151–52
Kierkegaard, Søren, 5–6, 259, 261–62
Kimball, Camilla, 165
Kimball, Helen Mar. *See* Whitney, Helen Mar Kimball.
Kimball, Sarah, 179
Kimball, Spencer W., 1, 134
kingdom of priests, 190. *See also* Relief Society.
Knowlton, David, 193–208
Korihor, 35–36
Kreeft, Peter, 4

L

Lady of the Temple, 175
Lamanite
  in Book of Mormon, 200, 203–4
  concept of, 193–208
  curse of, 197, 203

defined by opposition, 201–3
mark of, 203–4
and Native Americans, 201
as religious/political faction, 201
religious value of, 196–201
LDS Church Archives, 127
Lee, Harold B., 138
Lewis, C. S., 30
liberal theology, 11–15
liberalism, 11–15, 111, 236
   in twentieth-century Mormonism, 12
logic, 30
logos, 31–32
Loki's Wager, 64
love, 96, 115–17, 257, 265
   of God, 261
Luther, Martin, 3, 5

M

Macknick, Stephen L., 71
Marion, Jean-Luc, 237, 240
Martinez-Conde, Susana, 71
Martyr, Justin, 3, 253–54
Mary, 49, 176
   and Heavenly Mother, 177–78
Mason, Patrick, 89, 114
Mauss, Armand, 14, 120
Maxwell, Neal A., 22, 26, 55, 110–11, 132
McBaine, Neylan, 150, 152
McConkie, Bruce R., 165, 223–24
McGrath, Alister, 252
McLellin, William E., 36
McMurrin, Sterling M., 15n 51
Mendelberg, Tali, 151–52
Meridian Magazine, 147
Milner, Joseph, 171
miracles, 33
Modernism, 10–11, 119
Monson, Thomas S., 118
Mormon Doctrine, 223–24
Mormon Feminism, 152
Mormon Menace, The, 89

Mormon Stories Podcast, 99
Mormon Studies
   in academia, 88–89
   and apologetics, 77, 91
   broadening of, 103, 109, 117
   definition of, 91–92
   excludes conservatives, 112
   and faith, 94–97
   and institutional LDS support, 126
   insularity of, 85–86, 102–4, 107
   and meaning of life, 95
   and non-Mormon scholars, 87–88
   objectivity, 116
   secular nature of, 112
   and tone, 97–98
Mormon Studies Review
   book reviews, 111–16, 112n 43
   changes to, 111, 131–32, 135–36
   early mission of, 68, 111–12
   liberal, 116
   new mission, 107
   secular, 116
Mormon Women Stand, 147–48
Mormons on the Internet, 145
Moroni, 230–31
Morris, Wayne, 257
Mosser, Carl, 146

N

Native Americans, 200–201
Nauvoo temple, 179
Neal A. Maxwell Institute for Religious Scholarship, 21–22, 89, 99n 3, 219
   and apologetics, 131
   commits to Mormon Studies, 99
   and John Dehlin, 99
   mission statement, 21–22
   rebranding, 99–100, 113, 131, 135–36, 219n 21
   rejects bifurcation of faith and scholarship, 24
   tension around, 120

Near Eastern Studies, 130
negative apologetics, 2, 40, 65, 99, 108, 238
Nehemiah, 39–40
Nelson, Russell M., 1, 228
Nelson-Seawright, J., 148–49
Nephi, 46–48, 56–57, 230–31, 244–45
neuroscience, 69–77
New Mormon History, 85–87, 123
Nibley, Hugh, 49, 84, 129–30, 248
Nicene Creed, 249
Noah (king), 53–54

O

Oaks, Dallin H., 6–7, 160, 167
Olhasso, Mary Jane, 142
orthodoxy, 198
orthopraxy, 202
Ostler, Blake, 211
Owen, Paul, 106, 146
Oxford Center for Christian Apologetics, 140

P

Packer, Boyd K., 14, 17–18, 123–24
Park, Benjamin E., 83–90
    on Book of Mormon studies, 101–6
    in *Journal of Book of Mormon Studies*, 103–6
    in *Times and Seasons* (blog), 101–3
pastoral apologetics, 256–58, 264–66
pastors, 182
Patai, Raphael, 178
Paul, 32–34
Payne, Seth, 247–66
Pearcey, Nancy, 140–41
Peck, Steven L., 113–14
Peirce, C. S., 195
Penner, Myron, 261–62
Penrose, Charles W., 174
Peter, 181, 185
    on apologetics, 32, 91, 247, 250–52
    and Jesus, 216

Petersen, Zina, 111
Peterson, Daniel C., 27–41, 48–49, 67, 248
    and possibility of faith, 213–14
    defends apologetics, 130
    defines apologetics, 209–10
    dismissed from *Mormon Studies Review*, 131–32
    editor of *FARMS Review*, 130–31
    on Mormon Studies, 107–8
Peterson, Levi, 113–14
Peterson, Mark E., 13
Phillips, D. Z., 210–11, 216, 220–22
Planted, 89
Plantinga, Alvin, 6n 19
polygamy, 156, 211
    in afterlife, 157–58
    and gender roles, 157, 159, 164
    birthrate in, 158–59
    and women's rights, 166
positive apologetics, 2, 39–41, 65, 239
Pratt, Orson, 181
Preach My Gospel, 37
presuppositionalism, 15–19
priesthood
    gendered, 168
    women's ordination. *See* women's ordination.
priesthood and temple ban, 10, 169
Priscilla, 182
prophecy, 33

Q–R

Quetzalcoatl, 80
Quinn, Michael, 127n 12
race, 144
Radke-Moss, Andrea, 168
Rahab, 233–34
Rappleye, Neal, 43–62
reason, 3, 32, 262
Reeve, Paul, 89
Relief Society
    founding of, 162–65, 179–91

and kingdom of priests, 162–65
  naming of, 188–89
  patterned after priesthood, 180–86
Religion and Friendly Fire, 210–11
Religion of a Different Color, 89
religious claims, 210, 219–20
religious experience, 260–61
religious freedom, 83–84
religious studies, 91–92
Revelation, 242–45
Review of Books on the Book of Mormon. See *Mormon Studies Review*.
revisionist history, 81, 85–86
Reynolds, Juliann, 139–53
Reynolds, Noel, 46
Rhode, Deborah, 150, 152
Rigdon, Sidney, 175
righteousness, 202
Rise of Christianity, The, 182
Roberts, B. H., 12, 53, 120, 123n 6
Roberts, Kyle, 259
Robinson, Cal, 144
Roper, Matthew, 56
Ruth, 233–34

S

Salt Lake Temple, 175
same-sex marriage, 19, 111–12
scholarship
  and apologetics, vii, 258–59
  definition of, 210
  LDS embrace of, 9–10, 12, 19–22, 120–21, 125–29
  LDS suspicion of, 10, 12–15, 121–25, 135
School of the Prophets, 9
science, 77–78, 119
scripture
  fallible, 233
  human product, 227–34
Scruton, Roger, 99–100
secularism, 109, 134–36

Seminaries and Institutes, 13, 20, 124, 128–29
sexual morality, 114–16
Shermer, Michael, 70, 74, 79
Skaggs, Kathryn, 147–48
Skousen, Royal, 59
Smith, Emma, 183
  elected to preside, 189
  and keys to preside, 190
Smith, Gary Scott, 16
Smith, Gregory L., 112
Smith, Joseph
  claims unexplainable experiences, 7–8
  First Elder, 189
  First Vision, 217
  marriages, 220–21, 322
  prophet of God, 78, 212, 220–22
  and Relief Society, 162–63, 172
  restoration of priesthood, 171–91
  revelation to witness, 36–37
  views on women, 191
  vision of Heavenly Mother, 175
Smith, Joseph F., 12
Smith, Joseph Fielding, 12, 120, 123n 6
Smith, Julie M., 155–69
Snow, Eliza R., 179, 184, 189
Snow, Erastus, 174
Sophia, 188
Sorenson, John, 53, 57, 248
Spencer, Joseph, 235–46
  on Isaiah in Book of Mormon, 54
  on secular nature of apologetics, 210n 3
  on small plates, 51
Stackhouse, John G., 24–25
Starks, Rodney, 182
Statement on Symposia, 125
Steenblick, Rachel Hunt, 152
Story, Dan, 258
Sunday, Billy, 119, 138
Sunstone, 125
systematic theology, 249

T

Tacelli, Ronald, 4
Talmage, James E., 12
Tamar, 233–34
Taves, Ann, 110
Taylor, John, 188–89
Taysom, Stephen, 109
teachers, 182
temple
   ancient, 44–45, 176
   and Book of Mormon, 50–51
   modern, 49–52, 188
   parallels between ancient and modern, 50–51
Times and Seasons (periodical), 186
Times and Seasons (blog), 101–3
tone, viii, 28, 97–100, 209
   defense of, 98–100
tongue of angels, 51
Travis, Melissa Cain, 140
Tree of Life, 177, 188
   and Heavenly Mother, 48–49
   and Mary, 177–78
   vision of, 48–49, 177–78
Trinity, 172–73
   in Israelite Religion, 178–79
   in Mormonism, 173–74
truth, 92–93, 264
Turley, Gail, 202
Tvedtnes, John, 194–95, 203

U–V

University of Chicago Divinity School, 13, 122
University of Southern California, 88
University of Virginia, 126
Utah State University, 88, 126
Utah Valley University, 88, 126, 127n 12
Van Til, Cornelius, 16–17
Van Wagenen, Lola, 139
Vogel, Dan, 77
Von Feldt, Allison Skabelund, 49
wall of separation, 83–84, 90, 95

W

Welch, John, 54, 248
Wheelwright, Hannah, 152
Whitney, Helen Mar Kimball, 190, 221
Whitney, Newel K., 183
Widtsoe, John H., 12
Wisdom, 177, 188
Wittgenstein, Ludwig, 215
Wolterstorff, Nicholas, 137
women
   and apologetics, 139–53
   gender pay gap, 151
   in workplace, 150–51
   and priesthood, 162–63. *See also* women's ordination.
   status of, 156
   voices need in apologetics, 155–69
Women at Church, 150
women's ordination
   in early Christianity, 180–81
   explanations against, 168
   in LDS canon, 162–63
   possibility of, 166–67
Word of Wisdom, 85
Wright, Mark, 59–60

Y–Z

Young, Brigham, 165, 174
Young, Joseph Don Carlos, 175
Young, Persis, 190
Zen Buddhism, 258
Zeniff, 54

Also available from
GREG KOFFORD BOOKS

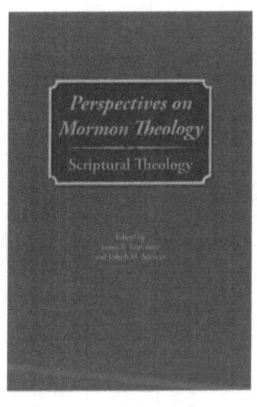

Perspectives on Mormon Theology: Scriptural Theology

Edited by James E. Faulconer and Joseph M. Spencer

Paperback, ISBN: 978-1-58958-712-0
Hardcover, ISBN: 978-1-58958-713-7

The phrase "theology of scripture" can be understood in two distinct ways. First, theology of scripture would be reflection on the nature of scripture, asking questions about what it means for a person or a people to be oriented by a written text (rather than or in addition to an oral tradition or a ritual tradition). In this first sense, theology of scripture would form a relatively minor part of the broader theological project, since the nature of scripture is just one of many things on which theologians reflect. Second, theology of scripture would be theological reflection guided by scripture, asking questions of scriptural texts and allowing those texts to shape the direction the theologian's thoughts pursue. In this second sense, theology of scripture would be less a part of the larger theological project than a way of doing theology, since whatever the theologian takes up reflectively, she investigates through the lens of scripture.

The essays making up this collection reflect attentiveness to both ways of understanding the phrase "theology of scripture." Each essay takes up the relatively un-self-conscious work of reading a scriptural text but then—at some point or another—asks the self-conscious question of exactly what she or he is doing in the work of reading scripture. We have thus attempted in this book (1) to create a dialogue concerning what scripture is for Latter-day Saints, and (2) to focus that dialogue on concrete examples of Latter-day Saints reading actual scripture texts.

Discourses in Mormon Theology: Philosophical and Theological Possibilities

Edited by
James M. McLachlan and Loyd Ericson

Hardcover, ISBN: 978-1-58958-103-6

A mere two hundred years old, Mormonism is still in its infancy compared to other theological disciplines (Judaism, Catholicism, Buddhism, etc.). This volume will introduce its reader to the rich blend of theological viewpoints that exist within Mormonism. The essays break new ground in Mormon studies by exploring the vast expanse of philosophical territory left largely untouched by traditional approaches to Mormon theology. It presents philosophical and theological essays by many of the finest minds associated with Mormonism in an organized and easy-to-understand manner and provides the reader with a window into the fascinating diversity amongst Mormon philosophers. Open-minded students of pure religion will appreciate this volume's thoughtful inquiries.

These essays were delivered at the first conference of the Society for Mormon Philosophy and Theology. Authors include Grant Underwood, Blake T. Ostler, Dennis Potter, Margaret Merrill Toscano, James E. Faulconer, and Robert L. Millet

Praise for *Discourses in Mormon Theology*:

"In short, *Discourses in Mormon Theology* is an excellent compilation of essays that are sure to feed both the mind and soul. It reminds all of us that beyond the white shirts and ties there exists a universe of theological and moral sensitivity that cries out for study and acclamation."
-Jeff Needle, Association for Mormon Letters

As Iron Sharpens Iron: Listening to the Various Voices of Scripture

Julie M. Smith

Paperback, ISBN: 978-1-58958-501-0

**2016 Best Religious Non-fiction Award,
Association for Mormon Letters**

Our scripture study and reading often assume that the prophetic figures within the texts are in complete agreement with each other. Because of this we can fail to recognize that those authors and personalities frequently have different—and sometimes competing—views on some of the most important doctrines of the Gospel, including the nature of God, the roles of scripture and prophecy, and the Atonement.

In this unique volume, fictionalized dialogues between the various voices of scripture illustrate how these differences and disagreements are not flaws of the texts but are rather essential features of the canon. These creative dialogues include Abraham and Job debating the utility of suffering and our submission to God, Alma and Abinidi disagreeing on the place of justice in the Atonement, and the authors Mark and Luke discussing the role of women in Jesus's ministry. It is by examining and embracing the different perspectives within the canon that readers are able to discover just how rich and invigorating the scriptures can be. The dialogues within this volume show how just as "iron sharpeneth iron," so can we sharpen our own thoughts and beliefs as we engage not just the various voices in the scriptures but also the various voices within our community (Proverbs 27:17).

Authoring the Old Testament: Genesis–Deuteronomy

David Bokovoy

Paperback, ISBN: 978-1-58958-588-1
Hardcover, ISBN: 978-1-58958-675-8

For the last two centuries, biblical scholars have made discoveries and insights about the Old Testament that have greatly changed the way in which the authorship of these ancient scriptures has been understood. In the first of three volumes spanning the entire Hebrew Bible, David Bokovoy dives into the Pentateuch, showing how and why textual criticism has led biblical scholars today to understand the first five books of the Bible as an amalgamation of multiple texts into a single, though often complicated narrative; and he discusses what implications those have for Latter-day Saint understandings of the Bible and modern scripture.

Praise for *Authoring the Old Testament*:

"*Authoring the Old Testament* is a welcome introduction, from a faithful Latter-day Saint perspective, to the academic world of Higher Criticism of the Hebrew Bible. . . . [R]eaders will be positively served and firmly impressed by the many strengths of this book, coupled with Bokovoy's genuine dedication to learning by study and also by faith." — John W. Welch, editor, *BYU Studies Quarterly*

"Bokovoy provides a lucid, insightful lens through which disciple-students can study intelligently LDS scripture. This is first rate scholarship made accessible to a broad audience—nourishing to the heart and mind alike." — Fiona Givens, co-author, *The God Who Weeps: How Mormonism Makes Sense of Life*

"I repeat: this is one of the most important books on Mormon scripture to be published recently. . . . [*Authoring the Old Testament*] has the potential to radically expand understanding and appreciation for not only the Old Testament, but scripture in general. It's really that good. Read it. Share it with your friends. Discuss it." — David Tayman, The Improvement Era: A Mormon Blog

For Zion:
A Mormon Theology of Hope

Joseph M. Spencer

Paperback, ISBN: 978-1-58958-568-3

What is hope? What is Zion? And what does it mean to hope for Zion? In this insightful book, Joseph Spencer explores these questions through the scriptures of two continents separated by nearly two millennia. In the first half, Spencer engages in a rich study of Paul's letter to the Roman to better understand how the apostle understood hope and what it means to have it. In the second half of the book, Spencer jumps to the early years of the Restoration and the various revelations on consecration to understand how Latter-day Saints are expected to strive for Zion. Between these halves is an interlude examining the hoped-for Zion that both thrived in the Book of Mormon and was hoped to be established again.

Praise for *For Zion*:

"Joseph Spencer is one of the most astute readers of sacred texts working in Mormon Studies. Blending theological savvy, historical grounding, and sensitive readings of scripture, he has produced an original and compelling case for consecration and the life of discipleship." — Terryl Givens, author, *Wrestling the Angel: The Foundations of Mormon Thought*

"*For Zion: A Mormon Theology of Hope* is more than a theological reflection. It also consists of able textual exegesis, historical contextualization, and philosophic exploration. Spencer's careful readings of Paul's focus on hope in Romans and on Joseph Smith's development of consecration in his early revelations, linking them as he does with the Book of Mormon, have provided an intriguing, intertextual avenue for understanding what true stewardship should be for us—now and in the future. As such he has set a new benchmark for solid, innovative Latter-day Saint scholarship that is at once provocative and challenging." — Eric D. Huntsman, author, *The Miracles of Jesus*

Mormonism at the Crossroads of Philosophy and Theology: Essays in Honor of David L. Paulsen

Edited by Jacob T. Baker

Paperback, ISBN: 978-1-58958-192-0

"There is no better measure of the growing importance of Mormon thought in contemporary religious debate than this volume of essays for David Paulsen. In a large part thanks to him, scholars from all over the map are discussing the questions Mormonism raises about the nature of God and the purpose of life. These essays let us in on a discussion in progress." —RICHARD LYMAN BUSHMAN, author of *Joseph Smith: Rough Stone Rolling*.

"This book makes it clear that there can be no real ecumenism without the riches of the Mormon mind. Professor Paulsen's impact on LDS thought is well known.... These original and insightful essays chart a new course for Christian intellectual life." —PETER A. HUFF, and author of *Vatican II and The Voice of Vatican II*

"This volume of smart, incisive essays advances the case for taking Mormonism seriously within the philosophy of religion–an accomplishment that all generations of Mormon thinkers should be proud of." —PATRICK Q. MASON, Howard W. Hunter Chair of Mormon Studies, Claremont Graduate University

"These essays accomplish a rare thing—bringing light rather than heat to an on-going conversation. And the array of substantial contributions from outstanding scholars and theologians within and outside Mormonism is itself a fitting tribute to a figure who has been at the forefront of bringing Mormonism into dialogue with larger traditions." —TERRYL L. GIVENS, author of *People of Paradox: A History of Mormon Culture*

"The emergence of a vibrant Mormon scholarship is nowhere more in evidence than in the excellent philosophical contributions of David Paulsen." —RICHARD J. MOUW, President, Fuller Theological Seminary, author of *Talking with Mormons: An Invitation to Evangelicals*

www.ingramcontent.com/pod-product-compliance
Lightning Source LLC
Chambersburg PA
CBHW020235170426
43202CB00008B/96